Boss Lady

The Luther H. Hodges Jr. and Luther H. Hodges Sr. Series on Business, Entrepreneurship, and Public Policy

Maryann Feldman, editor

This series provides a forum for social scientists, public policy scholars, historians, and others investigating the economic, political, societal, and geographic contexts and conditions that foster entrepreneurship, innovation, and economic development in the United States and around the world. As place-based inquiry has gained currency, scholarship in the areas of business, entrepreneurship, and public policy increasingly consider spatial and cultural issues. A basic aim of the series is to challenge analyses that privilege globalization with the view that place—and human attachment to place—influence the expression of creativity and innovation.

Boss Lady

How Three Women Entrepreneurs
Built Successful Big Businesses in the
Mid-Twentieth Century

···

EDITH SPARKS

The University of North Carolina Press Chapel Hill

Published with the assistance of the Luther H. Hodges Sr. and Luther H. Hodges Jr. Fund of the University of North Carolina Press.

© 2017 The University of North Carolina Press
All rights reserved
Set in Charis Regular by Westchester Publishing Services

The University of North Carolina Press has been a member of the Green Press Initiative since 2003.

Library of Congress Cataloging-in-Publication Data
Names: Sparks, Edith, author.
Title: Boss lady : how three women entrepreneurs built successful big businesses in the mid-twentieth century / Edith Sparks.
Other titles: Luther H. Hodges Jr. and Luther H. Hodges Sr. series on business, entrepreneurship, and public policy.
Description: Chapel Hill : University of North Carolina Press, [2017] |
    Series: The Luther H. Hodges Jr. and Luther H. Hodges Sr. series on business, entrepreneurship, and public policy | Includes bibliographical references and index.
Identifiers: LCCN 2016050513| ISBN 9781469633015 (cloth : alk. paper) |
    ISBN 9781469633022 (pbk : alk. paper) | ISBN 9781469633039 (ebook)
Subjects: LCSH: Women-owned business enterprises—United States—History—20th century. | Women executives—United States—History—20th century—Biography. | Businesswomen—United States—History—20th century—Biography. | Lewis, Tillie, 1896–1977. | Beech, Olive Ann, 1903–1993. | Rudkin, Margaret, 1897–1967.
Classification: LCC HD6054.4.U6 S67 2017 | DDC 338.092/520973—dc23
    LC record available at https://lccn.loc.gov/2016050513

Cover illustration: Background, from 1955 Annual Report of Flotill Products Incorporated (National Archives, A2-2000-Sharp363N-7@nara.gov _20130516_152739); left headshot, Margaret Rudkin (Wikipedia.com); middle headshot, Olive Ann Beech (Wichita State University Libraries, Special Collections and University Archives); right headshot, Myrtle "Tillie" Lewis (Palm Springs Historical Society).

For Rick, who has always believed in my leadership,

for Lucy, who has always believed it makes a difference,

and for Ada, who has always believed.

Contents

Illustrations

Acknowledgments

During the course of this project, I have benefited from the assistance and support of many individuals and institutions, and I am delighted to acknowledge them here. First, I'd like to thank my University of the Pacific colleague Ken Albala for initially pitching the idea of a book about Tillie Lewis, who was a resident of Stockton, California, where we both teach. Though we originally envisioned a cowritten book that would merge our respective areas of expertise in food and women's business history, Ken graciously agreed to yield the project to me as solo author after he published an article, "The Tomato Queen of San Joaquin," in *Gastronomica* in 2010. By then it had become clear to us both that I, a full-time administrator at the time (2006–12), would not be able to keep up with his pace of productivity. Because Ken had no shortage of projects, interests, or publishing opportunities (he is that awe-inspiring colleague who seems to churn out a book every other year), he was content to stop with his one article—but his decision nonetheless reflected his generosity of spirit as a colleague. Subsequently, Ken shared his research notes with me and provided both encouragement and valuable input on the book proposal, which contributed in no small way to the completion of the project.

Reshaping the project as a comparative one that treated the stories of Tillie Lewis, Olive Ann Beech, and Margaret Rudkin together was a turnaround inspired by the very helpful and enthusiastic feedback of my editor at UNC Press, Chuck Grench, and the many colleagues with whom he discussed the project in its proposal phase. Though I had always intended to use Beech and Rudkin for comparison, I had not planned to give their histories equal weight, and at the time I did not have sufficient sources to do so. Spurred on by the discussion with Chuck as well as my recollection of the kindly rejection I had received some time earlier from *Business History Review* suggesting that a comparative examination of three businesswomen would make the article I had submitted a better study, I went looking for more sources.

My archival research then and earlier was aided by the expertise and generosity of many people and institutions. Judy Schiffner generously shared memories and well as personal memorabilia pertaining to her great-aunt, Tillie Lewis, and those have enhanced my account. Thomas Rudkin, grandson of Margaret Rudkin, shared his memories and agreed to let me use his own collection of papers pertaining to Pepperidge Farm and his grandparents, and for that I am deeply grateful. It simply would not have been possible to incorporate Rudkin into the book in the way that I have without the resources he shared. Elizabeth Rose at the Fairfield Museum and History Center put me in touch with Tom and facilitated this arrangement as well as connecting me with the other relevant resources in the archive there. Mary Nelson at the Special Collections and University Archive at Wichita State University helped me to make the best use of the Walter and Olive Ann Beech Collection in the time I had there and oversaw the substantial photocopy order that I left behind after my visit. She has also been a helpful correspondent since. I also received help from Leigh Johnson at the San Joaquin County Historical Society and, early on, from Kimberley Bowden, then archivist at the Haggin Museum. A variety of archivists helped me to navigate the large and complex collections I utilized at the National Archives and Records Administration in both College Park, Maryland, and Washington, D.C., as well as the Library of Congress and Smithsonian National American History Museum. The same is true for the records of the Mexican American Legal Defense and Education Fund Collection at Stanford University and the various resources I consulted at the New-York Historical Society. I am grateful to all of them. My research trips were funded by generous support from the University of the Pacific, from which I received an Eberhardt Faculty Research Fellowship that funded five weeks of research on the East Coast. Annual support for conference travel, as well as a faculty development leave in 2014, was also invaluable in helping me to move the project to completion. I am grateful to be employed at a university that invests in the scholarly activities of its faculty. For research assistance, I'd like to thank Amy Eastburg, a recent graduate of Pacific. Early on I also received help from Paul Fraidenburgh, Kent Linthicum, and Heather Mellon, all professionals now but undergraduates at Pacific at the time.

Many colleagues have contributed to this project, and I am delighted to name them here. Jessica Weiss, Jennifer Helgren, and Carolyn (de la Pena) Thomas each read a chapter of the completed manuscript before it went to peer reviewers and provided both helpful suggestions and encouragement. Lisa Materson's oft-repeated prompt to "do more gender analysis" in the margins of chapter 5 turned into a general guide for me while revising the whole manuscript, and I feel certain that it is better because of this. Nikki Mandell also deserves special attention for the care with which she read chapter 3 and applied her expertise in both labor and business history to help chart a way to extensive revisions. I was humbled by the generosity with which she shared her time and grateful for her insights and suggestions. At several stages, Gesine Gerhard provided both suggestions and helpful discussions regarding the project, as did Laurie Johnson, my long-standing FSP partner. Thanks to the late Caroline Cox, my Pacific colleague who provided a steady drumbeat of support for me as a scholar over many years. And for encouragement as well as friendship, laughter, and good meals at several critical junctures, I'd like to thank Ellen Hartigan O'Connor, Cynthia Dobbs, and Jessica Weiss.

I am so grateful to be a UNC Press author once again and have benefited immensely from the wise counsel and compassion that I have enjoyed in UNC's hands. Thanks to Chuck Grench for thoughtful editorial guidance and support, and to everyone there who has contributed to the project. I especially appreciate the care and effort they put into recruiting peer reviewers. I benefited from insightful reads by two anonymous peer reviewers during the proposal stage, one of whom also read the whole manuscript and provided useful suggestions that have improved the completed project. A second peer reviewer who read the whole manuscript revealed herself to me, and I am delighted to be able to acknowledge her here. Pamela Walker Laird read the manuscript with great care, annotating each chapter with suggestions for improvement as well as providing holistic feedback on key areas of strength and areas to expand and improve. Her suggestions, comments, questions, and insights have substantially improved the completed manuscript and gave me the very important and satisfying feeling during the revision phase that I was "in conversation" with her and other scholars. This was incredibly valuable after working on the project for so many years and fueled me with the energy I needed to complete revisions. I have been so impressed and inspired by the delight with which she engages intellectual questions and am so grateful to have had the benefit of her wisdom here.

Special thanks to several women whom I admire deeply for inspiring me to think about women's leadership in new, deeper, and more personally meaningful ways: Elizabeth Griego, Corrie Martin, and my mother, Patricia Murar. For their abiding friendship and care, thanks to Lara Schultz; Stacey Mufson; Margaret Korosec; my sister, Elizabeth Brownlow; and Wendy Sheanin, who also shared her publishing and marketing expertise with me in the final stages. Thanks to my East Coast sisters, Maya, Ashley, Nicole, and Catherine, and to my stepmother Michelle, for helping to make my three-week research trip in 2013 (with kids in tow!) both productive and enjoyable. For their interest and cheers from the sidelines, thanks to my stepdad, Robert Murar, and my father, Frank Sparks, who is also the only person I know who reads everything I write!

Finally, I wish to acknowledge the support and encouragement that my husband, Rick Mendez, has provided, always believing in my ability to complete the project and to make a real contribution. And to my daughters, Lucy and Ada—it's finally done! We can go back to having some fun together now!

Boss Lady

Introduction

· ·

On 8 August 1959, the *Saturday Evening Post* published a sensationalized article about the female chief executive of Beech Aircraft titled "Danger: Boss Lady at Work." In it, the "Boss Lady," Olive Ann Beech, was caricatured as autocratic and austere, insecure yet self-righteous, and the author warned readers—as the title suggested—to beware. Reportedly, more than one businessman had declared, "I'm scared of that woman!" But according to the article, Beech herself was undaunted. "I never concerned myself with what people thought of me," she stated. "If I had, I'd have been pretty mousy."[1]

The idea that a "boss lady" at work was *dangerous* tells us a great deal about the historical context in which female business executives led and the obstacles they faced in the mid-twentieth century. Alarms about a crisis in American masculinity were de rigueur in popular magazines in the 1950s, and social commentators were quick to connect the problem to women. One result was a pronounced current in American popular culture of the 1950s that endeavored to prop up men at the expense of women and to demonize women who in their success appeared to embody an assault on men.[2] From this viewpoint, women who played a dominant role in American business *were* dangerous.

The remaining content of the 8 August 1959 issue of the magazine helped to emphasize the danger of powerful women by excoriating weakness in men and celebrating it in women. This same *Saturday Evening Post* featured an article titled "Our Fighting Men Have Gone Soft" by Hanson Baldwin, the longtime military editor at the *New York Times*, investigating the "harmful effects of leisure and consumption" and their deleterious impact on the fortitude of American military men.[3] And several pages into the magazine was a short story titled "New Girl" about the exploits of female office workers and their pursuit of male professionals as "eligible" marriage partners. It was a tale that portrayed office "girls" as both objects of desire and office schemers with marital ambitions and presented a business world populated with dominant male professionals and dependent female clerical staff who would rather be full-time wives.[4] A professional woman who led men in such an office environment threatened to unravel this gendered hierarchy. Representing a "boss lady" as dangerous aligned with this portrayal.

To become a "boss lady" in the middle of the twentieth century, therefore, was to fly in the face of a popular set of ideas about the proper roles for men and women in the business world. The term "girl"—eponymous label for not just the magazine story discussed above but a way of thinking about women, especially in an office setting—infantilized women at precisely the moment when a small but impactful group of female executives, including Olive Ann Beech, rose to the upper echelons of the business world. In contrast to the legions of female clerical workers who supported the business world—nearly one in three working women in the United States were employed in clerical jobs by 1960 and nearly two-thirds of all clerical workers were female—the women who led businesses in the middle of the twentieth century were transgressors whose very presence seemed a threat to those anxious to preserve men's power.

The notion that mid-twentieth-century female business leaders were dangerous also helps us to imagine what the path to the top of corporate America looked like for women—that is, how women such as Olive Ann Beech experienced it. Clearly, they could not afford to worry about such negative labels, for, as the *Saturday Evening Post* quote from Beech suggests, criticism was commonplace for women business leaders at this time and would have proved a formidable deterrent if they had not dismissed it. But even with such resolve, female executives faced the inherent challenge of figuring out how to navigate a business world that viewed them as fundamentally different simply because they were women. They were outsiders. To succeed, they needed to find a path into a professional world deeply ingrained with male privilege and steeped in rigid gender conventions that shaped both obstacles and opportunities. They needed to become the "boss lady," to inhabit both parts of that label and all that it implied.

This book takes up the stories of three boss ladies—women entrepreneurs who traveled to the top of the corporate world by building successful big businesses in the mid-twentieth century. Tillie Lewis, who founded Flotill Products, Inc., in Stockton, California, in 1934 as a tomato canning company, ultimately canned several fruits and vegetables and other foods (including Hormel chili) as well as C-rations for the military and created one of the nation's first saccharine-based diet-food lines. By 1966, Tillie Lewis Foods, as it was renamed, had grown into a multimillion-dollar, publicly traded company and was purchased by the Ogden Corporation. Olive Ann Beech cofounded Beech Aircraft in Wichita, Kansas, with her aviator husband

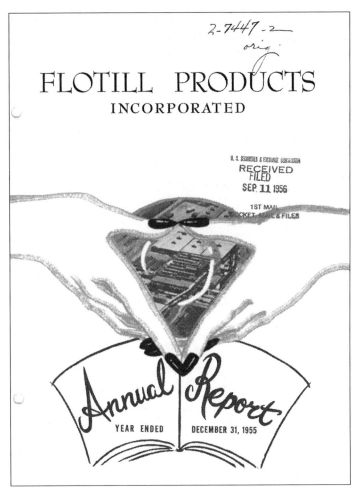

FLOTILL PRODUCTS
INCORPORATED

Annual Report

| YEAR ENDED | DECEMBER 31, 1955 |

This 1955 annual report cover for Flotill Products, Inc., filed with the Securities and Exchange Commission soon after the company launched its diet-foods business reveals the inherent tension in the label "Boss Lady." Branding focused on a "feminized" corporate image was conveyed by the stylized feminine hands with painted nails encompassing the Flotill manufacturing plant. Inside the cover, however, the update from the company's president, Tillie Lewis, was all business. Securities and Exchange Commission Records, National Archive and Records Administration, College Park, Maryland.

Walter Beech in 1932 but from the start took charge of the administrative side of the business. The company built training aircraft and eventually target missiles and cryogenic space equipment for the government and developed popular personal and commercial aircraft, pioneering instructional and purchasing programs that helped to expand private airplane owner-ship in the United States. When her husband was seriously impaired by an illness in 1940, Olive Ann stepped in to oversee company leadership, and when he died in 1950, she took over the company presidency, moving even-tually to board chair, a position she held even after the sale of the company to Raytheon in 1979. Margaret Rudkin founded Pepperidge Farm in Southport, Connecticut, in 1937 when demand for the health-oriented bread she made with stone-ground whole-wheat flour expanded from her doctor and his patients to local retailers and customers, eventually reach-ing national distribution. The company extended its product line to in-clude a variety of "high-end" bakery products including rolls, white sandwich bread, stuffing, European-style cookies, and frozen pastries as well as the ever-popular fish-shaped snack crackers called "Goldfish," drawing consumer loyalty as well as the attention of the Campbell Soup Company, which purchased Pepperidge Farm in 1961. All three women were elected and celebrated as the first female corporate board members of the corporations to which they sold their companies. And all three achieved national recognition for their business leadership and remarkable success, embodying the moniker "boss lady" in the press and in their day-to-day lives as business leaders.

How they did this is the focus of the book. It examines the business careers of each of these three women to identify the ways in which they accessed entrepreneurial success. Their careers and the business environ-ment within which they pursued them reveal common patterns and thus teach us a great deal. Together their stories illustrate the options and ob-stacles that ambitious and capable women encountered during this period in our history—in both the corporate and cultural contexts in which they worked. Mid-twentieth-century women could be "bosses" and "ladies," but to do so required them to effectively navigate the inherent tensions between these two labels, to seize opportunities wherever they found them, and sometimes to embrace stereotypical and status quo ideas that supported the success of their businesses.

Conventional ideas about the proper role for women fundamentally shaped their employment opportunities. All three women were married (one divorced and remarried) and two of them were mothers, and thus each of them faced the challenges of navigating professional work and family re-sponsibilities at a time in women's history when most Americans thought married women shouldn't be employed at all. Such biases could be found in workplace attitudes, but they were also encoded into formal employment policies. Marriage bars—prohibitions against hiring or retaining women who were married—affected 50 percent of the country's corporate and institutional employers, according to one study.[5] And in certain industries the rates were much higher. Such discriminatory policies led to restricted job options for married women and during the 1930s attracted the focus of business and professional women's clubs, which advocated their elimination. But cultural impediments to married women's employment persisted and stayed firmly rooted in the idea that "the place for a wife and mother is at home." A 1936 Gallup Poll highlighted this. When asked "if married women should work if their husbands were employed, 82 percent said no."[6] Of course, this didn't mean that married women didn't work outside the home, but it underscores what few choices they had and the social construction of women as family contributors but not workplace contributors. The trend certainly reflected the depressed economic conditions of the era but also long-standing ideas about the "family wage"—that is, that married men should earn more because they had families to support and married women shouldn't work for pay at all because they were the beneficiaries and dependents of their husbands.[7] Such ideas formed the context in which Lewis, Beech, and Rudkin worked, and their responses to them are part of the history examined here.

For all three women, their paths prior to entrepreneurship reflected the narrow set of choices facing most women at this time. None of the women attended college (a choice only the most elite women had), and just one of the three obtained a high school diploma, which was still uncommon in the United States at the beginning of the twentieth century.[8] Like many women of their generation, all three opted instead for "business training" (secretarial school) in order to access clerical jobs. This was one of the most reliable points of entry into the business world for unmarried women at the beginning of the twentieth century. Clerical jobs did not launch many women into higher level positions. Most stayed in low-level positions, supporting and serving the business needs of male professionals. When women did enter leadership positions in business, they did so in areas designated by their job functions or image as "female," either because of the traits needed for the job (such as the empathy demanded of personnel work) or because the job entailed dealing with female consumers (such as purchasing for department stores). Lewis, Beech, and Rudkin were unusual in that their secretarial jobs turned into launching pads for business ownership at the highest level. Yet while the business exposure they gained in clerical positions had something to do with this career trajectory, it was not the most important reason for their success. In fact, it was the relationships they formed with men while in those jobs that were the key to their entrepreneurial pathways. Two of the three married their bosses, and the third worked for her husband and other male family members. And in each case, it was these familial connections and the network of relationships into which they gained admission that opened up entrepreneurial possibilities. This is a long-standing theme in women's history. Connections to successful men provided opportunities and facilitated access to the business world. It was true generally for anyone trying to enter or rise in a professional business environment but was especially important for women trying to enter a corporate world that provided few choices for them and was overwhelmingly male and male-oriented.

Each of the women presented here operated a business in a sector of the manufacturing industry dominated by male business owners and executives and had to navigate a culture steeped in masculine bravado. Though Olive Ann Beech is the only one who was actually described as "dangerous" in the press, the term's implication—that she was a transgressor in an almost all-male executive business world—describes the experiences of all three women. For while it won't be surprising to learn that the aircraft industry was trenchantly male-dominated when Beech entered it as a business leader, it may come as a surprise to learn that the food canning and commercial baking industries that Lewis and Rudkin entered were also overwhelmingly filled with male business owners. Though both involved food production, which was a traditionally female form of labor in the home, on a mass scale and in an industrial setting, even these forms of production were masculinized commercial sectors. And for the most part, the men with whom they competed in these industries operated large, established companies. For example, Lewis's canning business operated in an industry where she competed with the likes of food giant Del Monte, a well-established company with nearly two hundred times the volume of sales in the same food category. To succeed in these industrial sectors—aircraft, canning, and commercial baking—was to succeed in a man's world on a big scale.

Most women business owners shied away from manufacturing sectors like these during the mid-twentieth century because they presented so many challenges. Constituting only 3.3 percent of all woman-owned businesses in one 1954 survey by the Federation of Business and Professional Women's Clubs (BPWC), female entrepreneurs in manufacturing were scarce.[9] Manufacturing was a capital-intensive, high-risk, complex sector. This discouraged women entrepreneurs who had a more difficult time accessing capital and for whom lower-risk investments had a particular appeal. In addition, this was a dynamic period in business history when all entrepreneurs, male and female, faced many ups and downs. For example, all three of the women highlighted in this book were plagued by the economic dislocations of the depression in the 1930s, when each of the businesses was launched. And each was simultaneously bolstered and hindered by wartime and postwar production, consumption, and economic recovery. In addition, once their businesses matured, all three operated manufacturing enterprises with mechanized production processes, high capital requirements for operation, a small professionalized management team and a much larger working-class production labor force, complicated challenges around sourcing and distribution, and a national customer base. These common challenges high-light the economic context in which Lewis, Beech, and Rudkin carved out their entrepreneurial paths.

Success in the manufacturing sector brought distinct advantages that distinguished the careers of all three women as well. Whether they produced and distributed canned foods, fresh bread, or aircraft, manufacturing businesses attracted the interest of large corporations looking to acquire or expand areas of production by purchasing smaller established companies. This was in fact a common trend during the 1960s merger spike, in which conglomerate mergers joining previously independent companies were especially high among manufacturing companies.[10] Previous scholarship has not documented the role of businesswomen in this historical process except to note the degree to which such mergers and acquisitions swallowed small businesses and thus truncated a historical pathway into economic enterprise for women who overwhelmingly operated small-scale businesses. But the stories of Lewis, Beech, and Rudkin add a new dimension to that perspective, revealing that the sale of a smaller company to a conglomerate was a strategy these women adopted that brought them wealth as well as seats of power. Thus, women could be and were agents and actors in the process of conversion to big business. This was not always a good outcome for the company or the community in which it was situated. And the degree to which these three female board members were able to exercise influence from their seats of corporate power is a topic of investigation in the book. Yet, importantly, all three women leaders examined here occupied this role, precursors to the yet unfulfilled hope of 1960s and present-day feminists for greater representation of women in corporate governance.

The histories of Lewis, Beech, and Rudkin push for a more complex and nuanced understanding of businesswomen's history. Because existing

scholarship has focused on earlier periods of history, small-scale proprietors, and entrepreneurs in feminized economic niches such as the beauty
industry, we know little about women who operated larger-scale businesses
with national markets in manufacturing sectors dominated by men, especially during the mid-twentieth century.[11] Yet as the National Association
of Manufacturers' 1950s film series *Industry on Parade* made clear to
American television audiences, women manufacturers were not novel and
they were not remarkable just because they were women. Instead, this
decade-long television program, which was broadcast on 270 stations nationwide, presented female manufacturing leaders in businesses of all sizes
as playing a crucial role in the country's economy as the creators of consumer
goods, jobs, and industrial growth. It was a celebratory perspective to be
sure, adopted to promote the interests of American manufacturers.[12] But it
was also the perspective shared by Lewis, Beech, and Rudkin themselves.
Although they operated in an overwhelmingly male business world, they resisted the notion that their story was remarkable because they were women.
Instead, they viewed themselves as remarkable manufacturers whose story
was worth telling because they were successful business leaders. By seizing strategic opportunities such as federal government loans and contracts
and tax recovery programs—which played a critical role in their business
success—these women eked out a place for themselves at the upper echelons of the corporate world. And it was for this business acumen, and not
because they were "boss ladies," that they viewed their status as high-profile
corporate leaders appropriate. Thus, these women teach us not just about
women's outsider status in the business world but also how they got inside
and thus reveal strategies of entrepreneurship about which we have known
little before now.

Understanding the stories of Lewis, Beech, and Rudkin is important
partly because they help to explain the emergence of the leaders who are
the face of female business success today. In the last twenty years, scholars
of the post–World War II period have asserted that incremental changes in
marriage, family, and work patterns among American women during the
late 1940s and 1950s are vital to understanding the dramatic changes that
occurred in conjunction with the feminism of the 1960s and 1970s. "Change
was already afoot" among the men and women of this previous generation,
historians demonstrated, but had been overlooked amid a focus on their
children—the baby boom generation whose radical activism as young adults
spearheaded so many changes for women.[13] In fact, the ongoing activism
of women—in a variety of feminist and social justice–oriented movements

that bridged the World War II era and the 1960s—has led some scholars to call for abandoning the "wave" metaphor in the history of American feminism, which inherently suggests periods of progress and stagnation or retraction.[14] In the arena of workplace activism, for example, extensive examples of "labor feminism" during the second half of the twentieth century suggest that a history focused on continuity rather than change is a more accurate framework for the examination of feminism.[15] This book contributes to that revision by positing that female leaders of large-scale businesses who operated in a national spotlight and national markets helped lay the groundwork for the businesswomen of the 1960s, 1970s, and thereafter whom we celebrate today as the forerunners of women's business leadership. If Lewis, Beech, and Rudkin had not *leaned in* during the middle of the twentieth century, then the Sheryl Sandbergs of today would not be gracing the covers of *Fortune* and *Businessweek* in the early twenty-first century. Even though they constituted a very small percentage of women business owners, they helped to groom the path toward leadership for subsequent generations. As they earned industry awards and honors for their success, served their nation on important government advisory committees as "leading women industrialists," garnered national media attention, and built wealth for their shareholders, they helped to chip away at the resistance to women's participation in the business world as leaders. Although business and popular publications made these women icons for the women's movement—all three appeared in one of *Fortune*'s features on leading businesswomen and *Cosmopolitan* included two in a story about successful women who could teach a younger generation about getting ahead—neither Lewis nor Beech nor Rudkin embraced feminist activism during their careers. But all three articulated powerful rationales for women's self-determination, resolve, and ambition, championing the idea that women's abilities were equal to men's and that they should have an equal opportunity to succeed. In so doing, this book argues, they contributed to incremental changes and helped to lay the foundation for later workplace triumphs for women.[16] It was a long road to pave.

Lewis, Beech, and Rudkin became entrepreneurs by adopting strategies for success that leveraged the opportunities they had to build a path to the top of corporate America. Through strategic marriages and alliances with male family members, they accessed "expert capital" and privilege to create successful entrepreneurial pathways for themselves in spite of limiting gender conventions about marriage and mothering (chapter 1). By forging effective relations with a growing federal government, they fended off intrusive regulatory practices associated with wartime powers and tapped into funding and contracting opportunities decades before legislation mandated equal access to government investments for women business owners (chapter 2). At a time of worker dissent and upheaval, all three conformed to the labor-management trends in their industries and time periods, reminding us that from the perspective of a business president, towing the line was often efficient, effective, and necessary for business success even if not progressive or admirable according to modern-day feminist and social justice advocates (chapter 3). In an era of growing competition, "differentiation [was] everything" and Lewis, Beech, and Rudkin used gender difference—ostensibly a handicap in the male-dominated manufacturing world of big business—to distinguish themselves from the competition, creating brands with distinctly gendered iconography, consumer appeals, and origin stories (chapter 4).[17] And finally, three-quarters of a century before Sheryl Sandberg reminded us that asserting self-worth was key to success as a woman business leader, these female entrepreneurs were carving out ways to advocate for themselves in business environments that were not prepared for women, let alone for women leaders (chapter 5).

Thus, this book examines the actions of Lewis, Beech, and Rudkin to reveal what it took to become successful female entrepreneurs in large-scale manufacturing businesses in the mid-twentieth century. It shows how women successfully traversed barriers to entry by identifying and seizing opportunities, manipulating commonly held ideas to their advantage, and asserting and advocating for themselves. Addressing what one scholar describes as "what the entrepreneur *does* and not who the entrepreneur *is*," it examines mid-twentieth-century female entrepreneurship in big business as a *process*, one that required vigilant and innovative investments in opportunity and self-advocacy.[18] Focusing on their strategies for success tells us not just that women made it, but how—the key to understanding their expanded opportunities and success.

Lewis, Beech, and Rudkin would have been glad for this focus on how they got there because it was their best defense against the common insistence that each of them was a "boss lady" rather than just a boss.

1   Constructing Entrepreneurial Pathways

· ·

"I know you, you go do it . . . six months from now you're going to be bored." That was what the husband of Virginia Rometty, IBM's first female CEO, said to her when earlier in her career she was offered a "big job" but worried that she did not have sufficient professional experience to be successful in it. She had "told the recruiter that she needed to think about it," but while reviewing the opportunity that evening with her husband, he said to her, "Do you think a man would have ever answered that question that way?" While Rometty reported that the experience had taught her the importance of confidence, the story also reveals the supportive role that husbands have played in the lives of some successful businesswomen. Such emotional support can help facilitate the kind of risk-taking inherent in business leadership for which confidence is a necessary ingredient. And as Rometty has been quick to emphasize, in addition to providing emotional support, her husband has also been an equal partner in their marriage, helping to facilitate her rise to the top of corporate America.[1]

Rometty's relationship with her husband and the role his support and household participation have played in her success are emblematic of female business leaders more generally at the beginning of the twenty-first century. In fact, for many women in the upper echelons of the business world, marriage plays an important role in both their success and persistence, according to a variety of sources. One *Harvard Business Review* article titled "Manage Your Work, Manage Your Life," for example, reported that "many of those [executives] we surveyed consider[ed] emotional support the biggest contribution their partners have made to their careers."[2] But in other studies, the division of household labor is the focus and husbands are singled out for the impact their willingness or resistance to participate has on married women's professional careers and success. The 2014 national bestseller *Lean In: Women, Work, and the Will to Lead*, for example, includes a chapter titled "Make Your Partner a Real Partner," which documents the importance of sharing the work of house and family to women's success and encourages men to "lean in" to parenting. When professional women have husbands who do not share the work, it has a negative impact on their careers. In fact, a variety of research studies make clear that at the beginning of the twenty-first century, few women who are married to men will retain demanding professional jobs and remain married if they do not have the active support of their partners—both in the form of encouragement and participation in the day-to-day work of their household and parenting if they have children.[3] Thus, husbands figure prominently in the biographies of many married female business leaders at the beginning of the twenty-first century for the ways they help or hinder their wives' success.

This chapter takes up that topic—marriage and male family members— and examines the role both played in the careers of female entrepreneurs almost three-quarters of a century earlier, but not as sources of emotional support or household partnership. In fact, it is unlikely women received both or either of these forms of support from male relatives at this time in history. Rather, for women in the middle of the 1900s, marriage and male family members were stepping stones on the pathway to entrepreneurial opportunity.

Tillie Lewis, Olive Ann Beech, and Margaret Rudkin all provide examples of how successful mid-twentieth-century female entrepreneurs in large-scale manufacturing companies carved out a place for themselves at the top of the American business world by leveraging their relationships with the men in their personal and professional lives. This is different from arguing that men gave their wives [or sisters-in-law, in Lewis's case] a leg up. That was true too. But the goal here is to understand the way in which this generation of women, hampered by marriage bars, professionally crippling domestic expectations, and lack of access to higher education (none of the three received a college education, let alone an MBA), made the most of their relationships with male family members to plot their paths into business leadership and ownership.

For female entrepreneurs, who carry responsibility for a business's success or failure as opposed to female business professionals who manage it, connections gained through male relatives have been an especially important avenue to opportunity and success, and this is even clear in the lives of women at the start of the twenty-first century. Family studies scholars, for example, have coined the term "spousal social capital" to capture the "resource and interpersonal transactions" that entrepreneurial spouses provide and that studies confirm have a measurable impact on the sustainability of the firm. These include everything from time invested to participation in decision-making and representing the firm in the community. Wives have long played such a role in their husbands' businesses, often unnamed in official records yet essential in day-to-day operations. But women have often not been able to count on that same support from husbands and other male relatives. In fact, researchers theorize that because female entrepreneurs tend to have "less involved spouses during firm creation" relative to men, this may help explain what others have labeled the underperformance of woman-owned ventures.[4] Spousal contacts make a difference to female entrepreneurs too. For example, educated middle- and upper-class white women in the United States enjoy access to social capital and investors as an advantage of marriage because their husbands are likely to be employed professionally and to have connections to networks of power and privilege.[5] Thus, husbands' involvement, and their willingness and ability to share valuable connections, has tangible impact and can make a measurable difference in facilitating married women's entrepreneurship and success.

Studies of women entrepreneurs in American history have confirmed that marriage has played an important role in facilitating women's access to business ownership. Married and formerly married (widowed and divorced) women have constituted the majority of all female business owners, a finding that is consistent across several studies of women in colonial America up through the early twentieth century. They gained experience and expertise by working in businesses owned by their husbands, accessed capital through their husbands' income and property, and inherited their businesses when they died. The influence of a husband, however, was not always advantageous, as individual stories of profligate, foolhardy, and controlling spouses reveal. And during the nineteenth century, marriage also restricted women's legal independence, including their ability to own property and enter into contracts, both common aspects of entrepreneurship; this remained true in many states and hampered women's ability to "conduct business in their own name" until the laws were changed. Yet even then, as widows (or formerly married women), female business owners in the nineteenth century tapped into marital property and capital to independently operate enterprises now accessible because of their new status as "sole" traders. Thus, in spite of the important ways in which marriage restricted women's economic enterprise, in general historians of businesswomen agree that marriage also facilitated entrepreneurial opportunities for women by providing them access to capital and experience.[6]

Yet while a husband's resources might have provided access to entrepreneurship, women had to seize that opportunity. The frequency with which women married to business executives with contacts and capital did *not* launch entrepreneurial business careers clearly makes this point. Thus, to study mid-twentieth-century female entrepreneurs is to study women who actively pursued the opportunities before them to create pathways into business ownership.

For Lewis, Beech, and Rudkin, this was certainly true—all three leveraged the contacts, capital, and opportunities their husbands and other male family members provided to gain entry into the business world and business ownership. Lewis married a wholesaler and, while working in the business he owned jointly with several of her male relatives, gained experience and contacts that she used to launch Flotill Products. And both Olive Ann Beech and Margaret Rudkin were hired as secretaries to the men who later became their husbands and business partners and whose professional stature and contacts opened the doors to business ownership. But all three women walked through those opened doors themselves, leveraging their marital relationships and relationships with male relatives to create their own opportunities.

On the one hand, this is a familiar—even a clichéd—story. Marrying into opportunity is a literary trope with a long history and has been a driver of women's (and men's) social mobility over several decades. Stories about "office wives" abounded in the 1920s and 1930s—female secretaries who conducted the "housework of [the] business" for their male bosses in sociologist C. Wright Mills's conception and became romantically and sexually entangled with them in fictional accounts such as Faith Baldwin's *The Office Wife* (1930).[7] And historians have documented that during this period a popular conception was that unmarried women secured secretarial jobs in order to find husbands.[8]

But the history of female owners of large-scale businesses in the mid-twentieth century is not a story about "gold diggers" or sexual trysts but about the ways in which women leveraged marriage to access business entrepreneurship and leadership. As biographical accounts reveal, most successful businesswomen of the era gained opportunities through their husbands or other family members. *Fortune*'s 1973 article on "The Ten Highest-Ranking Women in Big Business," for example, reported that with only two exceptions, the executives featured "were helped along by a family connection, by marriage, or by the fact that they helped to create the organizations they now preside over." Though the article puts the emphasis on the help these women received rather than the opportunities they seized, it's clear that they actively pursued their leadership roles. As Dorothy Chandler of the Times Mirror Co. reported in the article, "If I had not been Mrs. Norman Chandler, I would not have had the opportunities I've had."[9]

The opportunities were associated with her married name, but the achievements were all Dorothy's.

Access to social capital was particularly key for women breaking into the male-dominated manufacturing fields Lewis, Beech, and Rudkin occupied, and male family members provided that connection. On the one hand, this did not distinguish them from men. Historian Pamela Laird, author of *Pull: Networking and Success since Benjamin Franklin* (2006), explains: "What the rare rags-to-riches story and *all* success stories prove . . . [with] no exception [is] . . . the necessity for connections and connectability—the rule of social capital."[10] But studies have shown that for women, social capital— access to mentors, networks, and information—has been a critical factor in "how and why [they] gain access to top leadership positions."[11] For female entrepreneurs in particular, breaking into industries in which few women have succeeded, connections to key players signaled expertise and legitimacy. One study of present-day entrepreneurship, for example, finds that this is even more important for women than it is for men. This is because they face a variety of barriers, especially in male-dominated industries, including doubts about their abilities and prospects for success—a particular problem when it is a perspective held by funders. Today, displaying ties to those perceived as "experts" in the industry—or "expert capital"—leads to strategic capital investments and venture longevity for female entrepreneurs because they are perceived as legitimate.[12] For female entrepreneurs in the mid-twentieth-century United States, "expert capital" required associations with men of influence and/or experience. Most times male family members in the business world provided this legitimacy; other times ties to leading men in the industry with whom female business leaders cultivated connections through family members or family responsibilities provided it. Either way, integrating "experts" into their social capital networks was a key step in their entrepreneurial pathways.

Privilege paved the way toward entrepreneurship and leadership for all three women too—another corollary of the ties they forged and leveraged through marriage. As is still true today, economic status afforded a degree of autonomy out of reach for most other women. For Lewis, this meant independent investments and travel—the latter tied also to the professional advantages of childlessness for women. Beech and Rudkin, on the other hand, both mothers of young children, used their wealth to craft versions of motherhood that relied on full-time, live-in childcare as well as other helpers to free them to devote time, energy, and attention to their businesses.

In interesting, important, and different ways, however, mothering and working overlapped for both of them, revealing the ways in which the separate identities and categories of labor we've imagined for mid-twentieth-century women were less clearly defined in the day-to-day lives of female entrepreneurs. Corporate jobs and motherhood were not irreconcilable for these women, but the "competing devotions" of career and family did collide. They mediated these conflicts by fashioning a version of motherhood that capitalized on pre–baby boom parenting definitions not yet saturated with what historian Jessica Weiss has called the "quest for togetherness" and relying on their wealth, allocating much of the work of day-to-day mothering to round-the-clock helpers.[13] Thus, wealth and the privileges it afforded, including social capital, all initiated through marriage and connections to male family members, enabled these mid-twentieth-century women to construct entrepreneurial pathways into positions of leadership and influence.

Tillie Lewis

For Tillie Lewis, relationships were everything—the escape route, the leg up, and the bridge to business ownership. And it's not that Lewis herself described her opportunities this way. Like many successful people, she tended to tell a tale of individual initiative when asked about her entrepreneurial pathway, underestimating both the degree of luck in her success and the contributions of the many other people who helped to facilitate her good fortune. Robert H. Frank's recent *Success and Luck: Good Fortune and the Myth of Meritocracy* reveals how common this tendency is even today and the ways in which it can be characterized as a psychological adaptation that fuels hard work even as it undermines appreciation for the many factors that contribute to success beyond individual enterprise.[14] But careful attention to the details of Lewis's life prior to and at the commencement of her entrepreneurship reveals that her connections to key individuals in business provided a conduit for her to acquire exposure, experience, contacts, and insights critical to her ability to launch her own enterprise.

Lewis's early biographical details reveal multiple encounters with the retail and wholesale business world and significant involvement in her family's business affairs. Born Myrtle Ehrlich in 1896 to Austrian Jewish immigrants, "Tillie"—as she came to be called—was raised by a father who, according to some accounts, operated a small phonograph store in Brooklyn, New York.[15] She left school early but reportedly completed secretarial and bookkeeping courses, which she utilized in subsequent jobs.[16] When she married in 1916 at the age of twenty, she chose Louis Weisberg, also an Austrian Jewish immigrant, who operated an established grocery business with his brother.[17] That Lewis's marital choice kept her engaged in the business world may have reflected parental expectation or personal interest. Countless Jewish American women before her had carved out important positions in their families and communities either as helpmates in their husbands' businesses or as independent business operators themselves. Multiple contemporary media accounts suggest that Lewis's involvement in her husband's business was significant.[18] In the census records for these early years, Tillie isn't listed as having an occupation. Yet when census takers indicated married women's occupation as "none" or "housewife," this obscured as much as it revealed, because many wives were in fact employed as unpaid family laborers in their husbands' businesses—hidden capital contributing to family well-being as well as their own acquisition of experience and skill.[19] This may well have been the case with Lewis in the early years. One family account indicates that in the business her husband eventually formed with her brother-in-law and father, she worked at the start as bookkeeper and that in fact it was she who had the vision for the family enterprise, suggesting that they open the wholesale business together in the first place.[20] Whatever the nature of her engagement, such experience provided valuable exposure to the day-to-day operations of business ownership that she would parlay into her own entrepreneurial pathway years later. This, in combination with the ambition and vision she seems to have displayed early on in conjunction with her family's business, provided the foundation for her successful foray into entrepreneurship herself years later.

Documentary evidence reveals that the family business afforded privileges that many immigrants or children of immigrants could ill afford and thus must have been a successful one. For example, by the mid-1920s, Tillie and Louis Weisberg resided in the Flatlands neighborhood of Brooklyn, a "suburban" area filled with "two-family brick row houses with garages" and populated with professionals and business owners, many of whom employed live-in servants, as was the case with the Weisbergs.[21] The incorporation of a new wholesale grocery business, Hochheiser & Weisberg, cofounded in 1923 by Louis Weisberg; Samuel Hochheiser, Tillie's brother-in-law who was also a longtime grocer; and her father, Jacob Ehrlich, facilitated the couple's upwardly mobile lifestyle and signaled business success.[22]

Privilege afforded comforts that also turned out to be opportunities for Lewis. For example, in 1924, at the age of twenty-eight, Lewis applied for

In 1924, Tillie Weisberg applied for a passport intending to travel for "health reasons." The trip was the first of many transoceanic voyages that took her to Italy, where she had the opportunity to learn about the Italian tomato business. In appearance and mobility, she was a "modern" woman. Passport Applications, National Archives and Records Administration, Washington, D.C., Ancestry.com database online.

her first passport with the intention of traveling to Europe "for health" reasons. And indeed, on May 28 of that year, she left aboard the *Aquitania* to visit France, England, Germany, Italy, Poland, and Czechoslovakia. On board Cunard's "Atlantic Lady," Lewis took part in the launch of "third class tourist travel" that became popular among the well-heeled but not super rich.[23] Sporting a Louise Brooks–style "bob" and quintessential "flapper" beads, Lewis was a fashionable, "modern" woman partaking in a new trend.[24] Upon her return to New York City some two months later, she was a woman with international experience, well poised to contribute to the import business her husband and male relatives had just launched.

Of course, the fact that Lewis remained childless during her marriage to Weisberg was a critical factor in her ability to do so. Though the number of economically active married women in the United States doubled between 1900 and 1930, their economic engagement was generally confined to those pursuits compatible with the high expectations of marriage and motherhood. This included taking in boarders, laundering clothes, and selling food—all traditional forms of work for women with families, especially those who were undereducated and racially marginalized as was Lewis. Though she had developed "business" skills at a vocational school, her status as a married woman barred her employment in many governmental and corporate jobs that had restrictive rules against hiring married women.[25] Applying her skills within a family-owned business, of course, solved this problem. Yet the role that Lewis would eventually play in her family's wholesale business involved travel—an activity that surely would have been off limits if she were parenting a young child. Though by the 1920s the white birth rate had declined significantly, childless marriages were still uncommon; on average, American women bore between 3.3 and 2.1 children each between 1920 and 1930.[26] Thus, Lewis was unusual in this respect, but the historical record leaves no indication of why—that is, we don't know whether she and her husband were physically unable to conceive or whether she deliberately practiced marital celibacy or contraception.[27] Historians have argued that a growing number of white middle-class women did the latter to "foster capital accumulation," though this strategy was typically paired with a reduction in the number of children and not childlessness altogether.[28] Not surprisingly for a woman in the early twentieth century, Lewis did not discuss her childless status, nor is there any evidence that she was asked about it in press accounts covering her later success. That she was a doting aunt, however, substantiated by her continuing involvement in the lives of her sister's three sons (two of whom she employed) and their children, suggests that she enacted the cultural expectations of women as family centered (and perhaps the dictates of her heart) in her own way. The result was that by avoiding the day-to-day responsibilities of motherhood, she was freed to engage in business on a scale unusual for a married woman.[29]

Transatlantic travel, for example, became a regular occurrence for Lewis over the course of the next several years and is key to understanding the network, expertise, and status she developed, which would later facilitate her own entrepreneurship. Extant ships' passenger lists reveal that Lewis traveled to Naples in 1926, 1928, and 1932 and to Genoa in 1933. On only one of those transatlantic voyages was she accompanied by a male relative— the 1932 trip to Naples during which she was accompanied by her husband Louis Weisberg. By the time Lewis began crisscrossing the Atlantic to Italy, she was in fact officially employed by her husband, brother-in-law, and father's business. In the 1925 New York City directory, under Hochheiser & Weisberg, Inc., Tillie Weisberg is listed as secretary of the company, with Louis Weisberg as president, Jacob Ehrlich as vice president, and Samuel Hochheiser as treasurer of their wholesale business.[30] As an officer of Hochheiser & Weisberg, Lewis may well have been expected to participate in international travel as one of her job responsibilities, since the company sold Italian imports. According to one study, many of the passengers on transatlantic ocean liners during the 1920s were women working as buyers for U.S. companies.[31]

Lewis's professional status with Hochheiser and Weisberg begot both economic success and independence. While employed as secretary at the company, Lewis reportedly earned an income of $12,000 annually, four times the average yearly salary of many male professionals during the period. Some sources indicate that Lewis was employed selling stocks after the end of her marriage to Weisberg. In one account published at the end of her life, for example, Lewis reported, "My marriage came to end in five years and after that I went to business school, got a job selling securities for a stock exchange firm and saved my money." Yet because the dates of such employment conflict with both records of her employment in the family firm and a much longer marriage to Weisberg, the chronology and accuracy of such a claim is unclear.[32] But it is possible that investment income may have constituted at least a portion of this, since she was an avid investor. In this she was not unusual. According to historian Julia Ott, by the end of the 1920s "1.5 million Americans held trading accounts with brokers." Stock market investing had become a lot more accessible thanks to the New York Stock Exchange's efforts to create a "people's market" by reaching out to retail investors. And as "the Dow Jones Industrial Average nearly doubled between March 1928 and September 1929," the attraction of stock investments seemed clear.[33] Lewis invested her money independently of her husband, and that meant she gained and lost her earnings on her own too. By 1932, unpaid liabilities totaling $57,716 incurred from stock transactions forced her to declare personal bankruptcy.[34] This was the height of the depression— a year when such declarations were commonplace. But before the Great Crash, she could have earned an equal amount.

Her ability to trade stock independent of her husband, her solo travels, and her employment in the family business as an officer reveal a great deal about Lewis, her marriage, and her entrepreneurial pathway. Clearly she expected to be able to negotiate the world independent of her husband. This, in fact, may have been the source of the "irreconcilable differences" cited as the reason for her eventual divorce from Louis Weisberg.[35] One account suggests that Lewis's independence from her husband is best explained by a public extramarital love affair (and perhaps more than one) though the evidence for this interpretation is not conclusive.[36] Regardless, long before her divorce, Lewis behaved as an *un*married woman was expected to behave rather than a married woman, carving out a degree of autonomy that ran counter to the marriage prescriptions of the day. Years later when Dun & Bradstreet evaluated her business's credit-worthiness, she was still married to Louis Weisberg, but he had "no financial interest in the business and

[was] not active" in it.[37] Evidence does not reveal whether the end of the Weisbergs' marriage was congenial or acrimonious, but they seemed to be practical about it because they maintained a business relationship after their divorce. Fourteen years after Lewis launched her business and left her marriage, 2 percent of her company's total sales were to Moosalina Products Corporation in New York, an importer and wholesaler of groceries where Louis Weisberg was employed as secretary-treasurer.[38] Lewis's marriage to Weisberg had helped her to gain access to the business world— it provided experience, contacts, and wealth that she leveraged to launch her entry into entrepreneurship. This, in combination with her penchant for independence and her aforementioned business vision, situated her well for entrepreneurship.

Lewis's knowledge about Italian tomatoes, the product with which she launched her business in 1934, also developed through her involvement with Hochheiser & Weisberg, which had a long-standing specialization with Italian foods. This was an economic sector that Samuel Hochheiser, the husband of Tillie Lewis's sister Beatrice, knew well. He began as a grocery manager in 1912 and within three years had succeeded as a business owner in the Bronx in a neighborhood populated largely by Jews and Italians.[39] Hochheiser first brought his business interests together with Louis Weisberg in 1920. It was a natural partnership given the closeness of the two families, who also were neighbors.[40] They operated retail groceries in three locations in Belmont, a Bronx neighborhood densely populated by Italian immigrants in the early 1900s that "eventually became known as the Little Italy of the Bronx."[41] Grocery shopping was primarily a local affair in the early twentieth century, an excursion undertaken within one's own neighborhood, and thus it stands to reason that the preponderance of their customers were Italian.[42] And for Italian Americans and Italian immigrants, this must have included imported, canned tomatoes, since, as reported in a 1903 New York newspaper article titled "Things Little Italy Eats," "no people [were] more devoted to their native foods than the Italians, and Italian groceries filled with imported edibles" were the norm. Canned tomatoes from Italy were among the many imports that were in demand.[43] When Hochheiser & Weisberg commenced in the wholesale grocery business three years later, they located their warehouse in an industrial section of Lower Manhattan that was "the principal conduit for New York City's consumer food" economy and in close proximity to Manhattan's "Little Italy."[44]

In press accounts, Lewis emphasized a singular and romanticized version of her initial encounter with *pomodoros*, but her business experience with

Hochheiser & Weisberg and their specialization in Italian foods provided her ample opportunity to gain extensive product knowledge. Reportedly, the tomatoes had first caught her attention on the warehouse shelf: "I was taking inventory in this dusty old grocery store warehouse in New York City. I took down the small can and looked at it. It was a fancy little thing, decorated in red, yellow and green. The label said: 'Pomodori Pelati, imported from Italy.' . . . That evening on the way home I bought a can of the peeled Italian tomatoes I had seen on the self and tried them for supper. I loved their tangy flavor. I learned that these little pear-shaped tomatoes were popular in the United States."[45] Lewis's business experience with Italian tomatoes was probably much more substantial than this one encounter in the warehouse, however. During her voyages to Italy, she likely learned a great deal about Italian foods, especially tomatoes. Naples, thrice her port-of-call, was home to one of Italy's largest tomato-canning plants—a fact unlikely to be missed by an American wholesaler who distributed Italian foods. In addition, she must have learned about Madonna brand tomatoes through the business too—American-grown Italian tomatoes and paste canned by River Bank Canning Company, founded in California's Central Valley in 1923 by Italian immigrant Lorenzo Zerillo. His product dominated New York markets by the end of the 1930s, shipped out of Stockton, California, and was distributed to wholesalers from an office located less than half a mile from Hochheiser & Weisberg where she worked.[46] Thus, while several press reports indicate that Lewis researched the best conditions for growing *pomodoros* by contacting botanical experts and in this way chose Stockton in California's Central Valley as the location for her business, it is likely that her business experience and contacts had exposed her to the merits of California's climate for growing tomatoes.[47] In fact, one source indicates that it was Italian consul Harry Mazzera who "aided Tillie Lewis to see the possibility of that part of the country" [Stockton] for growing *pomodoros*.[48] But it is also possible that she simply imitated the River Bank Canning Company's business model after identifying the opportunity to capture market share in the nascent American-based Italian tomato industry. Countless entrepreneurs before her had launched enterprises by seizing a piece of an established but growing market with few competitors. It was a strategy that only an "insider" could pursue, since it required market insight—keen awareness about product, demand, and growth potential. Lewis had gained them all.

Contacts and connections within the Italian food trade were an important advantage for Lewis when she launched her own business. Most important, she developed a business relationship with Florindo Del Gaizo, agent in the United States for Del Gaizo, Santarsiero & Co., which operated a tomato canning plant outside Naples.[49] Del Gaizo was likely a longtime business associate. Lewis's personal secretary and her nephew both stated that she "probably knew Del Gaizo, or one of his associates, since the late 1920s from the wholesale food business."[50] Ship passenger lists also confirm that the two were on board the same ship twice, in 1928 and 1932, traveling between Naples and New York City. This may or may not have been a coincidence. Local historian Kyle Wood asserts that Lewis's trips to Italy with Del Gaizo were romantic rather than business-related and that the two had a long-standing extramarital affair.[51] Whether or not this conclusion is substantiated, it was certainly a fortuitous opportunity to have an audience with a member of the Del Gaizo family, leading tomato merchants in Italy especially at this point in time. Italian exports to the United States were severely depressed by a newly imposed 50 percent tariff on imported tomato products and Del Gaizo must have been primed for a new business opportunity.[52] He agreed to provide seeds, equipment, technicians to install it, and $10,000 to help Lewis start her business canning California-grown *pomodoros*. In exchange, he retained majority ownership in the company (85 percent) and gained a new revenue stream at a time when trade restrictions must have significantly hurt his sales. Lewis retained the title of secretary-treasurer, a 15 percent share of the company, and day-to-day management—it was a position she retained until becoming sole owner of the business. Though her relationship with Del Gaizo seemed to deteriorate over time, marked by fundamental disagreements about how to invest company profits and manage progress, which led to her efforts to buy out his interest, his association with Flotill was an important factor in its success.[53] In essence, his name signaled expert endorsement of Lewis as business manager, communicating to business owners, bankers, and others associated with the Italian food industry that she was legitimate and worthy of investment.[54]

Del Gaizo's backing was key to opening the distribution door too. An extensive network of contacts within the Italian American grocery business was critical to Lewis's early success. A handwritten account book reflecting company shipments between May and July 1936, for example, shows that most of Flotill's products were shipped to eastern and midwestern locations. Cities such as New York, Newark, Hoboken, Buffalo, Syracuse, Philadelphia, and Boston appear throughout the ledger, often in conjunction with Italian proprietors such as "Piccini," "Mazzini," and "Salvatore Lanza."[55] These were likely grocers to whom Del Gaizo had sold Italian food products and may have been known to Lewis herself through her own business experience at Hochheiser & Weisberg. Lewis personally attended to these sales, traveling all over the country by train and by bus, and when she appeared on their doorstep to sell her California-grown *pomodoros*, she got an audience with them because of her association with Del Gaizo and her experience in the industry.[56] Convincing them to buy Flotill tomatoes instead of or at least in addition to the competitors—by 1937 there were twelve California producers of canned *pomodoros* all marketing their tomatoes as "Italian"—became increasingly important. Early association with Del Gaizo and his excellent tomatoes—seeded from his very own Neopolitan plants—continued to distinguish her from the competition.[57]

Lewis's business associations and the connections they facilitated also provided the conduit for capital when she needed it most. After the initial startup funded by Del Gaizo's investment, Lewis found capital hard to come by. Like most small-scale entrepreneurs, especially women, she found loans on good terms nearly inaccessible. When she bought out the Del Gaizo interest in 1939, for example, $45,000—or 63 percent—of the total capital required came from Pacific Can, the company from whom she had originally leased the canning facility at her Stockton business site.[58] The money came in the form of a "personal loan repayable $15,000 yearly," but it came at a high cost: she had to agree to put up the "entire stock" of the company as collateral, signing "a second deed of trust mortgage on the real estate and buildings and a chattel mortgage on the machinery and equipment."[59] When she finally obtained a bank loan—$10,000 *unsecured*, the final piece of funding she needed to "commence operations on the 1939 pack"—it came from Banco di Napoli Trust Company in New York City.[60] The company was cash poor at the time of the loan, having been "bled dry" by Del Gaizo as well as Lewis's withdrawal to complete the buy-out. As she wrote in a letter to Charles Young, the executive vice president of the bank, "looking at our financial statement with a banking eye it may appear that we do not have enough working capital to warrant your generosity," but she assured him that her plans for the future were ambitious, prospects were good, and that "under many adverse conditions in the past I have weathered every storm." Her only interest now, she stated, "was to work and build up a reserve capital that must stay in the business and not be drawn out."[61] Specifically distancing herself from the Del Gaizo management strategy and assuring the banker that his investment in her would prove profitable, Lewis conveyed her characteristic level of enthusiasm and commitment. This quality no doubt helped convince Young to take a risk on her. As her nephew Arthur

Heiser stated in an interview years later, "She could have probably sold the Brooklyn Bridge if she tried," so compelling was her sales pitch.[62] But it was no coincidence that the bank loan she received was not from the local Bank of Stockton or Bank of America where she maintained her accounts but where she "couldn't get the California bankers to back [her]."[63] That it came from Banco di Napoli—an institution likely to have known and done business with Del Gaizo and which knew of Flotill—underscores the importance of connections as conduits for capital, most especially connections to those perceived as "experts." Clearly Del Gaizo and his status in the industry signaled this for Lewis, even after he was no longer associated with the business, legitimating her experience and expertise in the industry as sufficient qualifications to warrant investment.[64] For Lewis, expert capital and social capital more generally *were* the entrepreneurial pathway, one paved through marital and family connections.

Olive Ann Beech

Olive Ann Beech's entrepreneurial pathway was decidedly different from Tillie Lewis's because her entry into business leadership was an unplanned succession. Though she'd been intimately involved in Beech Aircraft's financial operations and overall business administration as cofounder and secretary-treasurer from the company's 1932 start (and director soon thereafter), it wasn't until her husband's serious illness in 1940 that she stepped in decisively to lead the company—a process that continued informally even after he returned to work and ultimately led to her being voted in as president of the company after his death in 1950. Yet for these reasons, evaluating Beech's "path" into the presidency requires a careful examination of the nature of her leadership within the company up to and including her succession. This evaluation reveals that relationships paved the path for Olive Ann Beech just as they had for Tillie Lewis. But for Beech, whose husband's associates included some men interested in ousting her and overtaking the helm of Beech Aircraft when her husband became incapacitated, business relationships provided positive as well as negative motivation. That is, the associations that she gained through her husband inspired both defensive action and initiative, propelling her toward greater entrepreneurial leadership. And privilege and the freedoms that it could provide, especially for a working mother, facilitated her progress.

The financial expertise that Beech displayed early on was key to her entrepreneurial leadership and evolved from deep roots and deliberate cultivation. According to family lore, Olive Ann had her own bank account at the age of seven and was "handling all the bill-paying for her parents by age 11."[65] This arrangement may have been born as much from their need as from her gumption. A carpenter by training, her father, Frank Mellor, supported a family of four children through inconsistent employment in the housing industry. For example, the 1910 U.S. Census noted that he was unemployed for sixteen weeks during the previous year. His wife, Susannah, was identified in census records as having no occupation but reportedly supplemented the family's income in a variety of ways, including raising animals. As the youngest member of the family, Olive Ann may have been most useful to their efforts for economic security as a budgeter, especially since she was likely too young to contribute in other ways. But it was a skill that she deliberately honed thereafter. Instead of attending high school, she was enrolled at the age of sixteen as a student at a local community college, where she reportedly studied "business," which for women at the time meant secretarial and bookkeeping courses.[66] Two years later she had her first job working at Staley Electric Co. in nearby Augusta, a position that provided her with the experience necessary to be hired, three years later, as secretary-bookkeeper for Travel Air Co., the first company Walter H. Beech founded.[67] She worked her way up to office manager and secretary to the company president, Beech himself, through hard work, attention to detail, skillful operational and organizational management, and financial know-how. Some twenty-five years later, upon being named president of Beech Aircraft, the second company that Walter Beech founded with her help, Olive Ann Beech was described in the internal company newsletter as "the retiring modest half of an outstanding husband-and-wife team of business builders" in which "Walter H. Beech was always the engineering design and production genius" and "[she was] devoted . . . to the finances and management of their enterprises."[68] These were the strengths and skills that Olive Ann Beech cultivated to earn an ongoing role in the company and the aviation industry.

To her, they reflected the special abilities of women. These were skills that men did not possess. She argued that organizations "need[ed] women . . . [for] the meticulous detailed work which bores men and which women can do so well"; "they need[ed] the initiative and imagination of women . . . [who had] a reputation for cool consideration, level-headed judgment and fairness in competition."[69] Though today we might disagree with Beech's characterization of these skills as the exclusive province of women, her description is revealing because it captures her own special area of expertise as well as her modesty about her own talent and sense that such expertise was common among women.

In addition to cultivating this skill set, earning the respect of male associates and building effective working relationships with them was key to Beech's entrepreneurial pathway. In the 1920s and 1930s, the aviation field, after all, was filled with men like her eventual husband—daredevil, "macho" pilots who enjoyed the masculine fraternity of the industry as much as they did grandstanding, especially in front of women. Breaking into this culture and community was something Olive Ann Beech did carefully and deliberately. As she told a Soroptomist Club in the 1940s, her experience at Travel Air, the first aviation company where she worked, was "not a path of roses." Because of the industry culture and because she was the company's first female employee, it entailed many challenges: "Young though I was, I had to be alert to see that I was not stepped on; I learned to be tactful in demanding my rights without precipitating crises. Travel Air in those early days was an organization of twelve men with Walter H. Beech owner. This dynamic young man informed me of certain things he expected, most important of which was in my conduct. Eleven of the men were married and he was too busy, so he said, to be interested. On the promise of my keeping a hands-off policy I was given the job."[70] Perhaps reflecting the 1920s American preoccupation with female employment as a way station to marriage, Walter Beech's insistence on a "hands-off policy" by Olive Ann indicated that she was viewed as a sexual distraction or threat as much as she was a "meticulous" detail-oriented worker with a "cool" head for tough decisions at the time she was hired. Indeed, one *Fortune* article reported that Walter's initial assessment of her was: "You've got pretty good-looking legs, I guess you'll do."[71] Such gendered humiliations may have been common for Beech, since more recent studies of what is now labeled sexual harassment suggest that between 35 and 45 percent of women who worked outside the home during this era experienced some version of this form of discrimination during the course of their working lives.[72]

Fighting the uphill battle to earned respect within this environment and withstanding the daily humiliations about her lack of airplane knowledge, which almost caused her to quit multiple times, was a carefully orchestrated endeavor. She stated, "Firmly and consistently I have insisted that my work be accepted on the basis of its own merit and, after a long struggle, I am happy to say that my men associates do accord me the respect and consideration they would accord a man in my position. They regard me as a person worthy of their business trust because I have met and coped with them fairly and squarely and at no time have resorted to the tricks and wiles usually thought to be the business secret of our sex."[73] Deliberately eschewing what she referred to as a "woman's game"—using flirtation and emotion to influence associates and outcomes—she set out to execute her job in a way that effectively "eliminate[d] from [her] . . . thoughts the idea of sex"; that is, she set aside gender difference and status as well as behavior she considered gendered, making it as irrelevant as possible in her day-to-day interactions with male colleagues, and insisted that they do the same.[74] This approach was key to Beech's path into entrepreneurship. While effective relationships with male associates were also important for Tillie Lewis, whose business was in the similarly male-dominated canning industry, Beech's singular status as a woman executive in the ultra-masculine aviation field continued to attract male doubters and challengers some twenty years into her entrance in the industry. She had to have a clear standard by which to measure her own professional conduct and by which to insist that others do the same—one that eschewed gender as a factor.

Of course, in spite of her interest in operating outside the bounds of gender, becoming the wife of Walter Beech was, ironically, key to Olive Ann's status in the company and industry, and her connection to him and his established expertise and stature in aviation—something she strategically leveraged over and over again—provided her pathway into entrepreneurial leadership. His skill in aviation was as deep-seated as Olive Ann's financial acumen. According to company history, "as an adventuresome 14-year old farm boy" in Pulaski, Tennessee, Walter "built a glider of his own design, using materials found around his home" and made his first solo flight in a biplane just ten years later in 1914—a set of actions that mimicked the famous Wright brothers' just eleven years earlier. Eventually becoming an award-winning pilot, Walter put his aviation skills to good use during the war effort. During World War I, he served as an Army Air Corps pilot, flight instructor, and engineer, and later he "toured every state in the union as a barnstormer [exhibition pilot], during which time he gathered many ideas for improvement in aircraft design and construction." It was this passion that motivated him to leave his job as test pilot, salesman, and then general manager at Swallow Airplane Company to "put his own ideas into practice" and start his own company, Travel Air, which preceded the company he cofounded with Olive Ann. The Beech Aircraft Company's twin-engine Model 18, one of its first planes, is credited with helping to "advance [the] growth of commercial aviation in the years before World War II." And during the war it was used by the army and navy to train pilots, gunners, bombardiers, and navigators. Though the Museum of Flight today pays scant attention to Walter Beech's role in the aviation industry, the company he founded with Olive Ann Beech continued to celebrate him as an "air pioneer." On its first page, *The Story of Beechcraft*, a company history published in 1969, described the Beech Aircraft factory as "a monument to the vision, courage and ingenuity of Walter H. Beech, whose pioneering spirit proved to be a significant factor in extending the horizons of powered flight." Olive Ann herself helped to direct this focus, frequently presenting herself in official poses with an image of Walter right behind her. The medallion commissioned to honor the twenty-fifth anniversary of the company is one example, as are countless images with Olive Ann Beech seated at the head of a conference table or on her couch with a painting of Walter on the wall just behind her.[75] Indeed Walter H. Beech's induction into the Aviation Hall of Fame in 1977, twenty-seven years after his death and fourteen years after the establishment of this commemorative organization, highlights the degree to which Olive Ann Beech and Beech Aircraft strategically kept his legacy alive. "Without a doubt, Walter Herschel Beech left a valued legacy to aviation," the tribute reads, underscoring the insistence on his ongoing influence in the industry.[76] And his influence on Olive Ann Beech was clear too. When she was inducted into the National Aviation Hall of Fame four years after him in 1981, the same year she was appointed the first female board member of Raytheon, which was now the parent company of Beech Aircraft, the tribute included a reference to her marriage to Walter: "One of the most important events in Olive Ann's life came when she married Walter Beech. Their union was more than a conventional marriage: they soon dug deep into their savings to form the Beech Aircraft Company." In contrast, their marriage was described as "memorable" rather than "important" in Walter's tribute from the same organization.[77] This rhetorical distinction reflected both the gender conventions of the day and the reality that Walter's stature in the industry had not only opened the door to Olive Ann's remarkable career path but also continued to pave the way.

Because Walter loomed so large in her career and in the industry and because he rather than she fit accepted norms of business entrepreneurship, Olive Ann Beech stepped out in front of her husband as company leader only in his absence, and when she did, her assertions of leadership triggered conflict with male associates. This first happened in 1940, eight years after the company's founding, when Walter Beech became incapacitated with encephalitis for a prolonged period of time. Details of Walter's condition are elusive and seem to have been guarded closely by the family, presumably for the sake of privacy and perhaps also for the sake of the company. But since in serious cases like his, symptoms of the disease can include mental confusion, lack of consciousness, and paralysis, it seems likely that Olive Ann may have been acting independently (and perhaps even without his knowledge) when she stepped into his place as leader of the company. In fact, she was in the hospital for childbirth at the same time he was for illness and thus made a dramatic return to the office to protect her own interests and those of her family and the company. Their second child, Mary Lynn, was born just as Walter became ill and as escalating war in Europe led to military buildup in the United States, greatly expanding company orders. "Because of the urgency of the situation and because of our general manager's absence in Washington called there to formulate plans for our part in the defense program," she reported in a speech, "I continued my work from my hospital bed," and after only "thirty days rest . . . I was back at my desk again."[78] What she didn't share in the speech is that at this very point—one of great vulnerability for the family and high profitability for the company—fourteen top executives at Beech Aircraft initiated a coup attempt to seize control of the company. In response, Olive Ann "discharged all 14 and came out of the hospital . . . to regain the corporate reins." In so doing, she "showed her mettle" and her willingness and ability to step in for her husband even before she officially succeeded him as the company's chief executive.[79] Though Walter eventually returned to the office and his role as the company's president, some reported that he was never the same again and that Olive Ann never retreated from this expanded leadership role in the company.[80]

The general manager's absence only partially explains why Olive Ann stepped in in such a substantial way, a move that is best understood as deliberate self-assertion. Her dismissal of all fourteen executives involved in the coup displayed assertiveness and authority and consolidated her family's control of the company as well as her own leadership. This must have been a key objective, since the company stayed in family hands for fifty years with Olive Ann presiding until 1968, when a nephew succeeded her as president and she became board chair. But Olive Ann's succession in 1940 had not been the original plan when Walter became incapacitated. A companywide memo from him, distributed as he was exiting to attend to his health problems, informed employees that longtime Beech employee and corporate vice president/general manager John "Jack" Gaty would be the "responsible chief executive" in his absence, not Olive Ann.[81] Thus, how she

The Beech Family (Olive Ann, Walter, Suzanne, and Mary Lynn) along with many family friends, right before Walter took off on a sales trip to Latin America. According to many accounts, Olive Ann Beech was already overseeing much of the company's business by this time. Wichita State University Libraries, Special Collections and University Archives.

had the authority to dismiss the conspirators is unclear, since Gaty rather than she had been officially sanctioned by her husband as the company leader in his stead. But Gaty was a trusted and loyal associate of both Walter and Olive Ann Beech who continued to work closely with her for years following this dramatic turn of events. One account, in fact, describes Gaty as "a family friend [who] often took the Beech daughters to the movies."[82] Trust must have been key to the outcome of the tense situation. Perhaps her actions were prenegotiated with Gaty and viewed by him as complementary to his efforts on behalf of the company. Perhaps practicality and logistics determined the turn of events—Gaty was needed in Washington, D.C., so Olive Ann had to step up to address problems at company headquarters in Wichita. Whatever the circumstances behind her initiative, she may have surprised many when she stepped in. But if anyone harbored doubts about her ability to lead the company, she did not. And the need to fend off challengers, to her husband as well as to herself, called her into action. It was something she had to do several times more; she forced the resignation of a company vice president and Beech family member on one occasion and, on another, the resignation of a board member. All of them tried to challenge her leadership as president of the company in the years following her official succession after Walter's death.[83] In so doing, they made a critical mistake: underestimating her stake in the company and its leadership. For even if they didn't think she belonged in the executive suite of an aviation company, she did. And as she had always done, Olive Ann demanded the respect and consideration that her position and the quality of her work afforded her and maintained her longevity, power, and position.

The struggle to assert her authority even shaped her relationship with her husband, which was for most of their marriage a business relationship as well as a personal one. In their twenty-five-year relationship, there were only two years when they were not professional colleagues—the two years immediately following their 1930 wedding when Olive Ann ceased working, a customary turn of events for a married woman during this era in American history. During these two years the couple lived in New York City, where Walter assumed the vice presidency of Curtiss-Wright, the company to which he sold his first aviation business, while Olive Ann committed herself to establishing the couple's posh new Manhattan lifestyle in an apartment blocks from Central Park. But it was short-lived. In 1932, they returned to Wichita to start Beech Aircraft together.

In extant archival records, the nature of Olive Ann and Walter's professional relationship is represented in contradictory ways, and this tells us a great deal about their collaboration. The contradictions themselves, in fact, indicate that it was a highly negotiated relationship, one in which both Walter and Olive Ann asserted themselves. Multiple company histories produced after Walter Beech died, for example, refer to Olive Ann as cofounder of Beech Aircraft. And certainly this seemed to be her conception of the company's founding, which she described early on as inspired by "our *united* efforts and interests."[84] But not so with all accounts by Walter Beech captured before his death. For example, the company's original 1932 "Prospectus" described his credentials and then stated, "With Mr. Beech will be associated Mr. K. K. Shaul, former Vice-President and General Manager of Curtiss-Wright Airplane Co., and Mr. T. A. Wells, Designing Engineer." There is no mention of Olive Ann Beech anywhere in the document. Nor was she listed as a stockholder at this time, though 2,000 shares were explicitly set aside for Shaul and Wells. Four years later, in a set of documents prepared for incorporation in Delaware (to replace the Kansas corporation), Walter Beech described the company's startup this way: "In April 1932, I returned to Wichita and with my own capital, [and] a few employees (an engineer, designer and helper) [and] started The Beech Aircraft Company." The "helper" in this scenario was Olive Ann. Later in the document, in response to questions presumably posed during the application process, Walter Beech described company personnel this way: "The executive and the factory personnel is composed of men who are thoroly [sic] trained and experienced in their duties—most of the men were employed with the Travel Air Company of Wichita, now a part of the Curtiss Wright Corporation." This time Olive Ann disappears in the gendered language used to describe the "men" who worked at the company. Later in the same document, however, she is singled out as secretary-treasurer along with Walter Beech as president; R. K. Beech, his brother, as vice president; T. A. Wells as chief engineer; and C. G. Yankey as director and chief counsel. Olive Ann Beech's description, like the others, emphasizes her relationship to Walter H. Beech and her experience working in the industry. The document was clearly aimed at justifying her position (as well as the other employees' positions) to outside evaluators.[85] But it also reveals a great deal about Walter's self-referential view of the company's genesis and its contrast with Olive Ann's more collaborative perspective.

As Walter's business associate, Olive Ann navigated their relationship assertively but carefully, since he was the key to her entrepreneurial pathway into the world of aviation. That she was the third-largest stockholder by 1936, owner of 552 shares, a small amount compared to Walter Beech's 10,080 shares and Harris Thompson's 3,750 shares yet more than those of twenty-eight other stockholders (with shares ranging from 1 to 300), belies her effectiveness in "demanding her rights."[86] Reportedly, when Olive Ann signed on as secretary-treasurer of the new company, she did so on the condition that she would be adequately compensated for her work. As she reported in a 1959 interview, "I made him pay me a salary or I wouldn't work. I wasn't willing to give my life's blood and not have it properly evaluated."[87] Such self-advocacy was an important ingredient in Olive Ann's relationship with her husband. And it reveals the degree to which she carved her own entrepreneurial pathway out of the opportunities presented by her association with Walter Beech.

Of course, for Olive Ann Beech, marriage brought children as well as entrepreneurial opportunities, and she seemed divided about how best to manage these competing interests. The couple's first daughter, Suzanne, was born in 1937, five years after Beech Aircraft was founded and just as her office manager resigned, requiring Beech to reinsert herself into office affairs. She had been planning to delegate such work in order "to divide [her] time between office and home" until circumstances prevented it. "How many other women have said the same thing?" she mused several years later in a 1940s speech.[88] The quip highlighted that in Olive Ann Beech's mind, she was not so unusual as a professional woman and mother who had responsibilities for managing a business and a family. But statistics indicate that while nearly 50 percent of white, married women in Beech's age bracket (ages forty-five to fifty-four in 1950) and an even higher percentage of professionals and managers were employed persistently throughout the period 1940–50, it was unusual for a woman of her age to have young children and even more so if she was working.[89] When Olive Ann Beech gave birth to her second daughter, Mary Lynn, in 1940, she was thirty-seven and occupied a group constituting only 4 percent of all mothers in the United States.[90] That she was an older mother with a professional career made Olive Ann Beech even more unusual. In accordance with the standards of the day for privileged women, she had planned "to go back home" after the birth of her second child in 1940, but it coincided with both the hospitalization of Walter and the company's ramp-up to wartime production, prompting Olive Ann's decision to return to the office almost immediately. Her decision helps to highlight that entrepreneurial opportunities had to be seized and were not preserved for mothers facing difficult choices about their priorities.

Beech's return to the helm of the company with two young children at home also illustrates the ways in which privilege enabled some mid-twentieth-century women to craft models of motherhood that incorporated professional jobs. Live-in hired help facilitated Beech's ability to respond to her company's needs. Since before the birth of their children, the Beeches had relied on Faye and Lauretta Buckner, a husband-and-wife team, to cook and serve them elaborate dinners at the end of their busy work days. We can imagine that the Buckners' responsibilities grew with the growth of the Beech family. They may have been joined by other hired help, but extant records do not reveal anyone else. What they do confirm is that in 1946, when the Beeches' daughters would have been nine and six years old, the Buckners lived at the Beeches' 48 Mission Road home with Faye listed as a houseman. Nearly ten years later, the 1955 Wichita city directory recorded a different residential address for the Buckners but still listed Faye Buckner as "houseman to Olive Ann Beech."[91] The death of Walter five years earlier must have made the consistent household labor that the Buckners provided even more important. A personal chauffeur was also employed by Olive Ann Beech and was sometimes used to transport her daughters to scheduled activities. One account of Beech based significantly on the reminiscences of family and friends recalls, "She didn't personally take Mary Lynn and her friends to cheerleader practice or to athletic events . . . she dispatched her chauffeur to take them." Reliance on others to stand in in her absence was, of course, a necessary part of working motherhood. Like so many professional working mothers today, Beech "didn't attend all of their school programs, but would send someone else to be there."[92] Family and friends as well as hired helpers may all have served in this role. Of course, only the wealthiest American women in the 1940s and 1950s could afford to pay for the help of at least three full-time employees dedicated to providing the family domestic, transportation, and personal services. This underscores the degree to which Beech's path was paved with privilege. It afforded her unique opportunities to combine motherhood (and partially single motherhood) with a spectacularly successful business career.

There is much evidence that in spite of her reliance on live-in, full-time staff and the help of friends and family, mothering inserted itself into Olive Ann's daily business affairs, intermingling with her job of presiding over Beech Aircraft. For example, a scrapbook titled "Olive Ann Beech" and dated 10 December 1941, which contains articles about her and photos of her being honored at a Soroptomist dinner, also has photographs of her two daughters mixed in with the careful documentation of her successful career. And stashed inside a scrapbook of the *Businessweek* article that appeared in 1956 was Mary Lynn's high school report card. It was signed by Olive Ann as the form required but perhaps never made it back to the school as was likely expected to provide proof of parental receipt. Beech also mixed personal favors into professional relationships, leveraging her stature to benefit her daughters. Photographs indicate that the Beech girls attended some business functions with their mother appearing alongside important professional figures.[93] And the archive contains a 1955 letter she wrote to President Dwight Eisenhower's secretary, Mr. Bernard Shanley, to thank him for including her in the president's breakfast meeting as well as to request autographed photographs of the president for both daughters, then ages fourteen and seventeen. Because she was intensely private, Beech did not discuss her daughters in interviews, but it also appears that she was not asked about them. In fact, in the midst of upheaval around the controversial *Saturday Evening Post* article published in 1955 that characterized her as hard and calculating, one friend noted with regret the omission of information about her daughters. It stated, "I felt that if Mary Lynn's collegiate standing had been brought out . . . the picture would have been a more correct one."[94] The comment underscores that in the minds of those who knew Olive Ann Beech, being a mother and a company president made her who she was and that both were necessary to truly understand her and her achievements.

Public confirmation of Beech's dual achievements as a mother and a leader highlighted that for some observers, it was the combination of these two roles that made her remarkable. In 1970, Olive Ann was named "one of the country's most outstanding women" by the American Mothers Committee. Organized in 1935 and incorporated in 1954, its purpose was to "develop and strengthen the moral and spiritual foundations of the American home and . . . highlight . . . the standards of ideal Motherhood and recognize . . . the important role of the mother in the home, the community, the nation and the world." The organization celebrated several specific qualifications in the mothers it honored, and Beech embodied them all: active membership in a religious body, exemplification of the Golden Rule (treat others as you would like to be treated), a sense of civic responsibility and engagement in public service, successful motherhood "as evidenced by the character and achievements" of one's children, and demonstration of "courage, cheerfulness, patience, affection, kindness, understanding and a homemaking ability," defined as "the traits highly regarded in mothers."[95] That Beech was viewed as an example of these desired qualities underscores that she successfully combined working motherhood as a parallel and even intersecting path with business leadership, one that privilege made possible and ambition made desirable, and this made her stand out.

Walter was the key that opened the door to her entrepreneurial success, but Olive Ann Beech didn't wait for him to offer it to her, instead seizing the chance to develop and display her expertise in a masculine industry, insisting that she be treated as an equal regardless of sex, leveraging her wealth and status to forge a career path that intersected with motherhood, and vanquishing challengers to her husband and herself while she stepped up and into the forefront of the business she and her husband founded together.

Margaret Rudkin

For Margaret Rudkin, who had a much more traditional path into business than either Lewis or Beech, connections to two key men—her husband and her doctor—enabled her to make the case that her bakery was more than a hobby. Commercializing what started as a personal pursuit of healthful bread was made possible by these relationships, which provided her access to customers and capital and enabled her to grow the business exponentially in its first year, putting her firmly en route to entrepreneurship. But like Lewis and Beech, she constructed this path herself, seizing opportunities, ideas, contacts, and connections to leverage a kitchen experiment to launch a commercial enterprise.

Like that of so many women business owners before and since, Rudkin's entrepreneurship grew out of her family role as cook and caretaker.[96] As a mother, she kept painstaking records on the health of her three sons, documenting their weight at birth through twenty-two years old and listing every illness, injury, and medical procedure for each one. Mark, the youngest son, who sparked the creation of the bread that started Pepperidge Farm (named for the family property in Fairfield, Connecticut), lagged in weight gain compared to his older brothers and had one ailment the other two did not: asthma.[97] When he was diagnosed, the doctor said there were two choices: move the family to a drier, healthier climate or enrich his diet with B vitamins. "Moving across the country with my three sons, husband, assorted dogs, cats and horses was impossible," she later reported, and so she turned to her kitchen to find ways to improve the nutritional content of his food.

Rudkin's experimentation in the kitchen was inspired by her son's asthma doctor, who emphasized nutrition and diet as the cure for a variety of ailments. Dr. Blake F. Donaldson dispensed advice that some consider to have been a precursor to the Atkins diet of the 1970s and the "paleo" diet of today. A New York City doctor with expertise in pediatrics and otolaryngology, a specialization focused on ear, nose, and throat health and often associated with treatment of allergies, Donaldson was best known for prescribing a high-fat, meat-focused diet derived from the nutritional practices of the Inuit. In *Strong Medicine*, published in 1962, he recounted his success treating patients for weight and allergy problems with this radical dietary formula.[98] His advice gained publicity in a *Holiday* article that Margaret Rudkin cut out for reference, and she went to see him herself for severe migraine headaches and underlying allergies. Donaldson's diet recommendations had at their center a concern about the body's conversion of simple carbohydrates to sugar, and it was this, in conjunction with the directive to enrich her son's diet with B vitamins, that pushed Rudkin to experiment with making whole-grain bread. A "nut on proper food for children," as one newspaper reported, she resurrected her Irish grandmother's recipe for traditional, stone-ground whole-wheat flour bread to create a healthful alternative to the impoverished bread available in stores at the time. Though Rudkin reported that the "first loaf should have been sent to the Smithsonian Institution as a sample of bread from the Stone Age, for it was hard as a rock and about one inch high," she continued to adapt the recipe until she had a tasty and nutritious loaf of bread, which she began to produce at the family's farm.[99]

When she shared a sample with Dr. Donaldson, he became one of her biggest advocates. He prescribed the bread to other patients in his own practice, driving the first sales of the product, and then urged other doctors to do the same. In the form letter he wrote to other doctors to help her generate business, he stated, "When [Mrs. Rudkin] makes bread she makes bread. . . . [She] has really studied the problem of making the finest bread the world has ever known . . . anything you would do to increase the use of this bread in your patients [would be] much appreciated by them as well as Mrs. Rudkin." The letter, in combination with word-of-mouth referrals, drew new customers. Extant company records include many written replies from doctors requesting the bread for their patients. For example, a letter to Mrs. Rudkin from Dr. Augustus McKelvey, dated 30 September 1937, requested that she "send to Mrs. Reese . . . a month's supply of bread." There are also letters from patients reporting that their doctors prescribed the bread and asking how to place an order.[100]

The doctor's support and advocacy played a critical role in putting Rudkin on the path to commercial baking. In some public accounts of the company's founding, Dr. Donaldson is overlooked in favor of an origin story about "friends" and "neighbors" liking Rudkin's bread so much that they convinced her to sell it commercially. But importantly, in the first company history written by Henry Rudkin one year after the business started, the official story distributed to prospective investors was that "the first sales of bread were made almost entirely to Doctor Donaldson's patients." Similarly, in several letters, Margaret Rudkin herself stated that she "started making these breads with the encouragement of Dr. Blake Donaldson, who wanted to find what he called 'an honest woman to make an honest loaf of bread.'"[101] Even Rudkin's cookbook/autobiography, *The Margaret Rudkin Pepperidge Farm Cookbook*, published in 1963, characterized her early success—a combination of "accidental circumstance and an opportunity to take advantage of it"—as hinging entirely on Dr. Donaldson's interest, encouragement, and endorsement:

> When I told the doctor I was making bread from the stone-ground flour, he wouldn't believe me because he "said it was too coarse and

I would have to add white flour to it. To convince him, I brought him some samples and told him exactly what I put in with the flour. Immediately he wanted to order it for himself and for his other patients. I was quite taken aback by this idea, but I knew the bread was nutritious, unique, delicious and was indeed an important part of the whole diet. I decided to work only through doctors. Armed with a letter from my specialist, I approached 3 or 4 doctors. Before I realized what could happen, they began telling patients about my product, and very soon I had a sizable mail order business."[102]

Thus, Dr. Donaldson was the "expert" Rudkin used to create a network of contacts with other doctors and their patients. The connection created legitimacy for her claim about the health benefits of her product, the key to the market niche she leveraged to appeal to customers who preferred wholegrain bread.[103]

Even though Margaret Rudkin's baking skills hardly distinguished her from other women of her time, the level of responsibility and ambition she displayed early on did and may help to explain her motivation to turn breadbaking into a business. Born Margaret Fogarty in 1897, daughter of an Irish American mother and Irish immigrant father whose ill-gotten gains as a contractor led to a two- or three-year imprisonment during her childhood, she bore much of the responsibility for her large family from a young age. Growing up in her grandmother's house, a "nice brownstone" on Prospect Place and 42nd Street, listed in Manhattan by the census enumerator but likely located across the East River in the Little Neck area, near Queens, she was pressed into the service of her family by her mother's reported lack of cooking skills and preoccupation with Margaret's younger siblings. In 1910, when she was twelve years old, "Peg," as she was called by family members, shared a home with six younger sisters and brothers, four of them five years old or younger, as well as two unmarried uncles and two male boarders. According to a younger brother, she did a substantial part of the cooking and other domestic labor required for the large household, contributing to the family's income as well as their upkeep since they kept boarders. Five years later, her grandmother's brownstone sold and she and her family occupied a small apartment in the Flushing area of Queens; there were no boarders and only four siblings, since the two youngest had died. As her father's earnings as a contractor often were consumed at the pub before he got home and her mother was occupied by the younger children, all of whom were students, Rudkin took a job after school as a stenographer at the local Chamber of Commerce, contributing an important share of the family's income once again. This she also leveraged to get her father a position with the Electric & Gas Company (a job he retained until his retirement), theoretically, at least, boosting the family's financial security in this way as well. Rudkin's persistent employment thereafter was essential to her family's maintenance for years to come, as she continued to live with them until her marriage in 1923, when she was twenty-five years of age—some thirteen years after she started contributing to the family's income and well-being.[104]

Rudkin began her business training immediately after she finished school and early on displayed a knack for business, which she turned into more opportunities. It was a pathway into business that many young women followed in the 1910s. The explosion of "pink-collar" jobs in the clerical sector during the beginning of the twentieth century drew increasing numbers of young, educated white women, often the daughters of immigrants like Rudkin. Such jobs paid well compared to others available to young women and provided a "respectable" environment attractive to the middle class and the upwardly mobile.[105] In particular, bank jobs for women as clerks, tellers, bookkeepers, and cashiers rose sharply in the 1910s due in part to the vacancies created by men's World War I enlistments.[106] Rudkin stepped into this burgeoning field immediately after graduating as valedictorian from Flushing High School, where she reportedly "majored" in business. Upon accepting a job as bookkeeper, she became the first female employee of Flushing Bank. After two years she was made a teller, about which she reported, "I liked [the job because] it gave me a chance to talk with people. I think the experience at the bank was invaluable. It taught me accuracy and responsibility and gave me a good background for business." When she was hired for the advertised position of "customer's woman" in a Manhattan stock brokerage, McClure, Jones & Reed, she gained valuable insight into the world of big business and the New York Stock Exchange, both of which would be instrumental in the creation of her eventual wealth as a business owner. But most important, she met her future husband, Henry A. Rudkin, a senior partner at the firm for whom she became secretary. An accomplished financier with lucrative ties to some of the nation's top capitalists, Mr. Rudkin became the single most important associate for Margaret Rudkin when she launched her baking business.[107]

For the young and hardworking Margaret Fogarty, marriage to Henry Rudkin in 1923 had a profound economic impact on her life, catapulting her into another class position altogether. In the tradition of the day for middle-class and upper-class, especially white Americans, Margaret Rudkin abandoned her employment as soon as they were married and depended on her husband for economic support—a big change for her after so many years of laboring to supply the needs of her natal family. In exchange, he relied on her to manage their household and the care of their soon-to-be-born sons. By 1930, the young family included three children ages six, four, and fourteen months and occupied a home on East 70th, on the tony Upper East Side of Manhattan, attended by six live-in servants.[108] Mr. Rudkin was a member of the Union Club, "an institution generally considered the cynosure of men's organizations in New York," whose membership was described by *Fortune* magazine in 1932 as "men who are, rather than men who do," indicating the depth and longevity of the wealth of its members, even at the nadir of the Great Depression.[109] Thus, through her marriage to Henry A. Rudkin, Margaret Fogarty was thrust into New York City's social and economic elite, where her husband's ties to the foremost businessmen of the 1920s yielded rich gifts—both literally, as her documentation of their many Tiffany wedding gifts reveals, and figuratively, as those connections would later be key to the capitalization of her business.[110]

Henry Albert Rudkin had worked his way up and into an influential role in the stock brokerage industry. His father had come to New York from Ireland as a child in the mid-1800s and by adulthood was associated with his father's firm, "William Rudkin's Sons," which dealt in "Bay Rhum." The venture funded a private education for the young Henry Albert, who graduated in 1901 from Clason Point Military Academy in the Bronx, a Catholic-administered military academy for high school boys. A veteran of the Spanish-American War, the young Rudkin subsequently served with the National Guard, the First New York Cavalry (1908–17), and the Mexican Border Service (1916–17). He pursued a career in finance by working his way up from a clerk position at a brokerage firm starting in 1907; by 1912 he had become a partner in the New York Stock Exchange firm McClure, Jones and Reed, where Margaret Rudkin would eventually work as well. He remained an active brokerage firm partner until 1946 and throughout his career was instrumental in funding historic ventures, including Warner Bros. Studios. In total he served on five corporate boards, including the studio's when it was first launching "talkies" in the 1920s.[111]

With this elite status and star role in the brokerage business during the lucrative 1920s, Henry Rudkin was well poised to leverage his connections to investors when Margaret Rudkin's Pepperidge Farm business required an infusion of capital to expand. Although the Rudkins had arrived at the pinnacle of New York City society by the end of the 1920s, marked by their purchase of 125 acres of land in Fairfield, Connecticut, on which they built a lavish, customized country estate, they suffered like most others dependent on stock income after the market crashed at the end of October 1929. Eventually they relocated the family to their country home, abandoning their city apartment, and engaged in raising poultry, pigs, and calves and growing their own fruits and vegetables on the property that they affectionately called "Pepperidge Farm"—the namesake for the business.[112] Henry Rudkin continued to commute into New York City by train, maintaining relationships with his firm's customers and generating what little money there was to be made in the brokerage business during the Depression. When in 1937 his wife's bread business started to take off, he assembled a small list of silent partners from his list of contacts, which included Donald Campbell, president of Chase Manhattan Bank, and Richard Gordon of the firm DeCoppet & Doremus, a Stock Exchange firm specializing in odd-lot deals. Together the "special" or silent partners' capital investment totaled $1,875, equivalent to $31,525.53 in 2014, with additional investments made by each at various points thereafter. Although Henry Rudkin was on friendly terms with both men, his correspondence about their investments in "Margaret Rudkin's Pepperidge Farm Company" was all business.[113]

From the start, Margaret Rudkin, her expertise, and her "good will" were the focus of the documents establishing her business partnership. Both she and Henry Rudkin were officially General Partners in the business, "authorized to transact the partnership business and sign the firm name." But the partnership agreement stipulated that only Margaret Rudkin was required "to give to the business of the partnership her full time and attention, so far as the best interests of the partnership shall require"; it did not obligate Henry Rudkin to work for the company, stating that he "[would] not be required to devote any particular time and attention" to it. For, after all, it was Margaret Rudkin's continuing dedication and labor, exacting standards, and expanding number of contacts that were the business's primary value. This is captured in the agreement's stipulation that the company maintain a $10,000 life insurance policy on Margaret Rudkin payable to the partnership and also that the agreement could be terminated by either Special Partner if she was incapacitated "for a consecutive period of two months because of accident or illness . . . from fully and effectually attending to the business." In exchange for such commitment and for investment of the total worth of her "Old Business"—the sole proprietorship under which she had commenced business, which was valued at $1,346.68 ($22,642.56 in 2014)—Margaret Rudkin would not earn a salary but would earn 84 percent of the net profits distributed among the partners. Henry Rudkin would earn 1 percent.[114]

Even though these specifications in the partnership agreement suggest a minor role for Henry Rudkin, his correspondence with the initial investors reveals that he was, in fact, deeply involved in the business affairs of the company. And this was true from the start. In a 27 May 1938 letter to a New York City businessman, for example, he reported, "I am now so imbued with the bread business that I can give you almost any figure even to the last mill." This was only one year after the business started, and knowing so much about the "figures" was required. It was a stated expectation that the company's investors be furnished "such financial statements as . . . may [be] request[ed] from time to time showing in reasonable detail the financial condition and operating results of the Partnership." Henry sent these nearly monthly during the first year and in them relayed considerable detail. On 7 June 1938, for example, he communicated, "Enclosed [find] . . . report of Pepperidge Farm operations for the four weeks ending May 28th, 1938. In my opinion we still have expenses that are incident to rapid growth but they should not increase even with considerably greater volume of business, so that in a few weeks I believe the percentage of profit on business done will be considerably better." Reading like a company annual report, the letters conveyed number of loaves sold, profit per loaf, conditions of the market (which were somewhat seasonal), plans for expansion, distribution channels, and reports on dividend disbursements. One year after the establishment of the initial partnership, Henry Rudkin provided an accountant's report and explained that the accountants had been hired "to set up a bookkeeping system" that had just been put into operation. Always emphasizing returns to investors and signaling that Pepperidge Farm management was competently and proactively managing both day-to-day affairs and growth, the correspondence provided by Henry Rudkin was critically important. It kept careful accounting and financial controls at the forefront as well as updating investors about the financial affairs of the company, and it freed Margaret Rudkin to manage production and sales—the centerpiece of any manufacturing business and her designated area of expertise and focus.[115]

It would be easy to conclude that Henry Rudkin handled the financial side of Pepperidge Farm's business in its early days because Margaret Rudkin did not have the financial know-how, but evidence suggests that was not the case. In fact, she characterized herself as particularly able when it came to staying on top of accurate figures for the business. "Of course," she reported in a 1948 *New Yorker* article, "figures have always been easy for me. Right this minute, I can go out to Cliff—he's the comptroller—and say 'What's the cash balance?' and I can tell offhand if it's correct. The average woman, of course, can't even balance her check book." She attributed this extraordinary ability to her early business training while working in the bank.[116] Correspondence from Margaret Rudkin to her husband's assistant in his New York City office asking her to ensure that he make certain required payments indicates that she was, in fact, engaged with the details of the financial side of the business. Yet first and foremost, she was occupied with ensuring the quality of production. Even when Pepperidge Farm production reached 500,000 loaves per week, as it did in 1954, she defined her job as "to make sure our quality is as consistently high as when I did the job myself."[117] Rapid growth of her customer base along with the focus on quality control, production, and personnel occupied Margaret Rudkin's time and drew Henry into the financial side of the company from its earliest days. It was not because she couldn't but because he could. The arrangement between them was a critical factor in Pepperidge Farm's success and the best example of the way in which she leveraged his skills and connections to ensure the success of her business.

That Margaret Rudkin thought of her relationship with her husband as a partnership, and even as a "business" partnership, is illustrated by a letter she wrote to him on the occasion of their twentieth wedding anniversary. Her tongue-in-cheek portrayal of their marriage partnership using business terminology and concepts reveals both her sense of humor, their apparent friendship and affection, and the degree to which their business provided a lens through which to view the relationship overall. In it she sketched the "Balance Sheet" of the "Rudkin-Fogarty Partnership for Period April 7, 1923 to April 6, 1943," calculating inventory, comprising "contentment, happiness, affection [and the] Rudkin sense of humor," at $4,000,000 total and liabilities, comprising the "Fogarty Sense of Gloom" ($1,000,000), "1 Boil on Chin" ($1.00), "1 Victory Garden" ($100) and Calypso, Saracen, and Alphousine (perhaps pets to be appraised). Original capital invested consisted of "Faith and Trust," and Fixed Assets included 1 Husband (valued at $1,000,000 with no depreciation), 1 Wife (valued at $1,000 and depreciated to $1.00), and 3 children (humorously valued at 90c with no depreciation). With surplus estimated at $4,000,033.13, she evaluated the partnership's net worth at $5,000,134.13. The document was handwritten on hotel stationery for the Madison Hotel in New York City, where we can imagine the two jovially celebrating their anniversary. It was addressed to "Henry A. Rudkin, Esquire, Senior Partner, Rudkin-Fogarty Co." Since he was not trained as an attorney, "Esquire" here is an appellation denoting her respect for and perhaps deference toward her husband, yet maintenance of her maiden name "Fogarty" in the name she gives to their "company" also suggests that she had a clear sense of her own value in the partnership in spite of her self-deprecating humor.[118]

Public accounts vary, however, in their explanation of the genesis of the business and the Rudkins' roles in it, not always portraying the partnership as generously as above. Some identify Henry and not Margaret as the founder of the business. For example, one obituary for Henry Rudkin reported: "A financier and founder of the Pepperidge Farm Baking Co. . . . He started in the baking business in the mid-1930s, utilizing his wife's personal recipe for whole wheat bread. . . . In the early years of the business, Mr. Rudkin used to carry loaves of bread with him in the morning. . . . But in 1947, he built a modern bakery in Norwalk, Conn."[119] Interestingly, in this account Margaret Rudkin is virtually erased from the company history, playing a role in its founding simply as supplier of the bread recipe that Henry utilized to launch the business. It's impossible to know where such an account originated, but one suspects that the inaccuracy may have been fueled by disbelief that a woman founded a multimillion-dollar corporation or that a high-powered stockbroker quit his job on Wall Street to join his wife's bakery business. Alternatively, when Margaret Rudkin was asked in a 1950s radio interview about her husband's role in the business early on, she affirmed his important involvement as an adviser but brushed over his essential role in financial management. Responding to the interviewer's question about whether she had been able to "lure" her husband into the bakery business, she replied, "Yes but I'm afraid it was the interest of the bakery business that lured him. You see at first . . . my husband's attitude was perhaps a very typical one, he was quite *tolerant* of my foolish idea and said well now I really don't think you have time to do this sort of thing. But the first thing you know I was turning to him sort of as the force behind the scenes . . . when it came to things like motors and automobiles and trucks I was lost so he *then* had to step right in and take over and now, well, we let him be the chairman of the board" [emphasis reflects intonation in interview.][120] Although affirming the interviewer's label of "senior adviser" for her husband, Margaret Rudkin does not refer to his financial expertise or involvement in the capitalization of the business but instead emphasizes her dependence on him to help with transportation—a stereotypically masculine role that reinforced her own feminine, domestic one. It is possible to view this interpretation through a marketing lens and see it simply as confirmation of the gendered roles the company had cast for each Rudkin by the 1950s. On the other hand, in the interview she also casts Henry's attraction to working in the business as authentic and self-motivated and acknowledges her need for his help. Yet this was after his initial doubts about the whole idea as a foolish waste of time. All together, this account, in combination with the first origin story captured in an obituary for Henry, suggests a more contested and negotiated business partnership between the Rudkins. What was certainly true, however, is that Henry Rudkin was a key factor in Margaret's ability to launch a successful business. While Dr. Donaldson helped her to identify an entrepreneurial pathway, Rudkin relied on her husband's expertise and contacts to follow it.

The advantages that Margaret Rudkin gained through her marriage to Henry also included a model of motherhood mediated by investment in full-time, live-in staff devoted to the care of her three school-aged sons, which allowed her to focus on the day-to-day needs of Pepperidge Farm. In fact, long before the bread business occupied Margaret's time, the wealth generated by Henry's stock brokerage business led the Rudkins to conceptualize parenting on elite terms in keeping with the social circles in which they traveled. According to Margaret's brother, when the Rudkins decided to start a family, they "were very social minded and decided to raise their children as other wealthy, social minded parents did. Turn the children over to governess's for training, etc." The three Rudkin boys had their own "quarters for training, eating, and sleeping," and the parents had "high expectations" for their sons' "progress" but "did not devote much time, energy or affection . . . toward them." The children spent their time with each other or with "the French sisters" employed as governesses, who taught them "excellent French." It was a parenting approach that was difficult for the youngest son, Mark, the asthmatic who had inspired her baking expedition in the first place. He was only eight when his mother started Pepperidge Farm and, according to his uncle's account, was "not strong" and was "unhappy and sensitive," a combination that "did not . . . [meet with] . . . parental understanding."[121] This was the one son who as an adult did not work in the business and who made a life for himself in Paris, far away from both his family and Pepperidge Farm—perhaps a legacy of these early difficulties. But like Olive Ann Beech, Margaret Rudkin did not spend much time discussing parenting in extant records—both private and public. Not surprisingly, she kept

The Rudkin Family: Margaret, Henry Sr., Henry Jr., and William (youngest son Mark not shown). Eventually everyone in the family but Mark was actively involved at Pepperidge Farm. Fairfield Museum and History Center, Fairfield, Connecticut.

the focus of interviews and publications on the business. When parenting did enter the story, it was in a way that Mark may have grown to resent. In an interview conducted in the 1950s, for example, Rudkin referred to him as a "feeding problem" and "one of these allergic children"—not language that conveyed care and concern, though certainly the actions she took to "find out what foods did or did not agree with him" did.[122] And for Rudkin, it seemed, food was more than nutrition but an expression and affirmation of love, affection, and appreciation. In the foreword to *The Margaret Rudkin Pepperidge Farm Cookbook*, for example, she described how when she cooked for "just the family" and heard "Golly, that's a good egg!" she "sort of" felt that "they mean you're a 'good egg' too."[123] Though it is hard to distinguish marketing from mothering in Rudkin's story, this remark suggests that preparing nutritious food *was* mothering to Rudkin and thus that work and family were overlapping spheres of activity, conceptually and to some degree practically, at least in the early stages of the business. Reliance on full-time staff to care for her children and home facilitated her ability to operate in both.

That the Rudkins' family life did not revolve around their children reflected both their wealth and American marital prescriptions between 1900 and 1930. As family historian Jessica Weiss writes, "Americans in the 1920s celebrated the image of the fun-loving, romantic couple. After their wedding vows, smaller families and the fun and amusement available outside the home encouraged couples to continue habits of companionship formed while dating." The onset of the baby boom "shifted the ideological emphasis in American marriage from the couple to the children"—a change that may have made Margaret Rudkin's approach to mothering appear anachronistic and distant to those assessing it in conjunction with 1950s models.[124]

Though Rudkin's commercial success was made possible by a less-engaged version of mothering that freed her to devote her time and attention to Pepperidge Farm, ironically the company's origin story remained integrally related to Rudkin's mothering. Domestic images of her in aprons and kitchens abounded in marketing material and media coverage. And as the chapter on marketing will later show, Rudkin successfully capitalized on her image as a caring grandmother whose "old-fashioned" bread was healthier for children and their parents. The opportunity to exploit a gendered image of herself as caretaker—in contrast to Beech—was of course determined by the food industry in which she operated her business. But it also shows her skill at harnessing the opportunities that wealth and connections provided her to traverse the confines of "mother" and "wife" to become an entrepreneurial leader. That one of her grandson's most memorable images of Rudkin was at her desk in her home office, with her secretary "Mr. Pendleton" posted just outside—a scene he and his brother viewed from an attic window they could swing open to look down on the second floor of the family's elaborate house—seems symbolic of the way in which she transformed domestic space, skills, and the privileges that came through her marriage and wealth into professional opportunities.[125]

Conclusion

For Lewis, Beech, and Rudkin, men were the key to opening the doors of opportunity. Husbands and other male family members as well as the men they were connected to were essential resources who facilitated their business experience in direct and indirect ways. As knowledgeable and successful businessmen themselves, they provided access to valuable experience, contacts, and eventually capital. They were the "gatekeepers" who pulled the women up into business ownership, a necessary component of success for all individuals, as Pamela Laird reminds us, but one that many women lacked. Yet none of the women examined here merely fell into her role as an entrepreneur. Each of these mid-twentieth-century business leaders paved her own entrepreneurial pathway by leveraging her connections to men of influence and expert status to gain entry into manufacturing sectors heavily dominated by men. Such "expert capital" legitimized their presence in business cultures fueled by male privilege and notions of workplace masculinity that excluded and even denigrated women. Asserting business personas of competence, all three women overcame lack of college or high school education and modest to difficult family backgrounds to blaze new trails into the upper echelons of the corporate world. Their success reflected a remarkable degree of autonomy, too, given the restrictive and demanding conventions of marriage and motherhood in the first half of the twentieth century. It was a freedom made possible through both conjugal and company wealth—another indication that marriage was a life choice with significant business implications for women and a reminder that economic status fueled opportunity. Thus, how Lewis, Beech, and Rudkin constructed their entrepreneurial pathways reveals that for mid-twentieth-century businesswomen without the advantages of advanced education and before the advantages of government incentive programs for female entrepreneurs, leveraging connections to men and wealth was essential to gaining the legitimacy and autonomy necessary to succeed. The spousal support these women relied on, in contrast to that offered twenty-first-century female business leaders, was fiduciary and business related. Rather than only giving them the confidence to take risks and the time to excel, marriage and male family members also gave these mid-twentieth-century female entrepreneurs tangible opportunities and assets, ones they turned into successful businesses.

In its 8 October 2014 issue, *Black Enterprise* featured Washington, D.C.–area female business owner LaKeisha Grant for her success at securing government contracts and the impact these have had on her business. Started in her home in 2007 with savings of just $11,000, Virtual Enterprise Architects (VEA) secured a subcontract through aerospace and defense contractor General Dynamics within its first three months. By her third year in business, Grant had secured certification under the Small Business Administration's "8a Business Development Program" designed for socially and economically disadvantaged business owners and shortly began providing services for nine different federal agencies. One of the largest was the U.S. Citizenship and Immigration Services. "VEA was able to capture all of the agency's records management business, technology, data, and security architecture for the millions of immigration and naturalization records and provide a road map for improvements to decrease processing time and analysis and ensure the storage and location of all records." This contract, along with the other government contracts she received, contributed to a 2,000 percent growth rate over two years, making VEA one of the fastest-growing technology companies in the country with total revenues of $3.8 million in 2012. The online article in *Black Enterprise* about Grant and VEA appears adjacent to a rotating video with tips from the magazine's "Small Business University" program; this placement underscores the publication's emphasis on government contracts as a strategy for success for small business owners who qualify for special certification programs.[1]

Female entrepreneurs such as Grant are newsworthy in part because they remain unusual. In spite of the federal government's commitment to award 5 percent of its total contracts to female business owners, it has continued to miss this mark until recently. At the end of 2014, for example, *Businessweek* reported that "about 4.3 percent of total contracts went to women-owned businesses," or "$2.3 billion short of the goal." Citing a report from the Senate Committee on Small Business and Entrepreneurship, the article stated that "the biggest culprit was the Department of Defense, which fell $3.3 billion short of its target for awarding contracts to women-owned small businesses."[2] As advocacy programs such as "Give Me My 5%" make clear, the persistent failure to hit the 5 percent government target has had a significant deleterious effect on opportunities for women business owners.[3] "Women own 29% of all businesses but only 2% of women-owned businesses grow beyond $1 million," according to the 2013 report on the state of women-owned businesses published by the American Express OPEN program for small business owners. One reason is that so few have secured contracts with the federal government, the largest single consumer in the United States with expenditures of $500 billion per year. One study found that "women-owned businesses that have gotten federal government contracts are 23 times more likely to break through that $1 million+ revenue barrier."[4] Thus, securing access to government business can make a significant difference in the degree of success experienced by women business owners.

This chapter reveals that the influence of government in female entrepreneurial success originated earlier than the twenty-first century. Nearly seventy years before LaKeisha Grant secured her first federal contract, mid-twentieth-century female business owners pursued advantageous relationships with the federal government. Lewis, Beech, and Rudkin all took advantage of government opportunities and actively resisted its intrusions, and this was essential to their success. Close examination of the World War II and Korean War eras—key episodes in the expansion of the federal government as regulator and customer—shows that for these businesswomen building a relationship with government was both necessary and important even three-quarters of a century ago. In some cases, they hardly had a choice. As Mark Wilson has argued, "U.S. mobilization for WWII . . . expos[ed] a large number of businesses to new regulatory action that often reached further than anything that they had experienced during the New Deal."[5] Examining how women business owners responded reveals the degree to which they actively constructed a relationship with the federal government that benefited their businesses, including accessing programs and funding opportunities. Prevailing scholarly interpretations have focused on the big-business biases and complex bureaucratic systems of mid-twentieth-century federal programs designed to aid business owners and concluded that they did not impact woman-owned businesses. Since most led small-scale enterprises, scholars have argued, women could not access government business programs and thus did not benefit from federal investments.[6] This chapter contributes a new dimension to our understanding of wartime programs and their relationship to female business owners. It argues that in fact, for those women who operated businesses big enough to cater to a national market, government programs were fundamental to their success and federal regulation threatened significant losses in profit. Both prompted female entrepreneurs' active engagement with the federal government.

Women acted out this new role energetically because it was in the best interest of their businesses—even when new forms of government regulation introduced during wartime required resistance. One of the new federal regulators with far-reaching impact for businesses was the Office of Price Administration (OPA) created in 1941 to curb inflation and boost consumption by dispensing rationing and price controls. "With its billions of ration stamps and thousands of field officers," Meg Jacobs tells us, "OPA had more regular contact with citizens than did any other government agency, even the United States Post Office or the Internal Revenue Service," and this certainly included business owners. For Rudkin, the OPA was central to her wartime experience, limiting access to key ingredients and restricting her ability to expand her manufacturing facilities as well as controlling prices. This shaped her relationship to government and drew her into active dissent of OPA policies both privately and publicly, aligning her objections with the National Association of Manufacturers, which "took out full page ads against [the OPA's] controls."[7] Ironically, the OPA's rationing policies led to expanded market opportunities for Pepperidge Farm by decreasing home baking, and thus in the long run Rudkin benefited from wartime regulation. But this was not clear at the time, and her experience encouraged her to view federal intervention in her business as invasive. In response, she crafted a defensive strategy in her relationship with government to minimize its impact, one that was key to her business's survival during World War II. It was a stance she retained for many years following the war.

The government was also the source of opportunity for women business owners during World War II and the Korean War and elicited proactive relationship-building from those eager to take advantage of this. For Lewis and Beech, government programs during this period led to clear and significant benefits that they actively pursued. First and foremost, Lewis and Beech were military suppliers. This was an opportunity and accomplishment of note for two medium-scale companies, given the well-documented bias for contracting with large, established companies. In 1942, for example, a Senate committee reported that "just 56 of the nation's 184,000 manufacturing establishments had received 75 percent of the value of the army and navy contracts awarded" to date for wartime supplies. Despite the steps taken by Congress to address such disadvantages to smaller businesses (for example, setting up a Smaller War Plants Division within the War Production Board to ensure that "a greater share" of defense contracts was awarded to smaller-scale businesses), contracts and even subcontracts overwhelmingly continued to flow to large-scale companies. Procurement officers within the military asserted that smaller firms were not "equipped with the plant and machinery, specially skilled workers, managerial know-how, financial stability, and established contracts with a wide variety of suppliers" that they believed were required to meet their needs for "vast quantities of goods on time."[8] This was a first challenge that both Lewis and Beech needed to overcome, since both businesses were small and financially insecure at the time that they obtained their military contracts and they competed with larger, established companies. They did so by starting small and building on early success by expanding their involvement in military contracting. It was a strategy that required determination, sometimes courage, and a long view of their potential as government business partners.

As this chapter will show, too, while there was no evidence of overt discrimination by the government against women-owned businesses, the process of awarding and regulating military contracts to both Lewis and Beech reveals the gendered assumptions embedded in the system. Procurement officers assumed they would be dealing with male business owners or officers and this elicited variable responses from both female entrepreneurs. Their recollections and actions avowed the need to overcome barriers that their gender created in working with the government. After all, this was long before the 1979 executive order calling on government agencies to aid woman-owned businesses through direct assistance and procurement opportunities and half a century before the 1994 act of Congress that established the goal of allocating 5 percent of all government contracts to woman-owned businesses.[9]

Lewis and Beech also boldly and aggressively accessed federal loans, which were essential to their survival as entrepreneurs. As defense contractors, they gained access to substantial government loans from the Reconstruction Finance Corporation (RFC). Founded in 1931 by a reluctant President Hoover as a lending institution to railroads and financial institutions to "restore banker confidence and stimulate an increase in commercial credit" during the Depression, the RFC took on a new role during World War II; it "ceased to be a recovery agency and came to resemble its ancestor, the War Finance Corporation," which made loans to war industries during World War I. By 1940, the RFC was financing new plant construction and making working capital loans to companies that had government contracts.[10] Loans to businesses continued until the RFC was terminated in 1953.[11] Lewis and

Beech both benefited, capturing large-scale government loans that were typically off-limits to female business owners. The loans enabled them to secure sizable military contracts. This brought them critical capital and substantial revenue at a time when both companies were barely financially viable and may have failed altogether if not for the government's business.

But the loans and government contracts came with a price—government regulation, intervention, and accountability, a challenge that both Lewis and Beech met head on. RFC loans, for example, stipulated repayment without regard to cancellation of government contracts and also sometimes enforced particular, invasive management expectations for company borrowers. Lewis and Beech navigated such interventions in varying ways but always with an eye toward how to benefit their companies. As military suppliers, they also found themselves targets of the excess profits tax (EPT) policy reintroduced in Congress in 1940. The tax was designed to eliminate wartime profiteering that had been rampant during World War I by reducing profits for contractors. The rate was raised almost yearly until, by 1944, a full 95 percent of earnings over peacetime "standard profits" were taxed. As participants in this process, historian Mark Wilson argues, "the military establishment served not only as an ally of business but also as a powerful bureaucratic regulator."[12] Both Lewis and Beech interacted with the military in this new regulatory role, launching lengthy legal battles to resist application of the EPT to their companies' World War II profits, which they won in 1957 and 1958, respectively.

Thus Lewis, Beech, and Rudkin proactively engaged in government relationship-building during wartime and in so doing fundamentally altered the course of their businesses. Effective use of mid-twentieth-century federal programs as well as resistance to regulation had a critical and long-term impact on their companies. All three contested, negotiated, and leveraged their relationship with government with an eye to enhancing and protecting their economic position. Sometimes they did so by relying on male employees to negotiate on their behalf, retreating to the background in discussions with federal government agencies—as in the case of Lewis, who was entirely absent in her company's interactions with military procurement officers. While there is no evidence to tell us why, this decision was likely more strategic than simply delegation, reflecting recognition of the hypermasculine, male-dominated sphere of military contracting in which being a woman was a liability. But for the most part, Lewis, Beech, and Rudkin were actively engaged in this process, orchestrating company responses and resources to take advantage of opportunities presented by federal spending and to fend off regulatory incursions. Doing so required strategic management of government relations at a time when female business leaders were rare, even unexpected by federal negotiators who contracted with and regulated businesses, and when the bureaucratic requirements of such relationships were enough to thwart many a company leader regardless of gender.

By the time each of these female entrepreneurs was at the helm of a commercial enterprise, interacting with the federal government was no longer a choice. By the mid-twentieth century, all business owners had expanded opportunities and responsibilities to engage with the government with varying degrees of impact on their enterprises. As it grew in response to depression, war, and postwar recovery, the national government carved out new roles as regulator, lender, and buyer and asserted greater and greater influence on the U.S. economy and in Americans' day-to-day lives more generally. The histories of Lewis, Beech, and Rudkin reveal how significant the influence was, eliciting decisive action from all three women when the government impeded their business interests and strategic action when government investments promised growth. For these female business owners in the middle of the twentieth century, this chapter argues, the role of government was critically important to their commercial operations, helping them to move from "small" to "big" business status. Without establishing effective government relations, in fact, none of the three women would have succeeded in business.

Tillie Lewis

Tillie Lewis saw government as an investor and buyer and took advantage of that opportunity as much as she could to grow her business. She submitted three applications for RFC loans and built a strategic partnership with the Quarter Master Corps, which earned her multiple contracts as a supplier to the U.S. military. The significant profits that Flotill earned during wartime led to a protracted excess profits tax fight that Lewis eventually won, cementing her strong business position by the 1950s. In fact, maximizing government opportunities was key to Lewis's early commercial success and made the difference in Flotill's survival as a company after she became its sole business owner.

Lewis first reached out to the federal government in 1939 when her business was in trouble and she needed funding. This was unusual for a business owner as small in scale as she was at that point and even more so for a businesswoman. According to historian of small businesses Mansel Blackford, savings as well as funds from family, friends, and business acquaintances and, to a much smaller degree, institutional loans funded business startup and expansion for small-scale proprietors, but "almost no use was made of borrowing from federal government agencies."[13] However, the circumstances for Lewis were desperate and drove her to seek out every possible source of support. Lewis first turned to the government for help when she had just bought out her business partner and his heirs and needed additional capital to complete the 1939 packing season. Typically, canners financed packing and warehousing costs by short-term borrowing and bank credit, but she could no longer procure such funding because earlier in the year she had exhausted her cash accounts and mortgaged the company to secure the capital required to become sole owner of the business. Even banks with whom she had long-standing commercial relationships would not lend to her.[14] So Lewis investigated the possibility of submitting an application for an RFC loan. But this avenue too was closed. A letter to Lewis regarding her interest in the loan stated, "It seems that they cannot do anything unless we can get the Pacific Can Company to step aside and subordinate itself in priority to the R. F. C. . . . that is about the only thing which can be done and which will satisfy the law and regulations as to the requirement that all loans must be covered by collateral."[15] But Pacific Can—the company from whom Lewis had borrowed $45,000 to buy out her business partner and to whom she had had to mortgage her company as collateral—was unwilling to subordinate its interest, and so she was unable to procure the 1939 RFC loan. Nonetheless, Lewis's application demonstrates that as a (then) small business owner, she was not intimidated or alienated by the federal government but rather saw it as a potential resource in her efforts to keep her company afloat.

Three years later, Lewis again turned to the federal government as a source of opportunity, and this time her application was successful. Flotill became a supplier to the U.S. military. Starting in 1942, "the company, with others in the canning industry, allocated portions of its production to government use." Flotill's military allocation grew from 8.7 percent of its sales to 31.06 percent of its sales at the peak in 1944 and then gradually declined again in 1947. Canning for military use during World War II occurred in the company's regular production facilities using standard equipment, and thus "upon cessation of hostilities no significant reconversion problems existed." Nonetheless, in Flotill's 1948 stock prospectus, it was reported that "almost all aspects of the Company's business have been affected by wartime and post-war conditions, such as increased demands for food products, short-ages of certain materials and products, price controls of purchases and sales, increased labor costs and taxes, and other economic factors."[16] Though some of these factors clearly impeded Flotill's day-to-day business operations, most were positive. At the peak of Lewis's military contract in 1944, ten years after the founding of her company and only seven years after she be-came its sole owner—a time when the company teetered on the brink of failure—a substantial portion of her earnings came from the military, and this business was key to her success.

The company also deliberately leveraged wartime conditions to expand sales, not just to the military but to consumers too. One large-scale ad fea-tured Tillie Lewis teaching consumers how to use Flotill's concentrated to-mato paste "wherever Tomato flavoring is desired" in order to save tin and shipping space—twin wartime goals throughout the country. To get across to consumers that Flotill was associated with patriotic wartime purchasing, the ad was bordered by marching Flotill tomato cans with military hats and bayonets shouting, "Use Flotill Tomato Paste," "Use concentrated foods," and "Save tin . . . Save space."[17] Thus, the overall positive impact of gov-ernment relations and wartime conditions for the company during World War II moved beyond military production.

Profit from war contracts during World War II drew the attention of the Internal Revenue Service (IRS), which levied additional taxes for Flotill, but Lewis fought back successfully.[18] The excess profits tax, a common tool used by many nations during both world wars to contain the profits (and thus the government's costs) from military contracts, was implemented in Octo-ber 1940. Starting as a 50 percent tax on earnings above peacetime "stan-dard profits," it grew progressively larger over the next several years: to 60 percent in 1941, 90 percent in 1942, and 95 percent in 1944.[19] Thus, when the IRS taxed the company for excess profits for the years 1941–46, it was levying an additional and sizable tax on Flotill's wartime profits. The stat-ute, aimed at "recovering excess war profits," targeted profits "in excess" of "normal" profits.[20] Although ostensibly measured as pre- and post-1940 profits, determining "normal" vs. "excess" profits involved a complicated and contested process for Lewis and other companies with meager earnings prior to the war—one that went well beyond measuring what came before and after 1940. For Lewis, this involved a protracted, seven-year battle with the government that did not end until Lewis won exoneration in 1957.[21]

Lewis fought the EPT by emphasizing her company's prewar weak-nesses when Flotill was still small and its future tenuous. Her tax attorney,

Mr. Willard C. Mills of San Francisco, filed the "Application for Relief under Section 722" of the tax code in 1950 under a provision of the law allowing corporations to appeal IRS determinations of excess profits. Doing so required substantial documentation of a company's prewar earnings and operations, since this was the point of comparison against which wartime profits were measured. The 1-inch-thick Section 722 supplementary document prepared by Lewis's tax attorney includes substantial evidence of Lewis's early financial challenges; the legal defense strategy she pursued was to prove that, in fact, her business profits in 1939—the crisis year that had precipitated her application for an RFC loan—had been depressed and were not an accurate reflection of "normal" profits. Thus, company profits during the years following, 1940–46, did not reflect as great a jump as it appeared and were not, therefore, excessive.

The burden to justify low profitability prior to the war in EPT appeal cases advantaged larger, more established companies. As historian Mark Wilson argues, this facet of the relief application process "unfairly reinforce[d] the prewar economic order" and "allow[ed] those firms that had been highly profitable in the late 1930s—including [notably large ones such as] Dupont and GM—to enjoy after-tax margins that could be triple or quadruple those allowed to other companies." In contrast, "any company with difficulties in the prewar 'base period,'" like Flotill, "was placed into the highest EPT bracket." This meant that smaller companies such as Flotill and others like it that had "a poor prewar profit record [were] likely to complain."[22]

Lewis was in good company in launching her fight against the IRS. By 1945, an estimated 35,000 applications for relief from excess profits taxes had been filed.[23] It was a long and costly legal battle, but it paid off. The "Certificate of Over-assessment" from the IRS that finally closed Lewis's case reveals that she had successfully reduced her tax liability by $129,478.90, an amount high enough (over $75,000) that it had to "be approved by the Joint Congressional Committee on Internal Revenue Taxation."[24] By any measure, this was success.

Yet Lewis negotiated reduction of her tax burden in a highly gendered environment. The public portrayal of one of her contemporaries underscores this point. Vivien Kellems, also a business owner (in conjunction with her brother), garnered national attention when she protested the federal withholding tax as unconstitutional and, with great fanfare, refused to implement it for her employees. Eventually she filed a lawsuit in federal court in 1950 but was never allowed to test the constitutionality of the law. The 1951 publication of her treatise against the federal income tax eventually earned her respect and acknowledgment of her expertise (she completed graduate work in economics at Columbia University focused on taxation). It did not, though, lead to a change in law or accession to her viewpoint. And according to one account, "most of the public thought of her as a cantankerous female hunting notoriety and emboldened by a womanly ignorance of the Law, and the mysteries of taxation." Evidently it seemed inconceivable to most mid-twentieth-century Americans that a woman would be able to understand the complexities of tax law.[25]

Furthermore, military representatives who endeavored to contain wartime profits by negotiating and renegotiating contracts with suppliers were portrayed in gendered terms. According to historian Mark Wilson, renegotiation was a "novel and uniquely American" approach to containing war profits and one that ignited ferocious political, legal, and public-relations battles between business leaders and military representatives. Not surprisingly, since it involved defining the limits of military power, business success, and American free enterprise, renegotiation debaters appropriated notions of masculinity to articulate their views. In 1944, members of the Senate Finance Committee considering changes to the law allowing military representatives to force renegotiation of contracts asserted that to blunt the statute "would emasculate it, opening the way for a new crop of war millionaires."[26] This gendered language is telling. If military leaders were somehow impotent—less masculine or lesser men—when challenged by business owners in this context, then challenges by *female* business owners must have been even more charged or perhaps threatening.

It is this context that must be remembered when Lewis's tax fight is considered. It was bold for Lewis to hire a tax attorney and contest the government's finding. Her actions in response to the EPT didn't distinguish her from the thousands of other business owners who filed suits resisting the excess profits tax, but it did lead her into a highly charged political and military environment in which resistance to the military's ability to reduce wartime business profits was defined as a threat to masculinity. Businesswomen's actions may have been viewed differently from men's in this forum.

Postwar conversion hit Flotill hard, and once again it was the government's RFC loan program that Lewis turned to for help to pull her through the crisis. Difficult times were almost universal in the canning industry at the end of the 1940s. "Like almost every other canner," *Time* magazine reported in 1951, "Tillie Lewis lost money in 1948 & '49." The reason was "high-cost inventories and over-production." These conditions were driven in large part by production for the military that suddenly dried up, leaving canners with extra inventory on their hands. Flotill's difficulties were deepened by its 1948 purchase of a 51 percent interest in the Tex-Mex Corporation, a Nevada company that imported and canned Mexican and Cuban pineapples. Lewis expected to use it to supply pineapple for the company's canned fruit cocktail, but it reportedly "went bust" and she lost an estimated $600,000 on the deal. She "squeaked through only by wrangling two RFC loans for a total of $1,600,000."[27]

It seems likely that Lewis's loan application was successful this time because she was a military supplier—both the reason for the greater financial security of her company and a reason that the RFC was confident in the company's future prospects. Although the RFC operated like a corporation, turning down more applications than critics thought it should due to insufficient capital or high risk of default, when applicants were government customers it had a reason to evaluate the applicant favorably, especially on the eve of the Korean War. Flotill was both a prior military contractor and a company on the cusp of becoming a military contractor again. From the perspective of the RFC, this was a reason to be confident in the company's future revenue and ability to repay a loan and thus ample justification to evaluate the company's application favorably.

Thus, for those women business owners who offered a product in demand by the military, government funds seemed to have been available in amounts sufficient to make a dramatic difference in a business's success. This suggests an opportunity to reevaluate previous scholarship that concluded that RFC funding was not available to businesswomen during this period. Instead, the mid-twentieth century appears to have been a unique episode in women's business history when government contracting provided access to government lending, both of which made a significant difference in female business success. The loan Lewis received kept the company afloat even as it shaped a new relationship with government for Lewis and Flotill Products.

The disbursement of Lewis's RFC loan was tightly controlled. The first loan, awarded to Flotill in 1949 for $1,100,000, was to satisfy the company's indebtedness and to provide working capital. Both investments facilitated the company's ability to contract with the military again one year later. But these allocations were not distributed in lump sums unencumbered by restrictions. Instead, the loan resolution stipulated that the money would be distributed directly to the following creditors: Pacific Can Company, which held a chattel mortgage on the company's property (not more than $75,000), trade accounts (not more than $319,864), accounts payable to growers (not more than $138,407), machinery contracts (not more than $73,329), and accrued property taxes (not more than $115,154). The remainder was to be used for operating expenses, but this too was carefully controlled. It was disbursed only when the RFC's San Francisco agency manager was "in receipt of evidence, satisfactory to him, that the disbursement . . . [was] needed and [would] be used . . . solely for Operating Expenses."[28] Thus, the terms of the loan inserted strict oversight by an RFC manager and compliance with a strict set of requirements.

The level of accountability and control imposed as a term of the RFC loan necessitated that Tillie Lewis—the guarantor of the loan—build a relationship with a federal organization and its agents. She had to earn their trust and satisfactorily prove how and why she was incurring operating expenses in order to access the remainder of her loan. Furthermore, the loan resolution stipulated that the company must supply monthly balance sheets and operating statements, that it must appoint a controller if asked, and that it must "make a study of the cost of operation of each of [its] . . . plants and . . . submit such study . . . with a view to consolidating its operations." These requirements may have seemed invasive to Lewis, but surely the one that rankled was the condition that the management "including but not limited to a new general manager" must be satisfactory. This appears to have been a specific reference to Lewis. For reasons not explained in the documentary evidence, Lewis entered into a five-year contract (1947–52) as the company's general manager—at the same time that she was officially listed as Flotill's president—that encompassed the start of the RFC loan period. Thus, the attention to the general manager focused on her own performance and suggests that the RFC and its agents had some concerns about her. Without comparative evidence, though, it is impossible to know whether such stipulations were gendered, reflecting apprehension about lending to a woman-owned company, or whether the added attention was commonplace or at least uniformly applied in the RFC loan process. Either way, active management of this new relationship with the federal government was required. Determining whether Lewis satisfactorily complied with each of the stipulations—including whether she proved herself as a manager—was left to the discretion of the local agency manager, an individual with whom she would need to interact regularly to access and sustain the loan benefits for her company.[29]

The trade-offs and "costs" of the RFC loan were steep, but the gains were substantial. In addition to the tight controls on her management, the agency also required collateral. For Lewis, this meant leveraging her company. She subordinated herself and mortgaged her company to the RFC—committing her life insurance policy and Flotill's land, buildings, machinery, and equipment as collateral. Yet the benefit to her was that the loan severed her obligations to several long-term creditors, in particular the Pacific Can Company. In addition, it offered a 4 percent interest rate and seven-year repayment schedule. That such "financial assistance . . . [was] not otherwise available . . . on reasonable terms" was in fact a signature requirement of the program that borrowers had to certify and substantiate with evidence.[30] For Lewis, this would have been easy. Even the small personal and collateral-free loans offered her by personal acquaintance Violet Greener, of the Agabeg Occult Church, Inc., in Los Angeles, which helped her to raise the required capital to buy out her business partner in 1939, came with a 6 percent interest rate.[31] The loan's benefits were so substantial, in fact, that in 1950 the company applied for and received an additional $500,000 from the RFC designated for use as working capital, which it repaid in one year.[32] Flotill used the loan to help it become a military supplier on a larger scale.

Lewis successfully capitalized on her company's experience and established relationship with the government to expand her role as a military contractor. In 1950, Flotill became a large ration assembler in addition to continuing to provide component parts from its own regular inventory of canned fruits. This was an opportunity generated by the Korean War as well as Cold War military buildup more generally. Consideration of "current bidders and World War II producers" was part of the producer-supplier selection process as stipulated by the Industrial Mobilization Planning Program of the military. "Know how," as it was called in some official evaluation reports, could make the difference between an assembler being able to produce rations "on time and in accordance with specifications" or not. While this narrowed access to military supply contracts for other, first-time bidders and was a topic of concern among small business owners and their political advocates, for Flotill this was advantageous.[33] Of course, in the canned fruit industry, it was no surprise to find a business with prior experience as a military supplier, since during World War II army procurement requirements for canned fruit and juice constituted some 56 percent of the "total allocable supply," according to one study.[34] Thus, it would have been hard to be a canned fruit producer and *not* become a military supplier during the early 1940s. Nonetheless, the experience that Flotill had accrued as a provisioner of canned fruit continued past World War II and was noted by the Quartermaster General Corps (QMC) in its 1950 "Potential

Wartime Ration Assembler Preparedness Plan" for the company. Flotill managers understood that their previous experience was an advantage, too, and they highlighted this on the required application form. It noted, "Management states facility has sold quantities of fruits and vegetables (canned) to the government in 1949 and is thoroughly familiar with government procurement and inspection procedures." This was one reason that in its plan, the QMC estimated that Flotill would need only thirty to forty-five days "between the receiving of [the] Quartermaster Corps Letter of Intent and the achieving of full volume assembly production"—a key criterion on which all potential assemblers were evaluated and selected, which was clearly linked to experience.[35]

Records indicate that location was also a significant factor in the selection of military ration assemblers during the Korean War, and this, too, was an advantage for Lewis. The Stockton, California, site that Lewis had originally selected when she established Flotill Products in 1934 was a strategic one for a company bidding to assemble rations for the military in 1950. It was in close proximity to all forms of transportation, nineteen of the twenty-three other companies providing parts for the rations being assembled, and the most important military supply centers for the Pacific-theater war. Equally important, it was outside a major population center that might become a military target. All these factors were key to Flotill's selection as one of the largest ration assemblers during the Korean War.[36]

Quality control was a chief goal of the Quartermaster Corps, especially when it came to food rations, and Lewis's strength in this area was highlighted in a promotional video. The 1950s television series *Industry on Parade*, produced by the National Association of Manufacturers (NAM), featured Lewis and Flotill Products in an episode titled "Caterers to Combat Men." Since the series was designed to promote the efficiency and importance of industry, the episode documenting Flotill's role as a C-ration assembler highlighted the company as "one of the largest and most efficient packing operations in the country."[37] But it spent more time focusing on quality control, separately featuring images of both army officers and Lewis walking the factory floor and inspecting the work of the women employed as seasonal laborers. Lewis did more than inspect, however, and the episode showed this by highlighting her hands-on approach to management. This was illustrated in footage of Lewis in hairnet and gloves "hold[ing] her own" on the assembly line preparing tomatoes for canning and in the scenes at her desk where she checked the quality of the ration packets assembled at her plant, even tasting the sausage and gravy that she poured out of a can

Flotill Products was the biggest assembler of C-rations for American troops during the Korean War. Each "combat" ration included Flotill canned fruit, imprinted with the company name as pictured here. National Archive and Records Administration, College Park, Maryland.

into a bowl in front of the camera. Although the company had "army inspectors always on duty observing how the food going into the cans meets the constant top standards" of the military, the episode reported, Lewis herself saw to product quality: "The woman who built this flourishing organization from nothing into the largest independent cannery in the world, refuses to accept any judgment but her own when it comes to the quality of the product. Tillie Lewis, the gal from Brooklyn who left the big city to find success in California's . . . San Joaquin Valley never forgets for a minute where this food is headed—to the men who deserve the best we can possibly give them."[38] Lewis's conscientious quality control may have been a standard feature of how she managed her business. Blind taste tests were, in fact, a regular occurrence in the fruit-canning business.[39] But the *Industry on Parade* episode emphasized that Lewis treated her military customers— the combat soldiers on the ground in Korea—with special care. This strategic alignment of patriotic interests and business interests made sense for a public-relations campaign launched by the National Association of Manufacturers to advance the cause of private enterprise.[40] Yet the episode and its emphasis on quality control also underscore that Lewis understood the value of her military contract and actively sought to sustain it.

In addition to helping her retain her contract as one of the nation's foremost ration assemblers, Lewis's active involvement in Flotill's quality control may have helped her to secure new customers as well. Each can of Flotill fruit packed within a C-ration arrived with the company name printed on it, indelibly etching it in the minds of soldiers. If the product they tasted was high quality, it would leave a positive impression. Press coverage of Flotill indicates that it did. One headline read, "GIs in Korea Tell Tillie They Like the Chow She Sends."[41] This positive evaluation by soldiers could have had a benefit after the war. The lucky ones would return home with a product memory that may have influenced their postwar consumption choices. It seems likely that Lewis and her managers (as well as those of the other companies featured in ration kits) understood this consumer advantage.[42]

Knowing how to successfully navigate a company relationship with the government was important for any leader, and in her relationship with the RFC, Lewis did so by casting herself as the official contact. This was in fact prescribed in the documents for the loan funding her military production. Occupying dual roles at this time as both her company's president and its general manager, Lewis was listed by the RFC as the "official with whom [the] contract should be negotiated and addressed."[43] The dual title Lewis occupied at this time may have intentionally emphasized that she was intimately involved in day-to-day operations. This helped reject the stereotype associated with some female business leaders as figureheads rather than active managers. And it conformed to the image of Lewis as a hands-on company president who paid close attention to quality control, as presented in the *Industry on Parade* episode described above.

While some companies also designated their presidents as the chief contact for military contracts, many viewed contracting with the military as a business function that required particular skills and developed a specific manager role for this purpose. Politicians told business owners that this was unnecessary and that they did not need to employ a representative in Washington to secure government business, but many companies did. Usually these business representatives were former military officials who had inside knowledge and contacts from the military that they could use to advantage the companies that employed them.[44] At large-scale companies, these positions focused exclusively on handling government contracts. Cal Pak (Del Monte), for example, one of Flotill's competitors in the California canning industry that was nearly 200 times bigger in terms of annual revenue in 1951, maintained a "Manager of Government Sales" who oversaw its C-ration assembly contract.[45]

At Flotill, no such role existed, but unlike in other companies, Lewis did not herself take on the role of managing military contracts as president and general manager either. Instead, she absented herself from day-to-day interactions with military procurement officers, delegating this function to male subordinates. Notes from the field visit of QMC captain Andrew J. Draper in January 1951 document interactions with a variety of Flotill Products personnel, but Lewis was not among them. Dr. Weast, identified as "Production Manager," led the company's recommendations for improving the ration assembly process with help from Vice President Heiser (one of Lewis's nephews). Mr. Sider and Mr. Mitchell also provided input and are noted in Draper's "Report of Travel," though their positions at the company are not noted. But Tillie Lewis herself was conspicuously absent from these discussions.[46]

Lewis's absence from interactions with military procurement officers is notable. Perhaps she was simply busy promoting Tasti-Diet, the company's new diet-food line, which was launched the same year, as chapter 4 will document.[47] But it may have also been prudent to keep herself out of this particular government relationship, since women were so rarely involved in military discussions in 1950. This was a lesson Olive Ann Beech was forced to confront in her interactions with the military too, as we shall see later in the chapter. Either way, careful management of the company's relationship with the military paid off, as the increasing importance of this line of business became clear over the course of the next several years.

The contracts that Flotill secured as a ration supplier and assembler during the 1950s buoyed the company's performance at a critical juncture in its history. In 1950 alone, "sales to United States Agencies . . . approximated $5,100,000," which amounted to 35 percent of its total gross sales ($14,642,640) for the year.[48] And most of the contracts contained renegotiation clauses, permitting Flotill to continue as a supplier to the military for several years. By the end of 1951, *Time* magazine reported that "Flotill [had become] the biggest packer of C rations for U.S. troops."[49] Ongoing government sales helped to sustain the company through a variety of market ups and downs for several years—which Lewis described in annual reports as "the food processing industry's . . . first post war test of overproduction and consequent price unsettlement"—and contributed to the record high posted in 1956. Once government sales were substantially reduced, as they were in 1957, the company showed a decrease in sales and earnings.[50]

Despite the decline of government sales by the end of the 1950s, however, the experience of canning and packing rations for the military had ongoing benefits. It helped Flotill to launch a significant sideline business as a private-label canner. The private-label market, a niche already constituting a third of its total sales in 1948, grew to a "big sideline" by 1951 when the company began canning for Hormel, Safeway grocery stores, and others. This helped attract the Ogden Corporation's purchase offer in 1966, since it was interested in entering industrial food production—processing food for other businesses rather than selling direct to consumers.[51]

Ration contracts also facilitated government investments in plant infrastructure as well as new liabilities. "Facilities costing $239,857.11 were constructed under Certificates of Necessity in 1951 for the assembly of Government rations," the company reported, and it was permitted by the government to amortize as much as 65 percent of the cost over five years.[52] But doing business with the government was not only profitable; it contributed to the company's legal liabilities too. In its 1958 annual report, the company reported an action brought against it by the United States of America "seeking recovery of approximately $595,000 plus interest . . . aris[ing] from sales of tomato paste in 1951 which the government contend[ed] did not conform to the provisions of the contract of sale." In response, the company refuted the claim and "filed an action for recovery of approximately $88,000 due it on these sales."[53]

Yet in spite of this liability and the excess profits tax liability it also fought, the net outcome of Flotill's relationship with the government—as a supplier and assembler of rations and as a borrower from the RFC—was positive. Contracting with the federal government provided a bridge that enabled the company to move successfully from its shaky startup phase at the end of the 1930s to its strong position as a producer of canned and dietetic foods with national brand recognition by the end of the 1950s. Lewis had successfully leveraged a relationship with the government to her advantage.

Olive Ann Beech

As she traveled around the country and the world in her private plane named *The Free Enterprise*, Olive Ann Beech championed each individual's ability to improve her position, yet she was also a patriot who believed in the wartime and Cold War buildup of American government. Couched as an investment in preserving American freedoms and strengthening America's position abroad, an expanded military was a cause she supported. Yet the role of the federal government as lender, buyer, and regulator in conjunction with military buildup directly impacted her business and her role in it, and it did so in negative as well as positive ways. Defense contracts, facilitated by government loans to expand production facilities, dramatically increased the size and scope of the company's output. But cancellation of the contracts had just as radical an effect, nearly sinking the company. Navigating the ups and downs, opportunities, and risks of contracting, borrowing, and profiting from the government, was a key phase in Beech's company leadership, and her success in this role was fundamental to Beech Aircraft's long-term outcomes.

Military production during World War II dramatically altered Beech Aircraft's output and profitability, moving its balance sheets from red to black in a short period of time. Before ramping up for wartime demand, the company's production levels were modest. It had only just emerged from the Depression, and the strong market for private aircraft had not yet developed. In 1938, the company delivered fifty-nine biplanes and eleven monoplanes and net sales for the year totaled $1,141,398.57. And it did so with 250 employees. At the invitation of the U.S. Army Air Corps, the company "submitted certain equipment in competition" and secured a $1 million order, nearly doubling its business.[54] This type of selective encouragement by the military was precisely what came under fire by most small business owners and politicians as unfair privilege—an advantage that usually favored large-scale companies. For Beech—still a small business at the time according to official government definitions—the privilege was likely connected to the fact that Walter H. Beech had served in the U.S. Army Air Corps from 1917 to 1920. He was "on the inside," having distinguished himself as a military pilot with substantial flying ability and aircraft know-how even before he became an award-winning commercial pilot.[55] The connection that Walter Beech's service record facilitated set the company on a new course.

The order from the Army Air Corps spurred production. By 1939, Beech Aircraft had increased its output to sixty-six biplanes and eight monoplanes and had a backlog of unfilled orders that by the end of the year had grown to $1,279,000. The company increased its labor force to 802, reoriented its production facilities and process to maximize efficiency, and by 1940 projected a monthly capacity of ten biplanes and four monoplanes—more than doubling its 1938 production level. By this time, however, Beech Aircraft was still not profitable. When the company filed a stock prospectus with the SEC in February 1940, it reported, "Up to the present time, through a period marked by the successful development of airplanes that are today outstanding in their classes, the Company has not had a sufficiently sustained volume of sales to establish its operations on a profitable basis."[56] That was the year that changed the fortunes of the company. "Midway through 1940, all commercial production was suspended, as the company geared up for defense manufacturing." Military demand for the Beechcraft 17 and Beechcraft 18, small planes used for training purposes, drove the company's assembly line to ever-increasing levels of productivity. Order backlogs reached $22 million in 1940 and $82 million in 1941, and employment grew to 2,100 in 1940 and 4,000 by 1942.[57] To meet this new demand, Beech Aircraft needed money—lots of it—and Olive Ann Beech was the leader who made that happen.

Beech turned to government loan programs to provide the capital necessary to outfit its facilities for wartime production. In June 1941, the company entered into a $2,316,019.07 loan agreement with the Reconstruction Finance Corporation "for the construction of emergency plant facilities." The company's contract with the government for military planes secured the loan and payments were made directly from the Defense Department to the Federal Reserve Bank of Kansas City as "Fiscal Agent" for the RFC. The government, in fact, would own the newly constructed facilities funded by the loan unless and until the company could purchase them, which it eventually did. Most small companies were not able to do so, but Beech did, paying back the loan "from current working capital" thanks to the tremendous volume of business it conducted with the military during the war. By the end of 1942, in fact, the company had acquired all the facilities paid for with the government's emergency construction loan. Amortizing the cost of this purchase for the duration of the war, as permitted once the company obtained "Certificates of Necessity" under Defense Department policy, added significant complication to the accounting and financial statements of the company but provided yet another advantage facilitated by government policy.[58] The next time the company turned to the government to help fund needed facilities for wartime production, it relied instead on the Defense Plant Corporation, which built and then leased the facility to the company—a significantly simpler financial transaction.[59]

Procuring sufficient capital for day-to-day operations was another problem, and Beech once again turned to the government for help. This was, in fact, a common challenge for wartime manufacturing firms during World War II. According to one contemporary analysis, the difficulty was tied to the rapidity with which wartime production was ramped up: "The rapid growth of many firms' scale of operations and the shift to new fields of production led to serious doubts as to the ability to complete contracts in a manner satisfactory to the contracting services. Growth in scale of operations was not matched in all cases by increases in capital funds; many contractors had financial needs far out of proportion to their net worth, indeed, so far out of proportion as to render them poor credit risks by normal standards."[60] Beech likely fit this description and thus had little choice but to rely on government-sponsored programs to supply its capital needs, since traditional commercial lenders were unlikely to provide loans on the scale the company required. Initially, it turned to the RFC for "Working Capital Loans," taking two loans totaling $8,647,335 that were secured by the company's military supply contracts and paid directly by the armed services upon receipt of completed orders.[61] In 1944, however, the company pursued a different method of financing under the Regulation V loan program.

This alternative financing program relied on federal financial institutions to guarantee loans to military contractors. Signed into law as Executive Order No. 9112 on 26 March 1942, the Regulation V program authorized military service departments to enter into contracts with the Federal Reserve Banks and the Reconstruction Finance Corporation and other financing institutions as a guarantor for contractors and subcontractors whose military production was "deemed necessary, appropriate or convenient for the prosecution of the war." The program provided "a means of assuring the financing of war production contracts through the utilization of the existing banking structure. The guaranteeing of large percentages of the loans by the Federal Reserve Banks as agents for the contracting services made it possible for local banks to finance local industries." Borrowers from the aircraft industry constituted 8 percent of the program total, and in this respect Beech Aircraft was in good company. But most authorizations in the program were for single loans; revolving lines of credit such as Beech had were much less common. And, according to one source, authorizations over $1,000,000 constituted less than 7 percent of the total loans in the program, with $4,000,000 being the largest authorized borrowing.[62] Thus, when Beech Aircraft secured a $50,000,000 revolving line of credit in March 1944, it made headlines.[63] Arranged under the "VT" loan program that dispensed money during a brief period between September 1943 and September 1944, the financing was specifically "intended to free working capital upon termination of contracts as well as to provide working capital to finance the contracts."[64]

This had been Olive Beech's concern—the need to secure the company's interests even in the face of military contract cancellation. As the resolution passed by the company's board of directors on 8 May 1944, reveals, the company had acted to "offer greater protection to the corporation's interest in the case of contract termination," which remained possible "at the convenience of the Government."[65] What the VT loan program offered that was better than the RFC loan program was that the loan remained intact if or when the government cancelled its war contract *and* the line of credit was facilitated by commercial banks. Because the Beech line of credit was so large, its loan came from thirty-six different banks in nine different states (mostly midwestern) facilitated by the Fourth National Bank as agent, which was "the company's local banking connection." The credit was extended for thirty months with a 90 percent guarantee from the government.[66] It was a substantial improvement to the company's financial position as a military contractor and a boon that catapulted Beech's productivity and profitability to record levels.

Olive Ann Beech was at the center of all the company's negotiations with government agencies for this loan. The photo that appeared in *Finance* in 1944 in conjunction with its article about Beech's "VT" loan illustrated this point. Seated at the head of a long conference table was Olive Ann Beech, flanked to her right by her husband and company president Walter H. Beech and to her left by vice presidents of the Fourth National Bank and the Federal Reserve Bank, the central institutions in the agreement acting as agent and guarantor, respectively. Also at the table or standing behind her were additional leaders from Beech and the Federal Reserve as well as the president of Fourth National Bank and military leaders—chief of the Fiscal Division at the Midwest Procurement District, an officer from the Department of the Fiscal Director, Army Service Forces, and a district financial officer, all holding the rank of "Major" or "Captain."[67] Needless to say, Beech was the only woman in the photo and presumably the only woman in the room. And she was clearly at the center of the day's work. Later accounts of Beech's leadership would credit her with securing the remarkable loan. A 1959 *Saturday Evening Post* article about Beech, for example, captured her key role in the negotiation: "She negotiated a revolving $50,000,000 credit with thirty-six banks; their chief negotiator still recalls how his clients thought the company had assigned too high a value to work in progress and questioned Mrs. Beech about it: 'She had good answers. She'd say, "How do you know?" Well, sometimes we didn't. She wasn't afraid of banks. She wasn't afraid of anything.' "[68] And why should she be afraid? One year before she brokered this deal, she had been named one of the twelve most distinguished women in America by the *New York Times* and was one of only five women invited to participate in a panel discussion of women's part in the war effort at the

American Bankers Association forum.[69] But it was more than just confidence that earned Beech her influence. "You have to be honest to pry that kind of money out of lenders," she reported in an interview years later with *Fortune*, "and you have to believe in what you're trying to borrow for."[70] Integrity and vision were two of the qualities that Beech leveraged to navigate her relationship with government. In conjunction with her well-established financial acumen, these qualities helped her secure substantial opportunities for the company during wartime.

Yet in spite of this success, for Olive Ann Beech, the only female executive in the entire American aircraft industry, gender was a liability she had to overcome in order to cultivate and sustain a successful relationship with government. Interacting with men almost exclusively on a day-to-day basis was familiar to Beech, and she had worked hard to earn her male colleagues' respect from the beginning, as documented in chapter 1. But interacting with government and military officials who did not know her and were surprised to find a woman at the helm of an airplane company brought additional challenges. In a speech she delivered to the Soroptomist Club in the 1940s, Beech reported, "At first the obstacles seemed unsurmountable, not the least of them being the blight of a female secretary-treasurer. Time and time again I was confronted with the surprise and consternation of men when they found the person with whom they were to deal, a woman. Largely because of the respect and loyalty of my fellow associates, men with whom I had worked side by side for years, was I able to live down the 'stigma' of being a woman at the head of a National Defense Project."[71] The particular trial for Beech as a woman in aviation in the 1940s—overseeing a "National Defense Project"—underscores the degree to which defense work, at the leadership level, was an almost exclusively male domain in the 1940s. Perhaps this is why her appointment several years later to the Defense Advisory Committee on Women in the Service (1963–65) was so important to her. She had experienced firsthand the challenges women faced working with male military personnel and was determined to improve the status quo for female members of the U.S. Armed Forces. With no such advocate for her own interactions with U.S. military men, however, Beech reportedly relied on the "respect and loyalty" toward her that was modeled by company colleagues to earn the trust of service members with whom she interacted during the course of Beechcraft business. The hypermasculine military context in which she exercised leadership as a contractor generated doubt about both her authority and her abilities, and Beech worked skillfully to eradicate both and assert herself and her financial expertise.

Supporting her success with these efforts was Beech's strong patriotism, which was both genuine and strategic to her interests as a military contractor. In her speech to the Soroptomist Club during World War II, she reported that upon returning from the Army-Navy game where she enjoyed watching thousands of midshipmen and cadets march, she had "a renewed determination to do my part and more in the emergencies that are now facing all of us." Of course, such a "do your part" attitude was precisely what the government tried to instill in all citizens on the home front during World War II, and there were many programs to help it achieve this. But as a producer of aircraft parts as well as planes used for training new recruits, Beech had the capacity to assist the war effort on a scale few others could. In addressing the Soroptomists, however, she modestly characterized herself as a "worker" like other American women during the war who were contributing to their country's defense: "I realize that your interest is centered on me not as a woman holding a responsible executive position, but as a worker very much concerned with our national defense program, and as such I join my talents and my ability with yours and all the other capable courageous women in the United States in our ALL-OUT-FOR-AMERICAN-DEFENSE!"[72] It was a rallying cry. And it was a message that normalized her atypical position as a female executive in the context of widespread and essential women's war work. This was an affective rhetorical strategy for her female audience. But it was also a useful way to position herself in relation to male military and government personnel who doubted her qualifications and authority as an aircraft company leader. A final comment revealed her passion for the country's defense program and communicated how invested she was in her work. She mused, "I, a woman, have a part in this vastly intriguing work—a work that grips your imagination at the same time that it puts the iron into your soul." Beech found challenging work satisfying and once remarked to a reporter that "the majority of people today don't know what the joy of work is."[73] Clearly, leading Beech Aircraft provided that stimulation. But what put "iron into [her] soul"—that is, gave her strength and fortitude—was the determination to play a role in helping to protect her country and its freedoms.

This was a sacred mission for Beech. She was an active member of the Freedom Foundation at Valley Forge, an organization chartered in 1949 that fellow Kansan and then Columbia University president Dwight Eisenhower helped to found. It was a nonprofit, nonsectarian organization "with a purpose to seek out and reward those who do outstanding work to further an understanding of the fundamentals of a free way of life." Beech was a director of the organization and later an award winner.[74] Her zeal for the organization's mission reflected a deep sense of commitment to preserve the American free enterprise system and triumph over both its foes and apathy toward it.

It was a set of principles expressed in part through explicit anticommunism. This was a sentiment she dispersed to her employees through internal communications. As one company newsletter highlighted, excerpting a diatribe from a speech by AFL-CIO president George Meany, there were many in the free world who failed to "see the real nature of Communism as the moral foe of everything that we hold dear."[75] Since U.S. Defense objectives were at the heart of this endeavor, especially in the 1950s in the midst of the Cold War, anticommunism aligned with the business interests of Beech Aircraft. But for Olive Ann Beech, anticommunism was both a business stance and a deeply held principle.

As for many Americans in the 1950s, patriotism for Beech was about the triumph of an economic system as well as an ideological one. Thus, when President Eisenhower reached out to her as a "leading industrialist," a Freedom Foundation member, and a longtime supporter—one of his "good friends in the business world"—to help make the case against communism and for investments in U.S. defense, he wrote in business terms, but she responded in ideological ones. A letter addressed to Olive Ann from Eisenhower explained "the crying need for Defense modernization" using a "comparison with corporate practices." In it he explained that the current defense organization was analogous to a business organization where each important subordinate reported directly to the board, bypassing the CEO. The letter ended with an appeal: "I hope that you, and others, will find it [the business analogy] useful in awakening the public to the grave seriousness of this matter." What Eisenhower was asking was for Beech (and other industrial leaders) to use their experience in the business world to help him explain the organizational inefficiencies of the government's defense sector and why they needed to be addressed. But Beech's response, sent via telegram, focused on moral and ideological standards rather than business ones: "The pioneer spirit of Kansas still lives, and those of us who have admired your years of forthright leadership are ready to back you up as you stand for what you and we believe is the right, the truth and the hope for the future of mankind." The response merged her roots, her principles, and her belief in the profound importance of the mission on which Eisenhower, the United States, and she had embarked. Thus, for Olive Ann Beech, patriotism was real and strategic both—helping her to establish a successful working relationship with military and government agencies and their personnel even as it animated the work she did for them with a passionate determination and sense of mission.[76]

Beech's patriotism did not mean her interactions with government were always positive, however; as for many business owners at this time, protecting the best interests of her company sometimes required resistance to government. One example came in the form of excess profits taxes (EPT). Like Lewis, Beech was charged excess profits tax on top of regular corporate income tax for the years 1942–49, paying a total of $1,458,633.77 above and beyond the $1,555,025.62 she paid in regular income tax. The problem, similar to that of Flotill, was that Beech Aircraft had not been profitable before the war. Furthermore, the company was concerned that containing wartime profits too low—especially as a percentage of costs as one bill proposed—"would not allow the aircraft industry to survive the postwar transition" when they anticipated that product demand would decline precipitously and companies would have to rely on previous wartime profits to get by.[77] For Beech, the fight against EPT came years later. Alert to the implications of a 1953 ruling on another company's tax claim, Beech Aircraft Corporation developed a legal theory that it had overpaid and that the operating losses of several years had not been taken into consideration to calculate a tax carryback refund. After having their claims denied by the Bureau of Internal Revenue, the company filed a suit in the U.S. Court of Claims in 1954. It was a case that Beech Aircraft finally won in 1958. The U.S. Treasury Department was ordered to issue a certificate of overassessment and, according to the terms of the settlement dismissing the case with prejudice, to pay the company $4,296,480.29 in refunded income and excess profits taxes as well as damages. Though Olive Ann Beech relied on a team of legal representatives to manage the case, her initials, signature, and notes on the related documents reveal her involvement. On a single sheet titled "Results of Tax Claim" with the awarded monetary figure at the top and her signature as president at the bottom, she listed "book value," "working capital," and "current ratio" as values measured on 7 May 1958 at 5:00 P.M. and again on 8 May 1958 at 8:00 A.M., the day the reward was deposited, showing how literally overnight the victory had measurably improved the financial picture of the corporation. Scribbled off to the side in handwriting unmistakably hers, Olive Ann wrote, "Coup de maître" with the date and the translation: "a master stroke." It was a sign that she took great pleasure and pride in the triumphs of her company, even at the expense of the government when she believed the outcome just—and that it was an outcome that reflected carefully calculated legal strategy.[78] Beech's role in this highlights the degree to which she occupied a liminal space with anti–big government, antiregulation, and pro–free enterprise on one side and pro-American, prodefense, and pro-Eisenhower on the other. It was the terrain many business leaders occupied in the middle of the twentieth century.[79]

The "peaks and valleys" of military contracting also tested Beech's mettle and resolve to win for her company regardless of government obstacles. In spite of dramatic layoffs, traumatic dips in sales, and two years of net losses, the company weathered the end of World War II by manufacturing all manner of implements for which there was a market: pie plates, aluminum vegetable crispers and meat preservers, components for cotton pickers and hay balers, plastic nozzles for hair dryers, parts for dishwashers, and even vending machines for soft drinks. As one account by a company executive revealed, "We didn't get rich from these ventures, nor did we escape from the wilderness of a deep post-war recession, but non-aircraft production did accomplish its primary objective: income to retain a nucleus of experienced employees." At the end of the Korean War, which had once again drawn the company into military production, cancellation of a $100,000,000 order for T-36 trainers for the Air Force's Air Material Command was both abrupt and devastating. "Not one flight in the T-36 was permitted even though it was just hours from its scheduled maiden flight." As a result, a newly constructed building adding 110,000 square feet in capacity and built especially for the project stood unused. And the 500 employees per month that the company had been adding to ramp up for T-36 production now had no work. Beech's recovery strategy was to enter into subcontracting, producing airplanes and component parts for other airplane manufacturers. Within two years, such "subcontract sales amounted to $25 million or approximately 30 per cent of gross sales." Thereafter, expansion of the Beech product line of commercial airplanes and diversification in 1955 into the space field as a pioneer in cryogenic engineering as well as a producer of missile targets enabled the company to weather the setback and emerge stronger than before.[80] While dependence on government contracts had almost brought Beech Aircraft to its knees, as the company feared would occur once military contracts declined, Olive Ann's vision and determination enabled the company to push on.

As it moved into new manufacturing ventures in conjunction with military and space programs of the United States, Beech remained, at its core, oriented toward a mission that strategically and philosophically aligned its interests with those of the nation. The twentieth-anniversary celebration

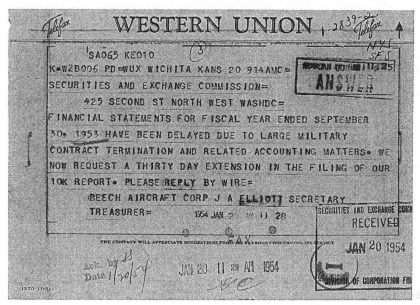

In 1953, Beech Aircraft sent an urgent telegram to the Securities and Exchange Commission requesting an extension on their filing deadline. The cancellation of their military contract wreaked havoc on their accounting records as well as the company's business generally. National Archive and Records Administration, Washington, D.C.

of Beech's Boulder Division, established in 1955, which set the course toward company production for the Gemini program, the Apollo explorations, and the Lunar module, acknowledged this perspective. The prayer delivered by "Father Pat" at the celebration captured the spirit of their work:

> Heavenly Father, we rejoice and give thanks for the years of productivity, friendship, cooperation and mutual regard of the Beech Aircraft Corporation and Boulder, Colorado.
>
> Our association, one with another, is now 20 years strong. Through it, our community has been enriched by the presence of fine people and good jobs, and our nation has moved through dreams and expectations into outer space.
>
> Now, we ask Thy Blessing on what lies (and flies) ahead of us. For each of us and for all of us, it is a journey of faith. Strengthen our courage, imbue us with wisdom, help us to discern the truth that we may act and plan for the future accordingly. Finally, keep in our

hearts and minds the knowledge that only those things begun, continued, and ended in Thee shall prosper and flourish.[81]

It was a set of ideas that moved Olive Ann, who was present for the occasion. She passed on the prayer to several Beech employees. What must have resonated with her was not just the importance of faith but also the theme of national mission and her company's contribution to it—a recurring refrain over many years of government contracting. For Beech, interacting with the government had ups and downs and sometimes pitted her and her company's interests against government agencies whose job it was to enforce policy, increase revenue, and reduce unnecessary costs. But she had learned to leverage government opportunities through loans and contracts that both bolstered the company's fortunes and aligned its mission and vision with that of the mid-twentieth-century national mission focused on military security and the space race. Though the company's private and commercial plane business became increasingly important after the Korean War, it never ceased supplying the military of the United States, and its explicit patriotism and contributions to the nation's military strength were among the affinities between Beech Aircraft and Raytheon, itself engaged in production for the military market, when the two companies merged years later.[82] Thus, for Olive Ann Beech, government was a source of inspiration as well as business. And she skillfully performed the role of government contractor to the great benefit of Beech Aircraft.

Margaret Rudkin

For Margaret Rudkin, for whom the government was neither a lender nor a buyer, it was the expanded regulatory function of the federal government that impacted her day-to-day business. In particular, the Office of Price Administration (OPA), both as a monitor of commodity pricing and as the initiator of domestic rationing during World War II, reached into Pepperidge Farm's affairs during the 1940s. Rudkin responded proactively, defensively, and strategically, galvanizing help from insiders and legal experts and sustaining a decline in profits to avoid compromising her brand. It was a courageous response and one that highlights that Rudkin, like Lewis and Beech, acted with the best interests of her business in mind and was not afraid to counter federal agency representatives when their actions threatened her company. Navigating this new relationship with government was key to her success.

The OPA was one of several new government agencies established under emergency wartime management powers during World War II, and it spurred Rudkin to action to protect her business interests. The agency, established in May 1941 as the Office of Price Administration and Civilian Supply (later simply OPA, under the War Production Board), was charged with stabilizing prices on commodities by setting price ceilings and rationing those that were scarce. But according to historian Lizbeth Cohen, it wasn't until the post–Pearl Harbor Emergency Price Control Act passed in January 1942 that it gained the "teeth" necessary to carry out its mission. Rationing started with rubber, automobiles, and sugar but quickly spread to include many other scarce commodities. By the end of the war, some 90 percent of goods sold were under price control, and these policies were administered by an agency that "had become the largest of the civilian war agencies." OPA's broad power to regulate the consumer marketplace was bolstered by consumers who embraced the notion of themselves as "consumer citizens" and the principle promoted by the government that "good citizenship and good consumership were . . . inseparable." Yet in spite of the OPA's popularity among American consumers and the evidence that mandatory wartime price controls worked—an 8 percent World War II inflation rate compared to a 62 percent World War I inflation rate when price controls were voluntary—business owners "were quick to complain that they cut disastrously into profits and favored some producers and distributors over others."[83] The OPA barreled ahead anyway but established several industry advisory committees that included experts from the various commercial sectors targeted by the agency's rules to help set pricing and rationing policies. For Rudkin and Pepperidge Farm, it was of course the baking branch that was of greatest importance. Charged with stabilizing prices of baked goods including bread and rationing scarce and essential baking ingredients such as sugar and butter, the OPA's baking division loomed large for the company and in fact had a real impact on how the company fared. Rudkin clearly understood this, and so when the agency reached into her affairs, she fought back.

The OPA's initial correspondence to Rudkin was decisive and demanding and reveals the far-reaching impact of its policies. On 28 May 1942, Fred W. Thomas, associate price executive of the Food and Food Products Branch of the Office of Price Administration in Washington, D.C., addressed a letter to Margaret Rudkin requesting information:

> We are desirous of obtaining certain information which will be
> helpful to us in the establishment of retail price on a commodity

similar to yours. In order that we may become more fully advised as the manufacture and distribution costs of this product we will appreciate your giving us the following information. We realize this information is of a confidential nature, and assure you that it will be treated as such. Please furnish us with the following: 1) Balance sheet and profit and loss statement for 1940, 1941, and first four months of 1942; 2) Breakdown of the present [cost?] of a loaf of your small white bread and small whole wheat bread showing such items as material, manufacturing labor, manufacturing expense, selling expense, delivery expense, advertising, administration and profit margin.[84]

The letter made it clear that the OPA relied on production cost information from producers, backed by documentary evidence such as that requested, to determine retail prices. Of course, providing annual profit-and-loss statements to the federal government was a standard requirement by the Securities and Exchange Commission (SEC) for any publicly traded company. But Pepperidge Farm was a privately owned company, and furthermore, even those firms that did supply the SEC with financial statements every year did not provide a breakdown of the production costs on a per-unit basis for individual items. The information requested in Price's letter was indeed "of a confidential nature," and providing it could have put Pepperidge Farm at risk of sabotage by competitors if it had fallen outside the hands of the OPA.

Rudkin's response, dispatched within fifteen days of receipt of the above communication, was cagey and calculated. In it she protested the utility of relying on Pepperidge Farm as a comparison at all, and though she provided some of the requested information, she reported that she did not have all the figures requested. She wrote, "I believe you are not familiar with my bread since you wish my figures to assist you in computing the cost of another loaf of bread which you describe as 'similar' to mine. Pepperidge Farm bread is unlike any other bread on the market from the standpoint of ingredients and method of manufacture. . . . There is no other bread on the market made as mine is and the cost would not be comparable. This is only a small family business, the general partners being myself and my husband. For four years the business was operated in the farm building on our home property."[85] With this response, Rudkin presented herself as a small-scale owner of a modest "family business" and seemed to suggest that the scale of her firm made her an unreasonable target for the OPA's bread price investigation. Furthermore, she asserted that Pepperidge Farm's novel ingredients (unprocessed and all natural) and "method of manufacturing" (hand knead-ing) once again made her product a poor choice as a comparison. What she did not explain is that her high price point reflected not just production and ingredient costs but was also essential to the brand—hers was a high-end loaf, not designed to appeal to the general public. This unique market niche meant that Rudkin had strong reasons to avoid revealing too much and also that application of a bread price ceiling determined by the cost of other, more typical and lower-cost loaves might be a serious problem for her business.

Rudkin also used subterfuge in her response, claiming that she simply did not have the information that the OPA wanted. For example, she stated that because the small loaf had been on the market for only six months, introduced for families whose food needs had been diminished by the de-parture of "so many men leaving . . . to go into the service," there was not enough information to provide reliable figures. And most important, Rudkin asserted that she simply did not have the information they wanted, stating, "I have made no breakdown of my small loaf such as you request as I find that rather complicated and difficult to do."[86] In this final assertion, Rudkin may have been simply stating the facts: she didn't know how to com-pute the figures requested. But it is more likely that this retort obscured at least as much as it revealed. After all, Henry Rudkin had been preparing detailed financial records and distributing them to the company's investors since its first year of operation.

Early company financial records, in fact, reveal that Rudkin knew a lot more than she represented. Already in 1938, someone had prepared a break-down of the cost and net profit of one loaf of bread showing all production costs including mileage, loss of profit on "comp" loaves and unsold bread, and supplies even down to the cost of "½ bowl of raisins, spoiled."[87] Whether the calculation requested by the OPA had actually been completed or not by June 1942 is impossible to know, but soon thereafter, profit-and-loss state-ments for the company had been prepared for 27 April 1942 to 15 Au-gust 1942 with a handwritten note attached stipulating that they be sent to the OPA. In the same "OPA" folder, just below but *not* attached to the note, are records documenting loaves produced and material cost per loaf, broken down by large loaves and small loaves, white and whole wheat. It seems, therefore, that the data existed—whether prepared at the request of the OPA or before their request was made we don't know—but that it was omitted from the information shared with the agency. What's important about this is that it provides a context for the correspondence that followed Rudkin's initial response to the OPA, letters that clearly demonstrate her proactive steps to avoid sharing information that she guarded as proprietary.

Sometime after she was contacted by the OPA, Margaret Rudkin also tried to utilize her influential network to subvert the agency's focus on Pepperidge Farm. She reached out to Charles Oliver, an OPA adviser who was a personal contact of hers, to try to derail the request for business information. Oliver was employed by Abbott, a nutrition company that produced powdered milk and egg products.[88] More important, he was a member of the OPA's Baking Division Advisory Committee and agreed to intervene on her behalf. He wrote, "I was in Washington yesterday at the meeting of the Advisory Council of the baking industry. . . . I took up the question of what had happened to your correspondence, and I find that they have accepted my recommendation that the entire matter be dropped as far as you are concerned, so . . . I am sure you will hear nothing further about it." But in spite of Oliver's confidence about the influence he wielded on the council, one month later the matter had not, in fact, been "dropped." He reported, "In the same mail came a letter from Washington in which they advised me that there is a possibility of their asking government accounting men to check on the costs of your bread, Arnold's and Gristede's. I am passing this along to you in strictest confidence and I am going to ask you not to take any steps to attempt to forestall this move until you get definite information from the proper parties. . . . I pointed out that there is no comparison to ingredients, method, or finished product between your bread and the others mentioned." This time Oliver shared council information with her rather than simply reporting what he had said to them and thus had to ask for "strictest confidence" in how she handled it and also that she not act until being officially notified by the OPA of their intended actions lest she reveal that she had been tipped off. His willingness to do so reveals the level of his support and commitment to helping Rudkin and Pepperidge Farm.

The letter also indicates that he was well informed about her business and was, therefore, a highly valuable ally. He seemed equipped to make precisely the same points to the council that she had made in her response letter to the OPA. Though we can't be certain, it is unlikely he knew all this without being prompted by Rudkin. For example, the letter states that among the competitor bakeries being included in the OPA's price investigation was Gristede Bros., about whom Rudkin had consulted an attorney in December 1939. This is a clue about what was at stake. The brief mention of Gristede Bros. in the attorney's billing statement does not specify the nature of the concern, stating simply "general services and disbursements

October 1 to date, including conferences with Mr. and Mrs. Rudkin re relations with Gristede Bros. and advice re possible suit." But commercial infringement was a topic of discussion in more than one letter with her legal advisors, and so it is highly possible that this structured her concern about the OPA's request for information. In the end, Oliver was unable to help her avoid the OPA's inquiry into her pricing structure. A third letter to Rudkin from Oliver nine days later gave her a "further confidential tip-off so [she could] be on the look-out for Uncle Sam's accountants" after he had learned that the OPA was "determined to go through with sending accountants to Pepperidge Farm." He had tried to make her case, but, he quipped, "apparently they think my advice is not worth much."[89] Rudkin's attempt to use Oliver to defend Pepperidge Farm from the OPA had failed, but it reveals a great deal about her network and how she used it.

The same connections that facilitated Rudkin's pathway into entrepreneurship provided a ready supply of social capital that Rudkin expended to proactively defend her business from the government. Charles Oliver was a powerful ally for someone in the baking business. Evidence indicates that she knew him not just as a supplier for Pepperidge Farm but as a personal acquaintance. In his letters, Oliver asked that she give his regards to her "charming husband" and also referred to their sons getting in touch with each other. He seems to have been an acquaintance, neighbor, or perhaps even a friend of the Rudkins. And this is no surprise given the circles in which they traveled—among elite New York stockbrokers and investors, members of rarified city social clubs, residents of exclusive Connecticut country estates, and even riders of polo ponies (a personal passion of Henry Rudkin and typically an elite pastime because of its expense). Like the original investors or "Special Partners" who had funded the launch of Pepperidge Farm five years earlier, Oliver was a valuable contact whom Margaret Rudkin and her husband knew how to cultivate as a business supporter or sponsor for Pepperidge Farm. As she reported in a twenty-five-year-anniversary retrospective, "My husband had always said 'When you want something, go right to the top man.' "[90] This was a philosophy that served her particularly well since she had contacts among many "top men" and could leverage those connections—as she did with Oliver—to try to influence favorable circumstances for her business. It was a testament to social capital and the privileges it afforded the well connected, including Margaret Rudkin. This was particularly valuable when it came to navigating relations with newly created government regulatory agencies in the mid-twentieth century that had broad discretionary powers.

Just how broad the powers of the OPA were was, in fact, one of Rudkin's concerns, and she turned to her attorney for an answer in order to clearly define the extent of her vulnerability and help her craft the most effective response. In a 1 September letter to Rudkin, Norman Parsells of the law firm Marsh, Day & Calhoun reported that the OPA had "very broad" powers to examine records, including "the power of subpoena." While there was a provision in the Emergency Price Control Act providing that any records that an owner requested be kept confidential would be treated that way, he admitted that "what such a provision is worth depends entirely upon the person with whom you are dealing." His solution was to propose that she refer to him any OPA representative interested in examining her books or records. Furthermore, he offered his safe: "If there are any records which you feel it would be harmful to your business for the OPA to have because of the danger that they might be seen by your competitors, I suggest that such records or other data be placed in our safe or in a safety deposit box so that they will not be subject to examination without your prior consent or court order. If you want to leave all of your books here temporarily, it is quite agreeable." Proactively utilizing the protection of the law and/or legal subterfuge along with the help of an attorney permitted Rudkin to avoid providing the information the OPA had originally requested. As already stated, the handwritten note with instructions to "Copy to OPA P. J. Fischer" was attached to statements of income and profit and loss but *not* to the breakdown of production costs per loaf. This was the data that Rudkin clearly believed would reveal too much, putting her at risk of competitor imitation if it got into the wrong hands and thus prompting her to call on the help of both her network and her attorney.

In the end, though it's not clear which strategy it was that helped her to achieve this outcome, it is evident that Rudkin successfully protected her business from the expanded powers of government regulators. No competitor copied her formula, nor did the OPA set price ceilings low enough to force her high-priced bread off retailers' shelves. The lack of any further correspondence regarding OPA suggests that the matter was closed. Rudkin had utilized every resource at her disposal—whether it was consulting legal professionals or calling on influential acquaintances—to stave off a federal investigation that she feared would undermine Pepperidge Farm and had succeeded in protecting her product's secret formula and viability.

What Rudkin could not avoid, however, was the OPA's rationing policy, and this had a profound impact on her day-to-day operations during the 1940s, prompting her to prioritize the long-term integrity of her brand over shorter-term profits. Pepperidge Farm bread relied on a small number of wholesome ingredients, and these included "natural sweetening in the form of unsulphured molasses" and "high-grade table" or "creamery butter," which was the only shortening used. These unique ingredients, along with the natural and stone-ground flour the recipe called for in combination with the hands-on production process used at the company, distinguished the company's bread from its competitors and allowed Rudkin to charge a premium price, one notably higher than that of other loaves available in groceries. So when the OPA began rationing sugar and sugar products including molasses as well as butter, Rudkin was forced to grapple with a "serious ingredient shortage." As she described in a company retrospective, "I was faced with the decision of either lowering the quality of our bread or limiting production. I chose to limit production if necessary and feel it was the right decision and a fateful one." Substitutions were made but not at the expense of the quality of the product. Thus, "when we couldn't get butter," she stated, "we used heavy cream. One full quart of real heavy cream as a substitute for one pound of butter. This contained the same amount of butter fat and we used it although it cost the company $1,000 more a week."[91] When adequate substitutions could not be located, then the number of loaves produced was lowered, limiting the company's ability to adequately respond to demand, as she reported in a letter to a customer: "We are, of course, limited in our production because of present day war conditions, but I will definitely see that Mr. Charles Karle of Geiger's Tatnuck Square Market is taken care of."[92] Even when ingredient restrictions meant the company was unable to meet demand, Rudkin worked hard to keep customers satisfied through individual interventions such as this one. In the end, she judged her decision to limit production rather than compromise the quality of her ingredients as "fateful"—a crucial decision in response to wartime government rationing that had a fundamental and positive impact on the long-term success of her high-end brand.

Complaints about rationing and price fixing by the OPA were legion during the war and affected both businesses and individual consumers alike. Although historian Lizbeth Cohen asserts that Gallup Polls consistently found that 80 to 90 percent of Americans supported OPA market interventions, congressional correspondence folders burst with concerns about the inadequacies and inefficiencies of price and supply controls implemented by the agency.[93] The records of the Senate's National Defense Committee during World War II are filled with correspondence regarding "food problems." The letters called attention to "the high prices [that the] (O.P.A.)

charged" for various food products and "the terrific waste" this caused.[94] Others written by business owners highlighted operational problems and inefficiencies. Mrs. Alexander H. Kerr, president of Alexander H. Kerr & Co., Inc., the glass jar company on which so many World War II–era homemakers relied for canning equipment, wrote about her inventory of 3 million mason jars that she could not ship because of the inability to procure corrugated cardboard partitions and boxes caused by the Government Conservation Order restricting distribution of paper products.[95] The vice president of California-based grocery Ralphs offered nearly five pages of criticism on national conditions in the industry best summed up in the statement: "We feel that the Office of Price Administration has been handicapped in its operations by doing nearly everything backwards." By this he meant that retail prices were fixed for consumers "without any apparent regard for the cost of material or labor to process such goods."[96]

Bread was a particular problem. It was composed of one "of the best foods to ship abroad"—flour—and thus government interventions were extensive. To meet its goal of feeding European allied powers, the United States intervened in the wheat market in several ways. First, it propped up wheat prices through mandated production restrictions to protect farmers from the deflation caused by oversupply; prices reportedly rose by as much as 75 percent during the war. Second, the government made substantial purchases of flour to meet military and allied consumption needs. This led to serious restrictions. By the end of the war, the wheat shortage was at a crisis worldwide. As a result, the U.S. government intervened in a third way, ordering "all bakeries to reduce use of all flour by 25%, effective immediately." This combination of price interventions and mandatory restrictions was a problem for bread producers because it ate into profits.[97] Rationing affected the supply of butter and shortening too. War needs dictated that shortening was set aside for use "in the manufacture of munitions" while butter was stockpiled for soldiers' rations.[98]

Bread producers commented on the negative impact of these interventions in correspondence with government representatives. One retailer with an in-store bakery explained in 1942 that because consumer bread prices were "frozen" while "the cost of flour ha[d] nearly doubled," the "cost of shortening ha[d] tripled," and labor costs had escalated, profit margins had evaporated. "If we were in the bread business exclusively," he reported, "we would be bankrupt."[99] For Rudkin, whose product was typically higher priced than others, this combination of price controls and increased production costs was a serious challenge, and unlike the retailer above, she *was* exclusively in the bread business.

Frustration with government policies regarding commodities and pricing led Rudkin to urge consumer action. While appearing as a guest on a radio talk show, she declared that it was the government that was responsible for inflated food prices. "Don't blame your grocer or the baker or the food manufacturer," she said. "Blame the foolishness of government guarantees to the farmer of minimum prices at a time of high demand and small supply. It's sheer economic nonsense." Engendering affinity with listeners, Rudkin described herself as "just a housewife" and "urged all other housewives . . . to follow her lead and write their congressmen."[100] In adopting such an identity, Rudkin both aligned herself with female "consumer citizens" and capitalized on the fact that during the war, women understood their civic participation in consumer terms. Thus, even as she promoted her own interests and those of food manufacturers more generally, Rudkin couched them in terms that appealed to already mobilized housewives highly attuned to wartime prices.

Mobilized consumers, like price controls and ingredient rationing, were an outcome of OPA policies. As historians have argued, "OPA reached down into communities and households everywhere and enlisted thousands of shoppers as its main shock troops in the fight against inflation," and women were the warriors on which the strategy relied. "Defined in consumerist ways, as keepers of the home front fires through their own disciplined, patriotic market behavior as well as through the enforcement of high moral standards in others," female citizens were loyal citizens when they were activist consumers who "kep[t] the home front pledge" to help keep prices down.[101] Consumption, especially the day-to-day consumer choices by housewives, was a key front in the war, one led by the OPA.

Thus, appealing to female consumers to get involved in reforming government policies was a move that made sense for a bread producer like Rudkin. Yet none of the issues surrounding farm commodities and price supports for farmers that were a problem for her were top of mind for the mainly East Coast, urban consumers on whom she depended. Trying to make them areas of concern for the housewives already primed to reject and renounce high prices on consumer goods was a calculated move. But it was one that awkwardly attempted to make the consumers who were the greatest champions of OPA price controls—housewives—the enemy of government price interventions. For if the OPA set price ceilings on consumer products including bread, then price supports for farmers ate only into the profits of bread producers and not into the pockets of housewife consumers. Yet for a housewife who instinctively saw high prices as grounds for resistance, it was a transfer of loyalty that might look sensible. And if food producers such as Pepperidge Farm had the mobilized housewife consumer on *their* side, Rudkin seemed to reason, then propped-up farm prices might get the attention of government leaders as a policy that required reexamination.

Rudkin's consumer appeal was strategic and reflected national advocacy by manufacturers. In the lobbying campaign led by the National Association of Manufacturers (NAM), OPA price regulation was characterized as a "drift toward collectivism." Cartoons published by the campaign "warned that the OPA's 'artificial prices' along with wasteful government spending and labor strife were the barriers blocking the typical American family from reaching prosperity." NAM advocated the housewife consumer as the proper mechanism of price control, not the government, and advocated elimination of price interventions altogether.[102] Likewise, profits were not an inequity of capitalism but a driver of American innovation and productivity that benefited manufacturer, laborer, and consumer. According to NAM, price controls hurt profits and thus impeded American progress.[103] Thus, Rudkin's appeal to housewives reflected a larger dynamic in this advocacy organization's campaign. And it was likely that she embraced it as a NAM advocate and participant herself. Pepperidge Farm appeared three times in NAM's 1950s television series *Industry on Parade*.[104] In addition, the organization invited her to speak at its fifty-eighth Annual Congress of American Industry some years later.[105] Her role was unique in the organization because she could position herself as both an activist housewife consumer *and* a business owner and thus urge consumer action that would benefit manufacturers. This made Rudkin's anti-OPA rhetoric especially useful within the nationwide efforts launched by NAM.

Rudkin's long-standing plans for expanding her production facilities were also foiled by wartime conditions, and this was a particular point of frustration for her. The delay in the design and construction of a new bakery facility was likely the result of production decreases, which reduced profit margins, as well as equipment shortages and construction restrictions. But it was a critical problem. By 1940, the company had outgrown its facilities in the remodeled garage of the family's estate and moved to a rented production facility in nearby Norwalk, Connecticut. Rudkin had plans to purchase land on which to build a new commercial facility to fit the company's

Pepperidge Farm quickly outgrew their company headquarters in Norwalk, Connecticut, pictured here, but because of the wartime moratorium on construction, Rudkin had to delay her plans to build a larger facility until the end of World War II. Fairfield Museum and History Center, Fairfield, Connecticut.

specific production needs and support its expansion, and she expected to pursue this shortly thereafter. But the outbreak of war with all its implications forced Pepperidge Farm to stay in the inefficient rented factory for seven years, long past its intended tenure. A company publication reported, "But the war came along and we had to stay in those buildings until it was over. And it was torture because they became too small as we grew. It was completely inefficient, and really a headache."[106] Although Rudkin emphasized proudly that this did not stop production, it did contract it, and it also delayed plans for new products.

Yet though government restrictions impeded Pepperidge Farm in a variety of ways, they also prompted an expansion in commercial bread purchases during the war, which had a long-term positive impact on Pepperidge Farm. Rationing was a particular concern of the flour milling industry, which went to great lengths to document the problem and to advocate that the OPA address it. What they discovered is that women did home baking less during the war. This was partly a response to the rationing of flour, butter, shortening, and sugar. As a home cook, even Rudkin herself had to learn to do without key ingredients in her baking and learned "to make icing for cakes by whipping egg whites with jam or jelly or orange marmalade" in place of sugar. It was "delicious," she reported, "but you had to eat it right away before the egg whites deflated."[107] Less resourceful bakers no doubt found the ingredient shortages daunting. But there were other reasons to purchase commercially produced bread instead of baking one's own. A consumer survey conducted by the Task Committee on Shortening for the Flour Milling Industry revealed that women also cited the cheaper price of store-bought bread, the reduced size of their families (with men away at war), the need to use their ration stamps for meat and cheese, and the fact that they had less time now that they were employed outside of the home. In total, 13 percent of those interviewed were now doing no baking at home, and of the remainder, 61 percent were "baking less than before rationing"—about 50 percent less. This reduction in homemade bread meant more demand for bakery bread. The Department of Agriculture estimated that "the business of the commercial baker has increased 20%."[108] By 1948, one article reported that "only five percent of Americans eat homemade bread."[109] Thus, even as ingredient shortages and price freezes dogged production and profits, the consumer market expanded for bakeries during the war. This meant that bakeries such as Pepperidge Farm sometimes could not meet their demand but continued to see that demand rise. Thus, as with Lewis and Beech, government ultimately aided Rudkin's long-term success. Though wartime interventions restricted production capacities in a variety of ways and cut into profit margins, they also changed the habits of consumers, turning home bakers into commercial bread consumers, thereby expanding the market on which her company relied.

The emergency powers of wartime government imposed restrictions and demands on Margaret Rudkin as a business leader, which she met. Always with an eye for what was best for Pepperidge Farm and its long-term prospects, she resisted the expanded powers of government regulation with a defensive strategy that called on legal professionals as well as influential contacts to help her protect what she considered confidential information about her product. And she endured wartime shortages by protecting her company's most important claim—uncompromising product quality derived from wholesome ingredients. In the end, she was well positioned to capture the expanded market for commercially baked bread that was created by government rationing.

Conclusion

Lewis, Beech, and Rudkin were proactive and defensive in their business interactions with the federal government depending on what was best for their companies. The newly expanded federal government, empowered by Depression, wartime, and postwar recovery, required this of business leaders, especially those who could take advantage of government loans and contracts. But business–government interactions went beyond advantageous investments. The long arm of the federal government reached into day-to-day business operations in other ways too—taxing and regulating corporations as part of its expanded capacity to intervene in commercial affairs. For advocates of the free enterprise system as these women were, such intrusions were unwelcome, yet they learned to protect their businesses from them and even to strategically align their interests with the government's. Gender was relevant to their experiences in working with the government when it affected the way that government or military officials judged their skill and status as company leaders. In such cases, they reacted by proving themselves and/or by delegating negotiations to male subordinates. But more important than gender in their government interactions was the business acumen that Lewis, Beech, and Rudkin all displayed. Demonstrating a savvy ability to master the federal bureaucracy, they leveraged federal investments for the long-term benefit of their companies and capitalized on growth opportunities created by the government's wartime restrictions. Indeed, all three women succeeded both *in spite* of and *because of* the government, which played a key role, though sometimes an indirect one, in their duration and rise as business leaders.

3 Labor-Management Relations

When Marissa Mayer, the newly hired CEO of Yahoo, announced that she was ending telecommuting for the company's employees in 2013, she attracted a lot of attention. Some pointed out that her policy was typical in the tech industry, where innovation and collaboration were a high priority. Silicon Valley giants Google and Facebook, for example, leave it to employees and their managers to arrange work-from-home opportunities as necessary but prefer that their employees report to work in person. According to a 2013 *San Jose Mercury News* article, both companies cite "the benefit in the creative sparks that come with random meetings in corridors or cafeterias" as the motivation for their policies. In fact, each encourages facetime and collaboration through open desk arrangements, common spaces furnished with couches and kitchen equipment, and free onsite services such as freshly prepared meals, massage, and yoga classes. The benefits are designed to keep their employees at work to increase opportunities for interaction.[1] But in spite of such policies and programs elsewhere, Mayer's decision shocked and angered a lot of people. Some called her a hypocrite, since she had recently installed a nursery adjacent to her office where an onsite nanny would care for the baby she gave birth to months earlier. According to one news article, "parents reacted furiously online accusing [the] Yahoo! President . . . of being out-of-touch with working-class families that depend on the flexibility of telecommuting." Editorial director of Working Mother Media, Jennifer Owens, stated, "We tried to make her our role model . . . [but instead she is taking] a step in the wrong direction. . . . It's incredibly disappointing." Others thought the "firestorm" Mayer's decision sparked revolved around the fact that she was a female CEO. One working mother reported, "I fully support Marissa Mayer. . . . This woman is just doing her job. . . . The thing that is really infuriating is that this is something that is done in business every day. What is really sexist is that people are looking at this call made by her simply because she's a woman."[2]

Expecting women to behave differently in business, especially as labor managers, has a long history. Starting at the turn of the twentieth century, the "assumption that women were better 'people persons' than men" created opportunities for them in certain areas of business, including what came to be called personnel management. Women in these roles early in the 1900s were referred to as "welfare secretaries" or "social secretaries" and viewed as a kind of translator between employer and employee. At the time, many thought that women were instinctively motherly and intuitively caring, communicative, and empathetic toward others. Perceived as essential differences between men and women, such qualities contributed to the idea that certain types of jobs required "female" skills and thus female employees. As a result, women were pigeonholed in support services roles including purchasing, personnel, and public relations, which were lower in status than line jobs such as production or sales and unlikely to lead to high-level promotions. Such expectations persisted beyond the first half of the twentieth century. By 1960, women's role as managers in large-scale American businesses was deeply inflected with the idea of women as nurturers, and a clear, well-defined "female" career path had been established. Devalued, lower paid, and with no chance for advancement to the upper echelons of the corporation, women's jobs were to support others.[3] Thus, while the idea that women possessed gender-specific abilities had created opportunities for them in the business world, it also shaped and limited the types of opportunities they could access.

Though research has shown marked similarities between men's and women's leadership abilities and styles in contemporary business settings, ongoing perceptions of gender difference influence expectations. For example, a November 2000 *Businessweek* article titled "As Leaders, Women Rule" reported on a new study conducted by Hagberg Consulting Group that revealed that female executives got the same or slightly higher marks than male executives in nearly all evaluative categories. This included the "soft skills" with which women have been historically associated as well as strategic thinking and other strengths traditionally associated with men. Yet women business leaders continue to be sidelined by their stereotypical association with "soft skills," the article emphasized. As the codirector of the Simmons Center on Gender & Organization reported, "Companies may say they want collaborative leaders, but they still hold deep-seated beliefs that top managers need to be heroic figures. Interpersonal skills may be recognized as important, she said, but they aren't explicitly seen as corner-office skills."[4] Similarly, a 2005 research report by Catalyst, a national research and policy organization dedicated to advancing women in business, found that "senior managers perceive differences between women and men leaders that may not exist." One explanation for the discrepancy between research and perception, the study finds, is gender stereotypes that the organization asserts still abound in corporate America. As the report's title captures, women "take care" while men "take charge"—stereotypes that typify thinking among corporate executives as well as others. While this has far-ranging effects on how female business leaders are evaluated for new opportunities and promotions, it also impacts how they are perceived by employees, the media, and the general public.[5] Such stereotypes go a long way in explaining recent reactions to Marissa Mayer's decision to rescind telecommuting at Yahoo—it did not reflect a "caring" orientation to the company's employees and thus did not "fit" widespread public expectations of her as a woman CEO.

Of course, expecting female business leaders to embrace and promote what are perceived to be progressive employment policies, especially those that impact other women, also illustrates feminist hopes and aspirations for the transformational potential of women's leadership—that is, the wishful idea that *if we can just get more women into leadership positions, we would finally be able to institute the women-friendly policies that we've been trying to pass for years*. Even historians have assumed or hoped that female business leaders would exhibit fundamentally different behaviors when it comes to managing their labor force. In *Cannery Women, Cannery Lives*, for example, Vicki Ruiz wondered whether the female workforce in California canning companies fared better or differently in a woman-owned company in comparison to the male-owned companies she had studied.[6] Her question was motivated by the idea that men and women manage differently, especially when it comes to managing people, even though the characteristics and qualities identified as leadership "potential" have consistently reinforced conformity to the same standardized behaviors, regardless of gender.[7]

Not unlike those of Melissa Mayer, the experiences of Tillie Lewis, Olive Ann Beech, and Margaret Rudkin nearly two generations earlier reveal that these female business leaders did *not* behave as champions of employees or of women as feminists then and now might have hoped. Instead, they acted in commonplace ways as architects of a "new welfare capitalism" characteristic of American companies starting in the 1930s and made labor-management decisions designed to blunt the impact of unions within their companies like so many business leaders in the middle of the twentieth century. Leveraging the language of family, they built companies that asserted overtly employee-oriented policies that rewarded loyalty and efficiency with strong wages, benefits, and noblesse oblige for the workers they wished to retain long term. When unionization came to their companies, they adopted strategies that reflected their particular labor needs.

Lewis participated in an industrywide contract with the Teamsters that ignored promotional opportunities for the large number of seasonal, unskilled laborers—most of them nonwhite women—on whom her canning production line depended but in whom she invested little training since she viewed their work as easily done by new recruits. Instead her labor policies privileged the much smaller number of year-round, skilled laborers, almost all white men, who were the targets of the company's retention efforts. Beech, whose aircraft manufacturing process depended on highly skilled labor and whose increased efficiency was the only way to improve profitability in contract-based work, cooperated with the union. And Rudkin, who invested in and depended on her workers' mastery of the company's special part-mechanized, part-handmade manufacturing process, oversaw a union-free company her whole lifetime. She was the only one of the three who was successful in using corporate welfarism to completely resist unionization. But all of them relied on the family-oriented language and programs typical of this mid-twentieth-century approach to labor management as a way to maintain control of labor-management relations and as an expedient business strategy.

Interpreting Lewis's, Beech's, and Rudkin's investments in the welfare of their workers through the lens of "caring" and as a reflection of traditionally feminine behavior would be shortsighted. That's not to say that their individual expressions of care about employees were disingenuous. But they *were* calculated, calibrated through the lens of corporate outcomes and bottom lines. Furthermore, as has been well documented by historians, such investments in corporate welfarism were common, adopted by many mid-twentieth-century *male* corporate leaders to enhance productivity, efficiency, longevity, and loyalty among employees. Although rooted in a Victorian ideal of the corporation as family and welfare work as labor done by company "mothers," welfare workers were never exclusively female, and during the early twentieth century, the job was recast from a maternal to an androgynous form of management, partly in recognition of the growing numbers of men who sought opportunities in this expanding field of management. As corporate welfare work evolved into personnel management by the 1920s, it became a tool to help sell the benefits of the company: to convince prospective employees to join and current employees to stay. Akin to salesmanship, such work gained status and even a manly association. Thus by the time Lewis, Beech, and Rudkin presided over their companies in the mid-twentieth century, corporate welfare—characterized by employee athletic and social activities, clubhouses, lunch rooms, suggestion systems, group insurance, paid vacation, and health and safety programs—was no longer work associated with women and had become commonplace in labor-management relations.[8]

After World War II, such corporate welfare programs continued but took on the new agenda of fighting New Deal liberalism and labor radicalism. Responding to what they interpreted as the ominous power of unions—exemplified by the largest strike wave in U.S. history, 1945–46—American business leaders coalesced around a vision that identified class harmony and business productivity as central to achieving nationalistic visions of the American way. To enact this, corporate personnel policies offered a variety of benefits and programs for workers designed to draw their loyalty away from organized labor and government. Such policies were an expression of the American business concept popular at the time that it was the responsibility of management and not unions and not the state to maintain its employees' well-being. It was a reciprocal relationship. In exchange, companies hoped such investments would yield higher employee morale, loyalty, and productivity. Enacting such programs reflected more grandiose goals for business leaders than simply selling their companies to employees and prospective employees, however; in fact, business leaders were selling the entire American system of free enterprise.[9]

Because corporate welfare was, in part, a reciprocal relationship between capital and labor, one built on social ties, individual business leaders loomed large in its perpetuation. The businesses most successful at wielding welfare capitalist policies in the mid-twentieth century had powerful leaders, often their founders, who saw personnel management as an essential part of their job and embraced the idea of creating a corporate Gemeinschaft—the German sociology term to describe a communal society characterized by personal relationships, well-defined and traditional social rules, and expressions of sentiment. They offered a corporate culture that offered security and a sense of solidarity.[10] In some companies the "corporate family" promised by welfare capitalism operated for generations but was often dependent on particular leaders, their personalities, and the relationships they built with employees. For example, in the Endicott Johnson shoe company, successors tried to imitate the company's longtime leader, George F. Johnson, but were unsuccessful. They could not re-create the intangible personal quality that imbued his relations with employees and was a key component of his successful corporate welfare programs. As a consequence, welfare capitalism at the company died with him. Even under popular company leaders such as Johnson, however, mid-twentieth-century corporate welfare existed alongside occasionally repressive policies, the other side of the coin that was explicitly antiunion and antistatist. Workers didn't need to be reminded that the "partnership" and "family" that corporate welfare celebrated was profoundly and inherently unequal.[11] Company presidents who dispensed welfare-oriented labor policies in the mid-twentieth century were thus remembered by some workers as both coercive and caring, but always memorable.[12]

Like the male business leaders described above, Lewis, Beech, and Rudkin were charismatic architects of corporate welfarism who embraced such industry standards as both the most expedient strategy for their companies and the most ideologically resonant with their own beliefs. They were beliefs shaped by conservatism, religion, devotion to free enterprise, and the popular ideal of bootstrapping or making it on one's own, all of which were characteristic of U.S. corporate leaders after World War II and informed the campaign against labor and government intervention that American business led following the war.[13] The female business executives featured here supported, founded, and/or participated in the organizations at the vanguard of these efforts—the National Association of Manufacturers, the Chamber of Commerce, and the Freedom's Foundation. Thus, while their labor policies and philosophies conformed to the standards of their day, their active participation in shaping those standards suggests that they were leaders rather followers in this process. Whether aligning themselves with traditional and exclusionary labor organizations such as the American Federation of Labor (AFL) over more radical and inclusive ones like the Congress of Industrial Organizations (CIO) as Lewis eventually did, investing in employee benefits and programs to avoid workforce radicalization as Beech did, or celebrating the lack of union in their plants altogether as Rudkin did, the three female leaders examined here acted in ways that they perceived to align with their own, their companies', and their shareholders' best interests. They were not crusaders for a more democratic workplace or one more welcoming to women. In fact, there is no evidence that they championed improved opportunities for women at all. And company pay scales (when they exist) reveal overtly unequal wages for female employees. Yet Lewis, Beech, and Rudkin were all business leaders of their time, evangelists for the free enterprise system, in favor of less government regulation, and in support of company cultures that treated their employees as resources with a responsibility to increase the company's profit margin. They were not heartless by any means. But they were also company founders with a sizable stake in the outcome of their employees' productivity and efficiency. And it was this orientation that took priority in their role as labor managers.

Tillie Lewis

Lewis's labor practices were consistently directed to ensuring her company the lowest operating costs and the most quiescent labor relations possible. In this she reflected both the specific nature of her company's labor needs and the common trend in California's canning industry. Though she relied on a small workforce of mostly white and male skilled workers year-round, the majority of her workers were seasonal and unskilled, consisting mainly of nonwhite women employed for several months during the packing season. With a heavy investment in perishable raw materials—the fruits and vegetables being canned—which varied in quantity, cost, and availability year to year and month to month, Lewis depended on being able to secure as much labor as she needed when she needed it for the price she was willing to pay. In this she resembled all canners and other agricultural producers. It is no surprise, therefore, that while Lewis's labor policies benefited year-round skilled workers, they largely missed or disadvantaged seasonal and unskilled workers. Keeping down the cost of such labor was the driving factor in her policies. Though she fostered a reputation early on as an employer who acted for the benefit of all her employees and was remembered as a larger-than-life personality liked by those who worked for her, her labor policies reflected an interest in keeping costs and conflict down and profits and productivity up—just like her competitors.

From the outset, the Flotill workforce disproportionately comprised unskilled, seasonal laborers on whom the company relied for cheap, fast work and long hours. One study of the canning industry characterized fourteen- to sixteen-hour days, piece-work rates, and exhortations by managers to work faster at lower wages as typical of the seasonal workers' experience.[14] This was as true of Flotill as it was of other canneries and structured the workforce there along a deep skill divide that mirrored racial and ethnic divides and created gender and class divides. In 1948, for example, by which time the company had a well-established workforce and labor policies, 93 percent of Flotill's employees were unskilled, seasonal workers and only 7 percent were year-round, skilled workers.[15] The latter were almost all white men, while the former—the larger population of seasonal laborers— came from a variety of racial, ethnic, and national backgrounds. Anglo- Americans, Mexican Americans, and Mexican immigrants were the largest groups, but there were also African Americans and large groups of first- and second-generation Italians, Portuguese, Japanese, and Chinese in the region's cannery workforce. And most were women. For many, working in the canneries was work that could be combined with caring for children and home precisely because it was seasonal. That is, for intense but temporary periods of time, they engaged in wage labor outside their homes to help support their families, but the rest of the year they devoted most of their time to the unpaid labor of household maintenance. Thus, the seasonal nature of the work was both the source of its inequalities and hardships and one of its attractions for the company's large female workforce.

In the press, Lewis was a manager who got to know even the seasonal workers in her factory and cared for them no matter the position they held in her company. Reportedly she was "on a first name basis with all her employees" and her "door [was] always open to anyone with a problem . . . everything from medical and financial needs to domestic and child care worries."[16] Another account attributed such kindnesses to a "heart [that] taught her to be a good employer."[17] And as one extensively syndicated article reported, she was an employer with a "heart [as] wide as the San Joaquin Valley . . . [who] gave the problems of every employee her full attention." This included female employees with Spanish names—a close stand-in for unskilled, seasonal laborers in the California canning industry. As the article continued, when Lewis received a phone call from Rosa, a former employee, whose daughter was sick with polio, she reportedly dropped everything to help: "Every night after her grueling day at the plant," the magazine story relayed, "Tillie bought food at a supermarket, went to Rosa's home and cooked dinner. Weekends, Tillie nursed the child so the mother could rest." This was a Tillie Lewis who did whatever it took to attend to the needs of her workers—all of them. And her largesse extended beyond the factory floor and included a commitment to their families and well-being outside the workplace. She was, in such accounts, a labor manager so generous and caring toward her workers that she was worthy of mythology.[18]

The origin of such fantastical stories was likely the widely syndicated biopic about Lewis published in 1952 because it was Christian inspired and designed to motivate imitation. Written by Dorothy Walworth and published in *Everywoman's Magazine*, it was several times summarized in other later publications without consideration of the author's penchant for morality tales. Walworth was, in fact, a novelist who published four Christian novels and was a regular *Reader's Digest* contributor who seemed

Images such as these, of Lewis posing with her factory workers during two different periods in Flotill's history, indicated her interest in being viewed as a compassionate employer who knew her employees. San Joaquin County Historical Society, Lodi, California.

to focus on inspirational biographies of women (she wrote one of civil rights activist Mary McLeod Bethune, for example). According to a review of her fourth novel, *Nicodemus* (Houghton Mifflin, 1946), Walworth was the "Daughter of a Methodist minister, [and] wife of *Reader's Digest* Editor Merle Crowell," whose friend said of her, "Her spiritual essence is a faith that permeates everything she does or thinks."[19] Indeed, a Christian moral economy does infuse the *Everywoman* article about Lewis, who in Walworth's hands emerges as something of a saint. Though it is not possible to check the validity of the story about Lewis caring for her former employee Rosa, other stories in the article are contradicted by extant records, and this raises doubts about the authenticity of the Rosa tale too. Indeed, inspiration rather than factual detail seemed to be the focus for the article's author.[20]

There is some evidence, however, that Lewis *was* an employer whose caring ways inspired appreciation among her workers. The local Japanese American Citizens' League, for example, gave Lewis an award in recognition of her open hiring practices for Japanese Americans returning from forced-relocation camps post–World War II.[21] One archived photograph of Lewis seems to illustrate the same idea. In it, Lewis is surrounded by dozens of female workers in headscarves and aprons (presumably seasonal workers) posed in front of the factory. Lewis felt an affinity for her laborers, it suggested, and managed them in ways that made them feel valued.[22] According to one account, Lewis was "a sort of banker, psychiatrist, and minister all in one" to her employees, helping to solve their problems, loan them money, and council them on challenging life decisions.[23] Some press accounts emphasized her humanity to employees too, citing workers who remembered her fondly. For example, one former worker, Max Martinez, described the "camaraderie and company spirit that everyone felt" as employees of Lewis's "family company." He "liked to go to work then but after she died it was dog eat dog."[24] Such esprit de corps may have been the inspiration for Lewis's 1970s nomination by an employee in her personnel department for the "Boss of the Year" award conferred by the local chapter of the American Business Women's Association too.[25] As her longtime secretary Alilea Haywood Martin reported, "She used to call the business her 'baby' and treated all of the employees as members of her 'family.' She was the matriarch—sometimes benevolent and sometimes exacting."[26]

Remembrances such as this underscore that Lewis presided over a firm organized on some level around familial employer–employee relations in keeping with the welfare capitalist orientation of American businesses of her day. While inflected with gendered language such as "baby" and "ma-triarch," these descriptions of Lewis and her employees in fact recall similar references to male business leaders and their employees during this era. For example, George F. Johnson, president of Endicott Johnson Shoe Company, addressed employees as "members of the Happy Family" and referred to himself as the "father" or "daddy" of the enterprise. Use of such language was a deliberate strategy and not simply a friendly affectation. Johnson crafted this role for himself and enacted it publicly with both aplomb and earnestness. His goal was to create the sense of belonging, security, and hierarchy associated with familial ties rather than industrial ones to secure labor continuity and management authority.[27] Use of family metaphors, therefore, was a common contemporary strategy that was designed to help achieve identified outcomes in employer–employee relations. And Lewis used it for these reasons too. Thus, while describing Flotill as "her baby" may have brought attention to her status as a female executive, her familial language did not differentiate her from businessmen since it was de rigueur in labor management in the mid-twentieth century.

Lewis's labor-management strategy was informed by the historical context in which she entered the industry as a business owner as well. In 1937, one year after she opened for business, the Stockton canning industry was embroiled in a violent confrontation between laborers and canning owners who sought to stop unionization of their companies. Organized into the California Processors and Growers (CPG), which one historian described as a "militant business association," spinach canners were determined to resist the demands for wage increases from organized workers, whom they viewed as communist activists. When local cannery workers affiliated with both the AFL and the more radical Agricultural Workers Organization (affiliated with the International Longshoremen's and Warehousemen's Union led by alleged communist Harry Bridges) demanded higher wages, improved working conditions, and a "closed shop" (requiring that all workers be members of the union), cannery owners balked. The workers in turn threatened to strike at the start of the spinach season, which would have prevented farmers and canners from getting their crops to market in the quick turnaround required for such delicate commodities. The confrontation that ensued came to be called the "Spinach Riot" and involved cannery and farm workers along with longshoremen and other sympathy strikers in conflict with a "posse" of farmers and nonunion workers deputized by the sheriff to help quell the revolt and force open the cannery. When a spinach truck attempting to cross the picket line was attacked by workers, law enforcement officials opened fire; workers fought back using rocks and clubs. The truce that was eventually mediated between canners and cannery workers with the help of California governor Frank Merriam led to some concessions by employers but, because it was not satisfactory to all workers, left Stockton's cannery unions divided and largely unorganized. Yet the episode provided a powerful lesson for a new cannery owner. Though Lewis was not yet in the spinach business or a member of the CPG, she well understood the importance of avoiding "trouble with the unions," and this would steer her actions as a cannery owner for years to come.[28]

When unionization came to Flotill in 1941, it was with great fanfare and highlighted the degree to which this labor-management partnership was for Lewis both a defensive and competitive strategy. The labor contract came about with the help of Meyer Lewis, western regional director of the AFL. Reportedly he had been contacted by Flotill workers discontented with a mandated industrywide strike. Conditions at Tillie Lewis's plant were comparatively better than those of other canneries, and they wanted his help to keep it that way. With his assistance, Tillie Lewis negotiated a contract, which she signed in November 1941, and immediately set out to celebrate it publicly.[29] In commemoration of the event, a dance hosted by the Cannery Workers Union of San Joaquin County (Local 20676) was held the same month. A "Souvenir Program" for the event featured, on the facing page, a photo of Lewis (then Tillie Weisberg) with the caption "Signing the first full union contract in the history of agricultural labor in the United States." A quote from Lewis herself followed: "I am happy to be the first industrialist in the agricultural field to place my signature to such a progressive and humane contract which will be an instrument of progress for both employer and employee. It has always been my ambition to work in harmony with labor and through an agreement of this kind which means better working conditions and working operations both parties cannot help but benefit materially."[30] Underneath the quote, Lewis's signature and "Flotill Products, Inc.," in large bold print, filled the rest of the page. It was not clear from the presentation whether it was Tillie Lewis or the union "writing labor history" (the title at the top of the page). But either way, Lewis was featured prominently, flanked by Meyer Lewis and other union officials. It was a policy decision and publicity opportunity that reaped benefits. Tillie Lewis promptly hired Meyer Lewis as general manager and kept the company strike free for the rest of the decade in spite of the general upheaval that gripped the industry, including the cataclysmic labor struggles of 1945–46.[31]

From the start, Lewis aligned her interests with the AFL, a union with a long history of championing the rights of white, male, craft (skilled) workers at the expense of unskilled, nonwhite, and female workers. Like most cannery owners, she rejected radical unions such as the International Longshore and Warehouse Union, which promoted a wage policy treating all workers as relatively equal. Instead, she preferred the more conservative AFL because it was committed to retaining the long-standing wage differentials between skilled crafts workers and unskilled seasonal workers that were customary in the canneries.[32] This kept wages down for the majority of the industry's workforce and thus kept the costs of production down for business owners.

Such bifurcation of the cannery workforce had been established early on. Canning required extensive manual labor during the harvesting season, when perishable fruits and vegetables had to be processed immediately. From the inception of the industry in the late 1800s, women had done this work, sometimes with their children working by their side and often jumping from plant to plant, depending on where the work was most plentiful. It was a casual owner–worker relationship mediated initially by foremen who procured groups of workers as needed. By the 1930s, widespread mechanization and multiproduct plants (which meant an extended processing schedule) drove a desire for two types of workers: "unskilled" workers who returned to the same plant for the length of the canning season to fill processing and canning jobs and year-round workers with specialized skills who did cook-room, warehouse, receiving, and maintenance work.

The first union contract in the industry—approved in 1937, the same year of the clash between owners and workers in Stockton's canneries—embodied this structure. It institutionalized jobs as female (unskilled, seasonal) and male (skilled, year-round), organized them hierarchically, and compensated accordingly. Seasonal workers gained preferential hiring or "seniority" for returning to the same company during the canning season but had almost no promotional opportunities. Higher-status year-round workers operated in a tiered skill system inherited from the long tradition of master and apprentice craftsmen with built-in promotional ladders.[33] And while it set a minimum hourly wage rate, the contract retained the existing piece-rate system for seasonal workers, embedding pay differentials for unskilled/female and skilled/male workers in the compensation structure and emphasizing the temporary and informal nature of seasonal work.[34]

This was precisely what the AFL reinforced—formal obligations between cannery employers and their year-round workers and informal ones between employers and seasonal workers. It was a stratified labor system that would remain attractive to Lewis and other cannery owners for its efficiency and cost savings and one they would fight for when radical unions threatened to upend it.[35] Certainly this was at the core of Lewis's decision to align her interests with the AFL's industrywide contract in 1947, but there were additional factors as well.

Lewis's relationship with the AFL was personal too. As mentioned above, shortly after Meyer Lewis of the AFL helped to settle the strike at her plant and oversaw implementation of a new union contract in 1941, she hired him as her general manager to oversee labor relations at the company. He had been operating as "personal representative" to AFL national president William Green when he was assigned the job of western regional director of the AFL that had brought him to Flotill.[36] The relationship between Meyer and Tillie turned personal sometime after he was hired, because seven years later they were married.[37] Tillie Lewis also retained a friendly relationship with AFL president Green, whom she likely met through Meyer. By 1942, Green and Tillie Lewis had their own reasons to correspond. She earned his appreciation for holiday gifts she sent his family and, on a later occasion, his respect for her company's subsidized war savings stamp program for employees.[38] Green would subsequently play a decisive role in what one scholar has called "The Great Northern California Cannery Struggle" of 1945–46. It seems plausible that Tillie Lewis's relationship with Green and Meyer Lewis's relationship with Green were factors in how Flotill navigated the contentious union organizing that embroiled the region's canning industry at that time, as we shall see. Thus, aligning her company's interests with the AFL reflected both longtime industry trends with regard to workforce stratification and the professional and personal ties between Flotill and the AFL forged through Meyer Lewis.

Tillie Lewis was not, in fact, the first canner to enter into a union contract in 1941, in spite of the congratulatory rhetoric at the celebration described above, but what that event acknowledged is that she seemed to be the first to do so independently. This distinguished her from 93 percent of the industry's regional leaders who had banded together in 1936 to present "a united front regarding labor issues." For the fifty-six canners who joined this alliance, the California Processors and Growers, their "strategy included avoiding individual labor problems by setting wage scales on an industrywide basis." Within one year, the group had grown so much that it "represented 93 percent of fruit- and vegetable-processing firms in northern California," including the big names in the industry such as Cal Pak (Del Monte), Libby, Hunt Brothers, and Heinz, many of whom had executives on the group's board.[39] CPG members were obligated to designate it as the "sole collective bargaining representative" and were bound to pay the wages specified and to abide by the agreements spelled out in the negotiations performed on their behalf.[40] Thus, the vast majority of the state's canners had committed to unionization years before Lewis's supposedly historic union contract but had done so collectively rather than individually.

Lewis finally endorsed the CPG contract in 1947, a delay most likely reflecting a lack of choice. In an interview, her nephew and longtime Flotill executive Albert Heiser revealed that it wasn't lack of interest that kept her out. CPG and the Canner's League, another contemporary professional organization for food-processing companies, he reported, "denied Flotill entrance to their organizations probably because the owner was Jewish."[41] Anti-Semitism by American business owners was not new; Henry Ford, for example, was an outspoken critic of Jews during the 1920s and 1930s.[42] And although northern California was a stronghold for Jewish merchants dating back to the gold rush, the 1930s were the apex of anti-Semitism in the United States, so perhaps it is predictable that such bigotry and xenophobia crept into the highest levels of the state's food-processing industry. As a barrier to entry, anti-Semitism may also have masked additional concerns by industry leaders, including the fact that Lewis was one of the only women in her position and the fact that she was rapidly carving out a niche in the field that stole market share from better-known brands.[43] Whichever of these reasons kept her out, Lewis did not join CPG until a decade after it was formed. Once she did, she remained a stalwart supporter and participant in industrywide labor trends.

While Lewis overwhelmingly exhibited conformity to industry trends in her role as a labor manager, there was one important example of her pioneering innovation. When World War II production engulfed the food industry in a labor crisis, Tillie Lewis stepped in for farmers as well as herself, since food processors fortunes were always tied to agricultural production. Her novel and innovative approach was to sponsor Mexican laborers through the Bracero Program to ensure that the crops would be harvested and prices would be kept low. The company ran an ad in the *Stockton Daily Evening Record* in 1944 that included testimonials from farmers expressing their appreciation for her intervention. Under the heading "Read What the Farmers Say about Flotill Service," the quotes lauded her action:

> Your bringing in of Mexican Nationals was of great benefit to us. If it had not been for this labor our crops would have suffered immeasur-

ably. . . . The men did good work, and Flotill Products is to be congratulated on this contribution to the war effort. [K. G. Stark, Patterson, 8 November 1943]

We feel indebted to Flotill Products for the cooperation which was afforded outside growers in allowing us to use the Nationals. We fully understand the expense and trouble that was necessary to arrange for bringing the Nationals in as well as the daily routine of housing, feeding, caring for them, and the responsibility of acting as paymaster and being responsible for all monies connected with the job. [E. A. Couture, Grower and Shipper, 10 November 1943]

I am pleased to assure you that from my point of view Flotill's Mexican Nationals Project is an outstanding success. [B. F. Hughes, Westley, 15 October 1943][44]

Lewis's initiative was made possible by the executive order first passed in 1942 in response to California (and other) growers who argued that because of the wartime labor shortage, they would not be able to harvest their crops. The program negotiated between the U.S. and Mexican governments made temporary exceptions to immigration prohibitions and allowed temporary workers to be transported across the border for the purpose of filling agricultural jobs. The Mexican government extracted a commitment from the United States that farmers would pay for the costs of transportation and wages equivalent to those of U.S. farm workers. On 29 September 1942, the first 500 Braceros arrived in Stockton, the heart of the San Joaquin Valley and the home of Flotill Products. Lewis must have caught on quickly, since farmer testimonials about her involvement were dated only one year later. There is no evidence in extant documents that Braceros were employed in the canneries of the company, but Flotill clearly operated as the employer, managing payment for the Mexican workers it sponsored and provided to local growers for field work.

Overall, the Bracero Program was such a success from the perspective of employers that it continued long past the war. Originally it was conceived as a temporary, wartime measure, and indeed the total number of temporary workers imported through the program peaked at 62,000 in 1944. But it was so profitable for growers—and by extension food canners and processors—that lobbying led to a variety of extensions of the law as well as complacence by the Immigration and Naturalization Service (INS), which "looked the other way" at the thousands of workers hired illegally, outside the structure of the program. The ongoing availability of Braceros until the program officially came to an end in 1965 fundamentally altered the California food-growing and -processing industry. The availability of imported Mexican workers supported labor-intensive cultivation of fruits and vegetables, established ties of dependency between rural Mexican communities and California growers, and drove wages down, which caused U.S. farm workers to seek jobs in other economic sectors. By the 1950s, the majority of crops such as citrus and tomatoes—Lewis's mainstay—were picked by low-paid Braceros, and farm wages as a percentage of manufacturing wages declined.[45] The program amounted to a "federal government subsidy for big business at the expense of organized labor" and "killed unionization efforts on California farms."[46] In sponsoring Braceros for the growers with whom she contracted, Lewis had a hand in this important transformation in the agricultural labor market—one that hurt farm workers but benefited her business and the food-processing industry.

In spite of this example of her novel approach to farm labor, Lewis's conformity to industry norms began early and is illustrated by her World War II–era policies. Hiring Braceros had been one way to address the wartime labor shortage for farmers. But locating and retaining workers was a problem for canners and manufacturers as well. As with others in the industry, this led to a variety of changes at Flotill Products. Some, such as the mechanization of the Modesto Plant, streamlined the production process, reducing the number of times operators "touched" the fruit being canned from three to one, ultimately achieving the same output with fewer workers. In the pages of the *Western Canner and Packer*, this was labeled "progressive management," though to workers this likely came as bad news since it meant a reduction in the number of jobs at that plant.[47] Other wartime programs introduced by Flotill were aimed at recruiting new workers and making the company a more competitive employer, given the contest for labor from other processors as well as nearby defense plants, a military hospital, and an important army supply depot. Plans such as relying on local college students and faculty spouses from nearby University of the Pacific and workers over fifty tapped into previously unused labor markets.[48] Newly introduced cafeterias, childcare, and transportation helped to recruit and retain such workers. The company even investigated the possibility of constructing low-cost employee housing on twenty acres of land adjacent to its production facilities in Stockton.[49] Such Flotill programs reflected national labor trends during the war, which prompted U.S. employers to introduce a variety of innovations in response to the severe labor shortage. And because they were viewed as emergency measures designed to address employment up-heavals associated with military mobilization, these progressive policies— at Flotill and elsewhere—were temporary, lasting only for the duration of the war.[50]

Lewis presented such wartime programs as evidence of a uniquely sup-portive environment in keeping with welfare capitalists of the day. In fact, such wartime programs were ubiquitous and not unique at all to Flotill. Yet the point for Lewis, as for other large-scale business owners, in the mid-twentieth century was to engender allegiance among employees to the company rather than the union or the state, both of which loomed large in the lives of American workers at this time and promised their own compet-ing forms of security. At Flotill, the introduction of services and benefits for employees was the first step. It invested in "excellent earnings, pleasant working surroundings, cafeterias, nurseries, transportation facilities, and individual financial assistance" for its workers. But the second and perhaps even more important step was telling workers about these benefits and tout-ing them as unique characteristics of employment at Flotill. Communication efforts such as company newsletters, pamphlets, and reports helped to get this message across and were increasingly common in mid-twentieth-century American businesses. Professional organizations such as the Na-tional Association of Manufacturers actually encouraged them. The aim was to make clear to employees that their goals and interests were shared by employers, that the company had the well-being of its workers top of mind, and that they were critical to its success and partners in it.

Flotill's 1946 multipage promotional pamphlet was a great example of such corporate communications. It clearly conveyed a vision common among employers at the time that workers and managers shared in a "community of interest" benevolently directed by the company.[51] The pamphlet dedi-cated a page to employee programs with the heading "Quality Standards Are Protected by Employee Cooperation." It explained:

A truly fine quality product necessarily reflects the interest of the individuals creating it. From top management to the very last employee, FLOTILL strives to help everyone like his work and be happy in it. As a result of the cooperative working relationship in the House of FLOTILL, each employee feels that he is important to FLOTILL and that FLOTILL is important to him.

FLOTILL'S liberal policy has insured uninterrupted plant operations. To accomplish this, FLOTILL provides the stimulus of reward for employee initiative. . . . No opportunity is overlooked to make working conditions most ideal for the FLOTILL employee.

Above all, each member of the House of FLOTILL knows that any life's work goal he is capable of attaining can be reached in the FLOTILL organization.[52]

Flotill's efforts to convey the importance of individual output and initiative and the abhorrence of interruptions to plant productivity were commonplace in corporate communications by the end of the 1940s. This reflected both the wartime spur for increased productivity and groundswell of labor activism and the Cold War impetus thereafter to illustrate the superiority of the American economic system over collectivist communist economies. Employers hoped that these investments and messages would yield an increase in loyalty, morale, and productivity among workers who might otherwise be tempted to seek union or state intervention.[53]

Key to the message that Flotill conveyed to its employees was the idea that they were part of a company family. It was meant to communicate the sense of belonging that American companies hoped to engender in their employees. One 1942 employee newsletter asked directly, "What can we do to build a better Flotill family?" and initiated a suggestion box system for collecting and rewarding workers' ideas.[54] The familial ideal was also captured in the description of the company as "the House of Flotill"—a workplace in which all employees would feel at home.[55] Though such language may seem to convey a particularly feminine approach to labor management, in fact it was standard messaging of the day among large-scale employers. In an era of intense labor competition, union upheaval, and what was perceived as the communist threat, the idea of family invoked American security.

After Flotill signed on with the industrywide labor contract brokered by CPG in 1947, the company's employee programs were more modest but continued to communicate the same emphasis. Helping each employee to "like his work and be happy in it" was the key because it benefited both the employee and the company. Flotill touted "fully equipped and modern first aid facilities," "a loud speaker system of entertainment," and "meals sold in Company cafeterias" in addition to modern-day insurance and benefits but none of the other programs that had been in place during the war.[56] That Flotill emphasized such benefits in its annual report filed with the Securities and Exchange Commission (SEC) reveals the degree to which such welfare programs were investments, ones calculated to avoid labor conflict and ensure profitability. It also underscores the importance of annual reports as a tool in the corporate communications strategy—a point emphasized for all employers by the National Association of Manufacturers, who saw them as a new frontier in the public-relations campaign they launched to convince consumers of the virtues of business.[57] Keeping workers, keeping them happy, and (employers hoped) keeping them away from costly strikes was well worth the investment in employee benefit programs.

Lewis's decision to sign on to the industrywide CPG union contract when she did—in 1947—was likely tied to the northern California canning industry's chaotic labor history post–World War II and perhaps to the personal ties she had to the AFL. For a period of two years between 1945 and 1946, a pitched battle ensued, pitting the American Federation of Labor against the more democratic Congress of Industrial Organizations (CIO) and cannery owners against cannery operatives, and Lewis and Flotill were almost certainly caught up in it. The conflict began in earnest when AFL president William Green, Meyer Lewis's former boss and a man with whom Tillie Lewis had maintained a correspondence, "granted jurisdiction over California food processing locals to the International Brotherhood of Teamsters (IBT)" in spite of bids for that role by other unions. The decision may have been the result of pressure and threats by David Beck, then a West Coast Teamster leader.[58] Beck would go on to national fame as the president of the IBT from 1952–57 and was later convicted of corruption, garnering attention for brazenly invoking the Fifth Amendment before a Senate Committee Hearing on union corruption. Described as "of the same tough mettle as James R. Hoffa," the famed Teamster president who succeeded him, Beck declared himself proud of this "rough and tough and bare knuckles" time in the union's history.[59] This helps explain why an AFL president would cave to his demands and why Lewis may have been sympathetic to that decision.

Yet the "Teamster Takeover," as cannery operatives called it, led to tremendous upheaval in the industry and the demise of more radical union representation. Northern California cannery workers preferred the CIO-affiliated Food, Tobacco, Agricultural, and Allied Workers of America (FTA). It appealed to female seasonal workers in particular by cultivating and recruiting a diverse group of women leaders and focusing on the issues that mattered to them. Under the leadership of women such as Luisa Moreno, a Mexican immigrant, it had achieved significant improvements in cannery wages and working conditions in the southern part of the state. The Teamsters, by contrast, had not pressed for such improvements and focused instead on the smaller number of year-round workers who were men. Thus, most cannery workers did not view the Teamsters as truly representing their interests. But in spite of a dedicated campaign with an influx of organizers from all over the Bay Area and Southern California, thousands of donated dollars, and an effort to prompt the National Labor Relations Board (NLRB) to support an industrywide vote, cannery operatives failed to secure representation by the FTA. Teamster lobbyists in Washington, D.C., toothless interventions by the NLRB, red-baiting, antidemonstrator violence, blockade of FTA-sympathetic plants, and massive lay-offs of Teamster-resistant employees all combined to ultimately end FTA's bid to represent northern California cannery workers. What the end of the FTA meant for the canneries was loss of more radical unionism but also that its largest population of employees remained disgruntled with the terms of their contract and their union representation.[60]

The Teamsters' win had a far-reaching impact. It gained a near universal hold on the California canning industry stretching from Oroville in the north (some seventy miles north of Sacramento) to Santa Maria in the south (some thirty-three miles south of San Luis Obispo).[61] While seasonal workers viewed this as a loss, cannery owners, on the other hand, viewed it as a win.[62] They saw the Teamsters as allies and the union contract as a "sweetheart deal" that bolstered their interests and blunted those of the vast majority of workers in the industry. It was a weakened position for unions generally, one that mirrored nationwide trends in 1947. This was the same year when labor lost and business owners won with the passage of the Taft-Hartley Act. Nicknamed the "slave labor bill" by detractors, it diminished the strength of unions and signaled the rising power and influence of business leaders.[63] This was a shift doggedly pursued by agribusiness in California that had begun more than a decade earlier. Farmers and big-business owners there had together launched a calculated antiunion campaign—an all-out war against "communist" labor organizers and union-friendly New Deal policies that would fundamentally shift the balance of power economically and politically in the state and eventually in the nation.[64] Thus, in 1947, a win for the Teamsters in the canning industry did not represent a strong win for labor, and it was only achieved through collusion with employers. It was a development with grave, long-term implications.

For Lewis, who signed the CPG contract right after the "Teamster Takeover," this development aligned with her own efforts to keep costs down and productivity up. The mostly white, male, year-round workers affiliated with the Teamsters and AFL were the workers she relied on throughout the year—the workers in whom she had invested the most in skill development. Privileging them over others may have seemed to be in the best interest of her business. And, importantly, this was the union of her soon-to-be husband and current labor manager, Meyer Lewis. Following his lead on this decision may have reflected gender convention—for example, a male company president may not have been expected to follow the advice of his soon-to-be wife/employee while a female president was. But it was also a decision that reflected self-interest over the interest of the many female, seasonal workers. She relied on their low pay, temporary status, and uninterrupted productivity to can her product for the lowest cost. This ensured the highest profit. Thus, while these were workers whom she had reportedly once known by name, Lewis did not endorse a contract with the union they preferred. If she had endorsed the FTA instead, their demands—a closed shop, a ten-cent raise in hourly and piece-rate scales, time and a half after eight hours a day and forty hours a week, double time for Sundays and holidays, three paid holidays, fifteen days of sick leave and time and a half after five hours' work without a meal period—would have increased her costs and lowered her productivity.[65] These were bottom-line concessions she was unwilling to make.

Instead, Lewis signed a contract that provided one category for all women workers at the bottom of the wage ladder with little access to benefits or opportunities for advancement. It contained a "Women" wage—a single level for all female workers—and a provision for 15c/hour additional for "floorladies" who performed "supervisory" duties. Needless to say, female supervisors (as floorladies) made the same amount as men in the lowest wage bracket.[66] Access to advancement and benefit opportunities were also restricted for seasonal workers. They could not, for example, access the company's much-touted profit-sharing plan.[67] This stratified wage system reflected long-standing racial and ethnic as well as gender "difference" in the seasonal labor pool that predated unionization in the canneries, as previously discussed. And it reflected the fact that Lewis viewed her seasonal workforce as informal (and thus pliable)—a clear advantage to her and disadvantage to Flotill's seasonal employees occupying the lowest rung in the hierarchy. It was a labor-management decision that reflected the industry norm.

Nearly three decades of such status quo employment practices at Flotill, with a separate track and pay scale for seasonal (primarily immigrant and female) and year-round (primarily native-born white and male) workers, came to an end when a group of employees filed a class action lawsuit alleging racial and gender discrimination.[68] Renamed Tillie Lewis Foods in 1961, the company faced legal and public scrutiny as the representative or lead defendant in a case that brought to the forefront the long-standing seg-regation of seasonal workers. In particular, it focused on their lack of ac-cess to promotional opportunities or year-round jobs and the failure of the union to include them and their concerns in its leadership or agenda. *Alaniz v. Tillie Lewis Foods et al.* (later renamed *Alaniz v. CPI*), which was liti-gated over the course of five years between 1973 and 1978,[69] named all seventy member companies in California Processors, Inc. (CPI), formerly CPG, as well as the California Council of Canneries, the Teamster organ-ization that bargained on behalf of all northern California cannery work-ers, as defendants in the case. Tried under the auspices of the Civil Rights Act of 1964, the case brought together the EEOC (Equal Employment Op-portunity Commission) with civil rights group MALDEF (Mexican Ameri-can Legal Defense and Education Foundation) as legal advocates for the plaintiff class, which included all seasonal laborers in the industry. In the end, the judge, EEOC, and MALDEF brokered a conciliation agreement requiring the unions to diversify their elected representatives, establishing an Office of Affirmative Action for the industry to redress employee griev-ances and pushing through new opportunities for seasonal laborers to gain access to year-round jobs. The case and its resolution were both extremely controversial throughout the region but did ultimately challenge the long-standing practice of favoring profit for cannery owners; status for year-round, male workers; and pliability for seasonal laborers.[70]

For Lewis, the case underscored her legacy as a business owner who cared first and foremost about containing costs and increasing profits in keeping with her peers in the canning industry. In spite of early press accounts that characterized her as an employer who was uniquely focused on the well-being of her workers, Lewis's labor-management strategies revealed instead that she was typical of canners in the middle of the twentieth century. And, in fact, because she was named in the title of the *Alaniz* suit, Lewis's name became forever intertwined with industrywide employment discrimination against women and nonwhite workers. It was the ultimate indication that as a labor manager she had sided with her peers—other cannery owners—and not with her employees. How Lewis reacted to this publicity is not recorded in extant records, particularly since it was filed two years after her retire-ment. But that was the same year she was awarded an Honorary Doctor of Business Administration degree from the University of the Pacific, for which she was lauded for her "longstanding practice of hiring without regard to race, color or creed." Thus, it is easy to imagine the case as unwanted pub-licity.[71] In fact, for a businesswoman who had reportedly prided herself on championing the rights of workers, the *Alaniz* case may have been an ethical as well as a legal disappointment to her. Yet in aligning her actions with industry standards, Lewis revealed that first and foremost she was a business owner interested in the success of her business as a profitable enterprise. Thus, she may have viewed *Alaniz* simply as another measure of the consolidation of her interests with peers in the industry and with American big business more generally. Certainly it was an indication of the fact that what had governed her business decisions all along was containing labor costs and conflict—the twin themes of her role as labor manager.

Olive Ann Beech

Under the leadership of Olive Ann Beech, Beech Aircraft erected a series of employee programs that were models of the new welfare capitalism. The company created an elaborate system of employee incentives ranging from years-of-service awards, cash incentives for ideas to improve efficiency, gifts, bonuses, luncheons with management, tuition grants for college-age children of longtime employees, a long-running employee newsletter that featured employee interests and activities as well as employer policies and procedures, and finally, an extensive recreational program for company employees and their families. These sizable investments reflected a desire to retain employees and keep union activity down and company profits up. At Beech, as at other companies at the time, these programs were tied to deep-seated principles about the free enterprise system, politics, and religion that were articulated in company publications and by Olive Ann Beech herself. The company's labor policies exceeded industry standards in many respects, and this reflected both a set of ideas about how to treat employees and the fact that Beech operated in a strongly unionized environment and a competitive local labor market. Thus, as a labor manager, Beech aligned with national standards and strategically confronted industry standards in a bid to best the offerings of her competitors to secure a loyal, long-term workforce. This was not empathy or managing "like a lady," but calculated business strategizing. In an industry entirely dependent on highly skilled labor and largely bound by fixed-price contracts and an era characterized by big-business investments in employee programs designed to blunt the influence of unions and engender long-term company affiliation, Beech was a model of the status quo and bottom-line management.

The particular labor needs of the aircraft-manufacturing industry shaped the policies of Beech. Like all companies in this sector, Beech Aircraft depended on workers with skill and experience in the aircraft-manufacturing process. And, as it articulated in its 1941 employee efficiency incentive plan, it was experience at Beech—not general industry experience—that was most valuable to the company: "The plan benefits the company by stabilizing its employee conditions and by reducing turnover of employees who otherwise might leave and take their valuable experience with them. It should be remembered that the experience of each employee is more valuable to the Beech Aircraft Corporation than it is to any other company where airplane models and productive systems are different and where his own particular experience is only partially usable."[72] The statement underscores both that employees did leave for other companies and that employee skill was only partially transferable. Wichita—still called the "Air Capitol" today—was home to several industry competitors, including Cessna and Boeing, throughout Beech's history.[73] Such geographic agglomeration—common across a variety of industries—both supported a deep pool of skilled labor and created a great deal of labor competition.[74] This problem was particularly acute during World War II. The wartime labor crunch made the competition for skilled employees fierce, since competitor aircraft companies in the Wichita area also had government contracts with accelerated timelines. During this period, obtaining and retaining workers with the needed know-how was a foremost concern. But the skill laborers acquired was company-specific and not easily substituted. Thus, Beech endeavored to formalize its ties to line workers. It invested a great deal of training in them, and their high level of skill and experience was particularly tailored to the company's production line and products. The value of keeping such skilled laborers at the company and avoiding labor conflicts that interrupted production had a formative impact on Beech's retention and efficiency policies for employees.

Unionization too must have contributed to the company's stance on employee value. Beech employees were the first in the Wichita aircraft industry to unionize. The company signed a contract with the Machinists' Union on 14 June 1940; Cessna and Boeing followed in the months and years ahead. According to one account, prior experience in a unionized work environment in a different industry predisposed many of the company's employees to seek the contract, and stories about indiscriminate lay-offs that had occurred elsewhere without respect to seniority were an influence. "The organizing drive took only a couple of months . . . and required no union vote. The company recognized the Machinists' Union as the representative of its workers on the basis of the election-authorization cards they signed."[75]

The *Beechcrafter* newsletter characterized relations between the union and the corporation as "friendly" thereafter.[76] During its entire history under Beech family leadership, in fact, company employees struck only once in 1969, and this was a track record of which the company was proud. One company-prepared biography of Olive Ann Beech emphasized that in response to the 1969 strike, "the company took positive steps that met the issues head on . . . [and] the work stoppage was ended after 26 days with the signing of a three-year agreement with the union."[77] An undated company advertise-ment addressed "to all Beechcrafters" captured the company's perspec-tive on ideal labor-management relations. Calling the Machinists' Union acceptance of a new three-year contract an "expression of confidence" in Beech Aircraft, it returned that sentiment, stating, "We are proud of the excellent work you have done in the past and are confident that you will continue these efforts as we move toward another record year. We believe you Beechcrafters are the best and want everyone in the world to know it."[78] The company's use of the term "Beechcrafters" to describe employees was a classic aspect of corporate welfare work because it defined them as members of the company family, in this case even imbuing them with the founding family's name. Even at unionized companies as Beech Aircraft was, such tactics were part of a larger strategy designed to contain the in-fluence of unions by establishing the corporation as employees' primary loyalty.[79]

Of course the union itself and not just company efforts to thwart its influence determined Beech's labor policies. This is well illustrated in the company's employee efficiency incentive plan, which was a product of labor-management negotiations and aimed at helping Beech achieve the rapid mobilization goals set by the wartime defense program. The plan, im-plemented in 1941, was essentially a profit-sharing plan, something only 6 percent of all manufacturers offered their hourly workers in 1940. But in-creasingly, this became a more common benefit. Firms "used these fringe benefits to bolster worker loyalty and to mitigate the effect of the wartime wage freeze." For unions, such benefits "were a way to expand the scope of bargaining." Triggered in part by the National War Labor Board's allowance of such policies even during the World War II wage freeze, such benefits continued to increase among American corporations well after wartime because of demand by workers.[80] At Beech, the union and the company re-sponse it helped to trigger appear to have been at the front edge of this trend. The policy set aside 50 percent of the "difference between the amount received by the company from the sale of its manufactured airplanes and their parts and its manufacturing costs of its products [including all costs, liabilities]." The amount set aside was devoted to added compensation. Executive incentive pay came from 5 percent of that total, while the remaining 45 percent was devoted to providing production workers with compensation above and beyond their normal rates of pay. Some version of this plan remained in existence for years at Beech, tying individual compensation to company productivity and motivating increased company efficiency across all levels of employment.[81] From the beginning, it was a cooperative program between the company and the union, which may have been its most distinguishing feature.[82] Less than a third of the Council of Profit Sharing Industries had contracts with organized labor.[83] Beech's profit-sharing plan was singled out for its generosity and effectiveness by *Time* magazine in 1942 and by Sen. Harry S. Truman in 1945, who commented on it from the Senate floor. By 1978, Beech's Productivity Council had attracted the attention of the American Productivity Center, which invited a team of company and union representatives to present the features of their program at a workshop.[84]

Individual initiative was also rewarded as an important contribution to company efficiency. Beech distributed "Busy Bee" badges to employees for high levels of productivity. Featuring a cartoon bee holding tools of the trade, these playful certificates of merit were designed by the Walt Disney Company, which created insignia for hundreds of defense-related efforts as well as propaganda and public service films during World War II. Cash rewards for employee suggestions about ways to cut costs and improve efficiency were also put in place in the 1940s and continued thereafter. Over the years, for example, many pages of the *Beechcrafter* were devoted to featuring the employees whose good ideas were adopted by the company, earning them recognition as well as cash rewards.[85] Along with the profit-sharing plan, these programs reflected the company's investment in increasing employee morale as well as efficiency.

Ultimately, however, company managers viewed enhanced productivity as the price that employees paid for high compensation. When a new union contract was finally settled in 1975 that increased wages and benefits, Olive Ann Beech and Frank E. Hedrick, Beech Aircraft chair and president, respectively, at that time, stated that because "our costs for each employee will sharply increase while costs for some of our competitors will hold," the company would need to redouble its efforts at efficiency.[86] Thus, Beech made clear that its copious investments in employees came with clearly identified strings attached. The company would invest in its workers, but in exchange its workers would have to invest their best efforts in Beech.

This management perspective grew from the profit structure in which the company operated, which is key to understanding the company's attention to employee relations. Because much of Beech's business starting in the 1940s and continuing through the 1970s came from government contracts that froze income levels for years at a time without regard for fluctuating prices in materials or labor—known as "fixed-price contracts"—one of the only ways for the company to increase its profit margin was to lower its production costs. Theoretically, it could have done this by lowering labor costs, but this would have resulted in less motivated workers, which typically depresses productivity. Instead, Beech sought to do this by increasing efficiency, which became a central tenet of its management strategy. The result was a focus on (1) employee retention, since training new employees was a "sunk cost" that was lost if employee turnover was high; (2) investments in employee training programs to incentivize ongoing learning and improvement, which boosted retention, increased the value of employees, and provided a pool of ready and experienced candidates when new positions opened up; (3) employee productivity, since increasing output per worker lowered costs; (4) teamwork, since cooperation between departments and individuals was an important component of the complex, multistep production process; and (5) error-free manufacturing, employee initiative, and ongoing improvement, since such examples of production efficiency contributed to profit margins.[87] Thus, Beech incentivized productivity and efficiency to improve company performance and the returns it provided to shareholders.

Enhancing employee loyalty was a chief component of productivity and efficiency programs as well as union containment and was a commonly articulated value among mid-twentieth-century American corporations, but for Olive Ann Beech, it also had a deeply personal significance. Several experiences engendered this priority. On the one hand, the departure of a carefully trained and highly valuable office manager early in Beech's tenure as secretary-treasurer of the company taught her the importance of retaining staff members in whom one had invested hours of training and upon whom one had come to rely. That disruption had forced her back to the office full time when she'd been trying to spend more time at home with her new baby daughter. Though she reported how much she loved her work in the same speech, the story highlighted the ways in which the departure of valuable employees hampered her own choices and possibilities; the potential she had and the opportunities she could imagine—in this case combining motherhood with an ambitious career—were dependent on the help of competent employees. Thus, finding ways to make those employees want to stay was an important investment.[88] The importance of loyalty was certainly also reinforced for Beech by the threat to her leadership from executive employees who challenged her authority and position on three documented occasions in 1940 and again in the early 1950s, as discussed in chapter 1. Loyal executive employees, therefore, became an essential ingredient not just in her success but in her survival as a business leader. This was a gendered outcome, since the personal experiences that had shaped this value concerned her ability to govern the company as a woman—as a mother whose attentions were divided between young children and her job responsibilities and as a woman executive surrounded by men eager to squeeze her out of the influential role she had in an industry they viewed as a male preserve.

The impact of these experiences was significant and fundamentally shaped her executive staffing plan. For the company's top leadership positions, she selected men who could be counted on to execute their jobs faithfully and competently and who exhibited loyalty to her as the company's chief leader. In 1950, when she officially took over leadership of the company after her husband's death, this became even more important. For the positions at the very top, she selected men with close ties to her and her husband: Frank E. Hedrick, her nephew, and Jack Gaty, a longtime employee and associate of her late husband. Others eventually joined them as the inner circle widened, but always Olive Ann Beech was the "boss lady" who explicitly cultivated trustworthiness as well as performance.

That Beech surrounded herself with loyal *male* executives reflects both the nature of the aircraft industry and also her own inclinations. There is little evidence that Beech paid attention to gender or even women as an employee manager. All of her top managers were men, and though she had two daughters, neither of them entered the business. Of course, the company's workforce was 40 percent female during World War II, like much of the aircraft industry, but this was temporary, and there is no indication that this state of affairs elicited particular action or support from Beech.[89] The one indication that female employees and their opportunities at the company *were* subjects she considered came at the end of her career when Beech became part of the Raytheon Corporation. That year, 1980, Frank Hedrick, her nephew and the company president, sent her "A List of BCX [Beech Aircraft] Salary ladies." The list contained the names of fifty-nine salaried female employees ranging from secretary to engineer, editor of the *Beech-crafter* to foreman of the spotwelding department, manager of the credit union to contract analyst. Alongside their names and titles were their hire dates and ages.[90] What Olive Ann Beech intended to do with this information and whether or not she carried it out is unknown. But what the compiled data suggest is that by the end of her tenure, someone at Beech Aircraft was thinking about female employees as a group, distinct from men who overwhelmingly constituted the company's workforce in production as well as professional ranks. But this likely had more to do with national efforts to spur equal access to business opportunities for women than it did with either the company or its leaders. By then the company employed an administrator of EEO (equal employment opportunity) programs prompted by new civil rights laws. Investigating discrimination allegations, developing management training programs "to promote consistent evaluation and treatment of employees," and career counseling "to prepare employees for promotional opportunities within the company" all came under the purview of the office.[91] Since such offices were de rigueur by the 1980s, it is unlikely that these programs reflected the gender of Beech's longtime leader.[92]

Beech cared about loyalty, not gender, and cultivated it among executive employees at Beech Aircraft through gifts and expressions of appreciation. Because her correspondence files fill nine boxes in the Beech archival collection, there is ample evidence of these exchanges. Thank-you notes document her generosity to others as well as her acknowledgment of others' generosity toward her. For example, her longtime personal secretary, Lucille Winters Edwards, wrote to say, "Thank you so much for another 'flower' for my ever growing garden," for a new "silver candle snuffer," and for "gifts to [my] present and future security."[93] This and other letters provide evidence that Beech provided personal gifts as well as monetary rewards to her closest associates to acknowledge and motivate performance and cultivate loyalty and long-term service. And on holidays and special occasions, they invested in her as well. In 1961 and 1965, for example, she wrote thank-you notes to the "Members of the Beechcraft Management Team" for their Christmas gift of a Dorothy Doughty porcelain bird—for sale on eBay today at prices ranging from $700 to over $2,000—to add to her collection. In addition, she acknowledged receipt of their Christmas poem, which seemed to be a holiday tradition.[94] Clearly the result of much care and effort, one humorous, rhyming, forty-nine-stanza creation is in the files. It told the tale of "The Day before Christmas at Beech" with lines devoted to each of the members of the management team—evidence that this lighthearted group of company executives had a sense of teamwork and community, something Beech herself acknowledged in a separate letter in 1965.[95] Members of the Beechcraft Management Team, she wrote on another occasion, were "a happy, healthy, loyal group—[who] love their Company and respect her ideals," and this gave her a "warm friendly feeling."[96] Those same executives were equally articulate about their appreciation of her, as several letters document. In 1984, two years after Olive Ann Beech had stepped down from the company, one longtime vice president wrote to tell her that he had decided to retire and said he had "missed the close association with [her] in the last couple of years." He continued, "I have always enjoyed our association, and here at Beech we miss the standards you personified. . . . I am grateful to you for the confidence you always had in me. It meant more than the welcome honors which came as the result of that confidence."[97]

The "welcome honors" referred to were, in fact, another important way in which Beech cultivated loyalty and longevity among both executive and production employees. These came in many forms. The company touted its excellent staff retention rates in all company publications, and employees were regularly honored for their "years of service."[98] Such recognition occurred throughout the year, not just at a once-a-year ceremony, and included a service pin as well as a feature in the *Beechcrafter* newsletter with a photo of each recognized employee at an "informal ceremony" presided over—almost without exception—by Olive Ann Beech herself. Most of the photos capturing these events featured the staff in her office or at her private conference table. One caption featuring the celebration of employees who had reached their fifteenth year with the company stated, "Events of fifteen years ago are 'rehashed' as the scrapbook in front of Mrs. Beech brings back memories of 1941, the year the men above joined the company." This was not an impersonal or stuffy ceremony, but one in which the president of the company herself sat with the staff to acknowledge and recognize their history with the company and value to it. Two employees recognized for twenty years of service in 1956 were provided with diamond lapel pins, gifted by Beech herself from her private desk, and a full-page feature in the company newsletter.[99] Those with a track record of distinguished service and promotions at the company received still more. One executive wrote to Beech to thank her for the "book of the history of my promotions and other important happenings from 1940 through 1975" as well as "a medallion commemorating the day . . . when I was appointed to Vice President." These "treasured items" and the recognition they conveyed, he stated, constituted "a very personal touch" that was particularly meaningful.[100] Another vice president said of his book that "it is easy to see that someone put a lot of time and care into its preparation."[101]

Imagining the preparation of such commemorative books—culling information from human resource files, reproducing copies, and arranging them all in a visually pleasing way in a special book and the staff hours all of this would require—underscores the investment of company resources in such employee recognition practices. It is also an example of a business practice—someone was paid to do this work and it was done for business reasons as discussed above—which was made to appear like a personal act of kindness. Such tactics aligned with the familial orientation of welfare capitalist policies in the mid-twentieth century. After all, it is usually our families and personal lives that we preserve in scrapbooks. Personalizing corporate–labor relations in this way, Beech endeavored to garner employee loyalty first and foremost to the company.

The promotions such books celebrated were themselves expressions of the company's commitment to retaining staff and generating company loyalty. This was increasingly common in American companies starting around World War II and was a direct result of union demands. The unions were helped along in these efforts by federal programs such as Training Within Industry (TWI), which in 1941 recommended implementation of job ladders and formalized promotional opportunities as "the American way." Beech Aircraft's policy responded to this business trend, emphasizing that it "Select[ed] for Advancement Those Individuals Already in the Organization in Preference to Importing Outsiders."[102] The company newsletter regularly published news about internal promotions, whether it involved executive staff or lower-level employees. There were other reasons to champion such programs too. An internal promotion plan was an opportunity to weaken union pressure to promote employees strictly based on seniority rather than merit.[103]

Rewards and recognition were also routine at the company and underscored the company's merit-centered orientation as well as Olive Ann's own commitment to employee loyalty. Beech distributed what she called "tangible token[s] of appreciation" to its highest-level employees, always accompanied by a letter summarizing and acknowledging achievements and spurring ever greater performance.[104] Such monetary awards ranged from less than $500 to $25,000 and came in the form of year-end checks and/or bonds accompanied by letters that were at least partially personalized.[105] "Special incentive awards" were also given for extraordinary service, as in the case of Assistant Treasurer Charles Dieker, who was recognized for his "personal dedication and extra effort," which helped lead to 1975 "being the best year in [the company's] forty-three year history."[106] Acknowledgment of "loyal devotion" was often a part of the text accompanying such awards.[107] Finally, recognition came in additional nonmonetary forms as well. Particularly cherished, in part because it was unusual, was the presentation of the "Oh Happy Day" flag for display outside an executive's office for a job especially well done.[108] When it was presented to an associate, it was a prized honor.[109]

Some members of the company staff received luncheon invitations from Beech herself, which facilitated what one scholar calls "a forum for face-to-face contact with management." Such affairs were often elaborate, as in the case of an appreciation luncheon for twenty-two instructors and other staff members (including secretaries) involved in the company's training program for owners and pilots. Each attendee's name was printed in the luncheon handout, which included the menu: "Fresh Spinach Salad, Prime Rib, Baby Asparagus with Hollandaise Sauce, [and] Strawberry Parfait."[110] One employee, an engineer, who attended a different lunch, wrote to Mrs. Beech thanking her for the opportunity: "I consider it an honor to be one of the Beechcraft team invited to attend your luncheon. I believe that it is through informal type meetings we can get to know each other better and thus do a better job for Beech Aircraft. I sincerely hope this program will continue."[111] Such "understanding luncheons" were in fact common among American firms in the mid-twentieth century and were promoted in industry publications such as *Factory Management and Maintenance*. They grew out of social science research suggesting that "employees with greater social and psychological satisfaction on the job" were more productive and less likely to align themselves first and foremost with unions and that inviting employees to discuss company matters "of deep concern to them" yielded dividends. Lockheed, a Beech competitor, clearly believed this, combining the opportunity to speak to managers with a company tour culminating in flights over Southern California in company-built planes.[112] At Beech, employees valued these opportunities, as their correspondence makes clear, underscoring that such nonmonetary recognition *was* meaningful to them and probably made a significant contribution toward long-term "loyal" employment at the company.

Loyalty in Beech's thousands of production workers—about 80 percent of the company's workforce—was engendered most importantly through strong wages and benefits. Certainly the union ensured this, and in fact, "To Pay the Highest Earnings Consistent with the Financial Soundness of the Company" became a stated policy of Beech as early as the 1950s.[113] On the eve of its merger with Raytheon some thirty years later, this was considered a strong selling point for Beech. The consulting firm evaluating the company reported that "wages and salaries are very competitive at all skill and experience levels," and this signaled that the company was successful in recruiting and retaining skilled workers.[114] Strong compensation and benefits were at the heart of the company's strategy for generating what it called "plain, every day, work-a-day loyalty—like the kind a man has for his job and the organization to which he belongs." But to generate what the *Beechcrafter* described as the kind of loyalty that "makes the individual part of an organization and thus makes the organization a part of you" took more than that.[115] It emerged from a sense of community, from what one chronicler of Beech Aircraft described as "a workplace that becomes 'home.'"[116] This conception of management-labor relations continued the idea of the corporation as family that was characteristic of early-twentieth-century corporate welfare but cultivated worker loyalty in some new ways.[117]

Corporate communications were a key part of this strategy. At Beech, as in other corporations in the decades after World War II, this came in the form of "an endless barrage" of company publications.[118] The *Beechcrafter* employee newsletter was key to this effort. The bimonthly publication carried announcements from management to employees, but it also contained retirement and birth announcements ("Heircrafters"), articles about children of employees who won Beech Aircraft Foundation scholarships for college, "notable events [and] worthy deeds etc." capturing employees' lives and achievements outside work, statistics on employees' blood donations and charitable contributions, a "Trading Post" (free advertising for items for sale by employees), thank-yous from employees to their colleagues, annual photo contests, and columns "For the Kids." "Departmental News," also a regular feature of the newsletter, included personal stories such as this entry for Departments 8 and 17 in 1973: "The Gerald Stichs, Lawrence Lees, Jim Bohanas and the family of Edna Mealmanns spent the weekend of July 28 at Milford Lake. Donna Lee baked a cake for her husband's birthday which was combined with homemade ice cream."[119] Such entries appeared to celebrate and give voice to Beech's employees and the minutiae of their lives both in and out of work and were designed to strengthen employee ties to the company, urging them to envision it as a fundamental part of themselves and their lives. They also drove readership of publications that had overt economic and policy messages that might not have been read otherwise.

the Beechcrafter

Vol. IX   March 1, 1956   No. 2

Published for the employees of the Beech Aircraft Corporation, Wichita, Kansas, by the Beechcraft Public Relations Department.

A Timely Message From General George Washington

Great leaders always have the gift of discrimination . . . they can distinguish true goals from false objectives and thus more properly direct and apply their energies.

George Washington, whose birthday all America celebrated recently, was no exception. His ideas were basic. He had the remarkable ability of interpreting and applying them to his period of history. For example, in his Presidential address to the First Congress on January 8, 1790, he said:

"To be prepared for war is one of the most effective means of preserving peace. A free people ought not only to be armed, but disciplined; to which end a uniform and well-digested plan is requisite; and their safety and interest require that they should promote such factories as tend to render them independent of others for essential, particularly military, supplies."

In President Washington's address to the Third Congress on December 3, 1793, he stated:

"I cannot recommend to your notice measures for the fulfillment of our duties to the rest of the world without again pressing upon you the necessity of placing ourselves in a condition of complete defense and of exacting from them the fulfillment of their duties toward us.

"The United States ought not to indulge a persuasion that, contrary to the order of human events, they will forever keep at a distance those painful appeals to arms with which the history of every other nation abounds.

"There is rank due to the United States among nations which will be withheld, if not absolutely lost, by the reputation of weakness. If we desire to avoid insult, we must be able to repel it; if we desire to secure peace, one of the most powerful instruments of rising prosperity, it must be known that we are at all times ready for war.

"The documents which will be presented to you will show

the amount and kinds of arms and military stores now in our magazines and arsenals; and yet an addition even to these supplies cannot with prudence be neglected, as it would leave nothing to the uncertainty of procuring war-like apparatus in the moment of public danger."

So long as some men will some nations selfishly strive for dominance over others, the fundamental truths outlined by George Washington will always apply.

We can well remember his studied analysis that clearly points out the necessity of preparedness, that spells out the dangers of failing to use the best of research and science in our planning, and that warns us against being unwilling to insure our freedom against aggression.

What Is Loyalty?

LOYALTY is a big word with a big meaning. It always wins praises and honors. Sometimes it is heroic and sensational, but more often it is just plain, everyday, work-a-day loyalty — like the kind a man has for his job and the organization to which he belongs.

LOYALTY is forever at your machine, your desk, your typewriter, your job, and at the customer's place of business. When you let up, loyalty bears down. It is a constant reminder of your obligations to the group to which you belong. It preaches of self respect, fair dealings and fair exchange. Then, the more you bear down, the less the pressure that is exerted by loyalty.

LOYALTY gives you that feeling that you want to brag about your job. It tells you to speak up when someone speaks harshly about the "best outfit in the world," your company.

LOYALTY cautions you to move cautiously in thinking that the other side of the fence is greener in flush times. Loyalty is an investment that pays dividends during days when "Help Wanted" is shortened to just plain "HELP".

LOYALTY is faithfulness and effort and enthusiasm. Loyalty is decency plus good common sense. It transcends the individual and in so doing makes the individual part of an organization and thus makes the organization a part of you.

I Believe

(The thirty-seventh in a series by Cliff Titus)

I believe in — up-grading.

Red Smith, writing in the New York Herald Tribune, took strong exception to the hue and cry, "Break up the Yankees" that used to follow every world series.

"Break up the Yankees," wrote Smith, "is a foolish slogan and sets an unworthy goal. The aim should never be to destroy excellence, to bring the best down to the common level of mediocrity. Don't break up the Yankees. Work harder, get better, and beat them."

Sometimes we get a kind of grim satisfaction when a competitor or another department or another worker slips or fails. It makes us seem better by comparison. But that is a pretty cheap and certainly the dead wrong way of grading ourselves. After all, it isn't much satisfaction to know that we are as good, or a little better, than someone else whose performance is poor.

To beat competition, we can't wait for competition to break up; we must work harder, get better, and beat them.

We can't beat the anti-democracies by waiting for them to break up; we have to beat them by our superior performance.

We can't make personal progress by down-grading someone else; we must up-grade ourselves. The only true standard for comparison is our own record of performance and progress day after day. A Hindu proverb says, "There is nothing noble in being superior to some other man. The true nobility is in being superior to your previous self."

COVER PHOTO

WORKING PARTNER to Glenn W. Peel, drilling operator, is this Beechcraft Model G35 Bonanza, framed dramatically in the entranceway to the new Wichita Municipal Airport terminal building. Peel's drilling interests, stretching from Louisiana to Nevada, keep him "on the go," but the job is eased by his two Beechcrafts — one above and on twin-engine Model 18. Peel lives on his purebred Hereford ranch near Newkirk, Oklahoma.

The *Beechcrafter* newsletter was one of the ways that Olive Ann Beech communicated both information and values to her employees to create a sense of *belonging*. Wichita State University Libraries, Special Collections and University Archives.

At Beech Aircraft, such economic and policy messages were communicated in ways that made them appear to reflect the personal values of the company leader even as they replicated the messages being distributed across corporate America in the postwar period. In fact, Olive Ann Beech *was* a deeply values-driven executive. She was a dedicated quote collector whose "inspirational messages" fill one full box (containing forty-nine file folders) in the archive. Favorites came from published advice to business executives as well as individuals including Abraham Lincoln and Norman Vincent Peale. And this reflected Beech's own personal values—she was a deeply religious person who contributed generously to her local Methodist Church and was an active supporter of conservatives who increasingly embraced Lincoln as an embodiment of their values after the publication of Harry Jaffa's *Crisis of the House Divided* in 1959.[120] By the 1950s, bestselling author and religious leader Rev. Peale was a fixture in the joint efforts of lawmakers, corporate leaders, and religious activists to imbue American ideas, ideals, icons, and rituals with religion. Beech's embrace of Peale reflected the trend among business owners around the country. Her staunch support of fellow Kansan President Eisenhower whose faith was an integral part of his "dynamic conservatism" reflects the same trend, as well as her commitment to regional values and Republican politics.[121] For Beech, as with many business leaders at the time, religion and politics went hand-in-hand with economic values, about which she was no less enthusiastic. The passion with which she championed the American economic system is best illustrated by the fact that she named her personal plane *Free Enterprise*, which she boldly displayed on the side of the fuselage. These were Beech's values, but they also reflected the values of mid-twentieth-century corporate America more generally.

After World War II, the messages American companies sent to their employees increasingly melded economics with religion—and, in particular, evangelical Christianity. At the urging of organizations such as Spiritual Mobilization and the Christian Freedom Foundation, which reflected the joint aims of conservative religious leaders such as Peale and top business managers who sat on their boards and drew support from the likes of General Motors, IBM, and United States Steel, businesses signed on to the Cold War idea that "the survival of religion depended upon the survival of capitalism" and vice versa. Radio programs, magazines, editorial columns, conferences, and seminars cosponsored by these groups taught that "the free market economy, informed with . . . moral and spiritual self-discipline . . . [and] stewardship, was the only known economic system consistent with Christian principles."[122] Mid-twentieth-century business leaders were "evangelists for free enterprise" whose vision was "Christian libertarianism"—a perfect melding of religion and business.[123]

For Olive Ann Beech, like many other corporate leaders and political conservatives, this guiding ideology was also deeply patriotic as well, and it was these three core values that came through in her messages to employees. For example, in her holiday message distributed in December 1950, one of her first as president of the company, she asserted, "Let us take a moment to remember that the foundation of our country was laid on Christian precepts, faith, courage and understanding to carry on the faith of our forefathers who blazed the trail for this very real and powerful nation of opportunity in which it is our distinct privilege to live and work today. . . . Let us keep our faith in our God, faith in our country, faith in our fellow-men, and always a grateful heart."[124] Overtly values-based messages such as this were common from Olive Ann Beech and appeared in Beech Aircraft publications regularly. Often containing quotes, stories, and excerpts from famous speeches and published material, they illustrate the degree to which Beech Aircraft, like other mid-twentieth-century American corporations, was communicating a common, values-driven message to employees, one that reflected patriotic, religious, and economic aims that were widely viewed as business-friendly values. These efforts were so ubiquitous and successful throughout the country that Americans came to understand religion as a founding principle of America and one inextricably linked to its system of economic enterprise—an idea invented and inculcated by business leaders between the 1930s and 1950s.[125] Getting on board with this trend reflected Olive Ann Beech's own values and what she viewed as the best interests of her company, since, as chapter 4 will document, corporations and their leaders were important customers for the private planes Beech Aircraft produced.

The opportunity to standardize business communications to employees to support this agenda was made possible by several post–World War II initiatives. First, pushing out such overt messages directly to employees was possible in part because of the Taft Hartley Act (1947), which scaled back the communications restrictions imposed on employers by the New Deal–era Wagner Act (1935). And wide distribution of examples and recommendations by industry associations including the National Manufacturers Association (NAM) and the Chamber of Commerce made it easier for firms like Beech Aircraft to launch and implement their own employee communications campaigns and also standardized what most firms communicated to their employees.[126] In fact, NAM's 1950s television series, a highly successful public relations campaign that featured celebratory vignettes about American manufacturers around the country interspersed with "messages from Industry" that reflected an overtly ideological agenda, promoted corporate communications as an essential component of successful business management. "Such a free and steady flow of facts and opinions both to and from employees help[ed] bring about better understanding, cooperation and harmony in working relationships," one episode declared, and made American employees "better informed than their counterparts anywhere else in the world."[127] The standardization of corporate communications in the middle of the twentieth century underscores that Beech's efforts in this regard were not unique.

Also central to the company's mission to cultivate loyal employees was the Beech Employees' Club, or BEC, and this too was typical of other companies during the period. Founded in 1940, it was still going strong forty years later. Aimed at providing recreational opportunities for employees during World War II when labor competition in Wichita was highest and production pressure from the government was fierce, the club hosted dances, semiprofessional baseball, picnics, and beach days, which helped bring "the corporate family together." Wartime experience with such programs was so positive that Beech expanded its recreational opportunities for employees after the war—an investment in keeping with spending on industrial recreation in American firms overall, which saw a 50 percent increase between 1948 and 1953.[128] Like other corporations such as Kodak, which "built an eighteen-hole golf course and a 300,000-square foot recreation center" after the war, or the Diamond Alkaline company, which was described as a "country club factory," Beech created an expansive outdoor space designated for the recreational use of employees and their families.[129] "Beech Lake" was a 340-acre area that provided opportunities for fishing, picnics, model airplane flying, and exercising as well as the many sports and other activities in which employees were already engaged. A "Good-Time Table" in the employee newsletter listed the variety of activities available to employees and their families each month. In March 1956, this included twenty-five classes and events.[130] It was a comprehensive recreational program that was touted as unique.

Even as Beech's recreational opportunities became increasingly independent from the company itself, they continued to reflect a commitment to fostering community as an advantageous business strategy. By 1980, the BEC was "supported mostly by club dues and income from the vending machines located throughout the company . . . [and had] grown to be a self-supporting organization with a budget exceeding $175,000." But as the twenty-year club manager reported, it was a thriving organization because company leaders believed in its benefits: "Ultimately, the club's purpose is to provide a fellowship of employees through social, cultural and athletic gatherings. Even though other companies have employee clubs, none are quite like ours. Beech management has always supported the concept that Beechcrafters who work together should play together."[131] Although the manager gave credit to the company for supporting opportunities for employees to "play together," what his syntax masked is that the company's support was, of course, an investment in fostering an improvement in how employees *worked* together. It was a sentiment expressed more transparently by the General Motors personnel manager in 1952 when he stated, "Employees who can play well together can work well together too." The fellowship engendered through company-sponsored recreational activities, the thinking went, helped tighten employees' ties to each other and to Beech Aircraft. It was a widely held view, one that mid-twentieth-century proponents saw as an investment in employee retention, loyalty, morale, and productivity.[132] And Beech did it well.

Beech's investments in staff programs were, in fact, business investments, a point emphasized when the company articulated its values and its value to merger partners. "The security and well-being of more than 10,000 hourly and salaried employees who depend upon Beech for their living" was second only to stockholder benefits when company leaders articulated the criteria most important in the search for a merger partner in 1979.[133] And when the consulting firm Beech hired to help manage the search completed its description and analysis of Beech Aircraft, it highlighted the company's approach to employees: "Beech Aircraft Corporation is a strong believer in and practitioner of the philosophy that its most valuable asset is its employees . . . the Company has developed an experienced work force of outstanding capability and an organization which, at all levels, is dedicated to product excellence and the Company's success. . . . Over 3300 of Beech's employees have been associated with the Company for more than 10 years, 2000 for more than 15 years, and 1500 for more than 20 years. . . . The Company's 46 executive managers have an average of 26 years of service."[134] The value of the company's labor force and its "good will"—carefully cultivated by Beech over the course of its history—were a selling point, according to the consulting firm completing the evaluation, and a characteristic clearly championed by those with whom the consultants had conferred. Raytheon, in turn, was attractive to Beech for the same reasons. Beech viewed it favorably in part because, as the press reported, "they don't spill blood." That is, their track record as a company that had already acquired or merged with several other smaller companies was to keep existing management and staff intact, allowing them to operate independently.[135] Once the merger with Raytheon had been announced, its approach to employee relations was kept at the forefront of discussions. Olive Ann Beech herself wrote to Raytheon president D. Brainerd Holmes to say, "Many of our people enjoyed having the opportunity to meet you and having your comments on the merger and the 'soul' of Raytheon, which concerns them greatly."[136] The guiding principles of the company, the values imbuing management strategy, the vision of its leaders—these, presumably, were what Beech meant by the "soul" of the company, especially as they pertained to its employees. What Beech employees were looking for when they peered into Raytheon's "soul" was likely how they treated their employees and whether they could expect to continue to enjoy the relatively conflict-free labor-management relations and corporate welfare–oriented policies and programs that they had experienced for so many years.

The fact that employees cared so much about this was a sign that Beech's investments in her employees had yielded the desired results. They felt invested in the company they worked for and anxious to know how the Raytheon merger might change this. Under Beech's leadership, the company successfully distinguished itself as a model of welfare capitalism, engendering company affiliation among its employees and improving its position in the marketplace through investments in labor programs. It was a calculated labor strategy that paid off for Beech, as the Raytheon merger proved.

Margaret Rudkin

For Rudkin, the most powerful tool of welfare capitalism was relationship-building, and it was one she wielded with skill and strategy at Pepperidge Farm to engender a loyal, long-lasting "family" of employees. In fact, having started her business at home and employed neighbors and their family members almost exclusively in the beginning, it was not at all a stretch for her to conceptualize her business this way. But carefully conceived employee policies, elaborate reward systems, and celebrations focused on employees' families reflect the fact that Pepperidge Farm's company culture was not born but made. She deliberately crafted and adopted policies and programs designed to achieve the desired outcome: hardworking, skilled employees who stayed because they were invested in the company they worked for just as it was invested in them. The scale of Rudkin's success with this may have been rare, but her strategies were not. In fact, while couched as a special characteristic of Pepperidge Farm, her employee programs and policies reflected national trends and norms among mid-twentieth-century American corporations that sought to personalize their relations with employees even as they standardized them across institutions and industries. This worked especially well at Pepperidge Farm, because the very welfare policies and programs other companies were using to cultivate employee loyalty and engender a familial corporate ethos were, in the hands of Margaret Rudkin, presented as an outgrowth of *her* family, which privately owned the company until 1961 and then continued to operate it for many years even after Campbell Soup purchased it. Thus, as a labor manager, Rudkin refined common tenets of mid-twentieth-century welfare capitalism into a personalized model of corporate benevolence that situated her as patron to her employees, a protector who looked out for their needs, and in return exacted their loyalty and longevity. It was a strategy that kept Pepperidge Farm union free her whole career—a point of pride for her and a distinction in the commercial baking industry, which was heavily unionized and conflict ridden on the East Coast during the mid-twentieth century. The outcome was both higher profits and a sense of satisfaction for Rudkin, who like many mid-twentieth-century American business leaders preferred the illusion of family to the reality of competing interests and implemented carefully calculated policies and programs to achieve it.

At Pepperidge Farm, family nomenclature was commonplace in descriptions of the company's employees and reflected Rudkin's investment in the idea of filial piety and patronage. A 1957 employee handbook, for example, instructed supervisors to "care for your people at work as you would care for your people at home." Because of this responsibility, it asserted, all supervisors "in a sense have two families."[137] This was a personal philosophy for Rudkin herself too. In her autobiographical cookbook, *The Margaret Rudkin Pepperidge Farm Cookbook*, published in 1963, she reminisced about her first employees as if they were additional children in her family: "I had to employ a young girl to help, and I taught her how to bake, for she had never made bread either. There we were on the farm in the hot August days of 1937, a pair of amateur bakers, mixing and kneading and baking like mad. . . . That girl celebrated her twenty-fifth year with the Pepperidge Farm Company last summer. Soon I employed her sister, her brother, her sister-in-law, her cousins, and at one time ten members of her family were Pepperidge Farm employees. Some of the girls married, but there are six of the family with us now."[138] Though her female employees remained "girls" to her long after they had become gray-haired women, her attachment to the diminutive term captured both mid-twentieth-century notions of gender and class and the representation of Pepperidge Farm as a family rather than a company. This grew in part from the fact that the company sprang up as a Rudkin family enterprise—one centered on their home turf—and expanded through the employment of Ference family members as described above. Mike and John Ference, both farmers, were neighbors to the Rudkins' Fairfield estate, and their large-sized families (each had five children) provided the first employees of Pepperidge Farm. The Ferences remained loyal champions and trusted staff for years to come. Several members of the family were employed at the company for decades—kneading dough, in the case of the women, and in the case of the men, overseeing the company's fleet of trucks, working in the laboratory, or managing maintenance. Reportedly, Bill Ference (Sr.) started working at the company at the age of sixteen and earned his plumber's and electrician's licenses at Margaret Rudkin's expense so that he could become head of maintenance—a job he held at the company for forty-four years. The Rudkins were patrons of other Ference family members too. Jean Ference, for example, the grandson of one of the original Ference brother neighbors, attended Cornell's Hotel School paid for in part by the Rudkins, who maintained an ongoing correspondence with him for four years. To Bill Ference, who reminisced over the phone with a Rudkin grandson, Margaret Rudkin was a "tough, driven person who cared for her employees." He remembered in particular that "she knew everyone by their first name."[139]

Though her employees did not call her by *her* first name—using instead the title "Mrs. Rudkin"—such deference did not mean that Margaret Rudkin was unwilling to work right alongside her employees if the conditions called for it, and this supported her ability to sell Pepperidge Farm's familial ideal. For example, she had no compunction about rolling up her sleeves and "getting her hands dirty" in the production process during the World War II labor shortage. After all, this was precisely how the company had started—Rudkin and Mary Ference, side by side, "mixing and kneading and baking like mad"—and she seemed never to forget that. Of course, despite such overtures toward a nonhierarchical structure, the "metaphor of corporation as family" was at least misleading if not false, because "what family would 'fire' its children when expediency so dictated?"[140] But Rudkin's "we're-all-in-it-together" approach to work undoubtedly bolstered her ability to characterize employer–employee relations at Pepperidge Farm as "family" relations—something that many companies tried to do but perhaps not always as convincingly.

At the end of her life and years after the company had become affiliated with corporate giant Campbell Soup, Pepperidge Farm still characterized employees in filial terms, and this helped to counter perceptions that the bigger the enterprise, the more insensitive or "soulless" it became. For example, in a March 1967 message printed in the *Conveyor*, the newsletter for employees, Rudkin's report about her visit to the company's Downingtown plant in Pennsylvania was rife with the language of family and friends: "Of course, I spent more time out of the cart than in because I kept seeing my old friends. Many, many of the men and women who started with us 18 years ago are still there. The reception to me couldn't have been more inspiring. Everyone seemed so glad to see me—old and new alike, it didn't seem to make much difference. And I was just as delighted to meet new members of our family as to greet the old. It's always reassuring to me to find that Pepperidge Farm continues to attract such fine, enthusiastic, dependable people."[141] For Rudkin, who by this time in her life was seventy years old and engaged in a serious battle with cancer, seeing longtime employees must have been genuinely heartwarming and especially meaningful. It provided evidence that others were also invested in the company she had started and that they would help to carry on her legacy there. But this was a management tactic too. Characterizing employees as "friends" and "family" was common among large corporations in the twentieth century and an essential component of efforts to create "the corporate soul." Pepperidge Farm wielded this device skillfully, invoking the company's modest founding by Margaret Rudkin, when a small number of employees worked side by side to turn out a superior "handmade" product, to emphasize that fifty years later the quality had not changed. The fiftieth Anniversary Edition of the *Conveyor* reported, "Her philosophy was simple and is the core of Pepperidge Farm. She believed that quality people made quality products and that people were the company's best investment and insurance for a successful future."[142] Such public demonstrations of compassion and appreciation for employees presented "the human face of American capitalism" and helped corporations "safeguard against perceptions of soullessness." Starting at the beginning of the twentieth century and continuing to its end, such appeals—whether published for employees, as in this case, or in public-facing advertisements—were increasingly common.[143] Rudkin's Pepperidge Farm provided a particularly good example.

The hands-on production techniques that Rudkin insisted on helped to define the nature of employee value at Pepperidge Farm. Handmade—in particular hand-kneaded—bread was a key attribute of the company's brand. As the *New Yorker* reported in 1948, "Pepperidge Farm bread is touched by human hands. Mrs. Rudkin has an antiquated notion, which she got from her grandmother, that only dough kneaded by hand makes good bread."[144] *How* to knead was also of great importance to Rudkin. It was her belief that it typically took a new employee three weeks to learn the proper method and "to develop her sense of touch to the point at which she can tell, by the feel of the dough, when the bubbles have been satisfactorily arranged."[145] To ensure that her employees developed the proper techniques with the dough and made Pepperidge Farm bread the way she wanted it made, Rudkin had a strict policy of hiring only those who had no prior baking experience. She didn't want to risk hiring someone who might introduce new steps in the carefully orchestrated production process she had developed. Thus, for Rudkin, controlling the knowledge and practice of breadmaking was an essential component of employee value; that is, it was the fact that employees' breadmaking skills were built from scratch by her that made them valuable to the company. Such personalized production techniques were key to the company's ability to carve out a niche market in the industry, and they also engendered its perspective on employees—one that viewed them as fundamental to product quality as long as they towed the company line.

Rudkin's employment philosophy for production workers was also overtly gendered, and while this distinguished her from competitors in some ways, in others she reenacted policies typical in the manufacturing industry. First and foremost, she hired only women as production workers. Using female employees in the bread business set her apart from other commercial bakeries, which in the 1930s were hiring men for this job. She stated in an interview recorded in 1958, "You see up to that time everyone thought that men were the only one who could make bread in large quantities. But I felt that traditionally baking bread is a woman's job so I employed only women." Of course, in choosing women for their "traditional" association with breadmaking, Rudkin glorified gender roles that assigned household labor to women because of biologically and socially driven arguments about the inherent abilities of female versus male family members. These same arguments were used to keep women out of most paid jobs and served as a powerful force in the gender segmentation of the job market. Yet in adopting the idea that to "nurture"—in this case through food—was "nature," Rudkin also knowingly challenged the status quo in the commercial baking industry, making specifically and exclusively female a job that had been traditionally unpaid in the home and remained inaccessible as a form of paid employment in the rest of the industry. In so doing, she inherently challenged the industry's predictable association of large-scale commercialized and mechanized baking with men and opened up a new job category for women at a time in U.S. history when employment options were slim and sorely needed. For this reason, Rudkin described her policy of hiring women as a "defiance" and perhaps ironically saw herself as undermining what had become conventional in the industry by boldly embracing women's traditional skills as homemakers in a paid environment.[146] This did not mean, however, that Rudkin compensated women equally with men. Like other manufacturing firms of the mid-twentieth century that employed women, Pepperidge Farm had a wage and job classification scale differentiated by gender, and the lowest starting wage for a male laborer ($1.75) was thirty cents, or 20 percent, more than the lowest starting wage for a female laborer ($1.46).[147] This was not a subject that Rudkin ever commented on in interviews, speeches, or company literature, nor does she seem to have been asked about it, so we do not have any insight into her thoughts on this gender disparity in the wages she paid. But in adopting this policy, she replicated the norms of the manufacturing industry and corporate America more generally, managing labor just as male employers did to maximize her firm's bottom line—and used gender as a strategy to achieve this goal.[148]

Even though Rudkin viewed herself as an upstart in the commercial baking arena, outsiders evaluated her as conventional in most of her employment practices, and in fact she generally managed employee relations in ways that resembled those of most other American company leaders at the time. The *New Yorker*, for example, described her as "follow[ing] the benevolent pattern popular among small New England firms." It reported that she paid slightly higher-than-average wages, provided bonuses and benefits, and provided "an infirmary, with a full-time nurse," a cafeteria where for forty cents employees could buy "a meat-and-potato lunch, with milk, dessert, and Pepperidge bread," and weekly discounts on company bread purchased for home consumption. Her policies, the article concluded sardonically, were "not dangerously radical."[149] Indeed, benefits packages, onsite healthcare, and cafeterias had deep roots and were all common among American corporations from the early to mid-twentieth century, and the examples of Lewis and Beech illustrate this too. Thus, while the *New Yorker*'s comment about Rudkin's employment policies suggests that it expected something more radical than it found—one suspects because she was a woman—it also affirms the degree to which her practices as a labor manager were unremarkable.[150]

Like other American companies in the middle of the twentieth century, Pepperidge Farm sought to generate the "family" feeling that was de rigueur in corporate capitalism, and it did so by wielding a variety of programs designed to personalize the relationship between the company and its employees. While some companies may have stopped at family rhetoric, Pepperidge Farm's investments in engendering the family ideal were more tangible. Beyond the onsite cafeteria and nurse and benefits package, Rudkin provided for her employees in a variety of additional ways, all of which took on the appearance of "gifts." The nature of such investments may have been influenced by the company's emphasis on hiring women workers for its production line. Some scholarship has found that in the Progressive Era, employers with substantial numbers of female workers tended to focus on corporate welfare programs that reflected their own notions of traditional gender roles in order to "enhance the femininity" of their workers.[151] At Pepperidge Farm in the mid-twentieth century, this took on the appearance of female gift-giving practices that resembled those prescribed for American elites by 1950s etiquette gurus Amy Vanderbilt or Emily Post. For example, the company provided wedding presents to employees ($5 for each year of employment completed at the time of marriage); Christmas gifts for each child (under age ten) of employees; baby presents for employees who became new parents (a monogrammed silver baby cup); Thanksgiving turkeys (one for each Pepperidge Farm family); an annual Christmas party that included dinner, dancing, and entertainment; summer picnics for employees and their families; and funeral flowers sent on the occasion of the death of an employee or an employee's immediate family member. All of these company investments in important and private occasions in the lives of employees and their families suggested that Pepperidge Farm considered its workers kinfolk. They showed that the company "took a human interest in [workers'] families"—a growing trend among American employers at this time who sought new ways to "tighten employee identification with the firm."[152]

Pepperidge Farm employees were meant to feel "seen." A good example was the way the Downingtown plant's tenth-anniversary celebration included an exhibit featuring employee hobbies ranging from salt-and-pepper shaker collections to home canning to charcoal drawing to homemade miniature trains, each of which was individually listed in the employee newsletter's coverage of the event.[153] Another was the way employee vacation news was published with photos and reports about how and where individuals spent their time off.[154] At Pepperidge Farm, the intended message was clear: the personal matters of employees were company business because it was not an impersonal place to work.

Rudkin also oversaw a community-giving campaign by the company. Such efforts were typical of mid-twentieth-century corporations, most of

4/1/57

C - #2

<u>Wedding Presents</u>

A wedding present of $5.00 for each year of employment completed at the time of marriage is given by Pepperidge Farm to the newly wed couple.

C - #3

<u>Christmas Toys for Children</u>

A gift is given at Christmas time to each child of an employee provided that the child will not have reached his or her tenth birthday by December 25th of that year.

C - #4

<u>Baby Presents</u>

A monogrammed silver baby cup is given at the time of birth to each new baby of any Pepperidge employee. Employee on maternity leave will also receive a cup for their child.

C - #5

<u>Thanksgiving Turkeys</u>

The practice was established in 1951 to give a turkey at Thanksgiving time to each Pepperidge family. This means that a husband and wife or mother and daughter living in the same house will receive one turkey. Any questionable cases can be decided as they occur.

Page from the "Welcome to Pepperidge Farm" packet distributed to company employees in 1957 showing the carefully prescribed gift-giving Rudkin used to create a sense of familial connection between her employees and the company. Fairfield Museum and History Center, Fairfield, Connecticut.

which were dedicated to crafting an image of themselves as "good neighbors" in the communities in which they were located. Thus, programs like Pepperidge Farm's were not new, but they were decidedly different from those that appeared in earlier decades. The difference in corporate–community relations programs after World War II was the "degree of conscious commitment, initiative, organization, and sophistication which companies were now prepared to pour into them" to establish themselves as congenial community members. Participation in community boards and agencies and fundraising for voluntary agencies were both typical. Rudkin may have advocated both, but what extant evidence certainly shows is that financial contributions to charitable organizations were a regular part of the company's budget, a practice first documented in its 1939 Partnership Return of Income form completed for the Internal Revenue Service. That year the company made contributions totaling $69, the next year $224.90, and two years later $491.50. By 1945, the final year for which the figure exists in extant records, the company made total contributions of $3,027.24 (0.2 percent of gross receipts), equivalent to $39,304.84 in today's dollars.[155]

But what is striking about the contributions is not so much the amount but the variety of recipients listed in the records, reflecting the individual commitments and affiliations of company employees. While some such as the Red Cross and Norwalk Hospital appear regularly, the other charitable institutions listed changed regularly and reflected remarkable diversity. The religious organizations alone, which included the White Plains Hebrew National Auxiliary, Church of the Seventh-Day Adventists, Lutheran Church of Manhattan, South Norwalk Colored Church, Hadassah, Jewish Argus, Hungarian Reformed Church, Christ Lutheran Church, and Grace Episcopal, demonstrate this.[156] Because it's hard to imagine why the Rudkins would be such supporters of religious pluralism in and of itself, it seems plausible that the contributions reflected the affiliations of Pepperidge Farm's employees. And, indeed, at least one local newspaper article suggested this. In conjunction with the announcement of a $5,000 contribution to the YMCA building fund from Pepperidge Farm, William Rudkin reportedly explained, "Many of our employees live in the . . . area and they and their families derive social benefits from the 'Y.'"[157] Such contributions played the dual role of enriching employer–employee ties and enhancing the company's image among a wide variety of community organizations. This charitable impulse typically reflected both "war-born profits and tax incentives" and the "desire for an improved public image" for American companies at mid-century and drove corporate giving up during and after World War II from 0.35 percent of profits in 1941 to 1.08 percent in 1960.[158] Of course, ultimately, such charitable contributions helped Rudkin to communicate to employees that she valued them and that what was important to them was important to her—precisely the sort of sentiment that contributed to a sense of family and to long-term employment.

At Pepperidge Farm, the personal relationship between employer and employee emphasized that the Rudkins themselves were the bearers of such gifts, not as the invisible power brokers of the company but as the patrons of its workers. For example, when the 1957 employee handbook described the Christmas bonus policy, it started with the statement: "For several years Mr. & Mrs. Rudkin have distributed a Christmas Bonus at Christmas time, basing the amount of the gift on the amount of company profit for that particular year." Even the sick pay policy was presented this way, stating, "Mrs. Rudkin has provided us with a sick pay program." The rejection of bureaucratic impersonal language here in favor of naming the company owners reminded employees who their benefactors were and to whom they owed their thanks or allegiance. Even employee loans were provided (interest free with repayment made through weekly paycheck deductions) at the discretion of localized management but with final approval by a Rudkin in the case of a repeat loan. All this communicated that employees worked not just for Pepperidge Farm, the company, but for the Rudkin family.[159]

Perhaps, then, it should come as no surprise that the appreciation of grateful employees at Pepperidge Farm was expressed in personal ways as well. The same year that the company articulated its comprehensive benefits and gifts program, Margaret Rudkin was the happy recipient of a surprise gift from her employees. Although gifts to managers by employees were explicitly prohibited in company policies, on 5 June 1957 "a 482-year-old cook book was presented [to her] . . . by 1,000 employees who pooled funds to present the gift in a surprise ceremony to celebrate the 20th anniversary of Pepperidge Farm." An enthusiastic collector of historic cookbooks, Rudkin was reportedly thrilled with the first-edition treasure, which was "described as the world's oldest printed cook book" and one of only seven in print in the world when it was bestowed upon her.[160] Such employee largesse belies cynical interpretations of whether genuine affection was possible between employer and employee in mid-twentieth-century corporate "families."

But as in all power relationships, gift-giving by employers to their employees conveyed more than simple appreciation—it communicated the idea popular among mid-twentieth-century employers that the company was the protector and benefactor of its employees. This was one of the ways American corporate leaders deliberately undermined the notion that New Deal welfare programs were necessary.[161] By "taking care" of their employees, companies made the implicit argument that the government did not need to.[162] The National Association of Manufacturers encouraged dissemination of information about such employee programs—what it called "the hidden payroll"—and focused a whole episode of its public film series *Industry on Parade* on "helping employees manage finances and understand the value of fringe benefits."[163] This is precisely what Pepperidge Farm did when one of its personnel managers calculated and communicated to employees the monetary worth of all the "gifts" and bonuses the company offered, determining the investment to be equal to $.044 per hour per employee. That such figures were determined and shared by personnel managers underscores that these were not spontaneous acts of generosity but rather investments mediated by corporate bureaucracy. Thus, while presented as a sort of personal gift to employees by the Rudkins, such largesse was clearly calculated and designed to recoup benefits to the company.

Outlays such as these designed to increase employee retention or "loyalty" were generally viewed by mid-twentieth-century business leaders as cost-effective investments that garnered benefits to the bottom line, but Margaret Rudkin professed to be after something less tangible—employee morale. It was a concern that preoccupied many business leaders, 73 percent of whom identified "a general indifference on the part of workers" as the chief reason for a decline in their productivity in one 1946 survey.[164] Indeed, improving employee attitudes about their work was a popular focus of mid-twentieth-century campaigns by industry associations such as the National Association of Manufacturers (NAM). One whole episode of its 1950s public film series, *Industry on Parade*, focused on improving company morale through employee opinion surveys, a technique used at the Garrett Corporation in Los Angeles, California, an aircraft and aerospace company.[165] And Sears Roebuck "continuously surveyed thousands of its employees, gathering data on their attitudes toward the company and other matters" to try to positively impact employee attitudes toward their work.[166] For Rudkin, achieving high employee morale was a labor-management priority that she presented as an ethical responsibility. In a speech to Harvard Business School MBA students, she argued that enjoying a "climate of satisfaction and pride [was something] which everybody ought to be able and share in."[167] Though she did not connect this viewpoint to the overtly political campaign in which so many American manufacturers were involved, Rudkin's principles aligned with those of other corporate employers who believed that "treating the worker with greater dignity and respect was expected to yield bigger payoffs." These included not just greater worker productivity but also strengthened ties between employees and their employers and workers' embrace of the idea that free enterprise was the engine of American progress rather than government and organized labor.[168] Thus, while the desired outcome—worker morale—may have been less tangible, it was nonetheless defined by many mid-twentieth-century employers as key to labor management.

At Pepperidge Farm, Rudkin pursued employee morale deliberately and methodically by putting in place a variety of highly bureaucratized and systematic policies and programs. Like Olive Ann Beech, she presided over an elaborate system for celebrating employee anniversaries with the company. Yearly anniversaries were recognized with a card and a check for increasing levels of extra pay: two days of pay on the first-year anniversary grew to four weeks of pay by the tenth-year anniversary. Additionally, five-year employment anniversaries were celebrated with a cake, ten years with a monogrammed silver platter with the name Pepperidge Farm and the date inscribed on the bottom, and fifteen years with a monogrammed silver carving set or silver cream-and-sugar set. As the 1957 employee handbook explained, such anniversary gifts recognized "those employees who have continued to work and to have kept their absenteeism to a minimum; thereby demonstrating their loyalty to Pepperidge Farm."[169] Scholars of business management today continue to recommend "reward systems that truly value good performance" as one of several essential ways to meet what they call employees' "deep needs"—a twenty-first-century way of understanding what Rudkin and her peers called "morale."[170] And companies and organizations still provide countless engraved platters, cups, clocks, and pens in recognition of employees' "years of service." But whereas employees today often have a choice in which reward they receive, Pepperidge Farm's 1950s prescriptive rewards system reflected paternalistic ideas about employers knowing what was best for their employees. And in this, the company was typical. Whereas companies with a primarily male workforce sometimes gave personalized gifts to the wives of long-term employees rather than the employees themselves, the goal was the same. "If you do it properly," one company manager stated, gifts could "mold" employee behavior and do a company "a lot of good."[171] Pepperidge Farm's carefully constructed rewards system was designed to achieve a particular "good" for the company—consistent attendance and long-term employment, which were both essential to a manufacturing process dependent on specialized knowledge that took a long time to cultivate among employees.

It was a point of pride for the Rudkins that Pepperidge Farms was a nonunion commercial bakery, and they fought to maintain that status. Margaret

Rudkin discussed this in her 1960 speech at Harvard, stating, "We have no unions in our plants. We've always more than met competitive wages with good fringe benefits in addition."[172] Rejecting the term "personnel work" in favor of "human relations," which had just come into vogue in 1946, Rudkin professed a belief in the common humanity of all employees. "We're all alike, college graduates or grammar school boys, we all feel that we want to be needed, we want to be doing something, and we want a pat on the back once in a while."[173] This human relations orientation was typical of antiunion employers at midcentury who, like Rudkin, embraced competitive wages and benefit plans, recognition and gift programs, access to onsite healthcare and subsidized food, and what they touted as a personalized relationship between company and employee as testament to their belief that unions were unnecessary. In the nonunion ideal, according to mid-twentieth-century business owners, employers acted benevolently toward their employees, and in exchange they retained control of their business free of interference from unions and government. It was an idea that appeared in the 1940s as "management rights," and NAM was its strongest advocate.[174] For Rudkin, who was an invited speaker to NAM and thrice-featured manufacturer in the organization's film series, the "climate of satisfaction and pride" that she said she desired—ostensibly a principled approach about how to treat workers—must have in fact reflected these same industry goals.[175] For, under her leadership, Pepperidge Farm took steps to keep unions out of Pepperidge Farm.

The company's performance-based bonus system was one such program that many employers used to keep unions out. At Pepperidge Farm, it was tightly controlled by the Rudkins or their deputies. Described in the employee handbook alternately as the "Christmas Gift Bonus" or profit-sharing plan, the end-of-year checks provided to employees were tied to an individual's earnings as well as company profits. But unlike the profit-sharing plans at Beech Aircraft and Flotill Products—both unionized companies—Pepperidge Farm's bonus was distributed at the discretion of the Plant Manager. Although employees "normally do receive it," the handbook stated, it was "a gift" that was "awarded in recognition of the co-operation and personal efficiency shown by the employees during the year." One consequence of this was that it could "be withheld for disciplinary reasons."[176] This degree of discretionary power over bonus pay highlighted the difference between unionized and nonunionized companies. Nonunion companies like Pepperidge Farm were more likely than unionized ones to have profit-sharing programs in the 1950s, but they were also more likely to dispense this largesse in tightly controlled and controlling ways. For many firms, profit-sharing programs were in fact important components of a "paternalistic personnel program" aimed at curbing the influence of unions and spurring worker productivity.[177] This description fits Pepperidge Farm, which used its bonus "gift" program to both motivate and punish its workers by retaining control over its dispensation.

Rudkin also embraced intracompany transfers based on seniority and voluntary severance to avoid layoffs as well as unions. This was, in fact, common among nonunionized firms because they had the freedom to explore layoff alternatives such as restructuring jobs, transferring employees to new jobs, and cross-training employees for flexible job placement. By contrast, unionized firms that were forced to respond to organized labor's emphasis on income security relied increasingly on seniority-based layoffs when they had to cut costs in response to a decline in demand.[178] Rudkin represented the practices she used to avoid layoffs as points of pride:

> We have never discharged our employees because of automation . . .
> we have no compulsory retirement . . . [and] where we have
> changed our methods because we were a growing concern we have
> always been able to carry the surplus labor for a certain length of
> time, work out new departments, give people a chance to transfer to
> them, with the older women where they didn't want to transfer, we
> have had a system of severance pay which was entirely voluntary
> with no compulsory severance whatsoever, and in many cases this
> severance pay was as much as $500 to 2,000. But generally we have
> those who have stayed with us—have been gradually absorbed into
> our new departments as we add new products and expand our
> present.[179]

Extant records provide no evidence of whether the company's actual practices reflected this benevolent description. But such actions would have been in keeping with those of other nonunionized companies, some of which were led by presidents who were willing to spend "more on wages and welfare programs than it would have cost to sign a union contract" just to keep organized labor out. Rudkin's comments came in the context of her speech to Harvard's MBA students, which emphasized overall the importance of crafting employer–employee relations governed by "mutual trust and respect" and not unions.[180] What she seemed to be after was "workers [who] are so well satisfied . . . that union leaders have not been able to organize them"—

it was a vision for labor management that captivated many employers in midcentury.[181]

The only evidence that Pepperidge Farm employees pursued unionization came after Margaret Rudkin's death, but the company relied on her vision of "human relations" to combat it. In 1968, her son William Rudkin, acting as chairman of the board of Pepperidge Farm, urged employees to reject the union:

> The country is plagued today with a kind of creeping impersonality. We are known to many people only by our social security number, our draft card number, our license number, our telephone number, our zip code, or our department store charge numbers. . . . Some of you at this very time are being asked to trade a portion of yourselves for still another number—this time a number on a union card. . . . Unions are dedicated to the principle that management and employees cannot get along together on a man-to-man on-the-job basis and that the union is a necessary third party. The way we have worked our problems out together here for 31 years is ample evidence that it can be done without the third party. . . . The fact that we remain one of the largest non-union bakeries in the United States makes us a prime target. . . . On election day I sincerely urge you to vote and to vote NO. . . . A No vote means NO UNION. A NO vote means continued faith in Pepperidge Farm, where people have always been much more than mere numbers.[182]

While it is impossible to know how Margaret Rudkin herself would have viewed such an outright assault on the unions had she been alive, the evidence suggests that she shared her son's conviction that problems between employees and employers could be worked out without a "third party." Years earlier, in a speech to the Drexel Institute of Technology, she explained that she expected only three things from her executives: "keep costs down, keep profits up, keep everybody happy."[183] That "keeping everybody happy" was one of the top priorities at the company underscores the commitment to working out labor troubles without the need of mediators, or unions. It was a vision for labor management that squared her policies with those of most American corporate leaders in the middle of the twentieth century.

Of course, unionization would have affected the bottom line as well as the company's culture. Though the company reportedly paid higher-than-average wages and thus would not have incurred increased payroll costs because of unionization, it did avoid most of the expenses of industrywide strikes that plagued other commercial bakeries. One company history (encompassing 1937–59) compiled by a longtime employee documented bakery industry strikes in New York, New England, and other regions in 1949, 1951, 1954, and 1959 that affected Pepperidge Farm. While in one case company deliveries were turned away by strikers blockading distribution centers, in other instances it seems the company benefitted. In 1954, for example, "extra bread [was] delivered to distributors in strike areas," taking advantage of the short-term opportunity to steal market share from the big-time producers who dominated the industry.[184] Thus, the Rudkins' antiunion stance is best interpreted as a financially as well as socially motivated company policy designed to maximize profits as well as Pepperidge Farm's carefully constructed "family" culture.

Conclusion

Lewis, Beech, and Rudkin were not crusaders who championed the cause of their employees, male or female. They were also not heartless corporate executives who implemented policies with the explicit intention of harming their employees. Instead, the evidence suggests that for all three, the most expedient strategy in labor-management relations was to follow the crowd. This is not to say that they did not have their own ideas about the kind of companies they wanted to create or the kind of company leaders they wanted to become, or that their labor-management decisions were preprogrammed rather than determined situation by situation. Overall, however, the vision they enacted conformed to the standards of their industries and their time. They were welfare capitalists who helped to usher in the new mid-twentieth-century version of this labor-management approach with roots in the nineteenth century. In so doing, they helped to introduce corporate policies designed to undercut union influence and strengthen company profits. For Lewis, Beech, and Rudkin this was the most expedient way to increase employee loyalty and longevity while at the same time increasing company profits and maintaining market position. It was a business decision through and through. But it was also a reflection of each woman's sense of herself as the head of a corporate "family" whose policies were benevolent as well as profitable.

· ·

"People aren't aware, always, that I'm a girl," quipped Mary Wells Lawrence, who many suspect served as the inspiration for the character of Peggy Olson, the female copywriter on the popular television series *Mad Men* about the world of American advertising in the 1960s. If one considers how male dominated the world of advertising remains even today, the comment won't be surprising coming from a woman who in 1970 was likely the country's highest-paid advertising executive. Her comment reflected the degree to which professional women were generally advised and perceived to "act like a man," but it also reveals the nature of her achievements in the advertising industry. After spectacular success as a lead creative director, she was refused the title of president as promised her at the agency where she worked because it was thought men "weren't ready" for a female agency president. As a consequence, she left to found her own agency in 1966, initiating a meteoric rise to fame and fortune in the advertising world that led to widespread recognition in the business press as "an outstanding female executive." When she took her company public in 1968, she became the first female CEO of a company traded on the New York Stock Exchange. In an industry dominated by iconic male leaders, she stood out. But she also challenged the widely held idea that women's value and expertise in advertising was limited to campaigns geared toward female consumers. Her own agency's most successful advertisements dodged such gendered pigeonholes, appealing to male as well as female consumers. Among them were "Plop plop, fizz fizz" (Alka-Seltzer), "I ♥ New York"; "Trust the Midas touch"; "At Ford, Quality is Job 1"; "Flick your Bic"; "Raise your hand if you're Sure" (Sure deodorant); and "Friends don't let friends drive drunk" (public service announcement).[1] None of these campaigns targeted exclusively female consumers, and none, in fact, offered a specifically gendered point of view. She was a successful woman in a male-dominated industry who breached not just the "C-suite" but also gendered content segregation.

In contrast to Mary Wells Lawrence, most women advertising professionals in the early to mid-twentieth century built their success on advertising to women—providing the "women's point of view." It was an "essentialist idea that women knew what other women wanted and that basically all women were after the same thing." This created opportunities for female professionals starting at the beginning of the twentieth century at a time in business history when they found few opportunities beyond clerical work and other support roles. The J. Walter Thompson Agency, for example, hired so many women in its "Women's Editorial Department" that by the 1920s it was "known as 'the women's agency.' "[2] The interest in female copywriters to script appealing messages for women was driven by the importance of reaching female consumers, who made some 85 percent of all consumer purchases in the United States starting in the early 1900s. Companies acted on this by developing their own internal departments geared toward women consumers and by seeking out advertising professionals who could help them to reach this lucrative segment of the market.[3]

Doing so became increasingly important by the second half of the twentieth century as competition fostered the emergence of modern marketing and in particular the creation of brand management. As growing numbers of companies offered ostensibly similar and similarly high-quality consumer products, companies were forced to seek opportunities to distinguish themselves from each other. Starting with packaged goods giants such as Proctor and Gamble, General Foods, and Unilever, they developed the discipline of brand management. A brand manager was "responsible for giving a product an identity that distinguished it from nearly indistinguishable competitors." Moving away from "straight 'reason-why' copy" that focused on utilitarian motives for purchasing a product, the new consumer appeals were psychologically oriented. A product's brand identity offered "not only functional but also emotional value" and pivoted on familiar or "already known" truths tapped into by advertising slogans and promises. Professional women in advertising whose job it was to capture female consumer dollars contributed to building brands by identifying "existing systems of meaning" of particular importance and appeal to women and exploiting them using emotionally captivating copy and images. Consumers were "buying into [a] promise" and not just buying a product.[4]

For female business *owners* in the middle of the twentieth century, such product appeals offered opportunities to leverage gender as a brand management strategy. This was both because company founder-operators could offer personal assurances to consumers about product quality—a trend in advertisements since the nineteenth century—and because, as female founder-operators, they could claim that gender was a distinction for them that contributed to their reliability.[5] If modern marketing started with the familiar and built product promises based on what consumers already knew, gender was a ubiquitous system of meanings that infused many areas of day-to-day life. And women executives were in a prime position to capitalize on it.

Lewis, Beech, and Rudkin did just this, positioning themselves in distinctly gendered ways relative to their products and their customers. For each one, their marketing messages changed over time, moving toward a more stereotyped presentation of themselves. Lewis, for example, whose early advertisements emphasized her role as a skilled and insightful female manager-owner, moved toward a constructed image of herself as "just a housewife" who struggled with weight problems and therefore was someone whom female consumers of her diet products could relate to and trust. Beech, whose marketing efforts aimed at convincing mainly male consumers to purchase personal aircraft and male distributors, dealers, and sales professionals to sell them, took an increasingly "backseat" role, crafting a persona for herself as the consummate hostess whose hospitality toward her consumer "guests" was a key feature of the brand's identity as a purveyor of quality and service. Rudkin, on the other hand, became the Pepperidge Farm "grandmother" whose homemade bread and bakery products promised traditional taste and high nutrition. As with Lewis and Beech, it was a marketing message that emerged over time in association with a brand identity that increasingly centered on the idea, image, and iconography of the old-fashioned.

Each of these promises—Lewis as housewife, Beech as hostess, and Rudkin as grandmother—was, of course, a gendered idea that leveraged the femaleness and femininity of the company leader to imprint its product with a particular emotion, value, and promise for mid-twentieth-century consumers and customers. If "brands are verbs," as one advertising executive has asserted, then Lewis's company eased, Beech's company indulged, and Rudkin's company nurtured.[6] And they did so in distinctly feminine ways. Each of the brands promised quality, but since this claim no longer was a point of distinction for most companies by the middle of the 1900s, all three businesswomen used gender to feminize their delivery of quality and in so doing to distinguish themselves from competitors.

Housewife, hostess, and grandmother were, of course, traditional and even stereotypical roles for women in the mid-twentieth century, but this is why embracing them made them effective marketing strategies. Such gender norms resonated with consumers and customers. This was not the strategy employed by Lewis, Beech, and Rudkin in all areas of their business operations, as the next chapter will show. For, when it came to asserting their value as company leaders, all three women went beyond rejecting normative gender roles and eschewed gender altogether, championing instead versions of themselves focused on their business contributions, skills, and accomplishments. But for marketing, embodying traditional ideas of womanhood was a successful way to convince consumers to invest in their brands—both as products and ideas.

Since Lewis, Beech, and Rudkin all operated their businesses and their marketing strategies from within a gender system that not only provided gendered meanings for their product promises but also created gendered obstacles to their success in male-dominated industries it is worth asking the question: was it really a choice? That is, did they deploy stereotyped images of themselves as housewife, hostess, and grandmother as a brand strategy, or were they cornered into that position by others or by a lack of alternative roles? One interesting factor that suggests it was a little bit of both is that all three companies relied on men to craft their marketing, advertising, and public-relations messages. There is some evidence in the case of Rudkin that the gendered version of her product's promise was pushed by male advertising executives intent on making the most of her potential to sell Pepperidge Farm as purveyor of old-fashioned baked goods— an idea traditionally and historically associated with women's home cooking. Yet it would be a mistake to understand this to mean that Rudkin or Lewis or Beech allowed stereotypical gender ideas to be imposed on them. To the contrary, ample evidence reveals that all three women actively championed the marketing messages of their companies, helping to shape consumer and customer opinion about their products.

The best interpretation of Lewis, Beech, and Rudkin as marketers, therefore, considers both their restriction by and use of gender. It captures both the degree to which mid-twentieth-century female business owners operated with and within stereotyped ideas about women and gender and the extent to which they leveraged such ideas to the advantage of their brands, their companies, and themselves by acting out gendered roles that advanced their products' promises. Thus essentialist ideas about women—the notion that women had intrinsic qualities and desires characteristic of their sex— were a "survival strategy" deployed by Lewis, Beech, and Rudkin in a male-dominated marketplace to benefit their businesses.[7] All three fashioned gendered narratives and even mythologies for themselves that followed and advanced the trajectory of their brand management. Housewife, hostess, and grandmother were marketing strategies rather than or in addition to restrictive roles. It was a complex and even contradictory identity for women at the helm of big businesses in the mid-twentieth century.

Tillie Lewis

Lewis's rise to fame and fortune as the founder of Flotill Products was both a carefully orchestrated marketing outcome and a key publicity trope. Lewis was both the marketer and the marketed in the company's promotions. From the 1940s onward, she figured prominently in promotional materials, but her role in the company's marketing campaign changed over time. Initially, promotions emphasized her role as a woman manager who understood the importance of quality to female consumers. She was central to the quality-focused messaging of the company but not the center of it. By the 1950s, however, with the introduction of the company's new artificially sweetened products for dieters under the label Tasti-Diet, Lewis became the center of the promotions, even gracing the company logo. Her story as a woman who created a diet plan to address her own problems with being overweight—constructed by the company—became the center of the company's marketing message. Paired with this story was Lewis's remarkable rise in the business world, reportedly achieved without the help of family, fortune, or education. The company seized on this message by characterizing her as an embodiment of the American Dream and proof that the country's free enterprise system worked—concepts that must have resonated with Cold War–era consumers. She was, the stories and ads argued, a woman worth emulating. By the 1960s, the company name was changed from Flotill Products to Tillie Lewis Foods, a testament to how embedded Lewis had become in her brand's image. Even as public relations and advertising professionals took over management of the company's marketing promotions, especially after it was purchased by the Ogden Corporation, Tillie Lewis as homemaker—a multimillionaire business executive who, she insisted, was "more interested in being and staying a woman and homemaker than anything else"—remained an enduring message. In the 1970s, when Lewis was celebrated in the pages of *Fortune* and *Cosmopolitan* as a "powerful" and "high-ranking" businesswoman and the company logo was redesigned without her image to align with new promotional goals, Lewis herself held on to the company's "origin" story as the one she wanted recorded for posterity.

To the end, Tillie Lewis Foods was a personal project for Lewis, one in which she was vested professionally, personally, figuratively, and, of course, financially. On the one hand, this did not distinguish Lewis from other, especially male, entrepreneurs, many of whom had long had an "intimate relationship . . . [with] their firms [and] their products" and remained highly involved in all public statements (including marketing messages) made by the company.[8] But the degree of Lewis's success in integrating herself into her brand using gendered ideas and language does set her apart. Tracing change over time in the company's marketing shows the ways in which Flotill Products increasingly relied on Tillie Lewis as the core identity for its brands. Moving from central to center to core in the company's branding between the 1940s and 1960s, Lewis was the magnet the company used to draw consumers to its products. As her company's trademark, she embodied a gendered identity that distinguished her from competitors and also changed over time.

Marketing at Flotill Products during the 1940s focused on quality and leveraged gender in service of that message. A 1948 multipage print promotion, for example, included a large-scale image of Lewis in the company's laboratory, demonstrating the quality of Flotill's canned *pomodoros*. The heading, "Founded and Operated by a Woman . . . for Women" reflected the gendered nature of the appeal. "As a woman," the copy read, "I recognize that other women demand quality above everything else when they buy canned food products." Of course, by this time there was a long history in the United States and elsewhere of women capitalizing on gendered assumptions about their expertise to capture a significant portion of the market for domestic goods and services. This promotional campaign clearly followed that lead, yet it stopped short of casting Lewis as a cook who shared with housewives the day-to-day challenge of putting a quality meal on the table. That marketing message would come later. In 1948, the copy emphasized Lewis's exacting production standards *as a business owner and manager*: "The industrial symphony that, today, is FLOTILL was inspired and is personally directed by a woman. Because a woman fully appreciated the universal feminine demand for the highest standard canned food production possible and insisted that quality—first, last and always—keynote every phase of operation, FLOTILL canned fruits and vegetables lead all other brands as the accepted criterion for quality—in eye-appeal, in taste-appeal, and in consistent uniformity."[9] In keeping with this message, the image of Lewis that accompanied this text did not in any way suggest a domestic setting. While she is demonstrating food in the picture, she does so in a scientific way—a point captured by the scientific beakers, labeled specimen bottles, scales, and other scientific equipment in the background. In stark contrast to the aproned female worker who also appears in the image, Lewis is in a suit—the only photograph of her in a suit in the archive. This emphasizes the manager–employee relationship captured in the shot and underscores Lewis's power and influence as an industrial leader, one with a finely tuned sensibility not for domesticity but for quality. That was the company's main marketing claim; as a company-issued deck of playing cards bragged, Flotill provided quality that was "out of this world."[10]

The company's insignia and logo in the 1940s echoed the emphasis on quality too, only hinting at the importance of gender to its brand. A crowned coat of arms emblazoned with FPI (Flotill Products, Inc.) included an image of wine and *pomodoros* set against contrasting red-and-black backgrounds. The imagery communicated tradition and bounty, while a banner below the coat of arms reminded consumers of the company's core message: "Quality in Quantity." Under that the logo stated, "The House of Flotill," recasting the corporate name "Flotill Products, Inc." into something simultaneously grander and simpler, suggesting a familial estate rather than a company. By using the word "house," the emblem communicated domesticity and family—gendered concepts for sure—but it did not reference Lewis herself as later company emblems would. Can labels followed this approach too, featuring the insignia as well as verdant agricultural scenes with a central but nameless "farm girl" and/or closeups of the fruit, meant to convey visual appeal and quality but omitting Lewis in name and face. Thus "house," "woman," and "feminine" were all central to the company's promotions but not yet in overtly connected ways. The name Tillie Weisberg never appeared on company product labels.

By this time, public outreach at Flotill Products was professionally managed and had a national reach. In 1947, Lewis's husband, Meyer Lewis, who is credited with orchestrating the company's marketing efforts in some sources, had resigned from active involvement in the company's day-to-day affairs.[11] Though he remained a director and would eventually return as a vice president at the company, he was at this time "engaged in the business of growing and selling dates commercially in Coachella, California." Starting that year, Lewis employed a professional public-relations director, Russell F. Bjorn, former manager of the Stockton Chamber of Commerce, who arrived at the company with some twenty-eight years of varied business experience.[12] Under his direction, the company pursued "a complete, well-rounded program of advertising, publicity and merchandising . . . keyed to the modern tempo . . . to make the buying public keenly aware of FLOTILL products and FLOTILL quality."[13] A 1948 stock prospectus for the company indicated that it would prioritize expenditure of the proceeds from stock sales on advertising. "The Company has not heretofore extensively advertised its products but is planning in 1948 to expend at least $300,000 in a nation-wide advertising and magazine advertising campaign to further acquaint consumers with the 'Flotta,' 'Flotill,' 'Stockton' and 'Penthouse' brand-name products," it reported.[14] The result of this sizeable investment—equivalent to nearly $3 million in today's dollars—was a flood of publicity between 1951 and 1952.[15] In newspapers around the country, with headlines ranging from "City Gal Has Fortune in Tomatoes" and "Tillie, Quite a Toiler Becomes Queen of Pear-Shaped Tomatoes" to "Tillie Lewis Builds Big Business through Curiosity, Plus an Idea," articles told the story of how Tillie started and succeeded as the only woman canner. Emphasizing Lewis's leadership of the company, the news articles brought national attention to her skills as an executive as well as her remarkable success as an entrepreneur.

National magazine stories followed in this vein with a sensationalized version of Lewis's biography as a businesswoman and helped to expand consumption of the company's products. Articles in *Time* (1951), *Parade: The Sunday Picture Magazine* (1952), *Everywoman's Woman* (1952), and *Reader's Digest* (1952) told a romanticized story about Lewis's rise from rags to riches. This version omitted attention to details and fact-checking and perpetuated a version of her story that failed to acknowledge her experience and connections in the wholesale food industry or difficulties in securing financing, preferring instead a romanticized, even mythic, presentation of Lewis's history. Yet it achieved what the company aimed to achieve. Production and sales went up, and Lewis's story was so well known that in 1952 she was chosen as the "Outstanding Woman of the Year in the Field of Business" by an annual poll of Women Editors of the Associated Press.[16]

The following year, Flotill Products introduced a new product line and new promotions staff, which together fundamentally shifted the company's marketing. The novel product, diet canned fruit sold under the name "Tasti-Diet," was the outcome of years of research by Clair Weast and his wife, Elsie Orr Weast. Clair Weast was a chemist by training and had been employed at Flotill for years in a variety of capacities, while Elsie Weast was a "stay-at-home mother with a master's degree in nutrition from University of California at Berkeley."[17] Through late-night experimentation, the Weasts had perfected a process for the "use of saccharine as a packing medium in the processing of fresh fruit." Lewis was eager to use it and signed an agreement with Clair Weast in June 1947 agreeing to pay as royalty 10 cents per case of fruit sold.[18] In 1951, the company also purchased Ditex Foods, an

Illinois corporation also "engaged . . . in the distribution of dietary food products."[19] This purchase augmented Flotill's resources as a purveyor of diet foods, adding diet dressing, gelatin, puddings, and dessert toppings to the Tasti-Diet brand.[20] By 1953, Flotill had set up Tasti-Diet Foods, Inc., as a wholly owned subsidiary and was ready to launch its diet products nationally.[21] In preparation, Lewis hired a new vice president to serve as the chief financial, advertising, and public-relations (PR) officer.

Lewis's new PR officer presided over a large-scale, high-profile, and expensive campaign in keeping with his history of creating such public-relations strategies for clients. Carl Byoir, who since 1930 had served as president of his own New York City public-relations firm, Carl Byoir & Associates, one of the largest and most successful PR firms in United States history, is widely lauded as a pioneer in the public-relations field. Referred to even today as "the Byoir Way," his techniques included "permanently installing staff executives in client headquarters offices" and requiring extensive prior newsroom experience for newly hired staff. His early experience in the field came from a stint working at the Hearst newspapers and with the Committee on Public Information wherein he contributed to the U.S. government's propaganda campaign during World War I. Cuban dictator Gerardo Machado, who hired him to promote U.S. tourism in Cuba, was his first client. Thereafter, his firm was employed by President Franklin Roosevelt's campaign to fight infantile paralysis and large-scale businesses such as the Great Atlantic & Pacific Tea Company, which hired him to help defeat a bill in Congress that chain stores saw as destructive to their interests. That Lewis successfully attracted a public-relations professional of Byoir's stature highlights her foresight, her familiarity with the public-relations field, and her company's prominence, since it must have been the option to purchase 120,000 shares of her company (at par value of $1 per share with a purchase price estimated at $4 per share) that enticed him to sign a five-year contract with her rather than the $500 per month she agreed to pay him in compensation.[22] The investment paid off for all parties. At the end of 1953, Lewis reported, "Tasti-Diet Foods, Inc. made a determined effort in 1953 to improve its dietetic food business and . . . increased considerably its advertising and sales promotion expenses [which] were no doubt substantially responsible for the increase of $3,292,246 in sales . . . or from $788,022.00 in 1952 to $4,080,268.00 in 1953."[23] It was success that could be measured another way too—brand recognition by consumers. A 1954 survey of customers administered by a professional research firm revealed that 19 percent of surveyed users of diet products identified Tasti-Diet as the best-known brand. All other brands combined achieved only 10 percent of consumers' vote as the best-known brand. This successful market penetration propelled the reported sales increases and secured the financial stability of the company at a time when industrywide inventory write-downs continued to cut into company profits.[24] Achieving this required a carefully constructed and new marketing strategy.

In marketing Tasti-Diet to American consumers, Flotill had several challenges. First, it faced considerable competition. In 1953, *Time* magazine reported that "more than 80 canners now turn out some 60 different low-calorie foods, ranging from applesauce and peanut butter to French dressing and puddings."[25] Competitors included food-processing giants Dole and Libby, who already had their own lines of diet fruits, so the company had to differentiate its products from competitors. One distinguishing feature of Tasti-Diet that was both an opportunity and a challenge was that it was "the first brand on the U.S. market with a full line of products."[26] This enabled the brand to market a diet menu and not just a diet product, but it also meant that it needed to convince consumers that adopting an entire regime of diet products was necessary. Thus, marketing Tasti-Diet involved not just market expansion but market creation. As historian Carolyn Thomas argues, what Lewis's diet-food promotional campaign achieved was to create "a set of meanings around the new artificially sweetened products." She was among the first to "tell compelling stories about what kind of people used such products, how these products could be combined with other foods to make meals, and, perhaps most importantly, how the use of these products was a fundamentally positive—even required—practice for women attempting 'healthy' living in the modern age . . . [In so doing she] removed the taint from saccharin and cyclamates and created a profitable dynasty."[27] Along with female journalists and Jean Nidetch, who founded Weight Watchers ten years later, Lewis created the diet consumer.

The campaign rolled out under Carl Byoir's leadership situated Lewis and Tasti-Diet as an innovation worthy of a high profile. One initiative, for example, was "Operation Waistline," strategically rolled out by California representative LeRoy Johnson, whose district encompassed Flotill Product's manufacturing plants in Stockton and Modesto. In a "Commendation to Congress" dated 13 July 1955, Johnson announced the Tasti-Diet line of products, recommended it to his fellow congressmen, distributed free samples, and captured photos of servicemen holding Tasti-Diet products. The message was clear: Tasti-Diet was for everyone.[28] But in spite of such high-profile stunts, the key to Lewis's Tasti-Diet campaign were the testimonials she used to personalize her brand and earn the trust of what was clearly her most important target audience: American housewives.

This new promotional campaign for Tasti-Diet made gender and Lewis herself central to the brand to appeal to housewife consumers. But it was not as a successful businesswoman that she appeared in Tasti-Diet promotions. Lewis was recast as an "everywoman"—a housewife just like "you" struggling to put a good meal on the table and keep her waistline trim. Because it was not advantageous for this marketing strategy to emphasize Lewis as the architect of her company's success, the new campaign did not feature Lewis as conductor of an "industrial symphony" as the 1948 promotion had but downplayed her role as businesswoman. Tillie Lewis never appeared in a suit again in promotional pieces. Instead she wore feminine dresses with soft necklines that showed off what became her signature triple-strand of pearls—an explicit rejection of what one 1951 newspaper article called "the starched female business executive" that Lewis herself associated with masculinity.[29] And instead of focusing on her business principles, such as insisting on high quality, the 1950s promotions emphasized her fictionalized experience as a woman struggling with obesity herself whose products helped her to lose weight.

Lewis's invented identity as a dieting housewife made her the icon of the new Tasti-Diet brand. There is no evidence that obesity was a problem for Lewis, and in fact, in one media interview she let slip that she managed her own weight by eating in moderation (rather than by eating diet foods). But the Weasts, the inventors of the Tasti-Diet formula, reported that they themselves had struggled with a weight problem and that this had motivated them to find a recipe for canned fruit using artificial sweetener. It's plausible, therefore, that the weight loss story was adapted from their own, but whatever its origin, Lewis used it with the Weasts' blessing and proceeded to weave a fictional biography of her own that was designed to communicate empathy and engender sales.[30] Even the logo underscored the degree to which Lewis and her origin story were at the center of the brand identity now. Whereas her name had not appeared at all on labels previously, "Tillie Lewis" was now emblazoned on each can or bottle produced as part of the brand. As one label for artificially sweetened chocolate-flavored pudding shows, the brand's logo put Tillie Lewis's name and image at the center of the Tasti-Diet name—literally inserting a rendering of her face between "Tasti" and "Diet." By 1966, Tasti-Diet and Tillie Lewis had become so embedded that the brand was renamed Tillie Lewis Tasti-Diet and the company itself changed names from Flotill Products, Inc., to Tillie Lewis Foods.[31]

This stylized image of Lewis with a tray of Tasti-Diet products illustrates the domestic role she played in the company's branding as "just a housewife" to whom consumers could relate. San Joaquin County Historical Society, Lodi, California.

The creation of Tillie Lewis as an "everywoman" whom consumers could relate to was a strategic decision and not just conformity to feminine stereotype, and this is illustrated by the company's multipronged approach to brand management. Starting with the marketing campaign to promote Tasti-Diet, the company channeled its original focus on scientifically derived quality and industrial efficiency—once associated with its management by a woman—into a strategy aligning product development with medical research. This messaging targeted medical practitioners as influencers who were in a position to promote Tasti-Diet products to patients as part of a weight-loss program. Highlighting an endorsement by the American Medical Association's Council on Foods and Nutrition, the company placed assertive advertising and validating articles in scientific and medical journals. Promotions included articles such as the one published in the *Bulletin of* the *Biological Science Foundation, Ltd.* in February 1955 titled "A New Approach to Obesity Management," which focused on Tasti-Diet in twelve of its nineteen paragraphs. Full-page advertisements such as the one published in the *Journal of the American Medical Association* in February 1955 offered a "Detailed Nutrient Evaluation for the Physician" as well as "A Simple-to-Follow Plan for the Patient." The centerpiece of the promotion was a direct-mail campaign. The kits mailed to doctors included copies of the 21 Day Menu Plan, which included use of the brand's products and convenient handouts for patients: charts showing "What You Should Weigh" based on height and size of frame and "Diet Diaries" for recording calories consumed at each meal for twenty-one days with "The Tillie Lewis Easy Calorie Counter" on the reverse side showing the calorie count of common foods. Doctors could mail a provided postcard to receive copies of the "Tasti-Diet Menu Plan Booklet" for their patients free of charge.[32]

Retailers, the company's key customer base, were told that these appeals to medical practitioners practically "presold" Tasti-Diet, assuring them that consumers would be driven to their shelves to buy the product. One four-page color brochure for customers claimed, "We are presenting the Tillie Lewis Tasti-Diet low-calorie dietetic foods, their superb quality and their advantages to every doctor, nurse, and dietician in your trade area." It went on, "Consider the Market! Medical authorities estimate that more than thirty million Americans must diet because of overweight, diabetes, etc. Their diets are prescribed by their physicians and looked after by their nurses and dieticians. That is why Tasti-Diet Dietetic Foods are so intensively advertised to these professions." Inside, the brochure featured images of *Modern Medicine, Postgraduate Medicine, New York State Journal of Medicine*, the *Illinois Medical Journal, Journal of Medical Economics*, the *Journal of the American Osteopathic Association*, the *American Heart Journal, California Medicine and Clinical Endocrinology and Metabolism*, the *American Journal of Nursing, Hospital Progress*, the *Journal of Obstetrics and Gynecology*, and even the *Journal of Pediatrics*—all professional medical journals in which the company was promoting the product. Tasti-Diet products were "the first real advance in food processing in decades," the brochure claimed, "up to 75% lower in calories," but still had the "look, taste, and feel . . . of ordinary foods of the highest quality."[33] One pop-up brochure for Tasti-Diet Low Calorie Sparkling Beverages appealed to store owners with the claim "Tasti-Diet = High Profits . . . Fast Turnover for You," emphasizing the advantages of the advertising investments made by the company to both healthcare professionals and consumers themselves.[34]

Tasti-Diet's direct-to-consumer appeal focused on Lewis herself, humanizing the brand by creating the impression that buying the label was a person-to-person transaction with a woman—albeit a fictionalized one—with whom other female dieters could relate.[35] In fact, ads even intimated that dieting using Tasti-Diet products could remain a secret—"only your figure will know" assured one ad—as if Lewis was a trusted friend that consumers could count on.[36] The campaign involved newspaper, magazine, radio, and television advertising focused on the company-constructed origin story for the brand, rooted in a personal doctor visit by Lewis to discuss her own weight problem:

> [She] appeared at her doctor's office with a familiar complaint. She was overweight. The doctor prescribed a diet. "It wasn't too bad at first," Mrs. Lewis reported afterward, "but how I yearned for those rich puddings I loved . . . and tasty salad dressings . . . all the things I couldn't have. How I hated that hungry empty feeling when I left the table." What happened to her followed a pattern all too familiar to those who have tried to lose weight. "First thing I knew," she confesses, "I was backsliding—cheating on my diet. But that didn't fool the scales." Her doctor's reaction when he found she wasn't losing weight was unexpected. "It happens all the time," he said. "Why don't you do something about it." Mrs. Lewis was startled. "What could I do?" "Why don't you, with your knowledge of food, and your research laboratories, do something about developing more low-calorie foods that people will like to eat." Tillie Lewis knew it had been tried, but only on a small scale. She went back to the plant and called a conference of her food technologists. Take the calorie out of vital foods? Well, it could be done, perhaps, but it would take time and be expensive, they told her. Yet when they had completed the job, what had seemed like a personal hobby of the proprietor suddenly became a major part of the Flotill enterprise.[37]

The story appeared in local newspapers all over the country as part of Tillie Lewis's 'whistle stop tour' of the nation.[38] Hitting medium-size and small cities like St. Louis, Missouri, and Armadillo, Texas, as well as New York City, Lewis did blitz publicity tours involving five days of radio and newspaper interviews, photo opportunities (which included the mayor and governor at the St. Louis stop, boxing heavyweight Rocky Marciano, and can-can dancer Pat Turner in New York), visits to hospitals, and, in St. Louis, even a visit to the St. Louis Cardinals' dugout. These visits were coordinated with extensive newspaper coverage during the same period or in the week following. Special promotions with local retailers paralleled the same schedule. The approach was the same in each city she visited.

The direct-to-consumer marketing campaign emphasized a personal relationship between Lewis and her customers. Many of the articles that appeared in the papers were attributed to Lewis as if authored directly by her. The columns all appeared alongside a photo of Lewis with the caption "Most famous woman in foods who has spent more than 10 years in intensive research in the field of sweetened low calorie dietetic foods," emphasizing diet expertise as well as personal experience.[39] But in the content of the articles, it was Lewis's relatability that was the focus. One *Chicago American* article described her as "a trim, slim, chic little woman with warm brown eyes and a lovely smile [who] didn't look like a captain of industry nor a woman who had ever needed a diet" but was both. It was an approach that helped sell the campaign headlines, which included "Folks Are So Very Human," "Lose Pounds Instead of Patience," and "Regain Your Figure This Painless Way," all of which relied on the idea that someone who had tried and failed herself at dieting had invented a new way to diet that was possible to sustain.[40]

The company counted on this messaging to appeal to America's white, middle-class urban women—the segment of the market its campaign clearly targeted. Tillie Lewis's carefully etched image—reddish, gently wavy hair and makeup-covered face—erased any reminder of her racial and original class identity as the daughter of a poor Jewish immigrant. Instead, it positioned Lewis as contemporary to a cast of female characters such as Betty Crocker created by American food companies to sell women food. "Known in the business world as 'live trademarks,'" historian Laura Shapiro argues, "these figures were designed to project specific, carefully researched characteristics to women shopping for their households."[41] Sometimes real but more often fictionalized, these corporate characters were, as a 1957 business publication explained, "ideally . . . wom[en], between the ages of 32 and 40, attractive, but not competitively so, mature but youthful-looking, competent yet warm, understanding but not sentimental, interested in the consumer but not involved with her."[42] And, according to Shapiro, Americans didn't always know whether or not the women whose advice they followed for recipes and product purchases were real or not. Thus, the Tillie Lewis female consumers got to know through company promotions—part real, part fiction—was familiar to white middle-class Americans and reflected a popular food industry strategy that relied on spokeswomen to market products.

That this was a strategic construction of Tillie Lewis leveraged to benefit the brand rather than a true-to-life portrayal is underscored by the very different coverage she received in *Fortune* in January 1966 announcing the purchase of Tillie Lewis Foods, Inc., by the Ogden Corporation. Focused on Lewis's management skills, that article eschewed the fabricated portrayal of her as the friendly and familiar "everywoman." Appearing in the "Businessmen in the News" section of the magazine, it reported that Ogden's president, Ralph Ablon, "plans no changes in the Tillie Lewis management" and assured readers of *Fortune*—shareholders, future investors, and business customers among them—that the woman at the helm was a calculating businesswoman whom they could trust to deliver profitable returns. Her photograph, the most serious one in any print format, said it all: she was not smiling and looked straight into the camera with an unwavering gaze. "Tillie Lewis," the magazine reported, "a shrewd and imaginative businesswoman, founded her company thirty years ago and nursed it to prosperity." With the exception of the gendered reference to Lewis "nurs[ing]" the company to its success, the portrayal characterized her in a gender-neutral way as a reliable and indeed desirable company leader with qualities that served businesses well. Thus, no matter the context, Lewis presented herself in the most advantageous way for her company. This time she purposely differentiated herself from the smiling face that shone out from product labels and magazine stories and instead presented herself as the kind of female entrepreneur who belonged in "Businessmen in the News," where she was surrounded by serious-looking men in suits being presented by *Fortune* as captains of industry.[43]

Elsewhere during the 1960s, however, Lewis perpetuated the carefully constructed image of her that had been designed to win over Tillie Lewis Foods customers rather than Ogden shareholders. A good example of the perpetuation of this public-relations trajectory is Lewis's speech to the Pilot Club in New York City in January 1968. A twenty-one-page typed, double-spaced speech titled "How to Get to the Top and Stay There," the speech ironically included the following paragraph in the middle: "However, in spite of all the 'action,' I am more interested in being and staying a woman and homemaker than anything else. This instinct dovetails nicely with my career because I've been in the food business all my life. In many ways, my problems in business have paralleled my problems as a homemaker and vice versa. In the food business, one must anticipate what masses of people are going to want to eat, and how much of each kind of vegetable, fruit or meat or dressing, the same as a homemaker does." In the middle of a speech that berated women for not seizing the opportunity to climb to the top, Lewis let listeners know that her heart was actually in the home—where "her problems as a homemaker" had paralleled "her problems in business." Casting herself as a homemaker positioned Lewis as a woman other homemakers could trust. It was a role for Lewis calculated to have an impact in the grocery aisle, where female consumers (who made the lion's share of food purchases) would have to decide which canned fruit and vegetable products to purchase from shelves filled with competing brands. The hope was that Lewis's friendly face and companionate profile would sway them to choose her brand.

Of course, this characterization of Lewis as a "homemaker" bore little resemblance to reality. With a seat on the board of directors of the Ogden Corporation and full-time management responsibilities for running a multimillion-dollar company that employed thousands, Lewis hardly had time to focus on making a home. And as a childless married woman—as chapter 1 outlined—her life bore little resemblance to that of the average American housewife with whom she tried to relate. Perhaps her statement that "I am more interested in being and staying a woman and homemaker than anything else" was a lament. After all, by 1968 when she delivered this speech, she had been divorced from Louis Weisberg; had been remarried to Meyer Lewis for twenty years, during which they lived apart for some time (as he pursued another business venture); and had become increasingly occupied with running her growing company. Yet while Lewis may not have spent much time engaged in typical mid-twentieth-century homemaking activities, she did craft a family life for herself that centered on those individuals most important to her. In one account, she is reportedly quoted as saying "I'm my husband's wife [at home]," representing herself as an adoring spouse who never missed a nightly phone call when she was traveling and away from her husband. And while she was childless, her life was not devoid of children or play. Gatherings at her Palm Springs home often included her nephews and their families and featured games of ping-pong, cards, and pool—the first two Lewis participated in herself—as well as informal meals that she served herself on the outdoor patio, all with young children underfoot. Lewis was also a lavish entertainer who appreciated fine furniture, art, and the accoutrements of success as befitted a company founder and president. According to one source, she decorated both of her homes (Palm Springs and Stockton) herself—enacting a form of elite mid-twentieth-century domesticity. Thus, when Lewis *did* focus on her family (and friends), she simultaneously embodied traditional gender roles as wife and hostess and her professional role as successful company executive. She crafted a meaningful home life for herself, but it was not one that would have been familiar to the average American housewife to whom her marketing materials appealed.[44]

By the time Lewis made her speech to the Pilot Club, professional agencies were stewarding the Tillie Lewis brand. Public-relations support from Hill and Knowlton, the Ogden Corporation's PR firm, as well as advertising by the Carson-Roberts Advertising Agency in Los Angeles (later Ogilvy-Mathers), a cutting-edge ad organization with clients that then included Mattel Toys, Max Factor, and Baskin-Robbins, helped Lewis manage her carefully constructed commercial image and underscores the degree to which hers was a manufactured image designed to help her succeed in business. And it paid off. Among the outcomes of the Pilot Club event were nationally syndicated radio and television interviews and newspaper features as well as coverage in "The Fast Gourmet," the regular column by famed food writer Poppy Cannon.[45] Arguably, this was the top for any executive in the food business.

Inclusion in two features on powerful women published in national magazines in the 1970s returned to an emphasis on Lewis's success as a self-made businesswoman. In *Fortune*'s April 1973 feature on "The Ten Highest-Ranking Women in Business," Lewis discussed the importance of being "inspired" to succeed. *Cosmopolitan*'s April 1975 article on "36 Women With Real Power Who Can Help You" identified "self-discipline" as Lewis's "secret of success" for independent businesswomen. Riding the tide of the women's movement, both publications avoided the company's characterizations of Lewis as a woman with modest hopes and altruistic values that housewives could relate to and instead characterized her as "daring," "perseveran[t]," and "a millionairess."[46]

In spite of new developments such as this, however, Lewis seemed committed to continuing the same core marketing messages and protecting the public image of her that had been so carefully crafted by the company to sell her products in the 1950s. A great example of this can be found in her corrections to Caroline Bird's book, *Enterprising Women* (1976 pub., correspondence re proofs 1974), in which Tillie Lewis was featured. In handwritten corrections to the proofs, Lewis crossed out the following: "As an independent canner, Tillie had to find some way to establish consumer recognition of her brand name. She early discovered that she could get publicity attention because she was a woman in a man's business, and she made the most of this advantage." In the sentence "She also kept a sharp lookout for specialty products the big canners were not offering," Lewis crossed out "the big canners were not offering." She also crossed out "She was, for instance, one of the first canners to spot the market for low calorie." She replaced it with "Having an obesity problem herself she produced the first artificially sweetened canned fruit to take the place of the Diabetic water pack for low calorie, low sugar and low sodium dieters." Interestingly, the sections that Lewis omitted from Bird's copy were the ones that characterized her as a savvy businesswoman who "had to find a way to establish consumer recognition," "made the most of [her ability to] . . . get publicity . . . [as] a woman in a man's world," looked for market niches that "big canners were not offering," and "[spotted] the market for low calorie" foods. Instead, she preferred that the manufactured image of herself be recorded in business history: a woman with an obesity problem who was the first to produce artificially sweetened canned fruit for dieters. Not only did this emphasize the company's longtime brand identity, but it also kept obscured the behind-the-scenes strategies that had made her company successful. In addition, she did not correct the statement that she borrowed $100,000 from the Banco di Napoli to buy out Florindo Del Gaizo, her investor and partner in 1937, although, as already mentioned in chapter 1, archived tax records indicate that that loan was a much more modest $10,000 loan. Lewis also did not object to Bird's description of her as "one of the few authentic Cinderellas of American industry" because she succeeded on her own. There was little mention of the family help and connections that had forged her entrepreneurial pathway per chapter 1. She seemed to prefer a touch of magical realism in how she was portrayed—as an overweight woman whose seemingly overnight success was born of an individual desire to make dieting delicious rather than as an entrepreneur whose dogged determination and strategic decisions built a successful brand.

Interestingly, after Tillie Lewis died in May 1977, she no longer had a conspicuous presence in the branding for the company's products. In a promotion dated 1978, retailers were urged to participate in a promotion between Tasti-Diet canned fruit and Sugar Free 7UP—"Two great names in dieting." Joint display and feature opportunities as well as a two-month coupon promotion promised retailers access to the "45 Million New Potential Tasti-Diet users," since that was the number of consumers in the diet drink category. This was a comarketing promotion between two consumer goods giants—the Ogden Corporation and Philip Morris, which purchased 7UP that same year. It promised retailers that "Bigger Advertising, Bigger Promotions [and] More Merchandising" would be the focus of the Tasti-Diet brand in 1978. And although the name Tillie Lewis still appeared in conjunction with the brand name Tasti-Diet, the image of Tillie Lewis that had graced the company's logo since the 1950s was conspicuously absent. Unlike some other popular brands, she did not live on as a disembodied icon for the company and its products. She may have been mythologized and parts of her story may have been constructed and shaped to help package and market the brand to the best effect, but unlike Betty Crocker, Tillie Lewis was a real woman whose real-life presence had been integral to the brand's promotions. Once she ceased being an integral part of the company, she ceased being an integral part of the brand's iconography.[47]

Olive Ann Beech

Over the course of her company's history, Olive Ann Beech moved from explicit to more subtle claims about gender in the company's marketing. Beginning with a focus on female pilots, product claims overtly associated ease of use with gender, and this was a contribution that Beech was proud to have made. But over time, as the company and its products became associated with an almost exclusively male consumer base and a sales culture that overtly celebrated heterosexual masculinity, it became more advantageous for gender to inform more subtle messages about product luxury. Beech herself came to embody the role of hostess, a gender performance through which she leveraged femininity to sell the brand. Yet she never became solely a symbol for the brand, consistently contributing to innovations including financing and training programs for consumers that strengthened brand loyalty and customer longevity. For Beech, gender was a useful tool but not the only one she deployed to market the company.

Some of the earliest promotions for Beech Aircraft put women and gender front and center to emphasize their planes' effortless operation. In its celebration of the winners of the 1936 Bendix Trophy, for example, the company's copy read:

> You Bet We're Proud. Louise Thaden and Blanche Noyes—plus the efficiency of a stock model Beechcraft—carried off the 1936 Bendix honors. It was a spectacular victory for the ladies—and for Beechcraft. . . . Officially the Bendix winners achieved four victories:

1. Won first place in the 1936 Bendix Trophy Race.
2. The first time this trophy has been won with a stock model airplane (C17R Beechcraft).
3. First women ever to win the Bendix Trophy.
4. Set a new transcontinental east-west record for women.

Only Beechcraft's inherent stability, ease of handling and high speed performance made such records possible—and Beechcraft is the only airplane that offers *low flying cost, ease of handling, high cruising speed* and an *extra margin of stability* in its regular production stock models.[48]

Associating the plane's "ease of handling" with women pilots had been Olive Ann Beech's idea. According to an article in *Businessweek*, she had "sold her husband on the idea that a woman should fly the Beech entry in the Bendix air races" by arguing that "this would demonstrate that Beech planes could be flown without brute strength."[49] The company's promotion credited her as the officer "in charge of [the] women's division of the company who sponsored the entry." No other extant document refers to a "women's division," suggesting that this organizational structure was invented to explain the company's novel reliance on female pilots. It was an idea that the company stuck with in at least one more promotional piece featuring the headline "Beechcraft Is Easy to Fly" followed by quotes and photos from four women pilots, all emphasizing that Beech planes were "the easiest plane to fly."[50] The strategy worked because it inherently argued that if women could fly Beech aircraft, then anyone could.

These early Beech Aircraft advertisements both subverted and reinforced common gender norms. Branding its planes as aircraft for the common man or woman, these ads ironically distanced the company from the popular association between masculinity, strength, and daring and the world of piloting that Walter H. Beech had been a celebrated part of and instead introduced the idea that flying was something anyone could do in a Beechcraft. Along with its ease-of-handling claims, the company also emphasized "dependability," "sturdiness," "unusual safety," the ability to navigate difficult conditions, "slow landing speeds," and "short take-off runs."[51] Such distinctive features were achieved through the good work of the company's excellent manufacturing staff, featured in close-up "on the job" photos with the copy: "Noting the intense interest expressed in faces and attitude of these men, is it any wonder that Beechcraft airplanes are of uniform excellence in construction and, hence, in performance?"[52] Juxtaposing the concentration of male workers who assembled the planes with the adventuresome spirit of the female pilots who flew them subverted some 1930s norms while reinforcing others. "Attentive" and "strong," the machinists made possible the arrival of the "girls," "feeling fresh" and "amazed"; it was terminology that celebrated gender difference. On the other hand, Olive Ann Beech and Beech Aircraft remained longtime supporters of this first generation of female pilots who were eager to push their way into the formerly all-male world of flight. As contemporary Amelia Earhart put it, they wanted "a chance to play the game as men play it, by rules established for participants as flyers, not as women."[53] Thus, although the company capitalized on gendered notions of the relative strength of men and weakness of women, it simultaneously helped to make the "game" of flight accessible to women.[54]

By the 1940s, Beech Aircraft had solidified its brand around efficiency and expert design and left gender behind. A one-page ad promised business and pleasure fliers that Beechcraft was "the modern 'cutter'": it "cuts flying time," "cuts flying cost," and "cuts landing space." Along with safety and speed, it was a "highly efficient" airplane.[55] Its design "features" and "refinements" growing out of "a score of years of experience" were "steps toward perfection."[56] Subsequent marketing publications followed this trend. In 1945, a marketing publication titled "The Grizzly" focused on the design features of a new attack airplane produced by Beech for the military (the XA38), the single most important customer for the company during that period. By the 1950s, the company was again pursuing pilots who flew for business and pleasure, and in 1954 it published a brochure for the Super 18 with close-up images of the interior and exterior of the plane.[57] As print marketing increasingly focused on the planes themselves, gender was no longer relevant in product brochures. The female pilots who had been prominently featured in the company's earliest brochures remained important to Olive Ann Beech and to the company in general, as shown by the "Beechcraft Parade of Champions" documenting the many female pilots flying Beech planes who had won air races and awards, including the O. A. Beech Trophy awarded for "fastest speed in [the] annual Skylady Derby."[58] But the company shifted its marketing brochures away from pilots and their testimonials and to the features of the planes themselves, reasoning, it seems, that the quality of a Beech plane would make the sale.

Although pilots were not featured in brochures any longer, the company went to great lengths to make them feel important and appreciated, and Olive Ann Beech was key to these efforts. As the quintessential hostess, Beech's femininity was a key component of this role, deployed to great effect in her campaign to "keep the customers happy," which she saw as her main job at the company.[59] In an article for the *National Aeronautic Association's Magazine,* visitor reception at the company was described with great fanfare and a focus on the feminine touches she insisted on for her visitors: "Flags representing customers from around the world who are visiting the company are . . . daily displayed, denoting her interest in making visitors feel at home. Guests are greeted by seasonal flowers neatly arranged in massive wooden boxes that flank the doorways—an expression of her deep appreciation for beauty. A pleasant and courteous security officer quickly completes registration and phones for a tour guide—an indication that all visitors to her company are important. . . . [In her office] she pours tea with an elegance that puts visitors at ease."[60] The emphasis on Beech's elegance, graciousness, and hospitality was an oft-repeated feature of articles documenting her role at the company. One reason was that she was so memorable. As one account by a visitor captured, "Upon first meeting her, I was a bit confused. She was wearing a blue-green silk dress, decorated with a gold biplane pin, as if she would soon be off to pour at a ladies tea. I could not mentally picture her as a tough-minded executive making hard decisions." Of course, this impression had more to do with gendered expectations about what "tough-minded executives" looked like during the second half of the twentieth century than it did with the unique self-presentation of Beech herself. And yet, impromptu invitations to lunch, as this visitor had been issued, hosted in Beech's elegant personal dining room, *were* meant to have an effect: to make visitors feel like they were the personal guests of Olive Ann Beech.

Beech herself went to great lengths to achieve her goal of hospitably and memorably entertaining company guests. Invitations to her personal office suite were central to these efforts. Although she casually explained the opulence of her office suite and the fanfare with which she entertained in it with the flippant remark, "If you spend half your life in your office, why not make it pleasant," Beech clearly took great pleasure in its impact on visitors and entertained in it with great flourish. When she invited guests to lunch with her, they dined in her personal dining room and received a twenty-page souvenir booklet with center pages devoted to the names and identities of those in attendance and the day's menu.[61] Such finely tuned attention to detail no doubt reflected Beech's own exacting standards, which the press made much of, but it was also a testament to the kinds of customers she entertained. "Among the customers who flew Beech airplanes," the *Saturday Evening Post* reported in 1959, "were Gene Autry, Winthrop Rockefeller,

King Hussein of Jordan, and Scott Crossfield, the first man scheduled to journey into space."[62] These were men accustomed to being treated as royalty, and so she obliged, entertaining lavishly in her personal office suite.

Intense interest in the famously blue-and-white private reception area, office, and dining room where Olive Ann entertained visitors—and her eagerness to share them—led to the creation of a thirty-five-page booklet devoted to its design and contents that celebrated gender difference in the executive suite. With a simple front cover graced with an image of the entry to her office and her signature, the booklet began, "For you who have expressed an interest, this booklet describes the appointments and décor of the private business suite and dining room of Mrs. O. A. Beech, President of Beech Aircraft Corporation." A combination of full-page photographs of each room and close-up etchings of every piece of furniture and special decoration in them, the pamphlet celebrated her taste, comportment, and status. Describing the Louis XVI style as "a meeting of quiet elegance and formality . . . interpreted for the affairs of business through selective use of the functional . . . highlighted with a gracious atmosphere of charm and cordiality," it captured Beech's universal achievement as an executive even as it highlighted a distinctly feminine expression of that success. This was one implicit message of the pamphlet: an executive suite in most mid-twentieth-century minds was a masculine space, but as Beech's office décor revealed, it could be a feminine space too.[63]

Olive Ann Beech emphasized her femininity even as she rejected prescribed roles for women. She stated in an interview for *Midwest Industry* magazine in 1969, "The only reason women don't go on in a business is that they are afraid of the future or they are afraid they will lose their femininity. There's no fear in my makeup and I haven't given up my femininity."[64] Wielding that femininity in her "homelike" private office suite, Beech dispensed company hospitality with a flourish that stuck in the minds of her customers as clearly gendered.[65] And she did this all the while parading the achievements of the company she helped to build with much bravado—a display of confidence characteristically masculinist. For Beech, the stereotypical roles of feminine hostess and unfeminine self-promoter not only coexisted but were inextricably intertwined. On the shelves of custom-designed cabinetry in her remarkable and feminine inner sanctum, she displayed models depicting the company's success and history, and in her private dining room she poured tea for guests at a custom-made walnut dining table inlaid with 24-carat-gold replicas of the twenty-two airplanes produced by the company up to that time. Olive Ann Beech was no "shrinking

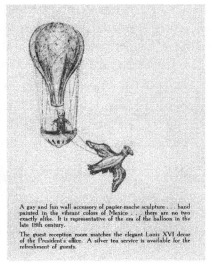

A gay and fun wall accessory of papier-mache sculpture . . . hand painted in the vibrant colors of Mexico . . . there are no two exactly alike. It is representative of the era of the balloon in the late 18th century.

The guest reception room matches the elegant Louis XVI decor of the President's office. A silver tea service is available for the refreshment of guests.

The thirty-five-page booklet Beech produced about her private executive suite emphasized the role she played as a hostess for company "guests." Wichita State University Libraries, Special Collections and University Archives.

violet," but neither was she "the brash, deep-voiced, masculine stereotype so often depicted in novels and movies" about successful women.[66] She was by design a combination of qualities perfectly pitched to "keep customers happy": she made them feel welcomed, important, and appreciated, as only an excellent hostess or host can achieve, while she simultaneously displayed her prowess as the leader "directing the course" of the successful company from which they made their purchases.[67] On the one hand, Beech famously eschewed being called a "female executive," but on the other hand she brazenly reminded everyone (and herself) that she was; it was a self-expression with both personal and strategic significance in the company's promotions, as the next chapter details.

To some degree, Beech's function as company hostess was a role crafted for marketing purposes that did not necessarily conform with her life outside Beech Aircraft. But unlike Lewis's image, it was not a fictional persona. Beech was, in fact, widely known as both extremely feminine and generous and as having impeccable taste and standards. She invested in fine things—jewelry, art, and clothes, for example—both for herself and others. But she was not a lavish entertainer like Lewis. It appears she preferred to host guests at the Wichita Country Club, where she was both a member and frequent diner. And when she did entertain at home, according to one account, her signature dish was resin-baked potatoes, which was an involved and even dangerous cooking process done in the backyard. This tells us both about her penchant for casual dinners at home as well as her sense of adventure and love of the outdoors. She regularly retreated to a modest Colorado log cabin adjacent to Rocky Mountain National Park named the Hide-Away, where she enjoyed the same casual, outdoor style of living. It was a remote location to which only a small number of close friends were invited. The name of the family cabin aptly captured that in her personal life, Beech's preference was for more private and casual endeavors. A well-developed sense of adventure also characterized Beech, and this, of course, took her away from home and hosting. The most striking example was her 1964 six-week tour of Europe, the Holy Land, and the Near East with friend Moya Lear (the wife of her competitor Bill Lear who was *not* her friend), which included a visit to the Great Sphinx and an Egyptian pyramid. One photograph commemorating the trip shows Beech sitting on a camel with both attractions in the background.[68] Thus in her private life, Olive Anne Beech was anything but the demure tea party hostess company records might have us imagine. She played the part expertly, but it was a constructed role that reflected the interests of the company rather than her own personal proclivities. And it was a gendered role that also reflected the expectations of the many male customers to whom she catered and for whom hostess was a more familiar (and perhaps comfortable) female role than executive.

That Beech knew her customers and was prepared to leverage gender in her brand management to reach them is also reflected in a 1955 ad that targeted executive wives. This was an era when the job of corporate executive or manager was termed "the two-person single career" by sociologist William H. Whyte because of the essential role that wives played in the career success of their businessmen husbands, both "provid[ing] unpaid labor and cultivat[ing] social networks crucial to promotions."[69] In keeping with this understanding of the executive wife as influencer, Beech Aircraft published an ad promising her benefits if she convinced her husband to rely on a Beechcraft for his business travel. It appeared with an image featuring a suited male traveler looking back at a well-dressed woman reclining on a comfortable-looking seat in an airplane cabin. The caption read, "When your husband travels in a roomy Super 18, think how little it would cost him to take you along occasionally." This overt promise of inclusion must have appealed especially to mid-twentieth-century women, who spent their week at home caring for children and household and often expressed a sense of isolation and loneliness.[70] The ad continued with the heading "How a

Beechcraft Super 18 can bring togetherness to you and your husband." It promised:

> In the Super 18's quiet, comfortable passenger lounge, he turns travel time into productive time as he speeds to his destination at more than 200 miles an hour. He gets more done during business hours, has less work to bring home. Freed of the delays and tensions of ordinary forms of travel, he returns relaxed, ready for fun and companionship . . . and with time to enjoy it. If you aren't seeing enough of your Man of Decision these days, is it because his means of transportation is no longer equal to the size of his responsibilities? Perhaps it's time you encouraged him to step up to a Beechcraft Super 18 . . . the aircraft that can make togetherness a reality again for you and your husband.[71]

Positioning Beech aircraft as "the air fleet of American business," the ad enlisted the wives of high-ranking executives and managers in the company's efforts by promising a return on investment that came in the form of time. It was time that would be restored to the family and the marriage for "togetherness"—the word coined by McCall's in 1954 to capture an emerging ideal that centered family on children and suggested (though it was rarely achieved) shared responsibility for childrearing and household maintenance. And it was women who generally bore the added responsibility of achieving this.[72] Beech's ad, therefore, capitalized on a trend and introduced gender and women back into its marketing at a time when leveraging the influence of executive wives provided the company with a new target market.

Innovative financing and training programs introduced during the 1960s, however, provide evidence that Olive Ann Beech's leadership was not limited to gender-centered marketing campaigns. During that decade the company increased its share of the private plane market by expanding its product line from three to twenty-one "to serve the growing demand for business aircraft throughout the world" and by providing new opportunities and incentives for purchase to individual and business customers. One example was the establishment of the Beech Acceptance Corporation, a wholly owned subsidiary, through which the company pioneered airplane leasing and financing services. This financially oriented marketing program—characteristic of Beech's long-standing distinction as a bold and innovative leader in the financial realm of the business—expanded the private plane market to smaller-scale businesses and individuals who would not be able to afford a plane on their own without these options. Another innovation introduced in 1964 was the establishment of an aviation education department. By 1982, some 31,034 attendees had attended Beechcraft training programs focused on piloting, maintenance, avionics, and mechanics associated with the company's many different planes.[73] This too was a marketing program designed to extend interest in and ability to use Beech products.[74] It was one way that the company kept customers long term and encouraged them to trade up to newer models. And as actor Christopher Reeve's story in the *Beechcraft Marketing Report* underscored, it worked; he had just completed pilot school for his new Beechcraft Baron 58P, his second plane purchased from the company in two years. "I'll use my airplane everywhere I go," he reported. "It's my form of business and personal transportation. In the movie business it's a great way to keep up with hectic schedules."[75]

These marketing innovations had a positive impact on the bottom line. By 1968, the company had "set an all-time high in commercial sales dollar volume of more than $122 million."[76] This constituted more than simply an increase in sales volume. It also marked a substantial shift away from overdependence on military contracts, which had been a concern about Beech Aircraft among industry watchers less than a decade earlier.[77]

What the company hoped to achieve with these marketing innovations was to convince business executives, traveling professionals, large-scale farmers, and movie actors alike that owning a plane made life more efficient and made traversing vast distances easy and fast. Olive Ann Beech was personally involved in championing this idea best captured in the company's slogan, "The World Is Small When You Fly a Beechcraft." Coined at least by 1957, it became a chief component of the Beech Aircraft brand.[78] While this idea did not differentiate the company from competitors in the small aircraft-manufacturing industry whose planes also, ostensibly, offered the same benefits, Olive Ann Beech was at the forefront of using this slogan to help build the market for privately owned small planes. To make the case that owning a plane for business and/or personal travel was a way to be more effective, she published articles in both *Sperryscope* (1961) and *National Aeronautics* (June 1964) about "The Future of Business Aviation." She asserted, "Thus a new era in business history is being written and bettered every year because of the benefits and the advantages of a proven new system of faster transportation for business. New concepts of business geography have been established by company-owned airplanes.

Modern business market opportunities stretch far beyond the limits of older travel and transport methods. Today there are some 8,000 airports throughout this nation, but fewer than 600 of them are served by scheduled commercial airlines. Thus the fast, comfortable, economical practical mobility of the private plane permits busy people to go where they want to go, when they want to go, on schedules that fit their business and professional requirements."[79]

Timed with the release of the Beechcraft King Air, which marked Beech's "entry into the turbine-powered airplane field," these articles helped to differentiate the company as a purveyor of corporate aircraft. The most sophisticated plane the company had yet produced, the King Air, "far exceeded expectations," attracting "customer acceptance even before the airplane's FAA certification." As the choice of top-line corporations such as Westinghouse and Gerber Products, the King Air remained the "undisputed sales leader among turbine-powered corporate aircraft" for four straight years, "accounting for nearly 77 per cent of all deliveries in its class."[80] And Olive Ann Beech herself was integrally involved in this company success.

The attention to detail that helped make the King Air such a success was a hallmark of Olive Ann Beech. By 1977, in addition to six variations on its popular King Air, the company offered the "Super King Air," which featured "a perfectly balanced performance profile unchallenged in speed, range, payload and handling ease" as well as superior passenger comfort with "a pressurized, air conditioned environment and handcrafted elegance in upholstery, carpeting, cabinetry and appointments."[81] Such high quality in performance and design helped draw the types of elite customers to whom Beech catered in her private office suite and so became an area of importance to her personally. Correspondence to company personnel about her own experience in Beech planes attests to this. In one November 1972 internal memo, Olive Ann Beech wrote:

> I was very disappointed on my trip to California in Beechcraft King Air 92B to find
>
> 1. There was no clock, air speed indicator, altimeter and heat control located in the cabin as usual
>   It is possibly too late and expensive to have these instruments installed at this time, but in the future please see that these items are installed in all of my airplanes.

2. The heating system needs regulating. It was either too hot or too cold, and the left side was always hot and the right side was always cold.
3. The sliding doors to the toilet were lousy and did not work, and there was no packet of towelettes in the toilet area.

Other than the above disappointments the airplane flew beautifully and we enjoyed a good trip.[82]

Beech's use of the term "my airplanes" captures how personal the issue of quality was to her. Every plane produced by Beech Aircraft was one of *her* planes, and thus she expected them all to meet her punctilious criteria. We can safely assume that the oversights she identified were attended to promptly and that such exacting standards contributed to the success of Beech aircraft among discriminating customers—precisely the market that the company was eager to please. By 1977, a brochure for the company's business and personal airplanes was titled "A Tradition of Excellence," branding Beech as *the* purveyor of quality planes.[83] It was a marketing effort in which Olive Ann Beech herself had been essential.

While Beech never imprinted her image on the brand she helped to create, she embodied Beechcraft's association with service as well as quality, both by sharing the company's name and by acting out the role of ambassador effectively and ambitiously. Whether entertaining customers in her private dining room at company headquarters or visiting them at their own locations, Beech was actively involved in building her brand's equity around the twin promises of quality products and personalized service. As one 1977 brochure asserted, "Wherever you go in the world, this emblem symbolizes the finest in aviation . . . a beacon to air travelers seeking the epitome of efficient service and personal attention."[84] Olive Ann Beech took this message wherever *she* went too, proactively seeking opportunities to advance the company's business.

International sales were a particular area of focus for the company and for Olive Ann Beech herself. Thus, when she was invited to the celebration of the openings of the Tokyo and Hong Kong Hilton Hotels in 1963, she stayed in Asia for several additional weeks to visit Beech distributors in Japan and the Philippines. During "many receptions, luncheons and dinners in [her] honor . . . the owners—be they government, business or private— and other aviation enthusiasts . . . [told her] over and over again what an outstanding, rugged, high performance airplane" Beech manufactured. But this visit was not simply ceremonial, nor was it limited to her visits to distributor installations. She also took the opportunity to sell Beech products. As she reported in the company employee newsletter, "I must say, a few prospects not flying the 'world's finest aircraft' were given every opportunity of being converted."[85] Attention to international distributors was a priority for the company that both drove and reflected the growth in international sales, which in 1961 increased 31.5 percent over the previous year. That same year, Beech Aircraft's $12 million in exports constituted "47 percent of all twin-engine business airplanes manufactured in the United States and sold in the international market." The company credited this accomplishment to its export distributors "who do pioneering work in their market area" and "who have the confidence to invest more capital in their Beechcraft operations."[86] Keeping those distributors and dealers happy and motivated was a job Olive Ann Beech helped accomplish by lavishing her personal attention and recognition on them. During the 1961 International Distributors and Dealers conference at Beech Aircraft, she presented the annual awards to outstanding sales leaders herself, shaking each winner's hand—some forty-three of them—at the banquet honoring the company's sales leaders.[87] As with the company's employee recognition program detailed in chapter 3, Beech was personally involved in recognizing the key partners in the company's sales and distribution program worldwide.

In spite of her personal involvement in ceremonial events for sales leaders, Olive Ann Beech played a sideline role in sales conferences. The 1961 conference was described as the "first of new concept conferences for retail management," and it set the tone for future events. As president of the company, Beech provided opening remarks, welcoming distributors and dealers "home to the family of Beechcrafters." This gendered language positioned her as hostess, perhaps even matriarch, both roles that suggested figurehead status rather than involvement in day-to-day management. And it left the content of the meeting to her male executives who presided (vice president, marketing) and presented a variety of addresses, including "a major policy address" on "Progress and Planning" (executive vice president), "Our Opportunities in the Domestic Market" (vice president, domestic sales), and "International Sales" (vice president, export sales) as well as updates on sales training, public relations, and advertising. Whether this was because she preferred not to speak in public settings—as suggested by one reporter—or because she was simply a good delegator, Beech adopted a supporting role to the central one played by the men who worked for her. But gender seems likely to have played a role in her decision. In a sea of white men in dark suits and ties, Olive Ann Beech stood out. And while this was an experience she was accustomed to, sales meetings were a certain type of business occasion when gender seems to have mattered.

In successive conferences, this became more and more plain. At the 1967 conference billed as the "Beechcraft Sales Spectacular," for example, salesmen were entertained by "pretty Natalie Di Silvio [who] captured considerable interest" while "blonde Gail Billings," clad in a form-fitting body suit, black seamed stockings (with a line up the back), and high heels, "corralled . . . the interest that Natalie Di Silvio didn't capture." Another image of a dancing chorus line of women in tight leather pants and high heels appeared with the caption "Girls were pretty, lively and melodic." Needless to say, what all of these acts had in common was that they drew attention to women as spectacles for a male audience. Described as "a fast-paced presentation of Beechcraft products and marketing programs for the coming year" that "effectively informed" salesmen as it entertained them, the show used heterosexually titillating, male-oriented innuendo and the display of women's bodies to help create a "rah, rah" masculine culture aimed at spurring salesmen "to work harder and sell more Beechcraft products." Coverage of the event in the *Beechcraft Altimeter,* the newsletter for distributors, dealers, and salesmen, emphasized this. It featured photos of a suit-clad man clapping as he walked by a group of women with the caption "You applaud what you like . . . I applaud what I like" and a smiling suit-clad man walking down the banquet hall aisle as he escorted a scantily-clad woman (per Gail Billings above) with the (tongue-in-cheek) caption "I'm walking her to the library." Both presented heterosexual, masculine humor focusing on the sex appeal of women as an "inside joke" well known among the company's salesmen.[88] Such content was no doubt designed to create camaraderie. But what it also did was sideline women *not* on display for the show, because it inherently communicated that the community it was meant to inspire to action was a community of men. There were only two references to women participating as attendees at the conference. One highlighted an award presented to Bob and Joan Wallick for setting an around-the-world flying record in a Beechcraft C55 Baron—a continuation of the company's early attention to pilots of company planes, including female pilots. The second reference focused on the wives attending the event, who were reportedly "unanimously and pleasantly impressed with the meeting," though there is little indication of what programming was designed for them.[89]

It is no surprise, really, that Olive Ann Beech may have had a hard time figuring out where she fit in to all of this testosterone-charged hoopla or simply decided not to try. Even as she declared in a newspaper interview the same year that "Being a Woman Is No Drawback to Holding Company's Top Post," she seems to have decided to stay out of the entertainment phase of the company's sales conference; there is no mention of her in any of the coverage of it.[90] To be fair, this was only one year before Beech stepped down as president of the company and continued on as chairwoman, so she may have deliberately pursued a less prominent role. But shunning the spotlight of the sales conferences that increasingly became simultaneous celebrations of salesmanship and heterosexual masculinity may have seemed prudent and desirable to this fearless female executive. By the 1982 sales conference, she had retreated to a "ladies luncheon" that she cohosted with the wives of her two nephews, both executives at the company.[91] Navigating the overwhelmingly male world of aviation as the only female executive in the industry undoubtedly presented many such challenges for Olive Ann Beech. Strategically occupying the sidelines to avoid confronting or being offended by the raucous, male sales culture may have seemed like the best course of action to a woman who prided herself on gender decorum, including a companywide rule that women employees could not smoke or consume coffee.[92] As president and then chairwoman of Beech Aircraft, she wanted and needed her salesmen to sell airplanes. She seemed prepared to turn her attention elsewhere when her marketing and sales departments proposed using stereotypical roles for women to help accomplish that goal.

Margaret Rudkin

From the first brochure to her bestselling autobiographical cookbook, Margaret Rudkin never stopped crafting the marketing message for Pepperidge Farm. While she did not work alone to create the brand's old-fashioned image and claim, relying instead on some of the public relations and advertising industry's finest innovators to help, she never stopped contributing. In fact, she was a master at leveraging free publicity to sell her product—a strategy she exploited for years before investing in professional marketers. Unlike Lewis, she did not *become* the brand, but she was an essential component of it. As friendly and domestic "Maggie Rudkin," she helped to bring to life the claim that Pepperidge Farm products tasted just like Grandma used to make. And in this capacity, she leveraged the brand's origin story to imbue its products with homemade quality, using gender to help her build a relationship with consumers that retained currency twenty-five years into the company's history. For Rudkin, gender served the interests of the brand by enhancing its association with old-fashioned quality.

From the start, Margaret Rudkin constructed the Pepperidge Farm brand around the idea that her bread was both "handmade" and "old-fashioned." Indeed, she reported that the original recipe came from her Irish grandmother, who used to bake bread at home when she was growing up. The first brochure Rudkin produced, which remained in circulation until at least 1940, celebrated the bread's traditional origin: "It is made by hand in small batches by skilled women in the old fashioned, homemade way."[93] Hand-kneading specifically by women, who she alleged had a historic association with breadmaking, became a signature part of her production process, starting in her own kitchen and continuing even as the company grew and moved into a modern manufacturing facility. The idea that "homemade" bread could be produced commercially, on a large scale and in a factory, which was precisely the claim of the brand, worked because of the company's integral connection to Pepperidge Farm, Rudkin's family property in the Connecticut countryside where she started making the bread in her own kitchen. Pepperidge Farm became emblematic of both old-fashioned, country living and homemade cooking by women using time-tested recipes that produced better quality than modern methods.

While Pepperidge Farm was a real place, it was the ideas it conveyed that mattered most for the brand. Named for its sour gum trees, which had "unusually gorgeous coloring in the autumn" and were popularly called "Pepperidge" trees, the property became the iconic backdrop to Rudkin's unfolding business empire. Pepperidge Farm comprised 125 acres of land in Connecticut "which had once been a farm," which she and her husband purchased in 1926. They "built a house and farm buildings and started [their] country life like babes-in-the-wood, for," as she explained years later, "neither of us knew anything about country ways." Over time, however, they raised their own vegetables, fruits, and poultry, and even pigs and steer for a short while, and learned to preserve and process their own foods.[94] Margaret Rudkin's homemade bread grew out of this lifestyle at the same time that it capitalized on it. She referenced "the farm" at every turn. In her first brochure, it appeared not only as her location written under her name at the end but also as the third line of text: "Made at Pepperidge Farm" just under "Pepperidge Farm Bread." That the bread was made on a farm was a key component of her sales pitch. Rudkin understood the value of her brand name and the marketing appeal of associating her bread with an earlier era and country location, even when the farm ceased to be the actual location of production.

That it was the *idea* of Pepperidge Farm rather than the actual place that mattered is illustrated by Rudkin's efforts to protect her brand from imitators. After only two years in business, she was pursuing a competitor whose "1800" loaf copied the same idea. She was able to pursue legal action because she had paid a law firm to trademark "Pepperidge Farm." The trademark allowed her to continue to utilize the name and to convey the brand image of handmade, old-fashioned bread even as her production process moved further and further away from its homemade origin. In 1942, her attorneys assured her, "About the move of your manufacturing business from Pepperidge Farm to Norwalk . . . you need not hesitate to do this on account of the trademark. It will not affect the validity of your trademark registration. . . . As a matter of fact, if you had had no farm at all, you could have picked the name Pepperidge Farm out of the air. . . . Pepperidge Farm applied to the bread does not mean a particular spot of ground where the bread is made. Instead it means that the product marked with that name is the product of the same organization that made some other products bearing the same name and to that extent the purchaser is assured that the quality is that of the products previously obtained bearing the same mark."[95] The attorney's reassurances captured the key point. Pepperidge Farm *the place* mattered little to her business. It was Pepperidge Farm *the idea* that was valuable and protected under her trademark registration.

For this reason, the disjuncture between Pepperidge Farm as an idea—the quintessential farm—and the actual place was immaterial. But it was stark. Margaret Rudkin's country or "rustic" life was an affectation. She did seem to be genuinely enamored with farm life, purchasing yet another country home in Ireland in 1953. But the term "farm" obscured the reality of both homes. Each was a country estate, lavishly appointed and maintained with full-time, live-in staff. When Pepperidge Farm was for sale in 1997, the *Fairfield County Times Monthly* described the home that the Rudkins had constructed on the property this way: "Craftsmen from Europe [were hired] to build the main house, a majestic English Tudor with thick stone walls, leaded-glass windows, a heavy slate roof, and a stable complex for [Henry Rudkin's] polo ponies at the opposite end of a long courtyard." The eighteen-room home included six fireplaces, one of which was reportedly a "twin to one at the Pitti Palace in Florence"; stained-glass windows featuring polo scenes (in the library) and children's fairy tales (in the nursery bathroom); a curved staircase with a railing of oak and forged iron; a brass chandelier; an au pair wing; a butler's pantry; and a dumbwaiter.[96] Thus, while Pepperidge

Farm *was* a farm, it wasn't the quaint country locale that the idea of home-made, rustic bread captured. It's not that Rudkin misrepresented the place. Early articles such as the 1939 article in *Reader's Digest* referred to "the Rudkin estate," and in her autobiographical cookbook Margaret Rudkin's chapter on the origin and history of the company featured an illustration of Pepperidge Farm that was unmistakably an estate and not a "farm." But over time, as the brand's association with all things old-fashioned and country was cemented through iconography, packaging, and advertising, the fact that Pepperidge Farm wasn't really a farm at all attracted some attention. "What Mr. and Mrs. Rudkin live on in Fairfield County is no more a farm, in the accepted sense of the term, than is The White House," explained one executive at the company's advertising agency in 1962. This was the chief reason, he stated, why the company had for many years been having "legal problems" with its "use of the word 'Farm.' "[97]

Why this was a problem in 1962 and not 1942 when Pepperidge Farm's lawyer had assured otherwise has everything to do with the way in which the brand had evolved. During that twenty-year period, Rudkin increasingly capitalized on a *notion*: that in turning out a rustic loaf of bread on her farm in Connecticut just like her grandmother used to make, she was delivering a little bit of old-fashioned, country goodness to American consumers. It was clever brand management. But it was a strategy that emerged over time.

The earliest packaging, brochures, and ads for Pepperidge Farm bread sold nutrition and taste as the key product benefits. Rudkin's first pamphlet, for example, began with the promise "As Nature Gives It to Man" featured prominently in large font. The inside text continued:

> Doctors and dieticians are generally agreed that man has treated the wise provisions of Nature wantonly. This is indeed true in the preparation of the "staff of life"—bread. Natural whole wheat meal keeps fresh only a very short time and the usual procedure by the millers of removing the valuable wheat germ by processing, in order to be able to market the flour without spoilage, unfortunately eliminates the stimulating effect of the wheat germ on the gastro-intestinal tract. The finished loaf is aerated to meet a size sales appeal and so processed all along the line that the "staff of life" is indeed a bent reed to lean upon. . . . Medical opinion considers this bread a most desirable part of the diet for children and adults—retaining as it does the natural balance of the important food values of wheat.

Though the dense text was leavened with enticing descriptions of the ingredients and taste of the bread, its overall emphasis was on health. *Eat this because it's good for you*, it promised; *we've made that easier by making it taste good*. An entire paragraph was devoted to explaining the significance and benefits of fresh, stone-ground, whole-wheat flour—a key differentiator between Pepperidge Farm bread and that of competitors—and early packaging highlighted this, featuring two stalks of wheat.[98] The Pepperidge Farm booklet, "designed and written" by Rudkin herself, used the "exact wording" from its inception in 1937 through 1940. Once imitators started to copy her loaf as well as her text—"copied word for word"—she inquired into whether a copyright on her booklet might protect her from such infringements.[99] She had found a market niche and a selling proposition that worked—healthful, good-tasting bread—and imitators were quick to try to steal some of her business.

Rudkin sold her bread through doctors initially, leveraging their endorsement to communicate the product's health benefits. "The first sales of bread were made almost entirely to Doctor Donaldson's patients," an early company history explained.[100] As chapter 1 detailed, Dr. Donaldson was her family physician whom she consulted regarding her son's health problems. His interest in the bread was an unexpected turn of events: "When I told the doctor I was making bread from the stone-ground flour, he wouldn't believe me because he said it was too coarse and I would have to add white flour to it. To convince him, I brought him some samples and told him exactly what I put in with the flour. Immediately he wanted to order it for himself and for his other patients. I was quite taken aback by this idea, but I knew the bread was nutritious, unique, and delicious and was indeed an important part of the whole diet."[101] Rudkin's clear preoccupation here with the health benefits of the bread was genuine, as substantiated through her correspondence with a variety of scientists with whom she exchanged nutritional information. This nutritional evangelism, in combination with Dr. Donaldson's backing, made a convincing case. A letter from him extolling the virtues of Pepperidge Farm bread became a regular part of her communications with other doctors. It was a strategy she was still using in 1947, ten years after starting the business, as in her response to a Dr. Greenberg who requested "a letter . . . giving me scientific and nutritional data and information." She replied, "I am not a scientist [but] I will endeavor to explain to you as best I can the value of my whole wheat bread." Citing her booklet, she continued, "You could see it is a highly nutritious food and because of its roughage [which is] very good as an intestinal stimulant." She ended by quoting the letter from Dr. Donaldson, which urged, "I think you would find anything you would do to increase the use of this bread in your patients much appreciated by them as well as by Mrs. Rudkin."[102] Rudkin's disciplined replies to the voluminous correspondence she received from doctors like Greenberg and their patients (as well as other consumers) was a key ingredient in her product's early and quick adoption.[103]

But some refused to accept Rudkin's certification of her product's nutritional values and sought expert insight into its health benefits. Dr. James R. Wilson, M.D., Secretary of the Council on Foods and Nutrition for the American Medical Association, wrote to Rudkin in 1949 for information about Pepperidge Farm bread so he could respond to the many inquiries he received:

> The inquiries that have come to me concerning your bread are questions such as "Please tell me about Pepperidge Farm Bread" or "What is the nutritive value of Pepperidge Farm Bread?" Questions of this sort are often sent to us because the doctor's patient has inquired and he in turn has asked us for information. This is the reason why I wrote you for some of the details of composition. I think that you may be surprised at the volume of inquiries that come to us from both physicians and laymen.
>
> p.s. From personal experience and from what I learned otherwise, all that I have written about your products has done you no harm, I'm sure. The samples you mailed were used up in no time flat.[104]

Wilson's endorsements helped to spread the product's acceptance as a "health food," and Rudkin understood this from the start. That's why she was quick to send samples as well as product information.

While this was especially smart brand management in correspondence with doctors, providing samples was, in fact, Rudkin's standard line of attack with all customers. Correspondence reveals how commonly she sent samples through the mail, along with product booklets, to interested parties. And she loved to tell the story of how in 1937 she had gone to her local grocer, Mercurios, with a loaf of bread, butter, and a knife in hand to provide samples and convince the proprietor to carry her bread. She repeated the same tactic at Charles & Company, a specialty grocery in Manhattan. In each case, the recipients declared the bread delicious, the best they had tasted since childhood, and readily agreed to stock it for sale to their customers.[105]

Pepperidge Farm's popularity until the early 1950s was generated by such in-store demonstrations, word-of-mouth testimonials, and publicity rather than by advertising. One result was that little money was designated for this purpose. During its second year in business, for example, the company reported that it had spent only $836.34 on advertising and $429.15 on promotional expenses for the year, a small fraction (less than 4 percent) of the total deductions for the year. Often that cost simply comprised complimentary samples of Pepperidge Farm bread as well as copies of the company's booklets.[106] The reason the company invested so little was that the extensive publicity it attracted was enough to drive sales. As Henry Rudkin explained in 1946, "Our business has been developed almost entirely without advertising of the conventional type. We have obtained extraordinarily good publicity. I am attaching herewith some reprints of these articles."[107] Favorable coverage commenced almost at the outset. A company timeline prepared by H. A. Baldwin, one of Pepperidge Farm's earliest employees, documented this. "One of our first publicity articles appeared in the New York Herald-Tribune," he recorded on 21 March 1938. Two months later, he revealed, an "article on Pepperidge Farm Bread appeared in Bakers Weekly," and three months after that, the "original article appeared in Vogue on this date. Ordered attractive reprints and proudly distributed them to our stores." Over and over again, Baldwin's company history documented the regular publicity Pepperidge Farm received between 1937 and 1959 (the dates of the chronology) as well as the way in which the company capitalized on it by distributing reprints of the articles. Sometimes he included comments about the boost it provided the company.[108]

The article with the highest impact on the business appeared on 23 November 1939 in *Reader's Digest*. Titled "Bread Deluxe," it reportedly prompted "letters [to] pour in" and "increased [orders] by leaps and bounds."[109] Another source credits the *Reader's Digest* article with helping to "make the company a household name" and to "increas[ing business] tenfold during the following decade."[110] Featured in a series titled "Depression Born Businesses," the article started with a statement of inspiration: "There is money to be wrung even from commonplace ideas—if mixed with imagination and industry. Margaret Rudkin, baker of old-fashioned, home-made bread, will illustrate." It went on to document the history and quick success of the business and then ended on another high note: "Born in a depression summer, when most people were thinking of retrenchment rather than expansion, conducted by a woman without previous business experience, it illustrates what wit and intelligence can do with an old idea." Bookended with universally appealing can-do statements, the article about Rudkin's bread attracted attention because her story did. It was a tale of enterprise and daring in spite of the Depression—a story of one individual whose innovative idea lead to employment for many and security for her family. As the article posited, "Hundreds of people in nearby Bridgeport needed work. Wall Street, which supplied the family income, was in the doldrums. Perhaps . . . [selling her bread] made sense."[111] Positioning Rudkin as family and community savior and her bread as an investment in employment and economic stimulation that a consumer could feel good about, the article reaped thousands of new customers for Pepperidge Farm and cost the company nothing.

Unsolicited endorsements, like free publicity, also helped to propel Pepperidge Farm bread to the fore of the popular imagination. In particular, a letter from popular journalist Dorothy Thompson, a columnist for *Ladies' Home Journal* between 1937 and 1961 who had garnered fame as a fearless reporter and cogent editorialist for her coverage of the expanding Nazi threat in Europe, which she published in a syndicated column, drew attention.[112] In her letter to Rudkin, Thompson wrote, "For years I have been trying to get some good bread. In fact, for years I have been trying to get something that was bread at all and not a sort of sponge that turns dry or mildews in two days. Your bread is excellent. I have only one thing against it. The ordinary Baker's bread removed bread from my diet. Your bread has put it back on and will, no doubt, put pounds back on me as well. I shall eat no other bread and although I have been solicited many times for testimonials this is a spontaneous one and a free one and you can use it wherever you like."[113] Cited in a *New Yorker* article published in 1948, this endorsement from a woman with such established influence over public opinion had a big impact on the interest in Pepperidge Farm bread. "Certain people who begin taking [the bread] regularly become addicts," the article reported. "Dorothy Thompson started using it in 1938. 'I shall eat no other bread,' she proclaimed soon thereafter in a letter to Mrs. Rudkin, and she hasn't." Positioning Pepperidge Farm as "addicting" using a free endorsement from a major U.S. opinion setter, the article reportedly made "sales start . . . to jump immediately."[114]

While such publicity was free and the endorsements unsolicited, these triumphs did not occur without help from Rudkin. In fact, she steered the train of publicity skillfully and deliberately. For example, one year after the *New Yorker* article had attracted so much attention for the company, Pepperidge Farm entertained members of the press at "A Day in June at Pepperidge Farm," no doubt an effort to capitalize on and expand the media coverage generated by the article.[115] A company publication highlighted that such publicity events remained a priority at the company for years, stating, "Emphasis has always been put on 'public relations.'" Even once the company had a formal public relations department it continued to rely on the free publicity that press coverage generated. The writers and editors of "women's pages" who reviewed Pepperidge Farm products in newspapers around the country were a key link in the company's strategy. Rudkin knew this and demonstrated her appreciation at the company's twenty-fifth-anniversary celebration, which included special invitations for these taste makers to several gala events.[116] She had a keen understanding of how to maximize publicity. As a member of a panel on public relations at a New York City convention of ad men, Mrs. Rudkin, according to a *World Telegram* account, really "taught them a thing or two." In her remarks she detailed examples such as hosting visitors, serving bread and butter, and other ways she and the company had ensured the people knew "Pepperidge Farm isn't just another bakery."[117] Rudkin's success with public relations at Pepperidge Farm was so great that one study of her leadership concluded that she had an "early background in public relations." Although extant primary records do not substantiate this claim, the misinterpretation is revealing because it highlights that Rudkin's success with public relations—in spite of her lack of training—was nearly unbelievable.[118]

Success with publicity may have overshadowed advertising as the preferred strategy for promoting the company partly because early ads struggled to find a unique selling proposition that gained traction with consumers. One of the company's only advertisements during its early years awkwardly navigated the twin promises of nutrition and taste by offering free samples but also sought female customers' attention by introducing a new product proposition—beauty. It promised to refund the cost of the bread and their postage if customers sent in their bread wrapper as proof of purchase and if they "drop[ped] us a note telling us . . . what you really think of it." But nutrition was a hard sell in 1955, the year the ad appeared. This was the era of canned foods and diet products made with artificial sweeteners, as Tillie Lewis's company history reveals. Pepperidge Farm sought to participate in the trend by emphasizing the importance of nutritious bread to achieve slimness and beauty as well as health. As with most food advertisements, women were the overt targets of the ad, but this one targeted women as dieters as well as household consumers. One-half of the full-page ad that appeared in the *New York Times Magazine* was a photograph of a stylishly dressed and classically beautiful woman with a man in the background glaring at her. The heading read, "How PEPPERIDGE FARM BREAD helps you keep that *radiant* look!" and was proceeded by the following text [emphasis original]:

> **True beauty** is not skin deep! Women with superb vitality have a *radiant* look . . . a warm *sunny* something about them that turns men's heads. **How does one** get such superb *vitality*? By the *right* rest, the *right* exercise, the *right* diet. **For example,** famous medical clinics prescribe a slice of bread like Pepperidge Farm at *every meal, every day,* for reducing diets as low as 1000 calories . . . far fewer than half the calories you need to maintain your ideal weight. Here is why: **Unlike** most energy foods, the long-lasting energy in Pepperidge Farm Bread is *slowly* released. This helps prevent that "hollow feeling" between meals which tempts you to over-eat. **Diet or no diet,** Pepperidge Farm Bread supplies you with certain essential nutrients you *must* have for your good health. **Pepperidge Farm Bread** is one of those rare kinds of food rich in *thiamine,* the great nerve and morale vitamin. It is lack of enough thiamine that can cause you to tire too easily, and to get upset and irritable "over nothing." **When you are** on a reducing diet, Pepperidge Farm Bread is particularly valuable because it is a natural aid to *digestion* and *regularity.*

Nutrition, it seems, was a hard sell on its own, so the company sought to pursue diet consumers promising a product that would help women to lose weight, attain more energy, maintain their equanimity, regularize elimination, *and* achieve radiance. It was a remarkable if exaggerated sales pitch, one that sold "grandmother's bread, fresh out of the oven" to a younger, self-conscious generation of women using stereotypically gendered categories for both seller and buyer.[119] This lengthy ad copy with a combination of "old-fashioned" and "modern" reasons to purchase Pepperidge Farm bread—what was referred to as "reason-why" copy—was an outmoded approach to advertising by the 1950s.[120] It is no surprise, therefore, that this approach did not appear in any other advertisements for the company, apparently abandoned as an ineffective sales pitch.

Years later when Pepperidge Farm returned to the "diet appeal," Rudkin herself was part of the proposed pitch, a key component of the branding strategy identified by the advertising agency she now employed. This reflected an important shift that sought to make Rudkin an icon of the old-fashioned appeal of the brand. In an internal memo, the advertising firm's president and chief creative professional proposed, "Could you build some . . . commercials around the charming idea that 'Maggie Rudkin plum forgot to put in the calories when she baked this morning'?"[121] Years earlier, the same firm had suggested "experiment[ing] with Margaret Rudkin" by "hav[ing] her start [a] commercial by belting out a few exuberant notes from a song, in the manner of a happy milkmaid saluting the dawn" to achieve the "gaiety" they were searching for in the ad.[122] There is no record of whether such an ad was created, but it is doubtful because other records reveal that Rudkin resisted inclusion in company advertisements. Advertising agency records reveal that by 1959, Margaret Rudkin had made clear that she did not want to appear in television commercials, and it appears to have been a sensitive topic; at the agency, this came in the form of an internal memo advising that it was "best to drop" the subject according to her son. In case the directive was unclear, the memo from the agency president concluded, "This is a decision."[123] Rudkin's resistance to television advertising could have been related to her health; at this point she had already gone through one struggle with serious illness, reportedly breast cancer. Yet there were likely other reasons that related to her refusal to become a brand icon.

Rudkin did, in fact, appear in the company's first television ad campaign, but the fact that it met with mixed results may have been a significant factor in her reluctance to do it again. In 1953, she starred in three one-minute commercials created by Kenyon & Eckhardt that featured her in a kitchen discussing her bread and its health benefits. A "Commercial Critique" published in *Billboard* magazine was extremely laudatory:

> Various sponsors have had varying degrees of success in finding
> someone within their organization who could handle these TV
> chores well, but for Pepperidge Farm Bakery it was easy. It went to
> the top and enlisted the services of the president of Pepperidge
> Farm, Margaret Rudkin. In three one-minute film commercials . . .
> Rudkin relates the amazing success story of the Pepperidge Farm
> company which literally started in her kitchen. . . . With no tricks, no
> dissolves and no supers, the commercials are simplicity itself. Just a
> handsome, dignified woman with a gentle voice and a sincerity that
> can't be doubted describing the wholesome ingredients that make
> her bread so distinctive in flavor and texture. Mrs. Rudkin exudes

that intangible quality best known as "class," which is particularly fortunate, since her bread is a premium product considerably more expensive than the mass produced commercial breads. If Mrs. Rudkin should burn the next batch of bread and go out of business, she has a bright future in TV selling.[124]

There was a lot to be proud of. Rudkin had acquitted herself well in the eyes of critics and in an activity that was "entirely new to her." But the stakes were high. This was the first major investment in advertising and promotions for the company. And according to one account, the campaign cost the company $200,000, equivalent to $1.7 million in today's dollars.[125] For this investment to pay off, the commercial had to do more than attract critical acclaim—it had to sell product. According to internal records, the commercial was a disappointment in this regard. When the company signed a contract to hire David Ogilvy as their new advertising agency a year later, he noted shortly thereafter that one of the primary goals to emerge from a meeting with Mrs. Rudkin was "to continue our search for the reasons why Kenyon & Eckhardt's TV campaign failed to sell Pepperidge." He also noted that "there seem[ed] to be an unspoken agreement that radio might be the better medium to use in New York. Whatever you do," he concluded, "stay away from TV on this account."[126] Rudkin, it seemed, had washed her hands of television advertising for the time being.

But she was not just skeptical of the medium; it was also the message to which she objected. For what emerged from the same meeting between Rudkin and Ogilvy was also the fact that she thought "the present generation has never experienced home-made bread and that any appeal to this particular nostalgia will be lost upon them."[127] Rudkin had reluctantly agreed to a new white sandwich bread as well as presliced bread, both of which flew in the face of the return to tradition that she had engendered and envisioned in founding Pepperidge Farm. For her the point was not nostalgia, it was nutritious bread—the kind that older traditions of flour milling, dough kneading, and bread-baking had produced. Twenty years after she founded the company, Rudkin still corresponded on letterhead featuring an image of "An Old New England Mill, 1742" with the caption "Old New England Grist Mills Today Still Stone-Grind Flour for Pepperidge Farm Whole Wheat Bread."[128] The inspiration for the image was the Wayside Inn Grist Mill in Sudbury, Massachusetts, a picturesque, working mill that was actually built in 1924 by Henry Ford as a museum to preserve eighteenth-century hydraulic milling technology. In 1952, Pepperidge Farm entered into a contract with the museum to utilize the mill for production of the company's stone-ground whole-wheat flour. During the course of the lease agreement, the mill ground approximately 9 million tons of flour for the company. The arrangement ended the year Margaret Rudkin died, perhaps underscoring the degree to which it was *her* vision and stubbornness that had kept it alive for fifteen years.[129] While the mill was picturesque, that was not the point for Rudkin—it was its utility that mattered.

But if Rudkin was skeptical about empty notions of nostalgia, the advertising agency was skeptical of her ability to sell Pepperidge Farm bread for its healthful qualities. One internal memo summarizing market research reported, "Women pay lip-service to vitamins and nutrition, but these factors are not too important in motivating actual purchase. Advertising claims about nutrition are not especially valuable."[130] The challenge was both that nutritional claims did not sell bread in the 1950s and that the price point of the product was so out of line with the market. The company had to appeal to consumers willing to pay more. David Ogilvy summed up the challenge: "I have a feeling that Pepperidge should always be well bred ('the well-bred bread'?) We want the egg-head trade." But he rejected "tongue in . . . cheek" advertising, asserting that food should be advertised "sincerely" "because food isn't frivolous, and housewives lack humor." Nutrition wasn't abandoned as a selling proposition altogether, but in and of itself it was insufficient. The agency needed another angle. The only other direction left, Ogilvy suggested, was to use "CHARM and a LIGHT HEART."[131] And perhaps this is what Rudkin was resisting when she declined to participate in television advertising herself after 1953. She was a serious woman who was serious about bread and nutrition. It would have been in keeping with her "class" and "dignity"—which came across in the first commercials she appeared in—to refuse to caricature herself in order to achieve an effect for the sake of advertising.

When the new Pepperidge Farm advertisements were produced, they achieved the desired lightheartedness by employing a male character actor and became wildly successful. Parker Fennelly had already earned some notoriety playing a character called Titus Moody on "The Fred Allen [radio] Show" in the 1930s and 1940s. Though a classically trained actor who got his start in Shakespearean roles, Fennelly became well-known by caricaturing his New England roots, playing old Yankee characters "whose accent he knew well." As Titus Moody, he "got laughs even before the start of a routine with his classic opening line, "Howdy, bub," and continued to receive chuckles with his rustic humor about farms and animals.[132] Reprised for the Pepperidge Farm commercials, the Titus Moody character was the equivalent of a celebrity endorsement and a character study. As such, it brought the desired effect—a charming and engaging interpretation of "old-fashioned." Immediately successful, the radio commercials and then television commercials received critical acclaim and, most important for Pepperidge Farm, convinced consumers to purchase the company's products.[133] For forty years, the character, eventually played by a second actor once Fennelly retired, was the icon of the company, appearing alongside the trademark horse-drawn bakery delivery wagon that had also been an invention of the advertising campaign pioneered by the David Ogilvy agency.[134]

Margaret Rudkin didn't disappear from company advertising altogether, but when she was included it was not as a caricature. In a 1957 Pepperidge Farm print ad for stuffing, for example, she appeared as "the genius who has created this 'instant' stuffing" and was described as "the red-haired New England housewife who bakes Pepperidge Farm bread."[135] And when the company finally introduced a white sandwich loaf—something that Ogilvy had urged from the beginning—she again figured prominently in the print ads proposed by the agency. The idea was to appeal to consumers with children who preferred a softer loaf. Roughly sketched by Ogilvy in an internal memo as an idea, the ad featured Rudkin as a grandmother who had capitulated to her grandchildren's preference: "We bake the best bread you can buy. It tastes better and it is more nutritious. The only problem is that my grandchildren don't like it. Poor misguided little things, they prefer ordinary bread—white and soft. So at long last I have given in to them, being a soft-hearted old grandma. Now I am baking a new kind of loaf which is much softer and whiter than the loaf which made me famous. Frankly, I don't like it nearly as well, but my grandchildren simply adore it, and I can assure you that it is just as nourishing as the old loaf."[136] Rudkin never saw this sketch, of course. But when she saw the final ad prepared by the agency, it was not an invented version of her—one with no basis in fact, as in the case of Lewis's diet ads, which leveraged a made-up story about her weight problems. Pepperidge Farm ads instead used Rudkin's origin story as a housewife and mother motivated to prepare nutritious food for her family—all based in fact—to craft a benevolent maternal figure to convince female consumers to buy her products because she was like them and wanted the same thing as they did. It was a page taken out of the book of General Mills, inventor of Betty Crocker, who was also an Ogilvy client.

As a grandmother in the ads, Rudkin's appearance was more of an affectation than a fiction. She was, in fact, a grandmother. By the end of her

Rudkin left the campy, country acting to Parker Fennelly, who played "Titus Moody" in Pepperidge Farm advertisements. But as "Maggie Rudkin," the grandmother, she posed in domestic settings and contributed to the brand's old-fashioned image. Fairfield Museum and History Center, Fairfield, Connecticut.

life, she had six grandchildren, raised partially in separate residences on the Pepperidge Farm property. But she was not the kind of doting grandmother who made homemade bread for her grandchildren that the above ad suggested. In actuality, she was remembered by one grandson as formal and perhaps a bit intimidating, like "traditional grandparents of that time." He recalled that they were "not allowed to walk the three hundred or so yards to the 'Big House'" from their cottage. And when they were invited to visit, especially at the holidays, a butler answered the door and a cook prepared the food. But such occasions were memorable, as were yearly trips to New York City with both grandparents, who took him and his brother to visit the Natural History museum and out to a fancy lunch. They had to dress in coat, tie, polished shoes, and "the itchiest wool pants ever," he remembered, but also that his grandmother saved him when the trout he ordered for lunch came with the head. She "sent it back to be cut up to look like tuna fish." Perhaps most meaningful was his grandmother's letter on his fifteenth birthday (the first letter she'd ever sent him), which suggested that he take as many courses and read as many books as he could on economics—a subject about which he knew nothing at the time but which proved important later in his life.[137] Thus, while the grandmother who appeared in Pepperidge Farm advertisements did not much resemble Margaret Rudkin, she was also not entirely a fiction. Rudkin *was* a grandmother and she *had* at one time made bread and other foods from scratch for her three young sons.

The Pepperidge Farm ads featuring Rudkin connected the performative role she played for promotional purposes with her actual and symbolic past as mother. Cooking for her family had been work imbued with meaning and emotion for her as a mother. As she recalled in 1963, "Now our children are married and off in their own homes and there's no need for that big storeroom, but I sadly miss the pleasures of those busy years."[138] Photographs created for the company's twenty-fifth anniversary in 1962 captured this visually, nostalgically featuring Rudkin in an attractive flowered dress crouching down to remove fresh baked turnovers from the oven.[139] These were a newer Pepperidge Farm product that consumers purchased frozen and baked themselves. This provided American housewives the opportunity to create in their own kitchens the high-quality homemade baked goods the company was known for and which, the image suggested, Rudkin had baked for her family. Thus, as she acted out her past as mother and home baker for the camera, Rudkin performed a role that embodied the product's homemade quality and the promise that any housewife could match

Rudkin's old-fashioned standards as a home baker if she purchased Pepperidge Farm products.

The role that Rudkin played for Pepperidge Farm's advertising and promotional materials was a gender performance, to be sure, but it stopped short of inventing the past. Even though the grandmother trope served a similar purpose to Lewis's invented housewife, the method by which the company sought to achieve it was decidedly different. It utilized normative gender roles as familiar icons to draw female consumers, but the stars were Rudkin as real-life family woman, cook, and entrepreneur and Titus Moody as the cartoonish punch line who helped to convey the brand's old-fashioned quality. The choice of name for Rudkin in ads—"Maggie," a name she never used in daily life, preferring "Peg" instead—helped to create some distance between the imagined and the real but stopped short of inventing a fictional character.[140]

By this time, Pepperidge Farm promotions were in the hands of very able professionals who championed a focus on Rudkin—or a version of her—as the centerpiece of the company's strategy. The award-winning Ogilvy & Mather advertising agency was joined by Ben Sonnenberg, one of the most well-known and effective public-relations professionals in New York City. He was on retainer to "build up Peg's [Margaret Rudkin's] name" along with her book, the *Margaret Rudkin Pepperidge Farm Cookbook*, published in 1963.[141] Part cookbook, part biography, the book was anticipated to "carry the Pepperidge Farm story to a great many people who have never been exposed to Pepperidge advertising or publicity" and "calculated to strengthen the image of Pepperidge Farm and to make the trade-mark more valuable for the future." Book promotions were multipronged. The publishing company advertised in the *New Yorker* and the *New York Times* book section, the company planned to insert leaflets in boxed cookies, and Campbell's Soup, Pepperidge Farm's parent company by 1963, "agreed to underwrite two or three pages in women's service magazines," such as *McCall's, Better Homes & Gardens,* or *Ladies' Home Journal,* promoting company products and announcing the book's availability.[142] The strategy worked. In the end, the cookbook was listed on the *New York Times* bestseller list—reportedly the only cookbook to have earned that distinction at the time—and helped to make Pepperidge Farm a household name.[143] It did so by making Rudkin the embodiment of a highly traditional role for women as wife, mother, and cook. Thus, whether Rudkin embraced the Ogilvy and Sonnenberg vision for her as the Pepperidge Farm grandmother in the brand's promotions or had capitulated to ongoing cajoling by these professionals is not entirely clear. But as the cookbook shows, ultimately she helped to construct the idea that cooking for family was among the most satisfying occupations she had. "Few things are more rewarding to a woman," she wrote, "than that happy feeling she has when she knows that the food she has prepared with love and interest brings pleasure to her family."[144] With the help of industry professionals, Rudkin had effectively leveraged gender to differentiate her brand.

Conclusion

Associating brands with gender roles worked because gender roles were familiar, even attractive, to consumers in the mid-twentieth century. It was not a socially progressive strategy, it did not challenge stereotypes, and it did not advance a brand persona that championed or even represented women as strong leaders. But it was the strategy that mid-twentieth-century big-business leaders Lewis, Beech, and Rudkin chose because they thought and hoped it would be effective. Casting themselves as housewife, hostess, and grandmother, respectively, advanced their business interests by distinguishing them from their competition. Thus, even as large-scale companies such as General Mills invented female icons for their brands to appeal to their consumers during this same period, these female entrepreneurs leveraged their own gender and allowed themselves to be cast in traditional roles to build brands that could claim a distinctive type of quality—a feminized form of quality—in contrast to their competitors. It was a strategy that stretched the truth, casting each of them in stereotypical, exaggerated, and even fictionalized roles. But it helped to achieve the goal of all mid-twentieth-century brands competing in ever-more-crowded markets against companies making almost identical claims about quality—to be remembered by consumers as different from and better than competitors. Using gender as a brand management strategy helped all three to accomplish this.

5 Asserting Self-Worth

In her popular 2014 book *Lean In: Women, Work, and the Will to Lead*, Facebook COO Sheryl Sandberg discusses the difficulties for women of asserting self-worth. She writes, "For women, taking credit comes at a real social and professional cost [and yet]. . . . Owning one's success is key to achieving more success." This quandary—the inherent contradictions of success and likability for women—is the subject of an entire chapter, which includes stories about executive women, including Sandberg herself, struggling with the cost of success. Case after case reveals that businesswomen face a double bind: the importance of ensuring that their successes are known so that their position and potential in a company are legitimized and the challenge of doing so without sacrificing the regard that others have for them—the typical outcome for a woman viewed as self-promoting. Even explaining why she is qualified or mentioning previous successes in a job interview, one study shows, can lower a woman's chances of getting hired. The result, in part, is a long trail of accomplished women reluctant to let others know about their achievements. Sandberg reports that *Fortune* magazine's annual conference, titled "Most Powerful Women Summit," is deliberately named to "force women to confront their own power"—an exercise that is uncomfortable for many of them.[1]

The idea that women need to "own" their success and the challenges it entails is a message that has been sounded before. A generation earlier, in *Women and Management*, Irene Place and Sylvia Plummer wrote, "Career women need to develop a degree of assertive behavior which will enable them to maintain leadership roles and to stand up for their rights without giving them the feeling they've compromised their femininity. They do not want to become aggressive to such an extent that they seem unpleasant or hard to work with."[2] Of course, the conflict between being assertive and being pleasant, being a leader and being feminine—categories that for women were viewed as incompatible in the 1980s—was one of the factors identified in the study published the same year that coined the now ubiquitous phrase "glass ceiling" to explain why so few women reached the top echelons of the business world. As one review of the study reported, to be successful, "women managers must be tough without appearing *macho*. And they must retain certain 'feminine' characteristics such as adaptability without appearing soft."[3] Navigating the fault lines of impression management, effectively projecting a competent yet not masculine persona, was challenging for women and yet essential to their success. Failing to do so could in fact cost a woman her career up until 1989, when the courts intervened on women's behalf in *Price Waterhouse v. Hopkins*. This was a landmark Supreme Court case that established that "sex role stereotyping was a legitimate grounds for suit." It found that the way in which the Price Waterhouse accounting firm had "used very different, sexually coded language to describe the same behavior" in Ann Hopkins, a candidate for partner, that was lauded in men but seen as a liability in her constituted sex discrimination.[4] The decision in favor of Hopkins was a watershed moment in American women's history that provided an important legal precedent for professional women, but there was still a long and challenging road ahead when it came to how women managed the twin goals of success and approval in the workplace. Self-presentation, therefore, and in particular how to project their success, was a complicated endeavor for businesswomen long before Sandberg helped a new generation to see its importance.[5]

Asserting self-worth was necessary for twentieth-century female business *owners* also because it enhanced their business's valuation. In business, "valuation" traditionally refers to the appraisal of a company's worth and in particular its potential for growth. Scholars have shown that through much of American history, judgment about the character of a business owner was at least as important as financial indicators in evaluations of a business's ability to steward expansion and/or its reliability for credit and investing.[6] Women faced this evaluation process with a disadvantage. Examinations of credit and lending, for example, have revealed the usually negative influence of being female, nonwhite, and nonnative to the assessments of creditworthiness from the nineteenth century to the present day. Other studies confirm discrepancies in salary and promotions for women in large corporations throughout the twentieth century, revealing the ways that they were evaluated and rewarded in different and diminishing ways compared to men. Theoretically, female business owners had the advantage of independence in contrast to professional women trying to work their way up corporate ladders; they were not dependent on others to provide their opportunities but created them themselves. On the other hand, to create those opportunities, like women employees in corporations they needed to earn and maintain the respect and esteem of a variety of people, in their case employees, board members, funders, customers, and peers in the industry, to name a few. And they had to generate a positive valuation of themselves at a time when gender roles and stereotypes triggered an automatic discount to their worth expressed in lower pay, questions about their abilities, and the trenchant hold of the "family claim" positing that their job, first and foremost, was to care for husbands, children, and homes. Articulating a counternarrative that established their value to their companies was important for female business owners and had an impact on the bottom line. How much stock they were allowed to issue, whether they would receive the price they asked when they sold their companies, and whether their terms of purchase would be met were all connected in some way to judgments about them that they could influence by asserting their self-worth.

For Lewis, Beech, and Rudkin, operating their enterprises two generations before the "glass ceiling" had even been identified, there were additional reasons that asserting self-worth was imperative to their success. First and foremost, they operated businesses at a time when one of the most common roles for women in business was as executive wives—women married to corporate executives and managers whose unpaid labor both at home and at professional social affairs played a key role in their husbands' success. The executive wife was a character "emphasized in films, novels, and advertising throughout the period," and its prevalence in the corporate world encouraged businessmen to see Lewis, Beech, and Rudkin as someone's wife rather than someone's president.[7] In addition, all three came from nontraditional backgrounds, making an unorthodox entrance into corporate leadership positions from secretarial jobs. This origin, in combination with a lack of formal education beyond high school or even elementary school in the cases of Lewis and Beech (except for vocational training), made it even harder to establish themselves and their reputations in the business world. And finally, because they operated manufacturing businesses, they had the added burden of breaking into an industry that was heavily male dominated. Of course, this was true of all businesses in the 1930s. But some industries—beauty, for example, about which we know a great deal—had several well-known female entrepreneurs. And this was increasingly the case over the course of the twentieth century as female professionals made their way into certain industries in increasing numbers and established high-profile careers.[8] But less than 5 percent of mid-twentieth-century women business owners launched manufacturing enterprises, so Lewis, Beech, and Rudkin operated in a sector with few peers.[9] Food processing, of course, was a field with roots in women's private domestic work, and there were many small-scale female proprietors in the field.[10] Yet scale set Rudkin apart from other niche producers as well as other women in the food industry—her distribution and advertising was nationwide and production volume was exponentially larger. For Lewis, the particular area of food processing she entered—canning—was already big business, one dependent on large teams of seasonal workers and complex and expensive equipment and populated by large, male-run operations. And not surprisingly, in the aircraft industry Beech was the only female business owner. Breaking into what many perceived as a man's world, each of the three women had to concern herself with how best to present her credentials so as to secure the most advantageous outcome for her company and herself. They positioned themselves not as challengers and not as women who "worked" the system but as skillful leaders who knew how to succeed within the existing corporate system.[11]

Each of these businesswomen asserted her self-worth differently. Lewis advocated her stature in the company and the industry, communicating this in a variety of ways, including doggedly pursuing compensation equal to other company presidents. Beech, on the other hand, viewed gender as irrelevant to leadership and insisted that she be judged solely on the basis of how she managed the company. And finally for Rudkin, whose leadership evolved from the most traditional origin, her home kitchen, expressions of competence including and beyond baking enabled her to present herself as integral to Pepperidge Farm's success. Whether asserting stature, the irrelevance of gender, or competence, these pioneering businesswomen made a convincing case for their own self-worth and the worth of their companies. In so doing, not only did they "own" their success, but they also created it.

Tillie Lewis

Lewis was savvy about pegging her self-presentation and self-advocacy to industry and corporate norms, selecting high-stature poses for photo opportunities, compensation commensurate with her title, and business trends and emphasizing her financial acumen as the chief skill to highlight. All together, these strategies helped her to position herself effectively in the eyes of customers, investors, and corporate board members. For Lewis, the payoffs were clear. She enacted the part of a successful corporate leader and became one.

One way Lewis portrayed this role was through carefully staged publicity photos to convey status and achievement. For example, a 1942 photo series, professionally captured by Van Covert Martin, Stockton's only commercial photographer at the time, seemed designed to capture both an important historical moment in Flotill's history—production of its millionth case of tomatoes—and Tillie Lewis herself as a business success. It featured Lewis in two main poses: seated behind her desk and smashing a bottle of champagne in the warehouse. Both settings included the same wooden crate imprinted to commemorate production of 1,000,000 cases of tomatoes. The office pictures in particular appear to have been deliberately set up to highlight the iconography of status. In the foreground, on the surface of a large executive-style wooden desk, sat a silver box, pen set, statuette (of a dog), and paperweight. Set against a darkly painted wall with white-trimmed wainscoting hung a large tapestry featuring a scene from classical Greece. This office setting—presumably Lewis's actual office at her company—communicated power, financial success, and mainstream status. In the background of the photograph, the viewer saw a miniature American flag and a model ship suggestive of the *Mayflower*. These objects subtly captured another side to this success story: its unique American cast whereby the daughter of an impoverished Jewish immigrant became a multimillionaire. Together these icons of success and status communicated the accomplishment of the subject—Tillie, always in the center of the photograph, sometimes surrounded by her nephews (both employed in the business) and/or by Meyer Lewis, a manager at the company and her future husband. But there is no doubting who the boss was or the reason for the celebration. Very clearly, Tillie Lewis was the subject of the promotion. Clothed in dark slacks rather than a more feminine skirt, a Peter-Pan collared blouse, and a celebratory corsage in these photographs, she was worker, manager, and executive—and very clearly the company driver. This professional photo shoot, commissioned only four years after Lewis became sole owner, conveys pride in her achievements and also a sense of self-importance.[12]

Tillie Lewis thought highly of herself. If salary is a proxy for how a company founder and president values her worth to the business, then Tillie Lewis judged her own contributions as its manager to be highly valuable. We know this because of extant tax records that permit a revealing glimpse into her business even before it was required to submit reports to the Securities and Exchange Commission recording officer salary information. When working under Del Gaizo ownership in 1936, Lewis earned an annual salary of $28,854, approximately two times the annual salary for women in professional jobs in 1930.[13] Though she lowered her own salary to $14,050 during the difficult year 1938–39, as soon as she became sole owner and increased the company's net taxable income the following year (turning the company around through heavy investments in new equipment for production), she raised her salary back up to $30,000. One year later, after achieving a nearly 20 percent increase in the company's net taxable income, she raised her salary to $40,000.[14] For Lewis, there was a clear and justified correlation between the company's performance and her compensation. When the company did well, it was substantially because of her efforts as its leader, and she believed she should be compensated accordingly.

In fact, Lewis fought for this valuation of her worth to Flotill Products in the multiyear battle she waged to resist paying excess profits taxes. In the "Application for Relief under Section 722" of the Internal Revenue Code (for 1941–46) filed by her attorney in 1950, Lewis leveraged a theory of value that rationalized a high salary for herself as the chief executive, without whom business decisions could not be made. Responding to the IRS assertion that her salary was both an example of the company's "excess profits" and itself excessive, she asserted that the $40,000 annually she paid herself was "not only not excessive, but less than the value of her services." The statement prepared by her attorney continued:

> Literally she was the company during this period; *all* decisions of importance in *all* phases of the taxpayer's [Flotill Products] operations were her responsibility. She determined the size of the pack, the type of operation, negotiated contracts with growers, negotiated loans and other financing, and finally made virtually all of the large sales. She had no assistant (with the possible exception of her plant superintendent) who was able to take independent managerial action. Even the plant superintendent was constantly forced to consult her in matters of plant operation, particularly in dealings with labor unions. . . . It was necessary for her to work long hours daily to complete all of her duties as president; she devoted from twelve to eighteen hours daily to the company's business virtually the entire year.[15]

The statement articulated Lewis's value to the company in terms of expertise, responsibility, and hours worked. In essence, it asserted, Lewis *was* Flotill Products, and thus the company's profits were appropriately distributed to

Tillie Lewis often posed for photographs sitting at her executive-style desk, surrounded by the accoutrements of success. Palm Springs Historical Society.

reflect the person who generated them. In conclusion, her attorney stated, "her intimate knowledge of all aspects of the business has been and now is the basis of the company's prosperity" and thus that "she ha[d] established beyond a doubt her ability as an executive." This was powerful and gendered language. "Executive" was a term that implied male. It conveyed status, power, and privilege, all of which were encoded as masculine qualities when defined in the context of the mid-twentieth-century business world. Thus, the claim her attorney made was that Lewis deserved a man's salary because she was as competent as a man and did the same job a man would have done in this position. The self-confidence and conviction that such an assertion required is palpable. She knew her value to the company and was prepared to assert it, even to the tax commissioner and the IRS that enforced the excess profits statute. Standing up for herself both reflected and helped to establish Lewis's "ability as an executive."

It was not coincidental that she made these salary decisions in the midst of World War II and defended them in the immediate postwar period. This was a new era, when women in the United States had access to "men's jobs for men's wages" for the first time in history.[16] Women moved into and dominated a variety of new economic sectors that had previously employed mainly men. Banking, for example, "took on so many women as managers, bookkeepers and tellers that the industry . . . became permanently feminized."[17] Wartime conditions also sparked initiatives to improve women's pay. For example, "Between 1943 and 1955, 16 states added equal pay laws to their books," and in 1945, "a federal law was introduced to Congress . . . and reintroduced periodically throughout the 1950s," even though it didn't pass until 1963.[18] Though scholars disagree on whether World War II marked a dramatic and long-standing shift in women's employment trends or whether it accelerated shifts already under way for unmarried women and sparked only short-lived change for married women, for those women who lived through it, it's clear that the period fomented a great deal of discussion and thought about women's work and their worth in the workplace.[19] This was the context in which Lewis asserted her value as Flotill's leader, reflecting the changes occurring around her and perhaps even helping to foment them in her own individual way.

Lewis's high salary was not indicative of a uniform compensation policy for company officers but specifically reflected her sense of self-worth. For when the company submitted its prospectus to the Securities and Exchange Commission in 1948, it reported an annual salary of $135,000 for Lewis as president and director and only $20,000 annually for each of her nephews who had appeared in the celebratory 1942 photos: Arthur H. Heiser, executive vice president and director, and Albert S. Heiser, secretary, general sales manager, and director. Even Claude O. Young, former president of the Banco Di Napoli who had provided the business-saving loan to Lewis in 1938 and was now employed at Flotill as vice president, treasurer, and director, was paid only $15,000, 11 percent of Lewis's $135,000 salary.[20] That salary was part of a five-year management contract that Lewis signed with the board for the years 1947 through 1952. Yet one year after the contract went into effect, it was amended with a reduced annual salary of $95,000. The change must have reflected the merging of Flotill Products, Inc., and Flotill Sales Company, both of which listed Lewis as president with two separate salaries, $99,999 and $35,000 respectively, totaling $135,000.[21] Whether the reduction in annual salary also signaled corporate concern about excessive executive compensation is impossible to know but is certainly a possibility.[22] What seems clear is that Lewis was particularly good at asserting her self-worth to the company's directors to secure an annual salary commensurate with her responsibility and leadership.[23]

Specific comparative salary figures are hard to come by, but those that exist make clear that Lewis's salary was similar to that of other senior executives, at the time nearly all of them men. For example, about the same year that she earned $99,000 annually at a company with a net income of $1.9 million, the president of Lorillard, a U.S. tobacco company with a net income of $5.6 million, earned a salary of $60,000, had $13,000 paid into his pension, and received a bonus equal to 1 percent of the company's net income, or $56,000. The bonus was part of a "new incentive compensation program" at Lorillard and brought the president's total compensation to $129,000, which exceeded Lewis's salary at the time but was similar to the larger amount she had first negotiated in 1947.[24] These figures were consistent with the average salary plus bonus earnings of top executives in manufacturing companies in 1947, according to one study. In that study, top executives in a sample of large manufacturing firms averaged $149,446 in salary plus bonus, and top executives in a sample of small manufacturing firms averaged $62,526 in salary plus bonus. Tillie Lewis's salary was almost exactly equivalent to the average of the two salary ranges, which was $105,986, making her compensation equivalent to that of top male executives in contemporary, "medium-sized" (as an average of small and large) manufacturing firms.[25]

This finding helps to contexualize Lewis's adamant assertion that she be compensated adequately for her leadership of the company. She was not requesting an excessive salary but essentially arguing that her compensation align with that of other executives at comparable companies during the same period. This, in itself, was a rhetorical strategy about self-worth, especially for a woman who had almost exclusively male executives with whom to compare her compensation. It was, in essence, a comparable-worth argument launched in an era when women made less than 63.9 cents for every dollar earned by a man and when female-led firms were still extremely rare.[26] Lewis, like most female corporate leaders at the time, denied feminism's appeals yet fought to be treated equally with male business executives when it came to compensation—a feminist argument if there ever was one.

In addition to salary compensation, Lewis sought to profit from her company's success through stock options. The 1948 stock prospectus she filed with the Securities and Exchange Commission reported that, as the sole owner of Flotill Products, Inc.'s stock, totaling 251,000 shares of Preferred Stock and 651,000 shares of Common Stock, she planned to sell a substantial portion of her shares (248,000 Preferred Shares and 250,000 Common Shares), with the proceeds from the sale projected to total $3,383,000 ($2,108,000 and $1,275,000, respectively), equivalent to $33.3 million today.[27] This was a sizable enhancement of her $99,000 annual salary, substantial additional compensation that she enjoyed because she had had the foresight in 1938 to buy out her business partner and investor, Florindo Del Gaizo, who held the controlling stake in the company at the time.

Lewis's stock holdings, like her salary, also reflected an implied equity argument. Stock ownership was just starting to emerge as an important executive benefit in U.S. businesses when she filed her stock prospectus in 1948. Average total executive compensation grew in conjunction with increasing use of stock options. It was a trend especially pronounced in the manufacturing sector, where by the late 1950s and early 1960s only one-third of total pay for top executives comprised salaries and bonuses, compared to three-fourths in the 1940s. Such "deferred and contingent" forms of compensation in an executive's "pay package" introduced "volatility" but also tremendous opportunity for substantially larger remuneration in conjunction with company performance.[28] Lewis took advantage of this trend. Aligning her interest in adequate compensation with the performance of her company and taking a salary cut at the same time that she issued a first sale of Flotill Products stock revealed the currency of her arguments. And it also revealed that she benchmarked her compensation against that of top male executives and pursued a compensatory strategy that reflected her commitment to being paid equally to businessmen in comparable leadership positions. It was another example of the way in which Lewis asserted her self-worth and value to the company.

The company biography of Lewis prepared during the 1970s that cast her as the embodiment of American economic freedom was also an example of skillful self-advocacy. This attention-grabbing story worked *because* she was a woman. The approach cashed in on several decades of Cold War–era Americanism to situate her success, pivoting on the idea that even though it was usually men who achieved executive status, in the United States women could and did too. Exemplifying an alternative to the domestic narrative that preoccupied cultural representations of women in the decades following World War II, Flotill Products' presentation aligned its female leader with a different current in American Cold War rhetoric—free enterprise.[29] Avoiding Lewis's childless home life altogether—a liability in the context of Cold War–era pronatalist nationalism—the prepared history of her life and achievements celebrated the ways in which she embodied the triumph of up-from-the-bootstraps economics. She was, the document claimed, "a Horatio Alger story in petticoats." The phrase highlighted the ways in which success was gendered male. Lewis couldn't be touted as a "Horatio Alger"—the "symbol for free market competition."[30] That story was inherently a story about the independent success of men. Instead, Lewis was a success story "in petticoats," underscoring that she turned on its head the classic "rags to riches" tale simply by virtue of being female. Titled "Who Is Tillie Lewis?," the biography emphasized her life as a quintessential American success story lauded around the country and even the globe precisely because she was a woman rather than a man.[31] The document cited an impressive list of reasons to view her as a remarkable businesswoman:

- Honored by the California Legislature as an outstanding citizen of that State. Since then, honored by many cities and states throughout the country for her outstanding accomplishments.
- Honored by resolution in the Congressional Record of the Congress of the United States for her exemplification that America's Frontiers have not yet been reached.
- Her story was broadcast over the Voice of America to the satellite countries exemplifying the American Way of Life and the free enterprise system afforded by our great country.
- Her story has been distributed to twenty-one countries in twenty-one different languages to show the opportunities that exist in America for women as well as men.

An "outstanding citizen," pioneer, and model American, Lewis, the document argued, was a product of all that made the United States great in this era of Cold War competition. This was precisely the purpose behind *Voice of America* (VOA), a shortwave radio program with origins in World War II propaganda that continued postwar to combat Russian communist propaganda and became an official State Department transmission between 1948 and 1953, when Lewis appeared on the program. The purpose of VOA transmissions—which were sent to countries all over the world in a variety of languages—was to "portray the variety and uniqueness of American society" and to "create a sympathetic understanding of its people and their beliefs." Though it was ostensibly charged with serving as an "objective reporter of news," some described VOA as an "unabashed advocate of American views."[32] Celebrating Lewis's rise to fame and fortune in this context worked because it illustrated a story the American government wanted to highlight: opportunities were universally available to men as well as women. It recast the achievements of the free-market system by putting a woman at its center. Lauding her and others like her was in the best interests of American economic and political policy at the time, but it was also in the company's best interest. Characterizing their leader as an exemplar of the "American way of life" confronted male models of success even as it capitalized on them by presenting Lewis as unique. It made a case for Lewis's achievements, because confidence in a company's leadership was key to attracting investors, business partners, government contracts, and even customers. It was a formula that both stimulated and reflected commercial success and strategically enhanced the value proposition of its female leader.

While it is impossible to know the degree to which this version of Lewis reflected company handling as opposed to self-presentation, other examples of Lewis's clear and intentional management of her public impression reveal a focus on financial aptitude rather than enterprise. Emphasizing discerning money management in contrast to initiative and innovation was a strategic and incisive move for a businesswoman in the decades following World War II. Lewis used her financial aptitude to make the case that she belonged at the helm of a multimillion dollar company—a rarified position, especially for a woman. A 1951 *Time* magazine article exemplified the trend: "In Manhattan's elegant St. Regis Hotel last week, a waiter carried two tomatoes on a tray into the suite of Mrs. Tillie Lewis of Stockton, Calif. She was aghast at the bill ($1). 'You tell Vincent Astor (who owns the St. Regis),' said Mrs. Lewis as she signed the check, 'that these tomatoes cost him no more than 5c apiece, that's 1,000% profit.' Said the waiter: 'I guess you know your tomatoes.'"[33] Focusing on her mastery of the financial intricacies of her business rather than, for example, her attention to the quality of the fruit, this opening story, like many others, highlighted Lewis's abilities as a fiscal manager. Another account reported, "Tillie Lewis had always been good at figures . . . mathematics was her best subject. She aimed for a career in finance."[34] Some stories reported that even as a young woman, she was good with numbers. "At school she studied hard, and got fine marks, especially in arithmetic, because she had a talent for figures," one account reported.[35] Such stories make clear that the version of her life story that Tillie Lewis told when asked included examples of her aptitude for financial computations—an emphasis she selected.

Lewis's focus on financial savvy was likely related to both gender and her lack of formal education. As discussed in the introduction, women's professional talents then (and even now) were typically associated with their supposedly superior people skills and not financial skills. While this shaped the opportunities women found as employees of large companies, it created serious impediments for a female company president who had to retain the trust of investors, lenders, customers, and employees as a sound fiscal manager. For Lewis, the gender stereotype of women as people rather than number experts was compounded by her educational deficits. Hers was an education gained in the "school of experience."[36] She had completed neither a high school nor college education, but she was careful to correct a headline describing her as a dropout. She stated, "I was not a drop out! Economic conditions made me a 'force out' after one year of high school, but I never stopped trying to make up for the scholarly deficiency by reading and studying as much as possible."[37] Smart money management could be learned outside formal education, she proved. And it was important that she prove this. Lenders and investors were "interested in a person's track record in financial dealings," something "women often have lacked experience with," and this could hurt their entrepreneurial and business prospects.[38] Lewis seemed determined to avoid this pitfall by helping to focus the media's attention on her financial abilities. In the same 1968 publicity speech to the Pilot Club in New York in which she positioned herself as "just a housewife"— per the marketing discussion in chapter 4—she also described herself as a financier: "My life in high finance so far has run pretty much along the same lines as the rest of my life. I approach problems with an eye to their simple elements. High finance is buying and selling, keeping costs down. It's producing a product good enough to warrant a profitable price in a competitive market. It's having capable people to help plan and carry out the work."[39] Thus, while the company's brand strategy was to downplay Lewis's role as manager and play up her similarities to her consumers, when she *did* discuss herself as a manager it wasn't her marketing or human resource skills that she emphasized but her financial management. It was an approach that explicitly avoided emphasizing her gender but that implicitly contradicted the predominant assumptions about women's abilities. Lewis positioned herself as someone especially skilled at procuring, managing, and making money in spite of her lack of education and the fact that she was a woman. Her use of the term "high finance" to describe her professional life helped to lay bare the way she wanted others to view her and the way she viewed herself: as someone who operated in the highest levels of money management and competently managed especially large sums. Clearly, this was an important part of her self-concept and self-presentation: an affinity for figures and finance that enabled her to advocate for and retain a powerful position in the male-dominated world of big business.

Lewis's sense of worth to her company and keen understanding of her business and its finances served her well when she sold Tillie Lewis Foods in 1966. The Ogden Corporation purchased the company for $16 million, and Lewis herself reportedly realized close to $9 million from the sale.[40] Perhaps as important to Lewis, she was appointed a director on the Ogden Corporation's Board. While the *Wall Street Journal*'s report on her election did not comment on the fact that she was its first female member, the *New York Times* did. With the heading "Ogden Corp. Stockholders Elect a Woman to Board" the brief article reported that she was "the company's first woman director."[41] Whether Ogden saw Lewis as a "token" appointment or a valued member of its management team is impossible to know. But early indications were that the company valued her expertise in the food industry, which was a new area of concentration for Ogden initiated by its investment in Tillie Lewis Foods. When the company acquired Wilson Foods (another Stockton canner) and International Products Corporation of Paraguay (a meat producer), it integrated both into Tillie Lewis Foods, which remained under Lewis's management.[42] Her ongoing active involvement in company affairs was reflected in how she was remembered. On the occasion of her death eleven years after her appointment to the board, Ogden chairman and president Ralph Ablon described Lewis as "a valued member of the Corporation's senior management since 1966." The year she died, she was scheduled to stand for reelection at the annual meeting, clearly intending to carry on with her role as director.[43] This commitment suggests that the board seat must have been an important part of the negotiation around Ogden's acquisition of Tillie Lewis Foods. For Lewis, the appointment affirmed what she had long advocated—that she was what was most valuable about her company. Its valuation was sound as long as she presided.

Whether Lewis wielded influence over the Ogden Corporation from her seat on its board is difficult to determine. Recent research has indicated that even one female board member contributes positively to a corporation's governance score as measured by business scholars.[44] Despite some contradictory findings, much of the research on the topic indicates that gender diversity on corporate boards has a positive impact on many levels, including financial performance and employee retention and morale.[45] Projecting these insights into the past to evaluate the impact of the first generation of female corporate board members such as Lewis is problematic because it does not enable us to account for historical context. Resistance to women's leadership, questions, and concerns in 1960s board rooms would have been much more stringent than today, when it is still a barrier. At the very least we can ask the question: did the appointment of the first female board member lead to the appointment of others? In the case of Ogden, it was a long time in coming; Terry Allen Kramer, the second female board member, was appointed in 1977, the same year Lewis died.[46] Thus, Lewis was the lone woman on the board for nearly the entire time she served. Present-day research suggests that women in this position are sometimes hesitant to speak out until there is at least a "critical mass" of female board members. This did not seem to be a problem for Lewis. She continued to demonstrate both ambition and ease with all-male environments, serving as the only female commissioner at the Port of Stockton and the only woman among U.S. representatives who participated in the 1974 World Food Agricultural Organization meeting convened in Rome by the United Nations.[47] These examples, in combination with her long-ranging service on Ogden's board, indicate that Lewis positioned herself to have influence even if her impact is hard to discern.

But Lewis walked a fine line between ambition and self-advocacy and conformity to traditional gender standards that persisted throughout her career. She complained that "women may get to the top of the heap at some low level, but they don't try to move up to the next plateau." The one "part of women's lib I think is good," she continued, was that it might succeed in inspiring women to do more. But at the same time she challenged women to push themselves, she assured them that at home, "I'm my husband's wife." Although she avoided the topic of childlessness, which was a particular liability for her in the context of traditional mid-twentieth-century gender norms, the comment placed her squarely in the domestic sphere in the role expected of women of her generation. It was a point of importance in many news stories about female executives at this time, which helps to explain why Lewis presented herself this way. *Fortune* magazine's 1973 article on "The Ten Highest-Ranking Women in Big Business," for example, assured readers that "careers apparently did not prove incompatible with husbands" and made a point of explaining that Lewis was the only woman on the list who had been divorced and that it was "from a man she married in her teens." This seemed to be an assurance to readers that her divorce did not constitute a rejection of marriage per se—a long-standing latent fear surrounding female leaders in mythology, fiction, and history. More important, it asserted, she had "been happily remarried since 1948."[48] Ambitious, self-promoting women such as Lewis challenged gender norms that prescribed adherence to supporting rather than leading roles for women in the business world. Even in the midst of feminist advocacy, stories such as *Fortune*'s and the one that appeared in *Cosmopolitan* in 1975 about "36 Women With Real Power Who Can Help You" were upbeat but warned that women were still "combating the myths that (1) they don't *need* to work, and (2) they are overly emotional and can't stand pressure or make decisions." Lewis's answer about how to navigate it all in the *Cosmopolitan* story was to "minimize your risks."[49] On the one hand, the message can be read as monetary strategy—apt advice from a female executive who had positioned her self-worth around financial acumen. But minimizing risk also referenced the liminal space female executives traveled, simultaneously challenging and enacting gender norms. Lewis seemed also to be emphasizing the importance for women leaders of figuring out how to present their success in ways that did not completely undo entrenched ideas about women's proper role and place in American society. When women failed to enact such norms even as they challenged them—in Lewis's case neglecting to emphasize her role as a wife at home even as she presented herself as a competent leader at work—it threatened others as well as their chance to succeed. Ultimately, Lewis had figured out how to walk that line in her self-presentation, and her advice to the Pilot's Club revealed this. Advocate for yourself, she seemed to say, but don't abandon all gender conventions and take precautions to ensure that it doesn't come back to "bite" you. This was a particularly important caution for a woman whose self-advocacy centered on asserting her stature and insisting that her worth be compensated and presented in comparable ways to male executives at the top of the business world. For Lewis, caution in conjunction with the courage to engage in self-advocacy was a winning formula.

Olive Ann Beech

For Olive Ann Beech, self-advocacy meant insisting on the irrelevance of gender. Though she was regularly confronted with gendered conventions and stereotypes that thrust her into roles and situations in which it was impossible to ignore her status as a *female* executive, it was precisely that characterization that she most abhorred. Though skillfully and graciously navigating the awkwardness that her rarified position as a businesswoman in the aviation industry sometimes engendered, she also advocated an assessment of her skill as a company leader and not a woman. Doing so was the only way she could be sure of her value, since only business leadership and not her gender were in her control and since she operated in an industry so intensively masculine and male-dominated that gender difference was a strategy destined to fail. Thus O. A. Beech, as she signed her name, deliberately erasing any indication of gender, asserted the radical notion that her self-worth had everything to do with her skill, experience, and track record and nothing to do with the fact that she was a woman.

When Olive Ann Beech was named "Man of the Month" by the National Aviation Club in 1959, it said a great deal about her challenges as a businesswoman in the aircraft field. Needless to say, she was the first woman to earn the honor, which was clearly conceptualized in masculine terms. Among the telegrams she received congratulating her were many that poked fun at the title: "We think 'man of the month' will be 'queen of the evening,'" "Congratulations but how can you be 'man' of the month [when] you're a mother," and most insightfully, "Aircraft 'man of the month' throws curves to industry." The last comment in particular acknowledged the degree to which having a woman at the helm of an aircraft company disrupted industry and social norms ill-equipped to adapt to her presence. From Beech employees came the quip, "On this grand occasion all of us here on the home front lift a toast to the most attractive 'man' of them all." Together the telegram messages reveal that Olive Ann Beech had a sense of humor— something admirers noted—and was comfortable joking about her status in the field as the only female aviation executive. But the awkwardly worded and male-centered award she received from the National Aviation Club that year highlighted the degree to which Beech's success depended on her ability to successfully navigate her nearly all-male world and advocate for herself in the process. The Beech guest list for the dinner reception that followed conferral of the award suggests that this was one of her strengths; it was filled with honorifics including colonels, commanders, captains, lieutenant colonels, and senators—all men of power who had influence over her opportunities and those of her company and were there to celebrate her achievements.

When Beech was appointed to the International Development Advisory Board (IDAB) by President Eisenhower the same year, she was, again, the only woman and unknown and underestimated by fellow board members. She was one of twelve named to the board, which was charged with advising the International Cooperation Administration, which "approve[d] foreign aid and assistance" to advance the mutual security of the United States and its allies. In particular, the board advised Undersecretary of State for Economic Affairs, Douglas Dillon, "on how to encourage free enterprise abroad." When Beech arrived in Washington on 3 February to attend the swearing-in ceremony, she must have been misjudged, perhaps as a "token" appointment. The IDAB board chair, Harry Bullis, retired board chairman of General Mills, wrote to Beech saying as much. After reading the high-profile *Saturday Evening Post* article featuring Olive Ann Beech that was published in August the same year, he admitted, "I did not realize what a tycoon we had on our IDAB. Seriously, I compliment you on your wonderful career with Beech Aircraft Corporation. I am looking forward to seeing you at the next meeting of our Board in Washington on September 16 and 17."[50] Being undervalued by male colleagues—at least on first impression—must have been a common experience for Beech and one that she labored to overcome.

One way she did this was by methodically documenting her achievements. Among the items preserved in the Walter and Olive Ann Beech Collection is a thirty-three-page typed list of her honors. Fronted with a Table of Contents, the honors were broken down into categories: (1) Special Appointments and Memberships; (2) Trophies, Plaques and Gifts; (3) Commendations and Citations; (4) Certificates of Appreciation; (5) Honorary Memberships; 6) Honorary Degrees and Fellowships; (7) Corporate Distinctions; (8) Corporate Elections; and (9) Offices Held (Non-Corporate). Her "Special Appointments and Memberships" included ten government appointments, six of which were national, as well as election to membership on the National Chamber of Commerce's Board of Directors in 1970, the first woman named to the post.[51] And while many of the items listed confirmed her national stature, the itemization of numerous small items too, such as an Eskimo art sculpture presented to her by an aircraft company in Canada as a token of appreciation for her leadership, demonstrate that to Beech, they were all evidence of the scope of her achievements.

Beech's résumé, too, captured the breadth of her accomplishments and the fact that she was confident about displaying them to present herself in the best light. When she received a letter from Dun & Bradstreet in 1961 soliciting her inclusion in a new publication titled *Top Management: The Officers and Principals* designed to celebrate the "universally recognized [idea] that success of a business is directly proportionate to the ability and experience of its management," she submitted a completed form for the book but one with many blank spaces as well as unconventional answers. After listing her present title as "President" and "Director" of Beech Aircraft Corporation, she found that the form presented some challenges for her. Under "previous positions," she could list only three: "Secretary-Treasurer & Director, Beech Aircraft Corporation," "Office Manager and Secretary to the President, Travel Air Company," and "Office Assistant and in Chg. of Bookkeeping, Staley Electric Co." This forced her to highlight her clerical work, something that advice books for upwardly mobile professional women at the time discouraged, and left eleven blank spaces below.[52] Both of these circumstances drove home the point that she was a nontraditional business executive, most of whom climbed the corporate ladder through a variety of leadership positions and not from humble origins as secretaries. In other sections of the résumé-type form, she included information that stretched the identified categories to improve her self-presentation. Under "other business connections [and] directorships," she listed her role as director in three companies, Fourth National Bank & Trust Co. and Union Center, Inc., both in Wichita, and Western Union Telegraph Company in New York, New York. These demonstrated that although her employment experiences had been limited, she provided executive leadership in other companies. In addition, she listed "Chairman of the Board" for both the Beech Acceptance Corporation, Inc., and Beechcraft Research & Development, Inc., both subsidiaries of Beech Aircraft. Arguably, this was what we'd refer to today as "padding" the résumé, since she was chair of those boards by virtue of her position as chair of the parent company. Yet listing them did convey the complexity of the organization that she oversaw.

Beech also emphasized her leadership ability by using the résumé to capture the variety of efforts she led beyond Beech Aircraft. Under "Business and Professional Membership," Beech listed three business-related professional organizations of which she was a member: the National Aeronautical Association (VP & Dir), the Wichita Chamber of Commerce (Board), and the Utility Airplane Council–Aerospace Industries Association. In addition, she listed two board memberships in organizations that promoted economic education and free enterprise—Freedoms Foundation and the Foundation for Economic Education. The remaining nineteen associational memberships listed captured the breadth of her philanthropy and community involvement, often in leadership positions, but not professional alliances in the business world as traditionally defined. These ranged from her seat on the Development Board for the University of Wichita to her trusteeship at Wesley Hospital and presidency for the local chapter of Junior Achievement. By broadening her list in this way, Beech boldly displayed the variety of ways in which she led.

A final example of self-advocacy on this résumé form came in the way she listed her education. The form's "educational background" section asked for "school, college or university," "dates" (of attendance), and "degrees" (earned). This was a problematic area for Beech, since she had not attended high school and earned no degrees. What she listed was "Paola, Kansas Elementary School, 1908–1916" and "American Business College, 1916–1920" with no degree, since this was a technical college. Most revealing, perhaps, she listed the honorary doctorate of business administration, awarded to her 16 March 1954 from Southwestern College in Winfield, Kansas, under her education rather than honors and awards. Traditionally, honorary degrees convey recognition of professional and community contributions. Since it is not an earned degree (and in fact Southwestern College did not even offer a doctorate in business administration), it is not customarily listed under education. Yet, for Beech, this honor helped to make up for her lack of actual education and set her apart from others listed in the book who likely had earned college and graduate degrees but perhaps not "doctorates" in business administration. How Beech responded to Dun & Bradstreet's definitions of what it meant to be "top management"—both in the education section and the experience sections it contained—illustrates her skill at self-presentation and an ability to navigate traditional and exclusionary definitions to assert her own self-worth on her own terms.

While such self-promotion was essential in the business world, Beech was often lauded for her modesty by admirers. For example, friend Lillian Whipple congratulated Olive Ann Beech "for having always been modest about [her] achievements and every inch a lady!"[53] This was something Beech truly cared about—there is ample evidence of this in archival material. But gendering modesty as feminine was a problem for Beech. This meant the inverse was also true: that self-advocacy might lead to perceptions of immodesty, which was characterized as "manlike" and "unfeminine." In one article, in fact, Beech described women's "universal tendency to avoid ungracious and undue publicity"—modesty—as a reason that women in business had "escaped proper evaluation."[54] Thus, while to be self-effacing was considered attractive for a woman, doing so meant she risked being undermined (as Beech had learned the hard way in her first decade as an executive, per chapter 1) or taken too lightly (as Harry Bullis had shown when she was sworn into the IDAB). Beech's detailed record of accomplishments—both in her own list and in her public résumé—suggests she was unwilling to take that risk of being undermined by the modesty that her friends admired in her. Thus, she asserted herself and her accomplishments because she knew she must.

One gets the impression from the many sources of inspiration that Beech called on in her work life that self-advocacy was a studied practice for her, and perhaps an uncomfortable one. In addition to the many individual quotes and sayings that she saved, E. F. G. Gerard's 1964 *Point Blank*, marketed as "A Gold Mine of Practical Inspiration for Men and Women in Business and Industry," was a favorite guidebook. The opening page begins, "You have powers you never dreamed of. You can do things you never thought you could do. There are no limitations in what you can do except the limitations in your mind. Don't think you cannot. Think you can. And you will!" Section headings included "Enthusiasm—Elixir of Success," "Faith and Confidence," "Brains Unlimited," "Find Out!" "Personality," "Common Sense," "You Can Sell Anything!" "Nuggets," "That Extra Something," "Be Polite and Live Longer," "Personal Efficiency," "Go-Getters and No-Getters," "Aim High!" "Pep and Go!" "Golden Minutes," "The Will to Win," "Opportunity Knocks and Knocks and Knocks," "Gumption!" and "Go to It!" For one dollar, the twenty-four-page booklet promised to provide "A Lifetime Gift of Priceless Goodwill."[55] Seeking inspiration and information for her role at Beech Aircraft was something Olive Ann Beech actually advertised. A 1979 advertisement for the *Wall Street Journal* actually featured her with the heading: "Olive Ann Beech, when did you start reading The Wall Street Journal?" Alongside pictures of Beech looking presidential was the quote: "When you're starting your own company and the country's in the middle of a depression . . . you need all the business help you can get. That's why I started reading The Journal—more than 40 years ago." The ad copy continued with the assertion that Beech found helpful business news in it every day, "information she can put to work for her company and for herself that same day." Identifying Beech as chairman of the board of Beech Aircraft and a "widely known and respected business leader," the advertisement celebrated Beech as a *student* of business—someone who pursued information and inspiration to shape her abilities as well as others' perception of her.[56] First she taught herself to think and act like an accomplished business leader, it seems, and then she convinced others of it.

Beech's insistence that she be evaluated on her performance and not her gender was a running theme in her speeches and interviews and an important way that she advocated for herself. It was, in fact, a point of irritation for her when she was referred to as a "woman executive" or when she was asked what it was like to be a female business leader. For example, in a speech to the Soroptomist Club during the 1940s, she described how the focus on her gender felt demoralizing:

> [There is] a letter now on my desk, notifying me that Time Magazine would like to publish in the near future a story on my work as Secretary-Treasurer of Beech Aircraft. When I read the letter I had the usual little thrill that accompanies the thought of one's name being in print. Upon closer examination, however, my self-importance was shattered—shattered by one word—"Female"; they should like to carry the story of my work as a *female* secretary-treasurer, and I realized that the interest in the story, so far as the editor was concerned at least, lay not in my ability as an executive but in my being a *female* in an important position. This, I am sorry to say, is typical, in a general sense, of the attitude of men toward women, who . . . have invaded the fields of work men have so long regarded as exclusively theirs.
>
> This attitude at times has amused me, at other times it has irritated me, but it has *ever* served as a challenge to me—to do my job along with the men in the business world, to be judged by the same standards, to be accepted on the same basis.[57]

Building her self-importance on the fact that she was a *female* executive rather than an *excellent* executive was a problem for Beech. If she was remarkable because she was a woman, then she had little to do with the accomplishment. But if her significance was because of the quality of her leadership, then she could rightfully claim the achievement and the sense of self-satisfaction and importance that went with it. For Beech, therefore, it was imperative that she be judged on her executive abilities alone.

The unremitting interest in Beech's status as a "woman executive" led her to articulate ever-clearer assertions of her worth as a leader regardless of gender. By 1961, she could address this obsession with more humor than irritation. In an article on the topic that she wrote for the *Michigan Business Review*, she quipped: "Women executives patiently expect to be called upon . . . to discuss their ideas 'about misapprehensions which are widely prevalent with regard to women executives' duties and performance.'" She went on to categorize the types of questions and inquiries that female business leaders received aimed at deciphering the secret around women's success in the corporate boardroom. But women executives, she insisted, "are no different than men executives." In answer to the question, "What kind of a woman" could succeed in such a role, she stated, "The correct answer from any board of directors of any business or industry would be, I believe, 'The foremost in the field; the best available.' "[58] And this was how she insisted others judge her—not as a female executive but as an executive who had earned her place at the top of an industry by her own efforts. She wanted to be judged an executive success.

Over the course of her career, Olive Ann Beech became just that. In the 1976 "Gallagher President's Report," marketed as "A Confidential Letter to Chief Executives," she was the number-one "Best Corporate Chief Executive of Achievement" in the Medium/Small Business Category (Under $1 Billion Sales). Beech must have been proud of the nature of the recognition: "for continued record earnings performance in competitive private aircraft manufacture market plus earning respect from male peers as successful business executive."[59] While her gender was implied in the statement, it wasn't referenced. The focus instead was on the fact that her peers were men and they respected her for her business ability, not because she was a female executive who had succeeded against the odds. Similarly, Muriel Siebert, chairman of Muriel Siebert & Co. and the first woman to purchase a seat on the New York Stock Exchange, named Beech Aircraft as the best investment she had made. Since purchasing the stock in 1972, she reported a thirty-five-fold gain fifteen years later.[60] In the world of investments, gender held no traction; stock performance alone made the difference. For Olive Ann Beech, this must have been the ultimate assessment of her achievement.

What Olive Ann Beech most wanted was for her gender to be irrelevant in the workplace, but it was almost always visible in the way others described her, some more subtly than others. At the dedication of the Olive Ann Beech Gallery in Wichita, for example, Gordon E. Evans, president of KG & E Electric Company, said of Beech, "In our many associations I usually think of her as any other business executive until I notice the 'blue' or 'pinkish blue' she wears—and if I should comment on this, her reply may be, 'Don't you think it is nice?' and 'I do.' "[61] For Beech, this subtle difference was the only difference between herself and any successful male executive. As the caption for her *Michigan Business Review* article read, "The office décor may vary but the daily problems are no different."[62] She dressed differently and decorated her office differently and that was it. Yet predictably, reporters who covered Beech during her many years as an executive were not so subtle about the role of gender in her career, even taking a jaundiced view of her success as viewed through the lens of mid-twentieth-century gender stereotypes.

Such was the case with the high-profile coverage she received in the *Saturday Evening Post* in a 1959 article tellingly titled "Danger: Boss Lady at Work." As the title suggests, the overall tenor of the article was that one must beware of female bosses. The lengthy story was written by Peter Wyden, a journalist who got his start at the *Wichita Eagle* and therefore is likely to have known about her beforehand. He went on to publish stories for *Newsweek* and *Ladies' Home Journal* as well as more than a dozen books. Characterizing Beech as both "autocratic" and "too shy to make the briefest speech without flushing, trembling and, occasionally, breaking out in tears," the article bowed to gender stereotypes on both ends of the spectrum. In Wyden's hands, she was proud, stubborn, formal, intimidating, handsome, regal, rich, hard-driving, unflappable, painfully lonely, smart but uneducated, unpretentious yet possessing an insatiable need for flattery, and contemptuous of the Europeans she encountered on holiday for "being poor and not doing something about it, as she had done for herself."[63] Overall, it was not a portrayal anyone would have wished for, and it generated an outpouring of letters from family, friends, employees, stockholders, and other supporters.

While some of the feedback was positive, congratulating Beech on the article and her achievements, most asserted that the portrayal did not accurately represent her and was unfavorably biased. As her daughter Mary Lynn wrote, "Well everyone . . . [here] is terribly incensed about the Post article. I agree with you that it sounds like one of your 'hating friends' wrote it. I really think it was done in a slanting way. . . . [It] just makes me mad everytime [*sic*] I think about it." Providing a window into how Beech herself may have felt—as if someone she thought she could trust had turned against her—the comments reveal that the article had indeed upset her. Friends who wrote to her about it identified specific shortcomings in the portrayal. From her friend Lucille came "I can't see you in the article—yes, you are a successful businesswoman—but never have you forgotten—first, a wife—a mother—a true and tried friend in need." From another friend: "That article in the Saturday Evening Post left me on a sour note. I felt that if Mary Lynn's collegiate standing had been brought out, and also the great love which Wichita has for you, the picture would have been a more correct one." This letter, discussed earlier in chapter 1, is worth repeating here because it reveals so much. The suggestion that Beech was first wife and mother and that her daughter's achievements and community stature should have been covered to highlight her mothering and selfless service reinforces longtime stereotypes associated with successful businesswomen as hardhearted, uncaring, and even incapable of mothering.[64] From another friend came the comment, "This character is not the O.A.B. that I know. Part of the facts are misconstrued terribly. If you were anything like the story, you could not build the organization that you have built here." And from an employee: "None of us here feel like man hours under your able direction." Suggesting that the evidence—her successful company and her many very loyal employees—contradicted the portrayal, these insights indicate that the article failed to grasp Beech's skill and complexity. Oversimplifying the story of Beech and her success was a common criticism in the messages from supporters. Famed pilot and longtime friend Louise Thaden added, "Gadzooks! I've just finished the Saturday Evening Post article about you and while impressed and pleased with this added recognition of your stature, I have also been (momentarily I suspect) thrown into a state of some confusion by the writers [sic] interpretation. It is a little too much to expect though—that a man in a relatively short period of time could do an adequate portrayal of anyone, much less a many faceted female . . . undoubtedly as in all writing there was the use of 'poetic license' to make for a sock-em-between-the-eyes article." Still others found the article inspirational, as two women professionals wrote, reporting that "it gave me courage to go ahead in my own job" and "I have for a long time saluted you for your contribution toward moving women up in business."[65]

In the end, Wyden's portrayal is perhaps best understood as an exposé rather than an article, one designed to sell magazines rather than provide even-handed coverage. He took a similar approach in his "unauthorized biography" of Lee Iacocca, the iconic chairman of Chrysler. As the *Fortune* magazine review of *The Unknown Iacocca* stated, "What you need most to understand about Lee Iacocca is the one thing Wyden lacks most: some experience around businessmen. Reading about the man's compulsion to be (as Wyden incessantly reminds us) Numero Uno, his single-minded drive, his occasionally ruthless behavior, his disregard for the niceties of social etiquette, and a dozen other attributes, I was struck by how similar he seemed to any number of other CEOs."[66] Interestingly, many of the qualities Wyden decried in Lee Iacocca were the same or similar to those he found in Beech. Yet in gendered terms, while these same attributes were evidence of over-the-top ambition in a man (a common quality in male CEOs, as the reviewer above stated), they made a woman "dangerous," as the article's title indicated. Beech never submitted to another lengthy interview or article again, and the scarring experience may have played an important role in her subsequent self-advocacy efforts.

The merger with Raytheon in 1979 revealed that even at the peak of her power and influence, Olive Ann Beech navigated stubborn gender conventions for women in business. Indeed, the business media's coverage of the company's merger cast Beech as a "wife" in her negotiations with corporate "suitors." Addressing speculations that Beech Aircraft might merge with General Dynamics in 1977, a *Time* article titled "Will Olive Ann Marry?" reported, "For a septuagenarian Wichita widow, Olive Ann Beech is quite a flirt. As chairman and co-founder of Kansas' Beech Aircraft Corp., which she has run since her husband Walter's death in 1950, she has been tempting— and turning down—various corporate suitors anxious to merge with her company for years. Now, after spurning such hopefuls as Lockheed and Grumann, Olive Ann may at last be ready to say 'I do'—and to one of their major competitors: General Dynamics."[67] Employing stereotypes of women as "flirts" and the metaphor of "marriage" for corporate mergers, the article framed the entire story as a gendered courting ritual rather than a serious business transaction. Two years later, the same framework was evident in *Fortune*'s report on Beech's confirmed merger with Raytheon in an article titled "Marrying Money," which began, "If all women chose mates as carefully as Olive Ann Beech, 76, chose partners for herself and for Beech Aircraft Corp., divorce lawyers would starve." Regional papers were similar, as in the Quincy, Massachusetts, *Patriot Ledger*'s article titled "Beech Aircraft Courted Its Buyer." These articles played on the idea that women would always be wives in the eyes of men—either someone else's or potentially their own. Such stereotypic roles also implied that women at the top of corporate America still somehow enacted their leadership in overtly "feminine" ways and in keeping with prescribed roles. Framing the Beech Aircraft merger this way ensured that readers and Olive Ann herself could not forget gender as a difference.

Even as they adopted gender stereotypes in the language they used to describe Olive Ann, the articles covering the Beech Aircraft–Raytheon merger were highly complimentary of her skill. In particular, the media coverage highlighted the care with which Beech had selected a buyer for her company. Unlike so many mergers in which a seller "ha[d] to be muscled into selling," Beech had initiated a search for the right buyer by hiring the investment banking firm of Loeb, Rhoades, Hornblower & Co. to prepare a report on the company's value, to propose a selling strategy, and to collect a list of potential buyers that met her criteria. Once the list was whittled down to ten potential buyers, Beech and her senior executives reviewed the prospects for "fit," which included maximizing financial outcomes for the company, its shareholders, and its employees but also matching a company culture overtly oriented toward Christian values and championing free enterprise.[68] When Raytheon was announced as the merger partner, the values of the company's leaders were described as very similar: "Raytheon . . . [is] extremely well-run. Solid. Competent . . . Phillips and Holmes [CEO and president, respectively] both have engineering backgrounds and are described as devout Christians whose management style is 'conservative' and 'straight arrow.'" The conservative label often has been pinned on Beech for the way its management has conducted its affairs. Like Beech, Raytheon's top management also has a reputation of actively singing the praises of patriotism and the free-market enterprise system.[69] The similarities in company culture made the match attractive to both companies. These were Olive Ann Beech's values—values she had inculcated into the company and values she wanted to make sure would endure. Their preeminence in the selection of a buyer underscores the degree to which Olive Ann Beech herself was driving the merger. But of course values alone did not drive the process. The business media in fact assessed the merger as a "sound" business decision and characterized Olive Ann as a "savvy business think[er]" because the partner she had found—Raytheon—would be able to "supply the money and know-how for the kind of R[esearch] and D[evelopment] program Beech [would] require" to maintain its strong market position.[70] The juxtaposition of such complimentary evaluations with the gendered stereotypes that framed the coverage of the Beech-Raytheon merger—Beech as flirt and wife and the merger as courting and marriage per above—highlights the degree to which Beech's goal of making gender irrelevant was a challenge to the end. Even when she was admired as a highly skilled, strategic company leader, both she and her actions were cast in gendered terms.

In her own mind, however, Beech saw the purchase by Raytheon as the realization of a long-term goal and plan that had everything to do with maximizing her own interests and that of her company and nothing to do with gender. As reported in internal company documents, she and the leaders of Beech Aircraft "knew there had to be a change" and that it was impossible for the company to "continue on the climb [it] experienced since 1970." Merging with Raytheon was good for the company because it meant that it wasn't "in these [difficult economic] conditions by [it]self." Anticipating this for the sake of the company and for the sake of the principal stockholders was prescient. The outcome, though it led ultimately to the departure of Beech and her two nephews—Frank Hedrick and Ed Burns—who together kept company management in family hands two years post-merger, was in fact planned. Even as the company roiled from the 1982 announcement of the retirements of its long-standing owner-managers, Beech was clear-eyed about the transition. Addressing company executives about the changes, Hedrick said, "I say to you as Mrs. Beech said it so simply—Mr. Hedrick we sold the farm. If they don't like us living on it that is their prerogative."[71] No sentimental corporate "bride" in spite of media portrayals to the contrary, Beech was all business. Perhaps a *New Yorker* cartoon tucked into the pages of her scrapbook on the merger says it all. Featuring an old man sitting at a desk in a well-appointed room, his cane propped nearby, it read, "Sans teeth, sans eyes, sans taste, sans everything. But a fifty-one-per-cent controlling interest."[72] For Beech, this must have summed up the outcome— she had finally made it to the top, and gender had nothing to do with it.

But even though gender was irrelevant in the mind of Olive Ann Beech, she never escaped it. Upon her arrival in Boston to attend her first Raytheon board meeting in 1980, she was greeted with a bouquet of flowers with a card signed "Welcome to Boston and to the Raytheon Family!" It was signed from Bobbie Holmes and Gert Phillips, the wives of the Raytheon president and chairman, respectively. Given the ubiquitous role of executive wives in the twentieth-century business world, it must have seemed fitting to have women welcome the first woman to Raytheon's executive team, which contained neither female vice presidents nor division directors nor presidents in any of its other acquired companies, let alone on its corporate board. It was a trope that repeated over and over again across corporate America: men conducted business while the women—all wives—constructed the social network. Olive Ann Beech navigated this double bind skillfully. In social events she was listed with her formal married name in keeping with the other married women in attendance, all executive wives:

> Mr. and Mrs. Thomas L. Phillips   (Gert)
> Mr. and Mrs. D. Brainerd Homes   (Bobbie)
> Mrs. Walter H. Beech   (Olive Ann)

In contrast, in official photographs after the merger took place, she was identified as simply O. A. Beech in keeping with the male executives, who were similarly identified by their first and last names and not the moniker "Mr." It was a simple yet telling indication of the multiple ways—big and small— that Beech engaged in strategic self-presentation.[73] Knowing when to advocate the irrelevance of gender and when to enact it seemed her best tactic for navigating the mid-twentieth-century corporate world as a leader.

Margaret Rudkin

For Margaret Rudkin, asserting self-worth meant presenting herself as competent. Over and over again, and in a variety of roles, she cast herself as skilled, experienced, and capable. It was a profile that she deployed in her own kitchen, in her marketing and manufacturing sensibility, and in the business world generally. Doing so provided a way to establish her value and to open up spheres of influence and importance. As a competent marketer, manufacturer, entrepreneur, and cook she became an authority who deployed her expertise on increasingly larger and more powerful "stages," from home kitchen to Harvard Business School, with expanding reach and impact, from local bread purveyor to national bestselling author. The progression reflected the growing valuation of her business, skill, and experience—by others and herself.

The position of influence that Rudkin enjoyed was hard won. Woven throughout the David Ogilvy account files for Pepperidge Farm are a handful of letters to and from Margaret Rudkin that reveal a woman inserting herself into the company's business, sometimes in spite of efforts to keep her out. By the time Pepperidge Farm had hired the Ogilvy Mather advertising agency to handle its advertising and branding work in 1956, Rudkin's sons had entered leadership roles in the company and she was sidelined from many of the day-to-day details of the business. As early as 1951, she and Henry Rudkin Sr. regularly sojourned at their homes in Florida and Ireland for months at a time.[74] A clear succession plan that empowered her two sons with significant leadership of the company facilitated this, but health problems also eventually forced her to temporarily relinquish engagement in Pepperidge Farm's business matters. In 1957, she was recovering from a serious illness and described her limitations with frustration: "We are off to Florida for two months. I have come along quite well but am still only able to operate at half speed which I find extremely annoying."[75] As a consequence, she was forbidden from participating in company affairs by her sons and husband. For Rudkin, however, this was a punishing exclusion. As she wrote in a letter to David Ogilvy in November 1957, "I am still not permitted to go to the office which is a frightful bore and I find that there is a subversive movement going on entitled 'Don't Tell Mother' but somehow I always seem to know how much money is being spent—for advertising!

Results?????"[76] This letter is a telling example of Rudkin's insistence on continued involvement in company affairs in spite of illness, absence, and surrender of significant aspects of company management to her sons. It also shows that even as her family tried to exclude her, ostensibly so she could focus on healing, she kept herself immersed in Pepperidge Farm's operation. In particular, a key way that she retained her company influence is that she regularly provided comments and issued requests to David Ogilvy at Ogilvy Mather regarding Pepperidge Farm advertising and branding.

Ogilvy and his staff understood well that when Margaret Rudkin spoke, they were expected to listen, even if her views contradicted their own or even those of her sons, and they navigated this relationship skillfully. For example, in April 1960, Ogilvy wrote an internal memo making it clear that responding positively to Rudkin's input was a top priority for the agency: "I discussed this with Mrs. Rudkin before her departure. She votes for #1 . . . I agree with her. So do you."[77] On another occasion, a letter from "Mrs. Rudkin" containing what she referred to as her "wild idea" for the company's new soft Sandwich Loaf caused Ogilvy to write to the account executives, "About three years ago I suggested that Pepperidge call their new loaf 'Angel Bread.' The idea was rejected by Hank Rudkin—with considerable asperity, as I was told at the time. Now comes this letter from Mrs. Rudkin. I don't know whether she is proposing it as an alternative to the advertisement we have proposed, featuring herself and her grand-children."[78] His response to Rudkin demonstrates that tact prevailed, as well as an interest in avoiding family conflict. Three weeks later he wrote, "About three years ago I suggested that we call the new loaf Angel Bread. However, I was told that it did badly in research. As a result, it was dropped from consideration. I have been brought up not to argue with research, but still. . . . Meanwhile, we have prepared an advertisement for the new loaf. I believe that Hank and Jim McCaffrey are going to show it to you next week. It doesn't contain the word 'Angel' but you may recognize the heroine. Hettie Green herself."[79] This exchange underscores that Rudkin herself still asserted significant influence over the company and its advertising even though she had ceased the same level of day-to-day engagement. And it also demonstrates that she was accorded a significant degree of respect, stature, and perhaps flattery, as is shown by his comparison of Rudkin to Hettie Green— the late-nineteenth-century tycoon who expanded her fortune through shrewd investments.

Ogilvy understood well that keeping Margaret Rudkin engaged and satisfied with the agency's work for Pepperidge Farm was of utmost

Kepperidge

Jill

MARGARET RUDKIN

PEPPERIDGE FARM, INC.
NORWALK, CONNECTICUT

November 1, 1957

"O lovely O most charming Man":

I thoroughly enjoyed reading the article about
Marjorie Fleming. Do you believe in reincarnation?
I am convinced that Minou Drouet is Marjorie Fleming
come back again because such wonderful spirits are
certainly not ordinary mortal's and could not be
wasted on one short lifetime.

I am still not permitted to go to the office which
is a frightful bore and I find that there is a
subversive movement going on entitled "Don't Tell
Mother" but somehow I always seem to know how much
money is being spent - - - - - for advertising!
Results??????

Sincerely yours,

Peg

Mr. David Ogilvy
589 Fifth Avenue
New York, New York

Margaret Rudkin's 1957 note to David Ogilvy reveals the breezy and personal
relationship they maintained. It also shows that she closely monitored the results
of her investments in advertising by his firm. Library of Congress, Washington, D.C.

importance, even if it was her son, Hank, who was now overseeing advertising for the brand. Carefully worded communications about strategic decisions were key to accomplishing this, but so were more personal interactions. Ogilvy adopted a client philosophy that included a preference for lots of friendly contact outside of day-to-day strategic decision-making to help establish a solid relationship and strengthen communication. As he stated in *Confessions of an Advertising Man,* "The head of an agency has so much on his plate that he is apt to see his clients only at times of crisis. This is a mistake. If you get into the habit of seeing clients when the weather is calm, you will establish an easy relationship which may save your life when a storm blows up."[80] With the Rudkins, Ogilvy put this philosophy into action by accepting and extending invitations to lunch and cultural events, by exchanging gifts, and by exchanging personal notes. For example, in November 1962, in a note addressed to "Dear Peg" at her home address, he accepted her invitation to "dine" and to "go and see the Lehman paintings" and added, "I had been increasingly afraid that you, Madame Chairman, had disappeared from my life. Indeed, I had written a valedictory passage about you in my book. Pat Knopf says that *your* book is terrific." The note is signed "Love to you both."[81] In other correspondence, Ogilvy sent Rudkin "a thousand thanks for Parsifal . . . a remarkable evening" as well as congratulating her on "splendid" articles in *Time* magazine and in Art Buchwald's column in the *New York Herald Tribune.* Rudkin thanked Ogilvy for "the article about Marjorie Fleming," and Henry Rudkin Sr. thanked him for a pocket journal.[82] The notes seem to reveal an appreciative and even affectionate relationship. But Ogilvy did *not* in fact write a valedictory passage to the Rudkins in his book, which only discussed Pepperidge Farm two times—in conjunction with his philosophy about always using clients' products and the story of how he thought up the Titus Moody commercial for the company. There is, in fact, no reference to the Rudkins at all. And he did describe other clients, such as Helena Rubenstein, the beauty industry entrepreneur, as a friend.[83] This could suggest that the relationship Ogilvy cultivated with the Rudkins was not the genuine friendship that the exchange of gifts, shared outings, and terms of endearment would suggest. But this is at least as revealing about Rudkin as it is Ogilvy. That is, she too invested in her relationship with Ogilvy because it kept her "in the loop" and enabled her to assert her views and preferences directly to him, in spite of the wishes of her family members.

While Rudkin's interest in Ogilvy and Pepperidge Farm advertising was about exerting influence, it was also about expertise. Account records reveal that Rudkin saw herself as a company founder who understood her brand and what would appeal to consumers and what wouldn't. During meetings with the agency, Rudkin asserted her opinions strongly. The appeal of home-made bread would be lost on the younger generation, she thought—a fact recorded in account notes early on, as discussed in chapter 4.[84] And two years later after a meeting that included Rudkin and several agency executives, Ogilvy recorded in an internal memo, "You need a U.S.P. [unique selling proposition] Mrs. Rudkin instinctively felt that. Your headline, like so many headlines around here, contains no direct promise of a consumer benefit."[85] Characterizing Rudkin as a client with an "instinct" for how to position a product to differentiate it from competitors, Ogilvy appears to have viewed her as a competent marketer. It was an impression that she worked to achieve.

Interestingly, it was this same sense of marketing competence by Pepperidge Farm leaders that was at the root of Ogilvy's frustration with their client. Several confidential memos prepared in 1962 outlined what was described as "deep-rooted areas of disagreement between OBM [Ogilvy Benson & Mather] and Pepperidge Farm on matters of marketing policy and client-agency relations." The account executive detailed eight key areas of difficulty. These included specific frustration with Hank Rudkin, Margaret Rudkin's son whom she had put in charge of marketing at Pepperidge Farm. They did not include specific complaints about Margaret Rudkin but did implicate all of "Pepperidge Farm management and key officers" in the critique: "While Pepperidge Farm management and key officers pay lip service to the principle of client-agency marketing partnership, they don't really believe in it. They choose to make virtually all *major* marketing decisions on their own, without calling on us for objective advice and counsel. They are rather arrogant in their opinions on their ability to do this well, but they lack real talent in this area. They are not a marketing-oriented company, and yet they pretend to be, often with disastrous results."[86] The problem, primarily, was that Pepperidge Farm and its leaders were too independent in their decision-making, overly confident in their abilities, and parsimonious in their advertising investments. From an agency standpoint, this was disadvantageous for business. Their ideal was to work with clients who viewed advertising as "a necessary cost of doing business," but Pepperidge Farm, in OBM's assessment, did "everything they possibly can to eliminate it from a given marketing equation." The greatest risk was that its parent company, Campbell Soup—which had deep advertising pockets and believed in investment spending—might come to the conclusion that the "amateurism" of Pepperidge Farm's marketing decisions was a reflection of OBM's work. Ogilvy executives acknowledged that these shortcomings reflected "the years when they were going it alone as an independent company . . . [and] had to produce immediate profits to keep the company in business." Though for Ogilvy this was a deep frustration, for Pepperidge Farm, such pluck, perseverance, and thrift may have been a point of pride, perhaps especially for Margaret Rudkin because these were signs of competence for an independent business owner—key to survival and success—and therefore a measure of her worth to the company as well.

Having a handle on Pepperidge Farm finances was also an important part of the way Margaret Rudkin presented herself and her self-worth. As already discussed in chapter 1, a 1948 *New Yorker* article recorded her pride in being able to best Pepperidge Farm's comptroller regarding the company's cash balance. She considered this a unique skill that set her apart from other women, most of whom, she asserted, "can't even balance [their] checkbook."[87] Distinguishing herself as superior to "the average woman" when it came to financial management may have seemed uncharitable to some, but it served her well as an entrepreneur, especially one who came from humble origins. Though she had a high school diploma, she entered the business world knowing little about manufacturing or business management and described herself as "too ignorant to know about these matters."[88] In fact, she reported that "I'm quite sure that if I knew as much as I know today I would never have had the nerve to try it."[89] Yet while on the one hand Rudkin revealed her lack of know-how as a starting business owner, she also assertively described how her work as a bookkeeper and then teller at a Flushing bank was "invaluable" in preparing her for the role of entrepreneur and company president. Her work there taught her "accuracy and responsibility" and provided "a good background for business."[90] Thus, Rudkin distinguished ignorance—a lack of knowledge, education, or awareness—from ability. She may not have known very much about running a business, but she came to the task with a sense of her own competence nonetheless.

Rudkin's narrative about her own competence extended into her work as a housekeeper and cook for her own family, too, and of course this was a reflection of the way in which gender shaped the definition of success for her. The 1948 *New Yorker* article documented this. It showed the degree to which she proudly represented her abilities in as well as out of the home:

> Mrs. Rudkin spends five days a week at her bakery and though she thoroughly enjoys her work, she looks forward to Saturdays, when

she has a chance to do some home baking. . . . Except for the assistance of a cleaning woman who comes in two days a week, Mrs. Rudkin does her own housework and cooking. During the week, she prepares meals for only her husband and herself. . . . On the weekends, when the family is usually at home, Mrs. Rudkin cooks for all hands and bakes some pies . . . and cakes . . . an assignment she handles with efficiency and good cheer. "I can whip up a cake in fifteen minutes," she says, "I've timed myself. And it doesn't take me more than forty minutes when I use the pressure cooker, to prepare a lamb-stew dinner for eight."

That she reportedly timed her ability to "whip up a cake" tells us a great deal about Margaret Rudkin. Her ability to prepare good food that her family enjoyed in a short amount of time seemed a litmus test of her competence as a busy working mother and wife—a notion familiar even to working women today who disproportionately carry on this role.[91] She seemed proud of both the skill with which she performed her domestic roles and of the fact that she did so with little assistance from hired help once her children were young adults. And Rudkin clearly was keen on improving her efficiency and seems to have seen this as a key measure of ability. The same article documented the fact that she considered bridge, golf, and cocktail parties "rather a waste of time" and even once "confronted" her husband and sons about the excessive amount of time they invested in golf-playing each week.[92] This insight reveals that Arlie Hochschild's 1989 phrase "the second shift" described the experience of women business owners like Rudkin a generation earlier too.[93] The labor that she performed at home— sometimes while her husband and sons played golf—underscored that she continued to occupy a traditional domestic role even as she grew a multimillion-dollar business. And she seemed proud of it. Her regimented schedule and home life suggest that for Rudkin, an ability to do it all was, in and of itself, a measure of her expertise. As with Lewis's insistence that at home she "was her husband's wife," Rudkin's focus on her domestic expertise was also a strategic self-presentation, one that conveyed adherence to some gender norms even as she challenged others. This was especially important for an executive in the food business whose brand, as documented in chapter 4, was itself gendered and emphasized "handmade" quality. Thus, Rudkin projected a particularly gendered construct of self-worth that emphasized that her conventional and prescribed role as wife and mother—represented by her cooking—had not been undermined by her entrepreneurship and business leadership and continued to be an area of competence.

Rudkin also presented herself as a skilled manufacturer—independent and capable, the chief architect of her successful business. When it came to building her new plant in Norwalk, Connecticut, on fourteen acres she had purchased on the Boston Post Road, this was quite literally the case. She "called in an architect, and handed him a large piece of cardboard on which she had pinned several dozen oblongs of paper, each representing a piece of bakery equipment." Rudkin knew exactly how she wanted them situated to support the most efficient and effective manufacturing process. It was a plan that had long been in the works as she and her employees labored in cramped quarters during the war years, stuck there for much longer than anticipated because of wartime restrictions on construction. When she finally hired and met the architect who would design the new building, she reportedly said, "This is how I want the inside laid out. Now, you figure out the exterior and the staircases. But don't you dare change my plans."[94] The comment reflected a sense that she knew better than anyone the best way to lay out the plant. Architectural credentials aside, she asserted herself as qualified and competent to design a building plan by virtue of her manufacturing experience and expertise.

Rudkin also conveyed her self-worth by emphasizing her role as inventor of the company's winning bread formula. That she suspiciously viewed competitors as eager to steal her recipe betrayed her sense of confidence and value. "When Mrs. Rudkin takes visitors through her bakery, she normally doesn't show them the room where the ingredients are mixed, for fear they may be spies in the pay of the big bakers who, she is convinced, are plotting to get her formula," the *New Yorker* article reported. Recording her remarks on the matter, the article continued, "Oh, ho," she says, looking arch, "wouldn't they just like to get their hands on *that!*"[95] As discussed in chapter 4, records reflect that early on Rudkin was highly aware of the threat of competitor imitation and had worked with attorneys to trademark Pepperidge Farm. The company's advertising also implicitly utilized "trade secret" language—in keeping with big-name brands of the era such as Coca Cola—although there is no evidence that she explicitly pursued establishing trade secret protection.[96] Even if she had tried to patent her recipe, it is unlikely she would have been successful given the strict requirements of intellectual property laws. Yet simply being attuned to her recipe *as* intellectual property was inherently an assertion of self-worth.[97] She understood that she had something of value that needed protection, and she vociferously asserted this. That it was "almost a recipe out of [her] head," as she explained it in one interview, helped to locate its worth in her and imbued her with clear value to the company.[98]

Both these self-assertions—her ability to design the best plant layout and her need to protect her bread formula—situated Rudkin as a business asset, of value to her company and, in fact, essential to its success. Perhaps this was especially important in an industry that grew out of a long history of women's domestic labor. That is, a woman who could bake a good loaf of bread, while increasingly uncommon in the mid-twentieth century, was not a dramatic point of distinction. Yet a woman who could leverage her bread-baking skills in combination with manufacturing expertise and a secret formula was one of a kind.

Addressing Harvard Business School MBA students in 1960 provided Rudkin with a professional forum to tell the story of her success, and she did so on her own terms, asserting *her* version of how to operate a manufacturing business. The opportunity arose out of a chance meeting with famed Harvard professor George Doriot, next to whom she was seated at a dinner party. Upon learning about the founding of Pepperidge Farm, Inc., Doriot invited Rudkin to address his "famous second-year MBA elective course" in manufacturing. A press release from the school described Doriot as a professor who "inspired and trained more leaders of U.S. corporations than any other person" during his forty-year tenure there. It estimated that some "7,000 MBA candidates took his course in Manufacturing," many of whom went on "to head such firms as American Express, Cummins Engine, Ford Motor Company, and Levi Strauss."[99] It was an impressive platform from which to expound her story of success and manufacturing principles, and for Rudkin it was a great thrill. "I had the time of my life," she said afterward.[100] Referred to as "The General" because of his promotion to Brigadier General for his World War II service as director of military planning for the quartermaster general and then deputy director of research and development for the War Department, Doriot had suggested a title for Rudkin's talk that she rejected. He thought that titling her talk to his MBA class "Anything I can do you can do better" was appropriate. She preferred "You never can tell." The distinction was an important one. While Doriot's conception was gendered and hinged on the idea that Harvard-trained business*men* could learn from and improve on Rudkin's successful strategies, Rudkin instead positioned herself as an embodiment of the American free-enterprise system in which *anyone*, not just the highly educated, privileged few (all men), could achieve great success in business.[101]

The assertion that business expertise could be learned and exercised by anyone supported Rudkin's authority and made her a champion of all those outside elite business circles. On the one hand, this was a common idea in her speeches—Americans were "blessed with the personal freedom to work for any goal we set for ourselves."[102] It was an inspiring notion. But it was also a daring message to deliver at Harvard Business School—the epitome of a closed system of opportunity that privileged white, educated men—especially in 1960, three years before women were admitted. Overthrowing Harvard's closed system, in fact, was on Rudkin's mind some five years before her appearance there. In a 1955 article, she gushed about her granddaughter and namesake, Margaret Rudkin, then ten months old, for whom she envisioned a Harvard future: "She's simply wonderful, has red hair just like mine and I'm going to see to it that she has a career. I'd like to see her go to Harvard Business School."[103] It was a vision that reveals how meaningful her appearance there years later must have been for her and also why she saw it as an opportunity to challenge commonplace ideas about how to run a business and who got to run one. In fact, in the first two sentences of her Harvard speech, she said, "I'm surprised, too, to be here. Actually talking to you, all these young men who have been told by all these professors just how to do everything, and all I have to tell you is to throw away the book." Simultaneously drawing attention to her outsider status as a woman with only a high school diploma and no formal business training and her confidence that what Harvard was teaching its MBA students was uninstructive, removed from the reality of operating a large-scale manufacturing business, Rudkin confidently asserted her expertise as know-how derived from experience. Framing her success as "the story of the business and how it . . . succeeded because it had never been run according to any of the accepted rules of manufacturing," Rudkin subverted the master narrative about manufacturing success.[104] Interweaving biography with detailed descriptions of the company's supply-chain procedures, distribution system, manufacturing processes, promotional efforts, new-product innovations, expansion efforts, personnel management, and pricing strategies, Rudkin held court for fifty-six minutes (the presentation was timed and recorded) before an audience of future manufacturing industry leaders.[105] It was a performance of both gender and business expertise and a powerful assertion of her worth—to Pepperidge Farm, to the business community, and to would-be manufacturing managers. She belonged, Rudkin seemed to argue, because her experience made her an expert on how to succeed in business.

Three years after her Harvard Business School debut, Rudkin published a book that would provide her with an even broader platform to spread the story of her success as the founder and leader of Pepperidge Farm. The book, *The Margaret Rudkin Pepperidge Farm Cookbook*, published in 1963, became a national bestseller, the only cookbook to appear on the list at that time in history. It was part biography, part cookbook, and included chapters devoted to her "childhood"; "country life" on her family's Connecticut estate; "Pepperidge Farm," which detailed the company's founding; "Cooking from Antique Cookbooks," a long-standing interest of hers; and "Ireland," where she and her husband maintained a country manor. While writing the book was an opportunity to indulge her interest in all things culinary, it was also a marketing document that enticed home cooks with adventuresome recipes as well as engaging tales of experimentation both in the kitchen and the business world. In fact, Campbell—by 1963 Pepperidge Farm's parent company—agreed to invest in advertising and promotion, hiring Ogilvy and famed public-relations guru Ben Sonnenberg to get exposure for the book and for Margaret Rudkin more generally. The expectation was not that the book would sell many copies, even though it did, or that the company should get into the business of selling and promoting books, which was not an interest, but that awareness about the book could help to generate consumers for Pepperidge Farm products. The results exceeded all expectations and put Rudkin on a national stage that she had not achieved prior to its publication. With charming original illustrations by Erik Blegvad, a renowned illustrator of children's books, the book took a cutesy and homey approach to the brand's core values—old-fashioned, handmade, quality baked goods aimed at high-end consumers. It was a paean to eating seasonally, cooking foods from scratch, and eating dinner at home for enthusiastic, even ambitious, cooks and positioned Rudkin as a culinary expert whom American consumers could trust for high-quality recipes and, by extension, high-quality prepared food products.[106] The book provided a window into her own life—a sort of "lifestyles of the rich and famous"—which must have been appealing to the target audience. This approach underscored that Rudkin deployed her assertions of competence on many stages, for many audiences, and in many dimensions. And it also shows that to the end, competence was the continuous thread in her strategies for self-assertion. For Rudkin, competence could be learned, practiced, and mastered through experience and developed into expertise. Asserting her worth in this way emphasized her mastery and explained and justified her ascendancy to the top of the business world.

Conclusion

At a time when the default assessment of a woman in the corporate business world was as an executive wife and her leadership skills were judged in gendered terms, Lewis, Beech, and Rudkin navigated the important job of image management by asserting their self-worth. Each did so in different ways. For Lewis, advocating her stature as a corporate leader and insisting on promotional and compensation parity with male executives, as well as an emphasis on her financial skills in keeping with corporate norms, enabled her to present herself as an essential component of her business's success. Beech adopted a different strategy, insisting that she be judged on gender-neutral terms, that is, as a successful executive and not as a female executive; for her, navigating prescribed gender roles meant alternately enacting and rejecting gender as a relevant factor in her presentation as a corporate leader. Rudkin, finally, asserted her competence—as a cook, as a marketer, as a manufacturer, as a business leader—to achieve status as an expert and reach increasing levels of influence. For all three, projecting self-worth required active engagement and was an important strategy for success. "Owning their success" and insisting that others acknowledge it was key to their ability to reach the heights they did. That they adopted a variety of strategies to do so underscores that there was not only one way to assert self-worth. Yet however a woman engaged this aspect of building a business, it was an essential ingredient in mid-twentieth-century female entrepreneurship.

Conclusion

· ·

Writing Lewis, Beech, and Rudkin into the "canon of business leaders" forces us to reconceptualize the 1930s–70s as a context for business entrepreneurship and leadership and also how we think about business success. In their study of "The Greatest Business Leaders of the Twentieth Century," Anthony J. Mayo and Nitin Nohria of the Harvard Business School emphasize that leaders must be considered, as their title suggests, *In Their Time*. They argue that context determines the nature of business opportunity in any period of time and that business leaders can be defined by how they pursue opportunities and, in particular, which ones. The term the authors use for this central idea is "contextual intelligence"—"the profound sensitivity to macro-level contextual factors in the creation, growth, or transformation of businesses," or more colloquially, "a nose for sensing opportunities and avoiding threats."[1] Yet even though both Beech and Rudkin appear in the book, what's missing from the study of context in Mayo and Nohria's examination of business leadership is gender. Lewis's exclusion from their list likely reflects this too. Her poor business performance the first five years (the period evaluated) reflected dependence on a controlling male investor—it was a particular vulnerability for women who had a hard time accessing capital and credit. Thus, the omission of gender as an analytic framework limits the story of entrepreneurship that the book tells—both who made it onto the list and what factors were considered in the analysis of performance. During the period 1932–79 when Lewis, Beech, and Rudkin all founded, managed, and sold their businesses, gender fundamentally shaped both their opportunities and threats, and thus their "nose" for business needed to be attuned to their gendered context. They needed to be able to navigate these gender-specific opportunities and threats along with those shaped by more general contextual factors in order to be successful. And we need to consider this in order to understand women's leadership during this period.

The absence of gender analysis in a book about great business leaders in the twentieth century like Mayo and Nohria's *In Their Time* will be no surprise to many readers. Business leadership literature is a genre steeped in male privilege. This reflects the essential role of gatekeepers in the American business world—those who preside over networks of connection and influence essential for success who have historically been white men. And it also illustrates the American tendency to ignore this legacy and celebrate instead the false idea that individuals make it to the top only because of talent and ambition.[2] Such origin stories and their omissions inherently suggest that gender had nothing to do with the preponderance of men who reside in the ranks of the greatest business leaders. And, conversely, they also communicate that being a woman had no bearing on the success (or lack of success) of female business leaders.

Yet the three women entrepreneurs whose stories form the basis for the history told here did not have the privilege of ignoring gender, for it was ever present as a context for their business leadership. Lewis, Beech, and Rudkin navigated the mid-twentieth-century business world in gendered ways and encountered gendered opportunities and obstacles at many turns, if not every turn. Even though they themselves insisted that gender was not an important factor in their histories, analysis of their stories reveals otherwise.

As the moniker "boss lady" implied, the environment in which Lewis, Beech, and Rudkin operated their businesses never let them forget that they were "ladies" as well as bosses. Gender, in fact, defined the context in which they led. The evidence makes this clear in their startup strategies, relations with government, labor management, marketing, and self-presentation. They constructed entrepreneurial pathways for themselves by relying on male family members and their associates to help them access the social, expert, and financial capital that was elusive for so many women and yet essential to accessing business opportunity and success. Their business success and longevity developed through their ability to tap into government opportunities and fend off government-related threats, and this commonality in their stories underscores that female business leaders could not afford to be excluded from such opportunities because of their gender. The stories of Lewis, Beech, and Rudkin as labor managers reveal that all three rejected the idea that they should manage labor differently as women and embraced the status quo in their efforts to curtail the impact of labor unions and implement commonplace welfare programs for employees. Conversely, when it was advantageous to leverage gender to advance their brands, they did so, embracing gender stereotypes in their marketing messages and stepping in to help enact them. Finally, as leaders at the helm of big businesses in male-dominated industries and a corporate world still accustomed to viewing women at work as secretaries or executive wives, Lewis, Beech, and Rudkin all learned to advocate for themselves by deemphasizing their gender and presenting themselves as bosses and not boss ladies. In all of these examples, gender played a critical role in their experience—how they were viewed by others, the opportunities and obstacles they encountered, and the choices they made as business leaders.

This matters, because if history is an important context for understanding business leadership, as Mayo and Nohria insist it is, then it must be a historical context relevant for all business leaders in the twenty-first century, female as well as male. Just as we do not live in a "post-racial" world, we do not live in a world in which gender has ceased to be an important factor in shaping the opportunities and obstacles facing women leaders in the business world. And thus, how Lewis, Beech, and Rudkin navigated gender during *their* historical context is relevant for women today trying to learn how to navigate gender in ours.

The relevance of Lewis, Beech, and Rudkin to women today is true in a general sense but also in the particularities of their stories. In fact, there are common threads tying together their experiences as presented here in all five thematic chapters with women business leaders at the beginning of the twenty-first century. "Pull" still shapes who can access opportunity in the business world and facilitates entry and advancement for those with connections to insiders or gatekeepers even today.[3] Present-day advocates for female entrepreneurs argue that government investment in woman-owned businesses makes the difference in the scale of success female entrepreneurs enjoy; thus, women business leaders cannot afford to ignore government contracts.[4] As long as we define business success in terms of the bottom line—profitability—then we may not see female business leaders stepping outside industry norms as labor managers or implementing employment programs to enhance gender equity for workers as some present-day feminists have expected. And finally, the experiences of Lewis, Beech, and Rudkin with marketing and self-presentation prompt questions about the utility of gender and the dangers of allowing gender to shape how others judge business leadership. Is there a way for female business leaders to use gender to their advantage? Does the gender of corporate leaders matter to early-twenty-first-century consumers? Finally, can women today lead businesses and manage their business career so that gender doesn't inhibit their success? Must they continue to insist, as Olive Ann Beech did, that their gender is irrelevant or, stated another way, are early-twenty-first-century women business leaders still *female* leaders or simply leaders?

Certainly, Lewis, Beech, and Rudkin worked for a day when women would be viewed as business executives and not women executives. And even though all three rejected the notion that they were advocates for women's rights, their insistence that gender should not shape how others judged them even as it shaped their opportunities and obstacles was an inherently equal-rights argument. In articulating such views, they made incremental contributions to paving the way for subsequent leaders and chipped away at the barriers women faced in the highest echelons of the business world. Even today, women are reaping the benefits of their work.

Notes

Introduction

1. Peter Wyden, "Danger: Boss Lady at Work," *Saturday Evening Post*, 8 August 1959, 26–27, 85–86, WOABC. Full issue of magazine in author's possession.

2. Gilbert, *Men in the Middle*, 221. Gilbert complicates the assertion found in so many previous accounts that a crisis in masculinity characterized the 1950s. He argues that this was neither universal nor uniform. Yet whether or not American middle-class men perceived a crisis in their own masculinity, social critics did. David Reisman's *The Lonely Crowd* (1950) epitomized this perspective.

3. The article by Baldwin, "Our Fighting Men Have Gone Soft," in the same issue of *Saturday Evening Post*, is cited and discussed in Fraterrigo, *Playboy and the Making of the Good Life*, chap. 4, n.18.

4. Gloria Amoury, "New Girl," *Saturday Evening Post*, 8 August 1959, 20, 79–81. Figures for clerical workers in subsequent paragraph from England and Boyer, "Women's Work," 309.

5. Goldin, *Understanding the Gender Gap*, chap. 6.

6. Kwolek-Folland, *Incorporating Women*, 144–45. The quote is from a letter to President Roosevelt from a private citizen dated 1933 and cited in Kwolek-Folland.

7. Kessler-Harris, *A Woman's Wage*.

8. Though all three came of age during a period when American high school graduation rates increased rapidly, in 1910 just 9 percent of seventeen-year-olds completed their secondary education. A college education was also uncommon, opening doors for only a wealthy few, and typically was a choice women made in place of marriage (Goldin, "America's Graduation from High School," 347; Goldin, "The Meaning of College." Figures are for the cohort born between 1895 and 1900, per Figure 1 in "America's Graduation from High School," and show that 10 percent of men and women attended college). Lewis was born in 1896, Rudkin in 1897, and Beech in 1904.

9. For the BPWC study, see Kwolek-Folland, *Incorporating Women*, 159.

10. Blackford, *History of Small Business in America*, 138.

11. Examples include Gamber, *Female Economy*; Kwolek-Folland, *Incorporating Women*; Sparks, *Capital Intentions*; Susan Ingalls Lewis, *Unexceptional Women*; Peiss, *Hope in a Jar*.

12. IOP.

13. Weiss, *To Have and to Hold*, 7–8; Meyerowitz, *Not June Cleaver*.

14. Cobble, Gordon, and Henry, *Feminism Unfinished*; Showalter, "Review: *Feminism Unfinished*."

15. Cobble, *Other Women's Movement*.

16. Stanley Buder characterizes this role as both "generator and reflector of American values"; see *Capitalizing on Change*. For quote, see http://www.uncpress .unc.edu/browse/book_detail?title_id=1572 (accessed 11 October 2015).

17. Moon, *Different*, 209.

18. Gartner, "Who Is an Entrepreneur? Is the Wrong Question." References here from 1989 version, 48, 57.

Chapter One

1. Miller, "Self-Confidence Is Rewarded," cited in Sandberg, *Lean In*, 36, and Stewart, "CEO's Support System"; Beck, "10 Fast Facts about Ginny Rometty."

2. Groysberg and Abrahams, "Manage Your Work." The article reported that an appreciation for the emotional support provided by a spouse characterized both men and women.

3. Sandberg, *Lean In*, 104–20. Study cited is Stone, *Opting Out*, 62. Male privilege is only a piece of the problem. Because masculinity is so closely aligned with the breadwinner role and because "current understandings of work commitment" require long hours, professional men's unwillingness to share household work reflects the inflexibility of professional models of male success as much as individual inflexibility. Williams, *Reshaping the Work–Family Debate*, 31.

4. Matzek, Gudmunson, and Danes, "Spousal Capital," 60–61, 70.

5. Cofield, "Minority Women Entrepreneurs."

6. See, for example, Kwolek-Folland, *Incorporating Women*; Sparks, *Capital Intentions*; Susan Ingalls Lewis, *Unexceptional Women*; Gamber, *Female Economy*; Deutsch, *Women and the City*; Hartigan O'Connor, *Ties That Buy*.

7. Peril, "Sex and Secretaries."

8. Berebitsky, *Sex and the Office*.

9. Wyndham Robertson, "The Ten Highest-Ranking Women in Big Business," *Fortune*, April 1973, 81–89, TLF.

10. The term "social capital" has been defined in a variety of ways: "key relationships with other individuals," "all those social assets that enable one to attract respect, generate confidence, evoke affection, and draw on loyalty in a specific setting," and "connections among individuals—social networks and the norms of reciprocity and trustworthiness that arise from them." Laird, *Pull*, 1–2. See also Murphy, Kickul, Barbosa, and Titus, "Expert Capital," 128; Putnam, *Bowling Alone*, 19.

11. Schipani et al., "Women and the New Corporate Governance," 523.

12. Murphy, Kickul, Barbosa, and Titus, "Expert Capital."

13. Weiss, *To Have and to Hold*, chap. 4. For more on the concept of "colliding" devotions to work and family, see Blair-Loy, *Competing Devotions*, 3.

14. The best example is Dorothy Walworth, "The First Lady of San Joaquin," *Everywoman's Woman*, August 1952, 5, 74–76, TLF; Frank, *Success and Luck*, 82. Thank you to Pamela Laird for bringing this book to my attention.

15. According to her 5 August 1924 passport application, Tillie was born 13 July 1896 in Brooklyn, New York, and resided in Austria from 1901 to 1904 and "uninterruptedly in the United States" from 1904 to 1924. According to the manuscript census, Tillie Weisberg was twenty-three years old in 1920. Tillie's given name was Myrtle Ehrlich. By the time of her first marriage, she was called "Tillie" and took her husband's last name of Weisberg—the name she retained when she started Flotill Products. But for the sake of simplicity and consistency, I refer to her throughout this essay as Tillie Lewis, or "Lewis" according to scholarly convention, the name she took with her second marriage to Meyer Lewis ("1924 Passport Application" and *Fourteenth Census of the United States, 1920*).

16. For biographical information see Walworth, "First Lady of San Joaquin"; Ruth Winters, "Tillie of the Valley: An Amazing Success Story," no date or place of publication; Tillie Lewis, "The Tomato Lady," *Guideposts*, April 1977; "Tillie's Unpunctured Romance," *Time*, 19 November 1951, all in TLF. One self-published account by a local historian suggests that Lewis was a cast member in the Ziegfield Follies stage show in New York City during her early years, but this conclusion is based on very little evidence and much speculation. Wood, *Tillie Lewis*, 21–22.

17. "1924 Passport Application" and *Fourteenth Census of the United States, 1920*. The manuscript census shows a "Brother, Joseph," several years older than Louis, living in their household, and also listed as a grocer.

18. One media account stated that Lewis's husband "resented the way she spruced up the place and added new equipment." Walworth, "First Lady of San Joaquin," 5, TLF.

19. Goldin, *Understanding the Gender Gap*.

20. "Speech and Notes by Saul Heiser," February 1964, on the occasion of the fiftieth wedding anniversary of Samuel and Beatrice Hochheiser (Tillie Lewis's sister and brother-in-law, with whom she entered into business), gift of Judy Schiffner, daughter to Saul Heiser, in the author's possession.

21. See Weinstein, "Flatlands," 459. The 1925 *New York State Census* listed the Weisbergs as residents at 1173 East 18th Street, Brooklyn; their household included a German immigrant woman employed as a servant.

22. "Certificate of Incorporation, Hochheiser & Weisberg, Inc.," 1 June 1923, copy (in author's possession) accessed from New York County Clerk's Office; interview with Judith Heiser Schiffner by the author, April 2014. A recently self-published history of Tillie Lewis by local historian Kyle Wood comes to different conclusions. Citing an interview with one of Lewis's nephews, Wood asserts that by 1924 Lewis had opened an Italian import business in conjunction with Florindo Del Gaizo (the Italian wholesaler who would later invest in the startup of Flotill—the combination of their two names) that doubled as a stock brokerage. This could explain the lifestyle Lewis enjoyed at this point in her life. However, the evidence for this conclusion (an interview with one family member, conducted decades after the fact) seems insufficient and the possibility improbable given that Lewis was listed as an officer in her family's wholesale business in the 1925 New York City Directory, as explained in the text above. Wood, *Tillie Lewis*, 31.

23. McCart, *SS Aquitania*.

24. "1924 Passport Application." According to local historian Kyle Wood, this was a romantic excursion paid for by Florindo Del Gaizo, with whom Lewis had a long-standing love affair (Wood, *Tillie Lewis*). I found no evidence of Del Gaizo on the Ship Passengers List on the return trip of the *Aquitania* in 1924 (*Passenger Lists of Vessels Arriving at New York, New York, 1897–1957*), but it was not possible to investigate the passenger list for the outgoing trip from New York. Del Gaizo did travel onboard on the same ship as Lewis in 1928 (when she traveled with no male family member) and 1932 (when she was accompanied by her husband). Ship passenger lists also reveal that Del Gaizo regularly crisscrossed the Atlantic between Italy and New York without Lewis and sometimes with his wife and children.

25. Campbell, *Women at War with America*, 105–11, cited in Kwolek-Folland, *Incorporating Women*, 144. Campbell reports that even in the 1930s, "84 percent of the nation's insurance companies, 65 percent of the banks, and 63 percent of public utilities had restrictive rules preventing [the employment of] married women."

26. Wetzel, "American Families."

27. Alternatively, Wood argues that Lewis's was a loveless marriage, a marriage of convenience, or perhaps even a fiction (Wood, *Tillie Lewis*). I do not find that the records support this conclusion. In particular, the only reason Lewis had to apply for a passport, having been born in the United States, was that she lost her citizenship status under the Expatriation Act of 1907 after marrying a foreign-born man (Louis Weisberg was born in Austria). (For more on this law, see Hacker, "When Saying 'I Do'.") It is possible, of course, that the Weisberg marriage was loveless and that Lewis was engaged in an extramarital affair with Del Gaizo as Wood alleges, though it is not my goal to substantiate this either way.

28. Kwolek-Folland, *Incorporating Women*, 55–56.

29. Schiffner interview; wedding announcement, gift from Judy Schiffner in possession of the author; residential pattern adjacent to the Hochheisers per census.

30. Trow's *General Directory of New York City*, 1925.

31. Murphy, "The Golden Age." Murphy reports that one-third of business travelers were women. He does not provide a specific citation for this fact.

32. Interview with Lewis's nephew Arthur Heiser as reported in Schleier, "Tillie the Toiler," 13. Heiser refers to a job trading stock as the source of this income, and some media accounts do, too. See, for example, Winter, "Tillie of the Valley," TLF. For quote, see "Margaret Kreiss, "Thoroughly Modern Tillie: Industrial Giant," *Sacramento Bee*, 1 February 1976, gift of Judy Schiffner in possession of the author. For documentary evidence confirming that Lewis was employed in her family's business and remained married to Louis Weisberg, see previous and subsequent notes. Comparative salary figures are from Goldin, *Understanding the Gender Gap*, 64. These figures are for 1930.

33. Ott, *When Wall Street Met Main Street*, 211.

34. Dun & Bradstreet Credit Report for Flotill Products, Inc., 9 April 1941, TLF. This equates to $906,000 of purchasing power (using the consumer price index) in

2009 dollars according to the "Measuring Worth" calculator, http://eh.net/hmit/ (accessed 26 October 2010).

35. Interview with Lewis's nephew Arthur Heiser as reported in Schleier, "Tillie the Toiler," 13.

36. Wood, *Tillie Lewis*. Wood sometimes takes great liberties with her interpretations. She substantiates her conclusion about the Lewis-Del Gaizo affair with interviews conducted with a small number of family members one and two generations younger than Lewis and a set of photographs of Lewis and Del Gaizo—reportedly in Italy and onboard ship. Wood contends that there was also a collection of love letters that the family discarded. I remain unconvinced. As subsequent chapters here will discuss and the many different versions of her life in press accounts show, Lewis was a woman unafraid to mythologize her own story (who knows what she told family) so the possibilities abound. I don't think we have enough evidence to know much for certain about Lewis's personal life.

37. Dun & Bradstreet Credit Report, TLF; a certificate of dissolution for Hochheiser & Weisberg, Inc., was not issued until 13 October 1944. Record obtained from the New York City Clerk's office, August 2013, in author's possession.

38. Prospectus, filed with the Securities and Exchange Commission, 5 May 1948, TLF. A credit evaluation of Flotill Products, Inc., in April 1941 listed Louis Weisberg as the husband of Tillie still but stated he had "no financial interest in [her] business"; it stated that Louis Weisberg was the secretary and treasurer of Moosalina Products Corporation, "importers and wholesalers of groceries in Brooklyn" (Dun & Bradstreet Credit Report, TLF). According to Wood, this was the name of the wholesale business jointly established by Lewis's brother-in-law, her husband, and his brother on her suggestion years earlier (Wood, *Tillie Lewis*, 29). The documentary evidence I've gathered and reviewed above indicates only that their commercial collaboration was called Hochheiser & Weisberg, Inc.

39. *Trow's New York Business Directory*, 1912, 1913, 1915, 1916; Gurock, Holder, Taylore, and Jackson, "Harlem"; Ultan, "Williamsbridge." In the 1915 *New York State Census*, he is listed as a grocer, and his brother, also listed in his household along with his wife Beatrice, is listed as a grocery clerk. Though Beatrice is listed as a "housewife" in extant records, she likely was involved in some way in the family business too, as was common for the wives of small business owners. In at least one publication, Tillie Lewis references this, stating, "My sister had a grocery store," as reported in the *Jerusalem Post*, 5 April 1966, Folder 3, Box 1, SJCHS.

40. Trow's *General Directory of New York City*, 1920–21; Trow's *General Directory of New York City*, 1925, listed the Hochheisers and Weisbergs as neighbors, living at 1169 and 1173 East 18th Street, respectively, in Brooklyn.

41. Ultan, "Belmont," 114.

42. See Sewell, *Women and the Everyday City*, chap. 2 ("Errands").

43. "Things Little Italy Eats," quoted in Ziegelman, *97 Orchard*, 194.

44. Sparberg, "Hudson Yards," 627; Mary Elizabeth Brown, "Little Italy," 758.

45. "Tillie's Unpunctured Romance," 104, TLF. There are many accounts of how Lewis learned about *pomodoros* that differ in some details, but they all originate in her husband's business. The quote here is from Lewis, "Tomato Lady," 19–20, TLF. By 1977, Tillie Lewis Foods was owned by the Ogden Corporation, and a well-oiled publicity department must have overseen all such publications. It is doubtful that this is truly Tillie Lewis's "voice," but it represents at least an approximation of the true story, since, in broad outline if not in specific detail, it is the story repeated in multiple published accounts of the origin of her idea for the business.

46. Cinotto, *Italian American Table*, 143–44. Cinotto cites 99 Hudson Street as the New York address of Riverbank's wholesale office. Hochheiser & Weisberg's wholesale office was located at 469 Greenwich (Trow's *General Directory of New York City*, 1925). Both Google Maps and Sparberg, "Hudson Yards," 627, confirm the proximity of the two offices. For Lewis's three trips to Naples, see New York passenger lists for the *Duilio*, departing Naples 19 June 1926, the *Corte Grande*, departing Naples 13 June 1928, and the *Roma*, departing Naples 8 July 1932 (all in Records of U.S. Customs Service, Washington, D.C.).

47. Google Maps confirms that Lewis's address was within walking distance of the Botanical Garden in the Bronx. Ultan, "Belmont," 114, and Mary Elizabeth Brown, "Little Italy," 758, also shed light on the proximity. For accounts suggesting that Lewis researched tomatoes there, see Winters, "Tillie of the Valley," TLF.

48. "Italian Canners Step into the American Picture," Western Canner & Packer, September 1935, Folder 2, Box 1, SJCHS.

49. Albala, "Tomato Queen of San Joaquin," 55–63. Senatore Luigi Del Gaizo was also the director and head of the Italian branch of Bank of America and head of the Italian Corporate State, "one of the most influential and important divisions of Il Duce's government," in addition to being president of Scentarsieno, the largest canning company in Italy. Florindo Del Gaizo was related to Luigi and appears to have been in charge of the Naples plant and to be chiefly engaged in the export of canned tomatoes to the United States ("Italian Canners Step into the American Picture," SJCHS).

50. For the interviews referenced here, see Schleier, "Tillie the Toiler," 9–23. Schleier conducted interviews with Arthur Heiser, Lewis's nephew and an officer in the company, and Alilea Haywood Martin, her longtime secretary, both of whom stated that Lewis met Del Gaizo on a boat trip to Italy on her way to research tomatoes; she had probably known him or one of his associates from the wholesale business of her former husband, Louis Weisberg, since the 1920s.

51. See New York passenger lists for the *Conte Grande*, departing Naples 13 June 1928, and the *Roma*, departing Naples 9 July 1932 (Records of U.S. Customs Service, Washington, D.C.). Tillie and Louis Weisberg were both on this second ship. Tax records confirm that a boat trip to Italy to meet with the Del Gaizos occurred in 1933 as well (*Flotill Products, Inc. v. Commissioner of Internal Revenue, Tax Court of the United States*, 30 April 1956, 4, TLF). Some press accounts claim that the two met serendipitously while en route (see, for example, Walworth, "First Lady of San

Joaquin," 74, TLF). Amy Goldman, who describes Tillie Lewis as a cousin, writes, "My mother told me what the *Brooklyn Eagle, Reader's Digest, and the Stockton Record* never did: Tillie and Florindo had fallen madly in love. . . . The pair were lovers for more than ten years, until Flo's death in 1937. . . . The photographs from the family album of Tillie and Florindo aboard transoceanic liners and relaxing in Monopoli, Italy, are images that I hold dear" (Goldman, *Heirloom Tomato*, 1–2). Wood comes to the same conclusion, spurred on in part by Goldman (Wood, *Tillie Lewis*). See note 36 above on the nature of the evidence for this conclusion. Among other things, the very obvious frustration and even contempt for Del Gaizo's handling of the business before he died that is recorded in the pages of Lewis's Application for Relief from the Excess Profits Tax casts doubt on this version of the story.

52. With passage of the Smoot-Hawley Tariff in the United States in 1930, "the tariff on imported tomato products [was raised] to 50%," heavily reducing American demand for the now extremely expensive *pomodoros* (Gentilcore, *Pomodoro*, 116).

53. Supplement, Flotill Products Application for Relief under Section 722, filed with the Excess Profits Tax Council 30 June 1950, 1–3, TLF.

54. Wood asserts that the Stockton-based business was the Del Gaizo family's idea from the start and that Lewis was essentially the happy beneficiary—in the right place at the right time and sufficiently impressive to capture their imaginations as a partner. She does not cite evidence for this conclusion. Wood, *Tillie Lewis*, 38, 46.

55. Account Book, TLF.

56. Dorothy Walworth's article stated, "Then she set out to sell the anticipated pack of 200,000 cases. Traveling through the middle west and east, she sat up all night on trains and buses and ate little, walked weary miles to the wholesalers. They, too, were skeptical, but besieged by this spirited woman who wouldn't take no for an answer, they agreed to take a gamble. Tillie sold every case in advance" ("First Lady of San Joaquin," 4–5, 74–76, TLF).

57. Gentilcore, *Pomodoro*, 117–18.

58. The remainder of the money ($20,000) came from the Flotill Products, Inc., bank account, which she repaid later.

59. Letter to Mr. E. J. Wait, 14 April 1939, Supplement, Application for Relief, TLF. Also see text of statement prepared by tax attorney contained in the application. The Pacific Can Company loaned Lewis an additional $4,110.29 later in the same year.

60. Supplement, Application for Relief, 1–3, TLF.

61. Letter to Mr. C. H. Young, 24 May 1939, Supplement, Application for Relief, TLF.

62. Schleier, "Tillie the Toiler," 14. Interview conducted by Schleier.

63. Phyllis Battelle, "America's Fabulous Self-Made Women: Tomatoes Grow a Fortune," Fourth of a Series, in Women's World column, *Los Angeles Herald-Examiner*, April 2, 1974, B7, gift of Judy Schiffner in possession of the author.

64. In a letter to Young, Lewis stated, "I understand that . . . from a banking standpoint we haven't given you too great a volume of business in the past," suggesting that Flotill had conducted some business with Banco di Napoli and thus that the two must have known each other. Years later, she hired him as her company's treasurer when he lost his job during the war and wrote to her for help (letter to Claude Young, Executive Vice President, Banco di Napoli Trust Company, New York, 24 May 1939, in Supplement, Flotill Products Application for Relief, TLF).

65. Farney, *Barnstormer and the Lady*, 38.

66. *Fourteenth Census of the United States, 1920*; Farney, *Barnstormer and the Lady*.

67. "Beechcraft Takes Off on the Wings of a Jet," *Businessweek*, 25 February 1956, Box 7, Folder 2, WOABC.

68. Unnamed article, *Beechcrafter*, 22 December 1950, WOABC.

69. Soroptomist Club speech, Box 6, Folder 3, WOABC.

70. Ibid.

71. Arthur M. Louis, "The Hall of Fame for U.S. Business Leadership: Olive Ann Beech," *Fortune*, 4 April 1983, Box 28, Folder 18, WOABC.

72. Kwolek-Folland, *Incorporating Women*, 189. The author reports that sexual harassment was "more prevalent" in blue-collar and military workplaces than in white-collar jobs.

73. Soroptomist Club speech, WOABC.

74. Ibid.

75. *The Story of Beechcraft*, 1969 company publication, Box 27, Folder 1, WOABC. An image of the medallion is published in the publication. There are many examples of such poses, which remained a consistent pattern throughout Beech's history at the company. See, for example, Louis, "Hall of Fame," WOABC, which underscores that even thirty-three years after his death, Walter Beech loomed large in the background of Olive Ann's career and leadership at the company at her direction. See Museum of Flight, "Beech C-45H Expeditor."

76. National Aviation Hall of Fame, "List of Enshrinees."

77. Ibid.

78. Soroptomist Club speech, WOABC.

79. "Mrs. Beech a Tough Pilot," *New York Times*, 2 October 1979, Box 15, Folder 7, WOABC.

80. Unnamed article, *Fortune*, 1947, n.p., cited in Farney, *Barnstormer and the Lady*, 76.

81. Ibid.

82. Farney, *Barnstormer and the Lady*, 75, photo caption.

83. Ibid., chap. 9, especially 100; Wyden, "Danger," 26–27, 85–86, WOABC.

84. Soroptomist Club speech, WOABC.

85. Delaware Incorporation document (no label or title), Box 26, Folder 1, WOABC.

86. List of stockholders, 13 August 1936, Box 26, Folder 1, WOABC; "Demanding Her Rights" from Soroptomist Club speech, WOABC.

87. Wyden, "Danger," WOABC.

88. Soroptomist Club speech, WOABC.

89. Goldin, "Role of WWII," 745, 751, tables 2 and 5.

90. According to the vital statistics rates published by the U.S. Department of Health, Education, and Welfare, only 40 in every 1,000 live births that year occurred for mothers ages thirty-five to thirty-nine. See Grove and Hetzel, "Vital Statistics," 62, figure 4. This is a lower rate than in 2013, when the birth rates for women ages thirty-five to thirty-nine were 49.6 births per 1,000. See Hamilton, Martin, Osterman, and Curtin, "Births."

91. Farney, *Barnstormer and the Lady*, 69; *Wichita City Directory*, 1946 and 1955.

92. Farney, *Barnstormer and the Lady*, 69, 117–18. Farney is a distinguished journalist who was commissioned by Mary Lynn Oliver, the Beeches' second daughter, to write their biography. Oliver collected recollections about her parents from family, friends, and former employees, which contributed to the project. Farney supplemented this source material with fifty interviews he conducted himself as well as the Beech archives at Wichita State University, on which this book is also based. See foreword and preface to the Farney book.

93. See, for example, the photograph of Olive Ann Beech and both her daughters with Lt. Gen. Jimmy Doolittle and his wife (Farney, *Barnstormer and the Lady*, 104).

94. "Olive Ann Beech, December 10, 1941" scrapbook, Series 2.2, Box 6, FF4; letter to Mr. Bernard Shanley, Secretary to the President (Eisenhower), White House, from Olive Ann Beech, 24 May 1955, Box 17, FF3; scrapbook about President Eisenhower, including invitation to his inauguration; letter to Olive Ann Beech from June H. Mayer, 5 August 1959, Series 2.2, Box 7, FF4, all in WOABC.

95. "39th Anniversary Year Booklet," American Mothers Committee, Box 20, Folder 9, WOABC.

96. See Sparks, *Capital Intentions*; Kwolek-Folland, *Incorporating Women*; Susan Ingalls Lewis, *Unexceptional Women*.

97. Handwritten notes by Margaret Rudkin, Folder 1, MHRC.

98. Donaldson and Heyd, *Strong Medicine*.

99. "Margaret Rudkin: Champion of the Old-Fashioned," *Time*, 21 March 1960, MS B106, ELS; clipping from *Holiday* magazine, May/June, no year, MHRC; Margaret Rudkin, *Margaret Rudkin Cookbook*, 199; letter to Mark Rudkin from Dr. Blake Donaldson, 22 August 1942, MHRC; Ray Josephs, "Old Formula + High Price = Thriving," *American Business*, September 1954, MHRC.

100. Letter from Dr. Blake F. Donaldson to Dear Doctor, 12 November 1937; letter to Mrs. Rudkin from Augustus McKelvey, M.D., 30 September 1937; both in Folder 20, MHRC.

101. Letter from Dr. Blake F. Donaldson to Dear Doctor, 12 November 1937; letter to Mrs. Rudkin from Augustus McKelvey, M.D., 30 September 1937; letter to Dr. Byard from Margaret Rudkin, no date; letter to Dr. Arthur Holland from Margaret Rudkin, 24 May 1938, File 20, MHRC (patient letters in same file); "History," undated but in file with hand-drawn graph of sales for August 1937–July 1938, File 29, MHRC.

For an example of an article that overlooks the important involvement of Dr. Donaldson, see J. D. Ratcliff, "Bread, de Luxe," *Readers' Digest*, December 1939, ELS, which emphasizes that "friends who tasted these early batches of bread asked her why she didn't sell" and only that "doctors gave an initial push by recommending the bread to patients."

102. Margaret Rudkin, *Margaret Rudkin Cookbook*, 200.

103. See Blackford, *A History of Small Business*, for specialty products and niche markets as a common strategy for small businesses.

104. Letter to Mark Rudkin (youngest son of Margaret Rudkin) from Lincoln Fogarty (youngest brother of Margaret Rudkin), 11, 12, and 13 November, no year, Folder 3, MHRC; *Thirteenth Census of the United States, 1910—Population*; *New York State Census, 1915*; *Fourteenth Census of the United States, 1920*.

105. See, for example, Davies, *Woman's Place Is at the Typewriter*, and Strom, *Beyond the Typewriter*, both cited in Sparks, *Capital Intentions*, 66.

106. Kwolek-Folland, *Incorporating Women*, 109. See also Kwolek-Folland, *Engendering Business*, which focuses on the life insurance and banking industries.

107. John Bainbridge, "Profiles: Striking a Blow for Grandma," *New Yorker*, 22 May 1948, ELS.

108. *Fifteenth Census of the United States, 1930*.

109. "Biography of Henry Albert Rudkin," Folder 2, MHRC; *Fortune* story cited in Gray, "Inside the Union Club."

110. See her list in leather-bound "My Trip Abroad" journal, recorded April 1923 on board the *Cedric* on the White Star Line, Folder 2, MHRC.

111. "Biography of Henry Albert Rudkin," MHRC; Fischler, "Long Island Journal"; *Fifteenth Census of the United States, 1930*.

112. Margaret Rudkin, *Margaret Rudkin Cookbook*, 64.

113. "Document for Certificate of Formation of Limited Partnership," File 12, MHRC; correspondence, File 13, MHRC.

114. Ibid.

115. Ibid.

116. Bainbridge, "Profiles," 40, ELS.

117. Josephs, "Old Formula + High Price = Thriving," MHRC; letter to "Jo" (employee of J. R. Williston & Co., presumably assistant to Henry Rudkin) from Margaret Rudkin, 6 June 1946, File 7, MHRC.

118. "Balance Sheet of the Rudkin-Fogarty Partnership for Period April 7, 1923 to April 6, 1943," Folder 3, MHRC.

119. Obituary, place of publication unlisted, Folder 2, MHRC.

120. Margaret Rudkin interview, undated but approximated as late 1950s, recorded on vinyl, ELS.

121. Ibid.; letter to Mark Rudkin from Lincoln Fogarty, MHRC.

122. Margaret Rudkin interview, ELS.

123. Margaret Rudkin, *Margaret Rudkin Cookbook*, foreword.

124. Weiss, *To Have and to Hold*, 117–18.

125. Thomas R. Rudkin, "Overview: The "Life and Times" of Henry Albert Rudkin & Margaret Fogarty Rudkin," MHRC.

Chapter Two

1. Carolyn M. Brown, "How One Female Business Owner Won."

2. Clark, "Government Agencies Fail to Hire Women."

3. See Give Me 5%, http://www.giveme5.com/. The government hit its 5 percent target for the first time in 2015, as reported in Cowley, "Government Hits Goal."

4. "Women and Minority Small Business Contractors: Divergent Paths to Equal Success," research summary for the American Express OPEN for Government Contracts: Victory in Procurement (VIP) for Small Business Program, 2011, https://c401345.ssl.cf1.rackcdn.com/pdf/VIP_Survey2_Final.pdf, cited in Stengel, "How Women Can Up Their Chances." The federal spending figure is cited in a variety of locations. One clear explanation is in U.S. Environmental Protection Agency, "Selling Greener Products and Services to the Federal Government."

5. Wilson, " 'Taking a Nickle out of the Cash Register,' " 349.

6. Kwolek-Folland, *Incorporating Women*, chap. 5. Because Kwolek-Folland emphasizes the focus on government investments in large-scale businesses rather than small businesses, she advances the view that programs such as the Reconstruction Finance Corporation's loan program missed women business owners altogether.

7. Jacobs, " 'How about Some Meat?' " 911, 934.

8. Blackford, *History of Small Business*, 100–101.

9. For the text of the 1979 executive order, see http://www.archives.gov/federal-register/codification/executive-order/12138.html (accessed 13 June 2016). For more on the 1994 Federal Acquisition and Streamlining Act that set a goal of awarding 5 percent of federal contract dollars to women owners of small businesses, see National Association of Women Business Owners, "Federal Procurement."

10. Olson, *Saving Capitalism*, 17–18, 13.

11. Butkiewcz, "Reconstruction Finance Corporation."

12. Wilson, " 'Taking a Nickle out of the Cash Register,' " 350, 383. Wilson also documents renegotiation of military contracts, but extant evidence does not indicate that Lewis or Beech was subject to renegotiation, only EPT.

13. Blackford, *History of Small Business*, 105.

14. Supplement, Flotill Products Application for Relief under Section 722, filed with the Excess Profits Tax Council 30 June 1950, 3, TLF.

15. Letter to Mrs. Weisberg re. R. F. C. Loan, 30 August 1938, TLF; Supplement, Flotill Products Application for Relief, TLF.

16. Flotill Products, Inc., stock prospectus, 5 May 1948, p. 10, TLF.

17. Copy of advertisement provided by Judy Schiffner, in possession of author.

18. Lewis was also sued by the Office of Price Administration for overcharging on her products but was able to show that she had not violated policy ("Local Cannery Sued by OPA on Sales," *Stockton Record*, 1942, as cited in Wood, *Tillie Lewis*,

130–31). The citation in Wood is incomplete. Because there is much less evidence on this battle with the government, I focus on the EPT here instead.

19. Wilson, "'Taking a Nickle out of the Cash Register,'" 350.

20. Chizek, Review of *Tax Relief*, 223–24. By 1945, an estimated 35,000 applications for relief from excess profits tax had been filed.

21. According to Mark Wilson, the final report of the War Contracts Price Adjustment Board regarding World War II military contracts was issued in 1951. As Lewis's case highlights, businesses fought assessments under the excess profits tax even later than that. See Wilson, "'Taking a Nickle out of the Cash Register,'" 382.

22. Wilson, "'Taking a Nickle out of the Cash Register,'" 361–62.

23. Austin, "Taxes after Victory," 92, cited in Chizek, Review of *Tax Relief*, 224.

24. Supplement, Flotill Products Application for Relief, TLF; letter to Mr. Claude O. Young, 18 January 1957, TLF; Chizek, Review of *Tax Relief*, 224.

25. Kellems, *Toil, Taxes and Trouble*. For the description of Kellems, see the introduction to the 1951 edition by Rupert Hughes. I would like to thank Mark Wilson for bringing Kellems to my attention.

26. Wilson, "'Taking a Nickle out of the Cash Register,'" 371, 375.

27. "Tillie's Unpunctured Romance," *Time*, 19 November 1951; Flotill 1948 stock prospectus, p. 20, TLF.

28. Resolution stipulating loan agreement between Reconstruction Finance Corporation and Flotill Products, Inc., 14 July 1949, Exhibit 1 for company annual report for fiscal year ending 31 December 1948 filed with the Securities and Exchange Commission, Folder 2-7447-2-1, Box 5459, SEC.

29. Local historian Kyle Wood presents a new possibility for why Lewis was closely monitored as a manager. According to her self-published history of Tillie Lewis, Wood argues that Lewis was under investigation by the FBI during this time because of the highly unsuccessful and messy purchase of the Texas-based pineapple canning company mentioned above. Allegedly, the concern of the FBI was that Lewis was pursuing bankruptcy and had violated bankruptcy law by paying some of her creditors. Wood cites a letter to J. Edgar Hoover from an RFC investigator asking for information about the agency's investigation because they were considering Lewis's request for an extension to pay off the RFC loan. Citing the FBI file she obtained through the Freedom of Information Act as well as interviews conducted with three family members/employees, Wood weaves a detailed and sordid tale about the difficulties involved in Lewis's failed pineapple venture. Because her book was released at the end of 2016, when this project was already in copyediting, it was not possible for me to obtain a copy of the cited FBI file to substantiate her claim. Parts of the story are also drawn from interviews conducted by the author. These do raise concerns for me as reliable sources of information, since they involve the distant memories of a small number of individuals. See Wood, *Tillie Lewis*, 168–76.

30. Resolution stipulating loan agreement between Reconstruction Finance Corporation and Flotill Products, Inc., 14 July 1949.

31. A number of documents substantiate these loans and their terms, including letters written on Flotill Products, Inc., letterhead and signed by Weisberg as well as typed receipts and copies of checks (Supplement, Flotill Products Application for Relief, TLF). All transactions were signed by Reverend Violet Greener, whom early California historian Carey McWilliams described as having "violet hair and green-painted eyelids" (quoted in Kevin Starr, *Dream Endures*). Evidently, she was one of many occult religious leaders in Los Angeles at this time. How Lewis knew her I can only surmise had something to do with the fact that she clearly knew people connected to the film industry, as evidenced by a letter to her from Don Lieberman, a producer with three film credits, who was associated with Coronado Films, Inc., in Hollywood, California (see Supplement cited above).

32. Flotill Products Inc., Form 10-K, annual report for fiscal year ending 31 December 1950, p. 2, SEC.

33. "Senate Group Probing Charge of Small Business Handicap," *Sunday Star* (Washington, D.C.), 5 November 1950, Folder 400-1411, "Time Allowed For Submission of Bids, '50, General Correspondence 1949–1950 (Subject File)," Box 118, QMG.

34. Hoos, "Determination of Military Subsistence Requirements," 983.

35. "Quartermaster General's Wartime Ration Assembly Plan for Flotill Products," 14 August 1950, Box 6, Entry 2112, "Procurement Schedules," QMG.

36. Ibid.

37. The efficiency of Flotill's industrial operation was also celebrated in newspaper coverage. See "Stockton Cans Rations for U.S. Troops," *Stockton Record*, 11 April 1951, Folder 3, Box 1, SJCHS.

38. *Industry on Parade* episode "Caterers to Combat Men," Reel 57, Box 3, IOP.

39. *Industry on Parade* untitled episode about the Canners League of California, Reel 174, Box 8, IOP.

40. There is more discussion of the *Industry on Parade* program in chaps. 3 and 4.

41. Article cut out, no attribution or date, Folder 3, Box 1, SJCHS.

42. See the photo of the C-ration kit, Box 68, QMG. For additional examples of photographs featuring the names of producers of ration contents, see Folder labeled "K Ration Photographs," Box 76 "K Rations," QMG. For more on the influence of military rations on consumer choices, see Salcedo, *Combat-Ready Kitchen*.

43. See "Quartermaster General's Wartime Ration," QMG.

44. "Senate Group Probing Charge of Small Business Handicap," QMG.

45. This comparison is based on the net income reported for Cal Pak in 1951 ("Del Monte Foods Company History") and for Flotill in 1953, annual report, Form 10-K, SEC.

46. "Extracts from Report of Travel of Captain Andrew J. Draper," 2 January 1951, Folder "Ration, Combat, Individual MIL-R-1504C (1951)," Box 68, "Quartermaster Food & Container Institute," QMG.

47. Form 10-K, annual report for year ending December 1951, Folder 2-7447-2-1, Box 5459, SEC.

48. Securities and Exchange Commission, Form 8-K, Current Report, Flotill Products, Inc., 1950, Folder 2-7447-2-1, Box 5459, SEC.

49. "Tillie's Unpunctured Romance," 105.

50. Flotill Products annual reports for the years ending 31 December 1957, 31 December 1956, and 31 December 1954, SEC. The decline in government sales may have reflected the concerns that emerged in QMG records about the wastefulness of stockpiling emergency rations, since they did not have a shelf life of more than a few years.

51. "Tillie's Unpunctured Romance," 105; Wyndham Robertson, "The Ten Highest-Ranking Women in Big Business," *Fortune*, April 1973, 81–89; Ogden Corporation annual report, 1967, all in TLF. Today, private-label or store-brand manufacturing by "copackers"—sometimes called contract manufacturing—is common. "At Safeway [supermarkets] almost 70% of self-branded items are co-packed. Safeway utilizes its 31 plants in the U.S. and Canada in dairy, grocery, bakery, beverages, pet foods and frozen desserts in addition to 900 or so co-packers for food and non-food items." This was a trend that got started much earlier in the twentieth century. In fact, Safeway's private dairy label—Lucerne—recently celebrated seventy-five years of private-label manufacturing, having made its start in the 1940s, the same period when Flotill began its private-label packing with Safeway, one of its key customers. Private-label manufacturing was so common by 1979 that the Private Label Manufacturers Association was founded to help connect manufacturers and retailers, and it remains an active and growing business organization (Adapa and Chakraborty, "The Supermarket Industry"; Private Label Manufacturers Association, http://plma .com/).

52. Form 10-K, Flotill Products, Inc., annual report for year ending 31 December 1952, SEC.

53. Form 10-K, Flotill Products, Inc., annual report for year ending 31 December 1958, SEC.

54. Prospectus, Beech Aircraft Corporation, February 1940, Folder 2-4079-1, Box 2488, SEC. Beech's sales in 1938 would be equivalent to approximately $19.5 million in 2016. The contract it secured the same year would be equivalent to approximately $17 million.

55. "Add to the Roster of Aviation's Great: Walter Hershel Beech," *Aviation News Beacon*, 7 December 1950, 2, Box 6, Folder 2, WOABC.

56. Prospectus, Beech Aircraft Corporation, February 1940, Folder 2-4079-1, Box 2488, SEC.

57. Biography of Olive Ann Beech, prepared by Beech Aircraft upon announcement of her retirement, p. 5, Box 19, Folder 39, WOABC.

58. Form 10-K, Beech Aircraft, annual report, 1943, SEC.

59. Form 10-K, Beech Aircraft, annual report, 1942, SEC.

60. "Regulation V Loans in the Fifth District," 3–5.

61. "Form 8-K for Current Reports," Beech Aircraft, 1939, with attachments regarding fiscal year 1941, Folder 1-2839-1-1, Box 3028, SEC.

62. "Regulation V Loans in the Fifth District."

63. "Beech Aircraft Gets $50 Million 'VT' Loan," *Finance*, 10 April 1944, Box 6, Folder 1, WOABC.

64. "Regulation V Loans in the Fifth District."

65. "Certified Copy of Resolution of Board of Directors of Beech Aircraft Corporation," Exhibit B, Form 8-K for Corporations, Beech Aircraft, April 1944, Box 3029, Folder 1-2839-2-1, SEC.

66. "Beech Aircraft Gets $50 Million 'VT' Loan," WOABC.

67. Ibid.

68. Peter Wyden, "Danger: Boss Lady at Work," *Saturday Evening Post*, 8 August 1959, 86, WOABC.

69. "O. A. Beech Elected President," *Beechcrafter*, 22 December 1950, Box 6, Folder 4, WOABC.

70. Arthur M. Louis, "The Hall of Fame for U.S. Business Leadership: Olive Ann Beech," *Fortune*, 4 April 1983, 145, WOABC.

71. Soroptomist Club speech, Box 6, Folder 3, WOABC.

72. Ibid.

73. Wyden, "Danger," 85.

74. "Six Kansas Winners Receive Freedoms Foundation Awards," *Wichita Eagle*, 13 June 1955, Series 2.2, Box 7, Folder 1, WOABC.

75. George Meany, "'Liberals' Should Quit Being Soft on Communism," speech before the National Religion and Labor Foundation, New York, 14 December 1955, in *Beechcrafter*, 1 March 1956, reprinted from *U.S. News & World Report*, 23 December 1955, Box 7, Folder 2, WOABC.

76. Letter to Olive Ann Beech from President Dwight Eisenhower, 6 May 1958, and telegram from Olive Ann Beech to President Dwight Eisenhower, 17 May 1958, both in scrapbook about President Dwight Eisenhower, Box 17, Folder 3, WOABC. The same scrapbook also documents that Beech was an invited guest of the Republican National Committee, which organized a series of breakfasts with President Eisenhower for women leaders in 1955.

77. John P. Gaty, Beech Aircraft general manager, to Harry S. Truman, 17 October 1941, Folder "National Defense—Aircraft Production," Box 113, "Papers of Harry S. Truman, Senatorial File, Truman Library," quoted in Wilson, "'Taking a Nickel out of the Cash Register,'" 361fn59.

78. All the tax documents referenced here can be found in MS 97-02, Box 26, Folder 2, WOABC.

79. See Fones-Wolf, *Selling Free Enterprise*. Thank you to Jennifer Helgren for helping me to see and articulate this point more clearly.

80. Frank E. Hedrick, "Pageantry of Flight: The Story of Beech Aircraft Corporation," Newcomen Society Address, delivered at the National Meeting of the Newcomen Society in North America, New York City, 28 September 1967, pp. 21–29, Box 17, Folder 2, WOABC. Mrs. Beech and Mr. Hedrick were the guests of honor.

81. Handwritten prayer included in scrapbook given to Olive Ann Beech to commemorate twentieth-anniversary celebration of Beechcraft's Boulder Division, 1975, Series 2.3, Box 16, Folder 6A, WOABC. In a letter to the Boulder Division manager in the same scrapbook, she remarks on the prayer.

82. Lew Townsend, "Beech Agrees to Merger Offer of $615 million from Raytheon," *Wichita Beacon*, 2 October 1979, and Lew Townsend and Dan Bearth, "Personalities Played Big Role," *Wichita Eagle and Beacon*, 7 October 1979, Box 15, Folder 7, WOABC.

83. Cohen, *Consumer's Republic*, 65–67.

84. Letter to Margaret Rudkin from Fred W. Thomas, Associate Price Executive, Food and Food Products Branch, Office of Price Administration, Washington, D.C., 28 May 1942, File 25, "OPA," MHRC.

85. Letter to Fred W. Thomas, Associate Price Executive, Food and Food Products Branch, Office of Price Administration, Washington, D.C., 12 June 1942, File 25, "OPA," MHRC.

86. Ibid.

87. Pepperidge Farm, "Break-Down of One Loaf of Bread at 20c Based on Production of 4239 Loaves," Exhibit for 2 May 1938 partnership agreement, File 12, MHRC.

88. One of Oliver's letters to Margaret Rudkin is printed on Abbott letterhead. The company was founded in 1903 and now exists as Abbott Nutrition, maker of powdered baby formula and other nutrition supplements, which is a part of Abbott. See Abbott Nutrition, http://abbottnutrition.com/about-us/about-abbott-nutrition.

89. For references to Oliver letters in this paragraph and below, see Charles Oliver to Margaret Rudkin, 9 July, 12 August, and 21 August, File 25, MHRC.

90. *Pepperidge Farm Conveyor*, 25th Anniversary Issue, 1937–1962, p. 9, Box 1, Series B, Folder B, ELS.

91. *Pepperidge Farm Conveyor*, 20th Anniversary Issue, June 1957, Box 1, Series B, Folder 2, ELS. War needs dictated that shortening was set aside for use "in the manufacture of munitions," whereas butter was stockpiled for soldiers' rations.

92. Letter to Dr. Oliver Stansfield from Margaret Rudkin, 12 December 1944, File 20, MHRC.

93. Cohen, *Consumer's Republic*, 68–69.

94. Most of the letters were addressed to Senator Truman, who oversaw the special committee (known as "the Truman Committee") charged with investigating business, labor, and government agencies to seek ways to make all three cooperate. Letter to Honorable Harry S. Truman from Mrs. Rae M. Wentmouth of San Francisco, California, 6 October 1943, Senate 79A-F30, Box 314, "OP-9 Food: U.S. & Canada—Food Problems in Various Areas, Alabama—New Jersey," Folder "California," NDC. For a description of the committee and Truman's role on it, see U.S. Senate Historical Office, "Harry S. Truman, 34th Vice President."

95. Letter to Mr. Hugh Fulton, Chief Counsel, Special Committee Investigating the National Defense Program, United States Senate, from Mrs. Alexander H. Kerr (Ruth), President, Alexander H. Kerr & Co., Inc., 18 October 1943, NDC.

96. Letter to Mr. Hugh Felton, Chief Counsel, Special Committee Investigating the National Defense Program, United States Senate, from Walter H. Ralphs, Vice-President, Ralphs Grocery Company, 8 March 1943, NDC.

97. H. A. Baldwin, "A Chronological List of Events at Pepperidge Farm," 10, ELS. According to one representative of a Kansas wheat farmer group, "We would be getting about 25 cents a bushel for our wheat if it were not for the fixed price established under the AAA." With the price support provided by the wartime government agency, he reported that wheat prices were "flirting with the dollar mark" (cited in Hurt, *Great Plains*, 158–59). Similar price freezes were put into effect in conjunction with the Korean-American War.

98. According to one citizen who wrote to his elected representative in Congress, "the soldier [would] get 2 pounds of butter a week, whereas civilians . . . receive[d] ¼ pound per week." In combination with all the other food items in a standard soldier's ration, "the total [was] tremendous," he wrote, "and more than I believe any man could eat" (letter to Hon. John M. Costello, House of Representatives, Washington, D.C., from George W. Wilson, Los Angeles, California, 1 February 1943, NDC).

99. Letter to Mr. Hugh Felton from Walter H. Ralphs.

100. John Bainbridge, "Profiles: Striking a Blow for Grandma," *New Yorker*, 22 May 1948, 48, ELS.

101. Jacobs, " 'How about Some Meat?,' " 911; Cohen, *Consumer's Republic*, 75.

102. Fones-Wolf, *Selling Free Enterprise*, 33–35.

103. See *Industry on Parade* episode "A Message from Industry," Reel 375, Box 14, IOP.

104. *Industry on Parade* episode "Grandma's Methods Modernized!," Reel 109, Box 5, IOP; untitled feature on Pepperidge Farm's Downingtown, Pennsylvania, cookie plant, Reel 285, Box 11, IOP; *Industry on Parade* episode "Billion Dollar Breakfast," Reel 385, Box 14, IOP.

105. *Pepperidge Farm Conveyor*, 20th Anniversary Issue, June 1957, p. 22, Box 1, Series B, Folder 2, ELS.

106. *Pepperidge Farm Conveyor*, 25th Anniversary Issue, 1937–1962, p. 13, Box 1, Series B, Folder B, ELS.

107. Margaret Rudkin, *Margaret Rudkin Cookbook*, 66–67.

108. "Supplementary Brief in Behalf of Home Baking . . . Presented in the interest of the Flour Milling Industry by the Task Committee on Shortening for the Flour Milling Industry," 19 July 1943, NDC; letter to Dr. Harold F. Hollands, Food Distribution Administration, Civilian Requirements Division, Washington, D.C., from V. H. Englehard, Chairman, Shortening Committee of the Family Flour Industry, undated, NDC.

109. Bainbridge, "Profiles," 42.

Chapter Three

1. Bailey, "Yahoo CEO Marissa Mayer's Ban"; Surowiecki, "Face Time."

2. Pesce, "Marissa Mayer Bans Telecommuting."

3. Kwolek-Folland, *Incorporating Women*, 110–12, 200–201.

4. Sharpe, "As Leaders, Women Rule."

5. "Women 'Take Care,' Men 'Take Charge.' "

6. Ruiz, *Cannery Women, Cannery Lives*, 146fn8.

7. Laird, "Parallel Ladders to the Glass Ceiling," 21.

8. Mandell, *Corporation as Family*, 34, 156–59, 143–44, 10.

9. Fones-Wolf, *Selling Free Enterprise*, 5, 87–88.

10. Jacoby, *Modern Manors*, 5–7, 55–56; "Gemeinschaft and Gesellschaft."

11. Zahavi, *Workers, Managers, and Welfare Capitalism*, 202, 211–12, 215.

12. Diane Vecchio studied Italian immigrant women employed in the Endicott Johnson plant and argues that, for them, the choice between welfare capitalism or unionization was clear because the company's flexibility, benefits, and programs supported their participation in work and leisure activities as married and unmarried women and supported their personal and family aspirations. Yet at least one female employee also remembered that George F. Johnson himself, the Endicott Johnson president, would come onto the factory floor to convince workers not to unionize (*Merchants, Midwives, and Laboring Women*, 57–60).

13. Laird, "Making a Hero of Horatio Alger"; Fones-Wolf, *Selling Free Enterprise*.

14. Ruiz, *Cannery Women, Cannery Lives*.

15. Flotill Products, Inc., stock prospectus, 5 May 1948, p. 10, TLF.

16. Alice Packard, "Women Who Do: The Extraordinary Story of Tillie Lewis," place and date of publication not cited, TLF.

17. "How a (Female) High School Dropout Built a Business That Does More Than $150 Million a Year," *New Woman*, November/December 1973, TLF.

18. Dorothy Walworth, "First Lady of San Joaquin," *Everywoman's Magazine*, August 1952, 5, TLF. Wood's portrayal of Lewis's relations with her employees largely conforms with this favorable portrayal, although she reports that some employees were intimidated by Lewis. There are some exceptions to this rosy picture, however, as in the case of the Modesto plant employee who reportedly hated Lewis and left as soon as he could secure a job in the Richmond shipyards. Wood, *Tillie Lewis*, 124.

19. "Books: Faith for Straphangers."

20. This was also a familiar trope in Lewis's life, as chapter 4 on brand management will detail, and indicates that Lewis herself was comfortable with fabricating a fictionalized version of herself for public consumption to promote her company, its market position, and its best interests.

21. The award was confirmed by a phone message to the author from sitting president of the Stockton Japanese American Citizens' League, July 2009. See also "Tillie Lewis: Pioneer in the Food Industry," *Hornblower* (publication of the Northern California Section of the Institute of Food Technologists) 31, no. 2 (March/April 1977): 5, Folder 2, Box 1, SJCHS.

22. The professional photograph appears in Folder 2, Box 3, SJCHS.

23. Sidney Fields, "Only Human: Tillie Lewis, Tomatoes Wouldn't Wait," *Mirror*, 11 November 1951, 41, gift of Judy Schiffner in author's possession.

24. "Last Vestige Comes to a Close as Tillie Lewis Plant Shut Down," *Stockton Record*, February 1987, TLF.

25. "Tillie Lewis is 'Boss of Year' for Local ABWA Chapter," from Family Scrapbook, gift of Judy Schiffner in author's possession.

26. Letter to Gwen Thompson from Alilea Haywood Martin, 18 May 1983, TLF.

27. Zahavi, *Workers, Managers, and Welfare Capitalism*, 43–46.

28. Rose, "March Inland," 67–82, 155–76.

29. According to one account, Lewis's employees were on strike only by obligation to the AFL, which prompted one Flotill worker to write to Meyer Lewis "to protest that Tillie wasn't getting a fair deal." "Please let Tille's [*sic*] workers go back to work," he wrote. A different account emphasized that "a rival packer was paying [the local union agent] to keep [her] strikebound" by subverting all her attempts "to meet the strikers' terms" (Ruth Winter, "Tillie of the Valley: An Amazing Success Story," no date or place of publication, TLF; Tillie Lewis, "The Tomato Lady," *Guideposts*, April 1977, 20, TLF; Fields, "Only Human"), gift of Judy Schiffner in author's possession.

30. Cannery Workers Union Program, 15 November 1941, File "Getting Started Letters, Looking for Funding, Loans, Lawsuits 1935–1954," TLF.

31. Flotill 1948 stock prospectus, TLF; Ruiz, *Cannery Women, Cannery Lives*.

32. Brown and Philips, "Evolution of Labor Market Structure," 399–400.

33. Brown and Philips, "Decline of the Piece-Rate System," 585.

34. Ibid., 595.

35. Brown and Philips, "Evolution of Labor Market Structure," 399.

36. Obituary for Meyer Lewis, *New York Times*, 2 August 1976, TLF.

37. Wood suggests that this relationship was on-again, off-again, and started soon after Meyer Lewis began working at Flotill and before he divorced his first wife. Wood, *Tillie Lewis*, 153.

38. In fact, Green went out of his way to bring Flotill's wartime stamp purchase program to the attention of Treasury Secretary Henry Morgenthau (1934–45) as an "advanced step" in employer–employee relations in support of the nation's interests (Flotill 1948 stock prospectus, TLF; letters to Miss Weisberg from W. Green, president of the American Federation of Labor, 2 January 1942 and 9 July 1942, File "Getting Started Letters," TLF).

39. Ruiz, *Cannery Women, Cannery Lives*, 163–64fn17.

40. This language comes from the CPG contract Lewis signed in 1947. See "Labor Contract," Exhibit 15 (1), annual report for fiscal year ending 31 December 1948, Folder 2-7447-2-1, Box 5459, SEC.

41. Interview with Albert Heiser, 27 June 1994, conducted by Merrill Schleier, cited in Schleier, "Tillie the Toiler."

42. See, for example, Saker Woeste, "Insecure Equality."

43. Wood provides many examples of anti-Semitism and misogyny directed at Lewis gleaned from interviews with local residents. Wood, *Tillie Lewis*.

44. *Stockton Daily Evening Record*, 8 January 1944, TLF. Thanks to Ken Albala for bringing this to my attention; Martin, *Promise Unfulfilled*.

45. Martin, *Promise Unfulfilled*.

46. Olmsted, *Right out of California*, 227.

47. "Flotill Combats Labor Shortage," 70–72, TLF.

48. See photo feature and text labeled "canning tomatoes after classes" in *Naranjado* (student yearbook), 122–23, Holt Atherton Special Collections Library, University of the Pacific, Stockton, California, and Lewis, "Tomato Lady," 20, in which she refers to offering "siesta times for those over age 50."

49. Flotill Products, Inc., company pamphlet, undated but content indicates 1946, TLF; *Flotill Notes* 1, no. 1 (August 1942), gift of Judy Schiffner in author's possession.

50. In interviews with Albert Heiser and Alilea Haywood Martin (longtime secretary to Tillie Lewis), Schleier confirmed that these were not long-term company policies or programs (Schleier, "Tillie the Toiler," 19).

51. Fones-Wolf, *Selling Free Enterprise*, 71–80.

52. Flotill Products, Inc., company pamphlet, TLF.

53. Fones-Wolf, *Selling Free Enterprise*, 88.

54. *Flotill Notes* 1, no. 1 (August 1942), gift of Judy Schiffner in author's possession. According to Fones-Wolf, employee suggestion systems had been around since the late 1800s but began to flourish during and following World War II. Fones-Wolf, *Selling Free Enterprise*, 76.

55. Flotill Products, Inc., company pamphlet, TLF.

56. "Labor Contract," included as Exhibit 15 (1) with Flotill's 1948 filing, SEC.

57. See *Industry on Parade*, untitled episode, Reel 178, Box 8, IOP.

58. Ruiz, *Cannery Women, Cannery Lives*, chap. 6 ("Death of a Dream"), 103–123. The history of the northern California cannery fight in 1945–46, covered here and in subsequent paragraphs, all comes from Ruiz.

59. Obituary for David Beck, *New York Times*, 28 December 1993.

60. Ruiz, *Cannery Women, Cannery Lives*. The NLRB issued a tepid warning that employers could not engage in "preferential" treatment of any labor organization. While this was a win for cannery operatives, it was a weak strike at the powerful influence of the Teamsters. And it failed to circumscribe their power and influence.

61. Ruiz, *Cannery Women, Cannery Lives*.

62. Ibid. There were four northern California canneries that elected the FTA. These were Fruitvale Cannery (Oakland), Pacific Grape (Modesto), Califruit Co. (Manteca), Stanislaus Cannery Co. (Stanislaus), and Stockley Cannery (Modesto) ("CIO Challenges Cannery Vote Cites Intimidation," *Labor Herald*, No. California Edition, September 6, 1946), CWUC. Flotill Products was not among them. Thank you to the Labor Archives and Research Center at San Francisco State University for help in locating the edition that listed the names of these companies.

63. "National Affairs: Barrel No. 2."

64. Olmsted, *Right out of California.*

65. These were the terms won by the FTA in a contract with Pacific Grape Products (Ruiz, *Cannery Women, Cannery Lives,* 107).

66. "Collective Bargaining Agreement between California Processors and Growers, Inc., and California State Council of Cannery Unions, American Federation of Labor" and "Memorandum of Discussion between J. P. St. Sure and J. W. Bristow, December 26, 1947," both in "Labor Contracts," Exhibit 15 (1), Flotill Products, Inc., 1948, SEC. Because this is the only labor contract preserved in extant records for the company, it is not possible to compare it to the contract Lewis signed independently in 1941. There is no reference to other contracts signed independently after this first one, so it is impossible to know whether any changes were made or how conditions may have changed before Lewis signed on with the CPG contract in 1947.

67. "Flotill's Profit Sharing Plan," May 1955, TLF.

68. Extant company records document no other labor upheavals, contracts, or changes during the period between 1948 (when the company filed the 1947 CPG contract with its SEC report) and 1973.

69. The case finally came to a close when the Supreme Court denied a final petition to stop implementation of the settlement agreement in 1978.

70. A full explication of the complicated history and outcomes of the Alaniz case has been on my research agenda for a long time; I have an article on the subject in preparation. It is a fascinating case that deserves exploration outside the context of Tillie Lewis's business history.

71. "Doctor of Business Administration Conferred upon Tillie Lewis for Outstanding Leadership in the Field of Business," 25 May 1973, TLF.

72. "Explanation of the Proposed Beech Efficiency Incentive Plan," 19 December 1941, submitted to the SEC with "Form 8-K for Current Reports," filed 11 June 1942, Folder 1-2839-2-1, Box 3028, SEC.

73. "Wichita Tries to Boost Its Aviation Industry."

74. Ellison and Glaeser, "Geographic Concentration."

75. "Bumps Were Few as Union Landed," *Wichita Eagle-Beacon,* 13 May 1985, 1A, 7A, Folder 4, Box 16, WOABC.

76. "Company, Union Approve New Contract," *Beechcrafter,* August 1963, Box 17, Folder 5, WOABC.

77. "Olive Ann Beech, Chairman Emeritus, Beech Aircraft Corporation," biography prepared by the company, January 1984, Box 19, Folder 39, WOABC.

78. "An Announcement to All Beechcrafters," undated but filed with other items from the 1970s and 1980s, Box 18, Folder 22, WOABC.

79. Fones-Wolf, *Selling Free Enterprise,* 96; Jacoby, *Modern Manors,* 81.

80. Jacoby, *Employing Bureaucracy,* 198.

81. Beech Aircraft Corporation, "Extracts from Minutes of Meeting of Board of Directors, Duly Held on December 11, 1941, Relating to So-Called 'Beech Efficiency Incentive Plan,'" Form 8-K, filed 11 June 1942, Box 3028, Folder 1, 2839-2-1, SEC.

82. Appreciation for the leadership role played by the union in company history is revealed in a notice to employees (labeled "confidential") titled "Do It for Yourselves!" and signed by Jack Gaty, Vice President and General Manager, dated April 1956, Box 7, Folder 2, WOABC.

83. Fones-Wolf, *Selling Free Enterprise*, 89.

84. Farney, *The Barnstormer and the Lady*, 82; "Cooperation Key to Success in Beech's Productivity Council," *Beechcrafter*, 20 April 1978, 2, Box 27, Folder 9, WOABC.

85. Farney, *The Barnstormer and the Lady*, 81–82; "Patriotic Contributions" Gallery, Walt Disney Family Museum. A photograph featured in Farney's account shows Walt Disney himself playfully presenting toy Disney characters to Olive Ann Beech, suggesting that she may have received special treatment in her collaboration with the Disney company to produce the Busy Bee certificates. The museum exhibit also reveals that Walt Disney was the owner of a King Air, the signature plane of the Beech Aircraft company in the 1960s, suggesting the customer relationship between the two went both ways. For examples of awards for good ideas, see "$250 First Prize to Galloway and Anslinger in Beechcraft Semi-annual Award Evaluations," covering the year-end finalists in the employee suggestions program, and "Suggestion Prize for Month Shared by 5 Employees," both in *Beechcrafter*, Holiday Issue, 1961, Box 27, Folder 2, WOABC.

86. Letter to Mr. J. E. Isaacs from Olive Ann Beech and Frank E. Hedrick, 4 August 1975, Box 18, Folder 10, WOABC.

87. One example of many of these can be found in "Welcome to Beechcraft," a new employee handbook, undated but contents suggest 1957, Box 7, Folder 2, WOABC.

88. Soroptomist Club speech, Box 6, Folder 3, WOABC.

89. Farney, *Barnstomer and the Lady*, 81.

90. "Salary Payroll Employees List," Box 26, Folder 15, WOABC.

91. *Beechcrafter*, May 1986, Box 20, Folder 1, WOABC.

92. For more on government and corporate programs to incentivize inclusion of women in business during this period, see Laird, *Pull*.

93. Letter to Mrs. Beech from Lucille Winters Edwards, 5 January 1974, Box 18, Folder 10, WOABC.

94. Letters to Members of the Beech Management Team from O. A. Beech, 27 December 1965 and 29 December 1961, Box 26, Folder 3, WOABC. The birds and poems are mentioned in both letters.

95. "The Day before Christmas at Beech," undated, Box 18, Folder 10, WOABC; letter from the president, unsigned and with no addressee but clearly to employees, 16 December 1965, Box 26, Folder 3, WOABC.

96. Letter to Members of the Beechcraft Management Group from the President, 29 December 1961, Box 26, Folder 3, WOABC.

97. Letter to Mrs. Olive Ann Beech from Michael G. Neuburger, 26 June 1984, Box 26, Folder 6, WOABC.

98. See, for example, the 1968 Beech Aircraft Annual Report filed with the SEC, Box 26, Folder 4, WOABC; additional examples can be found in company marketing materials.

99. *Beechcrafter*, 29 March 1956, Box 7, Folder 2, WOABC. Such photos appeared regularly in the many years of *Beechcrafter* newsletters that are archived in the collection.

100. Letter to O. A. Beech from Glenn Ehling, 9 May 1975, Box 18, Folder 10, WOABC.

101. Letter to Mrs. O. A. Beech from John A. Pike, 6 May 1975, Box 18, Folder 10, WOABC.

102. Beechcraft employee handbook "Welcome to Beechcraft," undated but contents suggest 1957, Box 7, Folder 2, WOABC.

103. Jacoby, *Employing Bureaucracy*, 186, 196.

104. Letter from O. A. Beech, no addressee, 18 December 1964, Box 26, Folder 3, WOABC.

105. A 1974 year-end awards list categorized executive managers into eight groups, depending on the type and amount of award they received and therefore the letter they were to receive; another list has handwritten amounts for each employee. Frank Hedrick, O. A. Beech's nephew and by 1974 the president of the company, is the only executive who received $25,000; Beech herself was awarded $20,000 that year. Box 18, Folder 10, WOABC.

106. Letter to Mr. Charles W. Dieker from Frank E. Hedrick and Olive Ann Beech, 21 April 1976, Box 18, Folder 10, WOABC.

107. Letter from O. A. Beech and Frank E. Hedrick, no addressee but clearly to managers receiving year-end awards, Christmas 1966, Box 26, Folder 3, WOABC.

108. Letter to Mr. J. A. Elliott from Frank E. Hedrick and Olive Ann Beech, 21 April 1976, Box 18, Folder 10, WOABC.

109. Peter Wyden, "Danger: Boss Lady at Work," *Saturday Evening Post*, 8 August 1959, 86, WOABC.

110. Fones-Wolf, *Selling Free Enterprise*, 82; Handout for "Appreciation Luncheon, Wednesday, August 25, 1982, 12:15pm," Box 27, Folder 31, WOABC.

111. Letter to Mrs. Beech from H. A. Slingsby, 6 June 1975, Box 18, Folder 10, WOABC.

112. Fones-Wolf, *Selling Free Enterprise*, 73, 82, and fn70.

113. "Welcome to Beechcraft," WOABC.

114. Letter to Mr. Frank E. Hedrick from J. Paul Kinloch, Loeb Rhoades Hornblower, 18 April 1979, Box 26, Folder 13, WOABC.

115. "What Is Loyalty?" *Beechcrafter*, 1 March 1956, Box 7, Folder 2, WOABC. Percentage of workforce in production taken from the letter to Hedrick from Kinloch.

116. Frank Moore, "With a Grain of Salt," *Daily Facts* (Redlands, Calif.), 31 March 1979, B8, Box 20, Folder 9, WOABC.

117. See, for example, Mandell, *Corporation as Family*.

118. Jacoby, *Employing Bureaucracy*, 188.

119. *Beechcrafter*, 1 March 1956, Box 7, Folder 2; *Beechcrafter*, 8 August 1973, 3, Box 27, Folder 3; *Beechcrafter*, 17 November 1976, Box 27, Folder 5; *Beechcrafter*, 8 June 1977, all in WOABC.

120. See, for example, the partisan examination of Jaffa in Gottfried, "Harry Jaffa."

121. Kruse, *One Nation under God*; Smith, "Dwight David Eisenhower."

122. Fones-Wolf, *Selling Free Enterprise*, 223. I have edited this quote from the original ("the moral and spiritual self disciplines of stewardship") for ease of comprehension and trust I have not changed the original meaning.

123. Kruse, *One Nation under God*, xiv.

124. *Beechcrafter*, 22 December 1950, Box 6, Folder 4, WOABC.

125. Kruse, *One Nation under God*.

126. Fones-Wolf, *Selling Free Enterprise*, 78.

127. *Industry on Parade* untitled episode, Reel 178, Box 8, IOP.

128. Fones-Wolf, *Selling Free Enterprise*, 91.

129. Jacoby, *Modern Manors*, 80; *Industry on Parade* untitled episode, Reel 156, Box 7, IOP. Diamond Alkaline featured a country club that employees built themselves with the support of the company, which contributed land and materials. It featured a ten-acre manmade lake stocked with fish, a clubhouse, rifle range, playground, and two pools, and there were plans for developing a golf range.

130. "Good-Time Table," *Beechcrafter*, 1 March 1956, 25, Box 7, Folder 2, WOABC.

131. "The BEC: A Fellowship of Beechcrafters," *Beechcrafter*, 30 January 1980, 4–5, Box 27, Folder 9, WOABC.

132. Fones-Wolf, *Selling Free Enterprise*, 91.

133. Letter to Loeb Rhoades Hornblower & Co. (the firm hired to manage the search for a merger partner) from Frank E. Hedrick, 1 August 1979, Box 26, Folder 14, WOABC.

134. Study of Beech Aircraft by Loeb Rhoades Hornblower, p. 39, and "Employees" enclosure with letter to Frank E. Hedrick from J. Paul Kinloch, 18 April 1979, Box 26, Folder 13, WOABC.

135. Lew Townsend and Dan Bearth, "Personalities Played Big Role," *Wichita Eagle-Beacon*, 7 October 1979, 2B, Box 15, Folder 7, WOABC.

136. Letter to Mr. D. Brainerd Holmes from O. A. Beech, 24 October 1979, Box 19, Folder 60, WOABC.

137. Pepperidge Farm employee handbook "Ten Commandments of Safety for Supervisors," 1 April 1957, Series B, Folder 1, ELS.

138. Margaret Rudkin, *Margaret Rudkin Cookbook*, 200–201.

139. Description of 9 February 2014 phone conversation between Thomas G. Rudkin (grandson) and Bill Ference (Sr.) in "The Life and Times of Henry Albert Rudkin & Margaret Fogarty Rudkin," by Thomas G. Rudkin, provided to author in conjunction with permission to consult his collection of historical records in MHRC.

140. Marchand, *Creating the Corporate Soul*, 107, as quoted in book review by Fones-Wolf.

141. Pepperidge Farm *Conveyor* 15, no. 1, March 1967, Box 1, Series B, Folder 3, ELS.

142. Pepperidge Farm *Conveyor*, Fall 1987, 50th Anniversary Edition, Box 1, Series B, Folder 3, ELS.

143. Marchand, *Creating the Corporate Soul*, 15, as quoted in Fones-Wolf, Review of *Creating the Corporate Soul*.

144. John Bainbridge, "Profiles: Striking a Blow for Grandma," *New Yorker*, 22 May 1948, 38, ELS.

145. Ibid.

146. Margaret Rudkin interview, digitized from original vinyl recording, Series C, Folder 7, ELS.

There is no information in the file about who conducted the interview, what it was for, or when it was conducted, but since she refers to "21 years" having passed since the inception of the business, we can date it at 1958.

147. Employee records, 17 July 1960, Series B, Folder 1, ELS. The term "production worker" here describes jobs associated with the production of bakery products and excludes cafeteria jobs, which were gendered female and paid even less.

148. I have Nikki Mandell to thank for helping me to articulate this thought— she gave me feedback and words that enabled me to clarify my thoughts and arguments here and throughout the chapter.

149. Bainbridge, "Profiles," 38.

150. Fones-Wolf, Jacoby, and Mandell all document these employment trends.

151. Fones-Wolf, Book review of Tone, *Business of Benevolence*.

152. Ibid., 93–94.

153. Pepperidge Farm *Conveyor*, August 1959, coverage of the tenth-anniversary celebration at Downingtown, Box 1, Series B, Folder 3, ELS.

154. "Vacation . . . at Pepperidge Farm," *Conveyor*, May 1966, Box 1, Series B, Folder 3, ELS.

155. U.S. Department of Labor, "CPI Inflation Calculator."

156. Completed Form 1065, U.S. Internal Revenue Service, Treasury Department, Partnership Return of Income for the years 1938–45, Folder 18, MHRC.

157. "Pepperidge Farm Donates $5,000 to Y Building Fund," *Post*, 4 August 1963, PFBC. Thanks to Elizabeth Van Tuyl for providing me with copies of the articles in the file.

158. Fones-Wolf, *Selling Free Enterprise*, 159, 169, 173.

159. "Ten Commandments of Safety for Supervisors," Series B, Folder 1, ELS.

160. "Norwalk Ceremony Surprises Founder of Pepperidge Farm," *Post* (Norwalk), 5 June 1957, PFBC. Thanks to Elizabeth Van Tuyl for providing me with copies of the articles in the file.

161. Olmsted argues that the attack on government by big business in California that commenced during the 1930s was not prompted by a concern about big government per se but rather by the fact that some New Deal government programs were designed to benefit workers and not farmers or big business. As long as

they were the ones benefiting from large state subsidies, agribusiness leaders embraced New Deal policies. It wasn't until the turn to secure workers' economic status (at the expense of profits for growers and business owners) that they became critical of government policies (Olmsted, *Right out of California*).

162. Fones-Wolf, *Selling Free Enterprise*. The phrase "taking care of workers" was explicitly cited as a theme in an episode in the film series *Industry on Parade*, produced by the National Association of Manufacturers. "In Trust for Tomorrow," Reels 502 and 503, IOP.

163. *Industry on Parade* episode "The Hidden Payroll," Reel 447 (9 May 1959), IOP.

164. *Mill & Factory* survey, quoted in S. Avery Raube, "Nonfinancial Incentives," *MRec*, 8 December 1946, 395, cited in Fones-Wolf, *Selling Free Enterprise*, 72fn24.

165. *Industry on Parade* episode, no title, Reel 376, 28 December 1957, IOP.

166. Jacoby, *Modern Manors*, 111.

167. "Address by Mrs. Margaret Rudkin to Harvard Business School, 1960," transcript by the Rowland Company, Inc., MHRC.

168. Fones-Wolf, *Selling Free Enterprise*, 86.

169. "Ten Commandments of Safety for Supervisors," Series B, Folder 1, ELS.

170. Nohria, Groysberg, and Lee, "Employee Motivation."

171. Fones-Wolf, *Selling Free Enterprise*, 95.

172. "Address by Mrs. Margaret Rudkin," 30, MHRC.

173. See definition of "human relations" in the online *Merriam-Webster Dictionary*, http://www.merriam-webster.com/dictionary/human%20relations (accessed 8 September 2014).

174. Jacoby, *Modern Manors*, 49.

175. *Industry on Parade* episode "Grandma's Methods," Reel 109, 11 November 1952, featuring the Norwalk, Conn., plant; *Industry on Parade* episode, no title, Reel 258, 24 September 1955, featuring the Downingtown, Pa., plant; *Industry on Parade* episode "Billion Dollar Breakfast," Reel 358, 1 March 1958, featuring Pepperidge Farm as one of several manufacturing companies that "improves the quality, variety and freshness of food resulting in nutritious breakfasts," all from IOP.

176. "Ten Commandments of Safety for Supervisors," Series B, Folder 1, ELS.

177. Fones-Wolf, *Selling Free Enterprise*, 89.

178. Jacoby, *Modern Manors*, 252–53.

179. "Address by Mrs. Margaret Rudkin," MHRC.

180. Ibid., 30.

181. Fones-Wolf, *Selling Free Enterprise*, 86.

182. Memo from W. L. R (William L. Rudkin), printed in *Conveyor*, April 1968, Box 1, Series B, Folder 3, ELS.

183. Speech at Drexel Institute of Technology, 17 May 1962, given at the Convocation of the Home Economics Department, MHRC.

184. "A Chronological List of Events at Pepperidge Farm," compiled by H. A. Baldwin, 34, Box 1, Series C, Folder 8, ELS.

Chapter Four

1. Edwards, "Meet the 10 Most-Liked Ad Agency CEOs"; Kwolek-Folland, *Incorporating Women*, 201–2; "Lifetime Achievement: Mary Wells"; "Mary Wells Lawrence"; "Women in Business."

2. Sutton, *Globalizing Ideal Beauty*, 1–3.

3. Home economics departments at many companies reflected an internal company investment in the same idea. Goldstein, *Creating Consumers*.

4. Aron, "How Brands Were Born; Sutton, *Globalizing Beauty*, 3–4.

5. Laird, *Advertising Progress*, chap. 2 and pp. 107–8, on the relationship between founder-operators and advertising messages. Per Laird, Lydia Pinkham's advertisements for her Vegetable Compound, a tonic for women's "physical ailments" popular in the late 1800s that relied on Pinkham's image as the company's trademark, provide one specific example and illustrate a female entrepreneur's use of herself to help sell a product decades before Lewis, Beech, and Rudkin were utilizing a similar tactic, updated for the mid-twentieth-century marketplace.

6. Quote from Dan Wieden, founder of advertising agency Wieden & Kennedy, cited in Aron, "How Brands Were Born," 2.

7. Fuss, *Essentially Speaking*, 13.

8. Laird, *Advertising Progress*; the quote is from page 107, but the idea appears throughout, referring to both the late nineteenth century and the early-twentieth-century period covered in the book. Laird asserts that deep involvement in the advertising (and other day-to-day affairs) of a company by its leader remained common if the leader was also its founder.

9. Company brochure, dated approximately 1947, TLF.

10. Playing cards are in TLF.

11. See Albala, "Tomato Queen of San Joaquin."

12. Flotill Products, Inc., 1948 stock prospectus, TLF.

13. Company brochure, TLF, dated approximately 1947.

14. 1948 stock prospectus, TLF.

15. This calculation was derived using the U.S. Department of Labor's "CPI Inflation Calculator."

16. Program, testimonial dinner honoring Tillie Lewis, 3 March 1952, TLF. Newspaper article headlines are taken from a montage of such articles appearing on two pages of the program. Production figures come from annual reports for 1950, 1951, 1953, and 1954, SEC. The trend was upward from 1950 to 1952 and then inconsistent (2,211,843 cases for 1950; 3,829,948 cases for 1951; 4,100,914 cases for 1952; 2,910,532 cases for 1953; 3,349,303 cases for 1954).

17. Thomas de la Peña, *Empty Pleasures*, 109.

18. Exhibit 15(c): "Royalty Contract with Dr. C. A. Weast," submitted with annual report in May 1948, SEC.

19. Annual report, 1951, Folder 2-7447-2-1, Box 5460, #1, SEC.

20. Ditex Foods Inc.'s formula utilized sorbitol, which appears to have been incorporated into the Tasti-Diet process (Form 10-K, annual report, 1951, SEC). Ditex

reportedly carried "ten fruits, four salad dressings, three jellies, four puddings, four gelatins [and] a chocolate topping" ("Battle of the Bulge").

21. Tasti-Diet, Inc., was absorbed into Flotill Products, Inc., in 1955.

22. Byoir was a Jewish professional of high standing in New York City, and Lewis conducted a great deal of business in that city herself over the years after the Flotill Sales Company, which was eventually merged with Flotill Products, Inc., was located there. It is possible that they knew each other from this connection, but there is no way to confirm this. Agreement between Flotill Products, Inc., and Carl Byoir, 1 January 1953, submitted as an attachment to the company's annual report for 1953, Folder 2-7447-2-1, Box 54600, #2, SEC. Biographical information about Byoir comes from Truitt, "Byor, Carl." He was already a member of her board of directors in 1948. 1948 stock prospectus, TLF.

23. Form 10-K, annual report, 1953, Folder 2-7447-2-1, Box 5460, #2, SEC.

24. Annual report, 1953, SEC. In the 1954 annual report, Lewis described 1952 and 1953 as the "first post war test of overproduction and consequent price unsettlement" in the food-processing industry (annual report, 1954, SEC; "Survey of Customers," 1954, Folder 5, Box 2, SJCHS). Study was conducted by the Research Department at Erwin, Wasey & Co. in Los Angeles, California, 25 June 1954. Figures are based on interviews of 303 families who sent for the Tasti-Diet booklet in Dallas, Los Angeles, Indianapolis, and St. Louis in response to advertising in those cities.

25. "Battle of the Bulge."

26. Thomas de la Peña, *Empty Pleasures*, 114.

27. Ibid., 106, 114; Schwartz, *Never Satisfied*, 252, as quoted in Albala, "Tomato Queen of San Joaquin," 55.

28. For documentation of Operation Waistline, see Folder 2, Box 1, SJCHS. For Operation Waistline photo, with attribution to Carl Byoir & Associates on back, see Folder 2, Box 3, SJCHS. The campaign even reached out to child consumers, as evidenced in a photo (also attributed to Carl Byoir & Associates) of Tillie Lewis talking to "youngsters" eating Tasti-Diet saccharine-sweetened canned prunes. See Folder 1, Box 3, SJCHS.

29. "Success Story: Tillie and the Pomidori," *Sunday News* (New York), 18 November 1951, 14, gift of Judy Schiffner in possession of the author.

30. Thomas de la Peña, *Empty Pleasures*, 115, 109. For the quote "She keeps her figure not by dieting exactly . . . she just eats less of everything," see Alice Packard, "Women Who Do: The Extraordinary Story of Tillie Lewis," published in unnamed source, TLF.

31. For sample product labels, see "Sample Package Labels," undated, Box 2, Folder 4, SJCHS.

32. All sources cited here from TLF.

33. See "Tasti-Diet Foods Are Pre-sold for You!" brochure, which itemizes all of these advertising venues, TLF.

34. "Brochures and Recipes, 1948–ca. 1968," Box 2, Folder 2, SJCHS.

35. It helped to create what Roland Marchand has called a "soul"—a common strategy by large companies in post–World War II public-relations campaigns that were designed "to reassure consumers and politicians that their size and influence posed no threat to democracy or American values" (Marchand, *Creating the Corporate Soul*).

36. "Brochures and Recipes," SJCHS.

37. Madelyn Wood, "Fifty Non-Fattening Foods," *Coronet*, February 1955, 88–92, TLF.

38. "Whistle stop tour" is my phrase but adapts the political meaning to capture Lewis's multiple brief visits around the country in a short period.

39. Archived company records include several different scrapbooks with newspaper clippings and other evidence of her city visits with substantially the same information, showing how formulaic the approach was. Inside, one can find "articles" by different "authors" in each of the local newspapers that contain, word for word, the same copy. A different photo and heading accompanied each piece and obscured the similarities. See "Tasti-Diet Promotional Tour and Scrapbooks," Box 7, "Heiser Gift Box," TLF; "Testimonial Dinner" in recognition of her selection by Women Newspaper Editors and selection by New Institute of Dietetics as "Outstanding Woman in Food," 25 September 1952, "Awards and Honors," Box 1, Folder 4, SJCHS; and the many articles that appear in "Articles by Tillie Lewis, 1953–1977," in Box 2, Folder 1, and scrapbooks of Tasti-Diet advertising campaigns in Box 4, SJCHS. Thomas de la Peña argues that "the connection between the industry's promotional efforts and the copy that ran in these newspapers does not prove that newswomen were disingenuous in their promotions. . . . Many of these women writers likely believed they were doing something good for consumers" (*Empty Pleasures*, 129–30). Laird uses the phrase "puffing" to describe "paid insertions that appeared in publications as stories or reports without declaring themselves as advertisements." This describes Lewis's advertising campaign (Laird, *Advertising Progress*).

40. See "Articles by Tillie Lewis," Folder 1, Box 1, SJCHS.

41. Shapiro, " 'I Guarantee,' " 30.

42. "Current State of Live Trademarks," 28–30, quoted in Shapiro, " 'I Guarantee,' " 30.

43. "Businessmen in the News," *Fortune*, January, 1966, TLF.

44. Tillie and Meyer Lewis were married in her Highland Park, Los Angeles, home in 1948. According to the stock prospectus issued for Flotill Products, Inc., that same year, Lewis had left his job at Flotill and relocated to Coachella, California (near Palm Springs), to operate a date farm enterprise (1948 stock prospectus, TLF). Meyer Lewis later returned to the company as a vice president. Family film footage provided by Judy Schiffner, Tillie Lewis's great-niece and the daughter of Saul Heiser (the one son of her sister and brother-in-law whom she did not employ at Flotill), documents family gatherings, gift of Judy Schiffner in possession of the author. For the published reference to Lewis's home life, see Packard, "Women Who Do." The

article can be dated sometime in late 1960s or 1970s because of the reference to and an image of her service as part of the U.S. delegation to the world food conference in Rome, Italy. For photos of parties at her Stockton home, see the Tillie Lewis Foods Collection at the Haggin Museum, Stockton, California.

45. Poppy Cannon, "The Fast Gourmet," General Features Corp. Times Mirror Square, Los Angeles, February 5–10, 1968, TLF.

46. Wyndham Robertson, "The Ten Highest-Ranking Women in Business," *Fortune*, April 1973, 81–83, and Donna Israel Berliner and David C. Berliner, "36 Women with Real Power Who Can Help You," *Cosmopolitan*, April 1975, 191–98, both in TLF. Nonetheless, *Fortune* reassured readers that even though Lewis was the only woman among the featured ten who had been divorced, it was from "a man she married in her teens" and she had "been happily remarried since 1948."

47. See two-page 7UP advertisement, TLF. This mirrors Laird's findings in *Advertising Progress* in which she argues that founder-operator control of a company was the most important factor in determining how involved an owner and his or her name and ideas would be in a company's advertising.

48. "Laurels of Victory!" promotion for Beech Aircraft Corporation, ca. 1936, Box 27, Folder 22, WOABC.

49. "Beechcraft Takes Off on the Wings of a Jet," *Businessweek*, 25 February 1956, 181, Box 7, Folder 2, WOABC.

50. "Beechcraft Is Easy to Fly," company promotional brochure, ca. 1936, Box 27, Folder 22, WOABC.

51. "Beechcraft's General Catalogue," No. 11A, Box 27, Folder 22, WOABC.

52. "Studies in Concentration," company promotional brochure, ca. 1937, MS 97-02, Box 27, Folder 22, WOABC.

53. Amelia Earhart Museum, "Ninety Nines."

54. In fact, it was Walter and Olive Ann Beech who had arranged for Louise Thaden to learn to fly and who sponsored her entry into flight competitions beginning in 1929 (at Travel Air, the first airplane company founded by Walter H. Beech). Thereafter, Louise Thaden was a personal friend of Olive Ann Beech, and the two maintained a lifetime correspondence. Beech would go on to receive a special Amelia Earhart Medallion for outstanding contributions to the International Ninety-Nines, Inc., in 1971, the organization of female pilots of which both Earhart and Thaden were founding members. "Pioneer Aviatrix Louise Thaden Dies," *Beechcrafter*, 28 November 1979, 2, WOABC; "Honors: Olive Ann Beech," Box 18, Folder 20, WOABC. For correspondence, see WOABC correspondence files.

55. "Beechcraft Is the Modern 'Cutter'" one-page ad, ca. 1940s, Box 26, Folder 1, WOABC.

56. "Features Not Gadgets" promotional brochure, ca. 1940s, Box 27, Folder 22, WOABC.

57. "The Grizzly" marketing publication, ca. 1945, Box 27, Folder 23, WOABC; marketing brochure for the Super 18 Beech aircraft, Box 27, Folder 24, WOABC.

58. "The Story of Beechcraft," ca. 1969, Box 27, Folder 1, WOABC.

59. "Mrs. O. A. Beech," *Midwest Industry Magazine*, February 1969, 21, Box 28, Folder 25, WOABC.

60. "Main Article on Mrs. O. A. Beech for NAA Magazine" (dated 1980 or 1981 based on content), Box 20, Folder 9, WOABC.

61. Frank Moore, "With a Grain of Salt," *Daily Facts* (Redlands, Calif.), 31 March 1979, Box 20, Folder 9, WOABC. Moore was the guest of O. A. Beech when he accompanied a friend to Wichita to collect her new Beech aircraft and received the impromptu invitation to lunch upon that occasion.

62. Peter Wyden, "Danger: Boss Lady at Work," *Saturday Evening Post*, 8 August 1959, 26, Box 7, Folder 4, WOABC.

63. Untitled pamphlet (cover simply has picture of double doors and the signature of O. A. Beech), Box 27, Folder 31, WOABC.

64. "Mrs. O. A. Beech," *Midwest Industry Magazine*, 19, Box 28, Folder 25, WOABC.

65. Moore, "With a Grain of Salt."

66. "Mrs. O. A. Beech," 14.

67. The term "directing the course" comes from "Story of Beechcraft," WOABC.

68. Farney, *Barnstormer and the Lady*, 139–44.

69. Kwolek-Folland, *Incorporating Women*, 161.

70. Weiss, *To Have and to Hold*, 115–39.

71. The ad is reprinted in Farney, *Barnstormer and the Lady*, 120.

72. Weiss, *To Have and to Hold*, 115–39.

73. "Story of Beechcraft," 7, WOABC. Beech Acceptance Corporation was established in 1956.

74. Pamphlet for "Beech Aircraft Corporation Appreciation Luncheon" (for instructors), Wednesday, 25 August 1982, Box 27, Folder 31, WOABC. That the company considered this a marketing program is underscored by the fact that the vice president for domestic commercial marketing was the only other senior executive present at the luncheon along with Olive Ann Beech, then chairman of the board.

75. "Chris Reeve: Flying Like a Professional," *Beechcraft Marketing Report*, 1979, Box 27, Folder 21, WOABC.

76. "Story of Beechcraft," 6, WOABC.

77. Wyden, "Danger," 86. At the time of the article's publication in 1959, military contracts constituted two-thirds of Beech Aircraft's business.

78. The slogan was adopted by at least 1957, when it appeared on the special medallion created to celebrate the company's twenty-fifth anniversary. See "Story of Beechcraft," 7, WOABC.

79. Olive Ann Beech, "As I See: The Future of Business Aviation," *National Aeronautics*, June 1964, 3, Box 28, Folder 26, WOABC.

80. "Story of Beechcraft," 7, WOABC.

81. "Beechcraft Business and Personal Airplanes: A Tradition of Excellence," ca. 1977, Box 27, Folder 31, WOABC.

82. Memo from O. A. Beech to Mr. Roy H. McGregor and Mr. C. G. Parkhurst, 17 November 1972, Box 18, Folder 2, WOABC. Another memo in the same file addressed

to her personal assistant, Miss Winters, dated 27 November 1972, documents her displeasure with the fact that "the wastebaskets that were supposed to be aboard my plane were not aboard" and that "the fruit consisted of two measly apples." It concludes perfunctorily: "Please see in the future this does not occur."

83. "Beechcraft Business and Personal Airplanes," WOABC.

84. Ibid.

85. "My Visit to the Orient," *Beechcrafter*, August 1963, 3, Box 17, Folder 5, WOABC.

86. "Beechcraft International Distributors, Dealers Meet to Hear Future Plans, See New Airplanes," *Beechcrafter*, Holiday Issue, 1961, 5, Box 27, Folder 2, WOABC.

87. "Annual Awards Banquet Honors 1961 Sales Leaders," *Beechcrafter*, Holiday Issue, 1961, 6, Box 27, Folder 2, WOABC. The published photos of the event underscore Olive Ann Beech's personal involvement.

88. *Beechcraft Altimeter*, November/December 1966, 9, 8, 16, Box 27, Folder 21, WOABC.

89. Ibid.

90. John Wheeler, "Being a Woman Is No Drawback to Holding Company's Top Post," *Morris County's Daily Record*, 11 April 1967, 12, Box 17, Folder 5, WOABC.

91. *Beechcraft Marketing Report*, 1982 International Sales Conference, 2, Box 18, Folder 21, WOABC.

92. Wyden, "Danger," 35, WOABC.

93. Brochure, ca. 1938, in legal-size file in back of crate, MHRC. White bread, which is mentioned in this brochure, had been introduced by at least 1938 per letter to Dr. Arthur Holland from Margaret Rudkin, 24 May 1938, File 21, MHRC.

94. Margaret Rudkin, *Margaret Rudkin Cookbook*, 63–64 in the chapter titled "Country Life."

95. Bill from Pennie, Davis & Edmonds, 31 December 1939; letter to Margaret Rudkin from Dean Edmonds, attorney at Pennie, Davis, Marvin & Edmonds, 10 February 1942, File 23, MHRC. Also see "A Chronological List of Events at Pepperidge Farm," compiled by H. A. Baldwin, Box 2, Folder 8, ELS.

96. Jennifer Peyton, "Fairfield's Pepperidge Farm," *Fairfield County Times Monthly*, May 1997, Folder "1948 Sturges Hwy (Rudkin) Now 2 Fence Row Dr," FBC.

97. Memo to David Ogilvy from James McCaffrey, 5 April 1962, Box 58, Folder 2, DOP.

98. Brochure, ca. 1938, MHRC. For an image of early packaging, see photo included in Miller, "Consumers Will Pay for Quality," *Food Industries*, November 1938, ELS.

99. Letter to Dean Edmonds from Margaret Rudkin, 15 August 1940, File 23, MHRC.

100. "History," ca. 1938, in legal-size file in back of crate with other material on company in 1938, MHRC.

101. Margaret Rudkin, *Margaret Rudkin Cookbook*, 200.

102. Letter to Dr. Greenberg from Margaret Rudkin, 23 January 1947, Folder 21, MHRC; letter to Dear Doctor from Dr. Blake F. Donaldson (form letter), 12 November 1937, File 20, MHRC.

103. This is reminiscent of Lydia Pinkham's enterprise founded in the nineteenth century. Into the twentieth century, advertisements encouraged female customers to write to Lydia Pinkham for answers about their health problems. Long after Pinkham's death, the company continued this trend, employing a battery of female typists who used form letters to respond and always included a recommendation to use Pinkham's Vegetable Compound to improve their health and address their symptoms. See "Lydia Estes Pinkham (1819–1883)."

104. Letters to Margaret Rudkin from Dr. James R. Wilson, M.D., Secretary of Council on Foods and Nutrition of the American Medical Association, 3 January 1949 and 21 September 1948, File 20, MHRC.

105. J. D. Ratcliff, "Bread, de Luxe," *Reader's Digest*, December 1939, and "Champion of the Old-Fashioned: Margaret Rudkin," *Time*, March 21, 1960, both in ELS.

106. Completed Form 1065, U.S. Internal Revenue Service, 1938 Partnership Return of Income, prepared for Pepperidge Farm, 1939, File 18, MHRC; Pepperidge Farm, "Breakdown of One Loaf of Bread at $.20 Based on Production of 4293 Loaves," exhibit to partnership agreement, 1938, File 12, MHRC.

107. Memo to Banks & Ins Co. for mortgage from Henry A. Rudkin Sr., March 1946, in long manila envelope labeled "Rudkin . . . 1946 memo" in folder crate, MHRC. This was a form letter; the same text was utilized for a letter addressed to the vice president of Travelers Insurance Company and presumably to others as well.

108. Baldwin, "Chronological List of Events at Pepperidge Farm," ELS. Letters from Margaret Rudkin also confirm that including article reprints was a standard strategy for the company. See, for example, letter to Mrs. Mary Ann Reynolds from Margaret Rudkin, 24 August 1940, File 21, MHRC.

109. Baldwin, "Chronological List of Events at Pepperidge Farm," ELS.

110. "Pepperidge Farm."

111. Radcliff, "Bread, de Luxe," 102–3, ELS.

112. Sergio, "Biographical History" (Dorothy Thompson).

113. Letter to Margaret Rudkin from Dorothy Thompson (88 Central Park West), New York, 7 December 1938, File 20, MHRC.

114. John Bainbridge, "Profiles: Striking a Blow for Grandma," *New Yorker*, 22 May 1948, ELS; Baldwin, "Chronological List of Events at Pepperidge Farm," 22 May 1948, ELS.

115. Ibid., 11 June 1949.

116. "Press Releases, 1962," Box 1, Series C, Folder 1, ELS.

117. "Public Relations," *Conveyor*, March 1973, 12–13, ELS.

118. Mayo and Nohria, *In Their Time*, 126. The sources cited were checked, and no evidence supports this claim. More important, the biographical materials covered in this book indicate that Rudkin's work history included bookkeeping, working as a teller, and working as the personal assistant to Mr. Rudkin but not a job in

public relations. The error in interpretation appears to have been made in Fenster, *In the Words of Great Business Leaders,* 350, which suggested that Rudkin worked in public relations at her husband's firm, McClure, Jones & Company. Fenster is cited in Mayo and Nohria.

119. "How Pepperidge Farm Bread Helps You Keep That Radiant Look," *New York Times Magazine,* 1955 (only date visible is as cite for photograph; no date for issue of magazine visible or cited), DOP. To compress the quote, I have not followed the formatting of the ad, which was much more spread out, each bolded claim the start of a new section.

120. For more on the changes to advertising copy, see Laird, *Advertising Progress,* especially chap. 8 ("Taking Advertisements toward Modernity").

121. David Ogilvy to Dave McCall, internal memo, 1 April 1958, Folder 1, DOP.

122. David Ogilvy to Mr. Blair, internal memo, 17 September 1956, Folder 1, DOP.

123. David Ogilvy, internal memo, 5 October 1959, Folder 2, DOP.

124. Al Cantwell, "Commercial Critique," *Billboard* magazine, 6 March 1954, reprinted in *Conveyor,* Anniversary Issue, June 1957, 23, Box 1, Series B, Folder 2, ELS.

125. Baldwin, "Chronological List of Events at Pepperidge Farm," ELS; U.S. Department of Labor, "CPI Inflation Calculator."

126. David Ogilvy to Bill Blair, internal memo, 27 June 1956, DOP.

127. Ibid.

128. Letter to David Ogilvy, Ogilvy, Benson & Mather, Inc., from Margaret Rudkin, 12 December 1958, Folder 1, DOP.

129. Longfellow's Wayside Inn, "Grist Mill and Pepperidge Farm."

130. David Ogilvy to Stanley Canter, internal memo, 21 August 1958, DOP.

131. David Ogilvy to Reva Fine, internal memo, 11 November 1956, DOP; "36 Selling Propositions for Pepperidge Farm Bread," 14 April 1958, DOP; "Ogilvy's Selection of What He Guesses Are the Eight Strongest," undated, DOP.

132. Blau, "Parker W. Fennelly Dies"; "Actor Parker W. Fennelly, 96."

133. N. Peterzell to David Ogilvy, "Status Report—Pepperidge Farm," 22 November 1957, DOP. The report stated, "Verbal reports from Pepperidge indicate that the advertised markets are responding to the advertising." Letter to Mrs. Margaret Rudkin from Arthur H. McCoy, Executive Vice President, John Blair & Company, National Representatives of Radio Stations, 3 April 1958, DOP. The letter reported that Pepperidge Farm's radio commercials had "just been voted one of the six outstanding spots" in a nationwide survey involving over 228 product commercials judged by over 2,000 experts.

134. David Ogilvy to Mr. Booraem, internal memo, 5 November 1957, DOP. On the eve of producing the first commercial for Pepperidge Farm, the memo admonishes the head of the television department that the agency "must not do this job amateurishly" and details specific expectations for the bakery wagon, which he "want[ed] to make the symbol of all Pepperidge advertising—broadcast and print."

135. Pepperidge Farm stuffing ad copy for *Reader's Digest* advertisement published in November 1957, DOP.

136. David Ogilvy to Reva Korda, internal memo, 24 May 1962, DOP.

137. Thomas G. Rudkin, "Overview: The "Life and Times" of Henry Albert Rudkin & Margaret Fogarty Rudkin," MHRC.

138. Rudkin, *Margaret Rudkin Cookbook*, 67.

139. Photograph of Rudkin removing turnovers from oven, 14 October 1962, "Publicity Materials," Box 1, Series C, Folder 3, ELS.

140. One article in the local newspaper explicitly reassured readers that "Maggie" Rudkin was, in fact, real and that Pepperidge Farm's advertisements were not "just another attempt by Madison Avenue to create an advertising image" ("Pepperidge Farm Marking 25 Years of 'Home' Baking," *Post*, 30 September 1962, PFBC; thanks to Elizabeth Van Tuyl for providing me with copies of the articles in the PFBC file).

141. Letter to David Ogilvy from Alfred Knopf Jr., 29 January 1963, DOP.

142. Jim Heekin to David Ogilvy, internal memo, 8 July 1963, DOP.

143. For bestseller list reference, see Pepperidge Farm, "Margaret Rudkin."

144. Rudkin, *Margaret Rudkin Cookbook*, Foreword.

Chapter Five

1. Sandberg, *Lean In*, 44, 50–51; Laurie A. Rudman, "Self-Promotion as a Risk Factor for Women: The Costs and Benefits of Counterstereotypical Impression Management," *Journal of Personality and Social Psychology* 74, no. 3 (1998): 629–45; and Laurie A. Rudman and Peter Glick, "Prescriptive Gender Stereotypes and Backlash toward Agentic Women," *Journal of Social Issues* 57, no. 4 (2001): 743–62. Both cited in Sandberg, *Lean In*, 44.

2. Place and Plummer, *Women in Management*, 51.

3. Warfel, Review of *Breaking the Glass Ceiling*.

4. Lewin, "Partnership in Firm"; Kwolek-Folland, *Incorporating Women*, 203.

5. Allison Elias points out that Sandberg's recommendations for how individual women must behave in the business world to achieve success are "a new iteration of the advice literature of the 1970s and 1980s" that was inherently biased toward privileged professionals. It emphasized the importance for individual women of following "the rules of the game" rather than collectively addressing the structural barriers that impeded the largest number of women in the workforce. Elias, "Learning to Lead," 8–9.

6. Olegario, *Culture of Credit*; Gerber, "Cutting Out Shylock"; Laird, *Pull*; Kwolek-Folland, *Incorporating Women*.

7. Kwolek-Folland, *Incorporating Women*, 161.

8. Scanlon, *Bad Girls Go Everywhere*.

9. U.S. Department of Labor, *Women in Higher-Level Positions*, cited in Kwolek-Folland, *Incorporating Women*, 158.

10. See, for example, the story of Fanny Goldberg Stahl in Kwolek-Folland, *Incorporating Women*, 147.

11. See Scanlon, *Bad Girls Go Everywhere*, xi–xii, for her description of Helen Gurley Brown's belief in "working" rather than overthrowing the system. Brown was a contemporary of all three women in this book and couldn't be more different. Yet what they had in common with her was a belief in and commitment to capitalism and popular cultural ideals of femininity. None of the three women presented here represented herself as a feminist—and, in fact, they all explicitly rejected feminism— but they embraced some ideas that Brown did, such as insisting that men treat them as they believed women or "ladies" should be treated. Tillie Lewis was most explicit about this, stating, "I hear that being 'a lady' has gone out of style. I think a lot of career girls may find that's a mistake. Ye gods, what's the matter with being feminine? A woman is different from a man and I think that should be an asset." Phyllis Battelle, "Tomatoes Grow a Fortune," *Los Angeles Herald-Examiner*, 2 April 1974, B-7, gift from Judy Schiffner in possession of author.

12. Photos, Box A, TLF.

13. For annual earnings for women in 1930, see Goldin, *Understanding the Gender Gap*, 64.

14. "Before the Commissioner of Internal Revenue: In the Matter of the Income Tax Liability of Flotill Products, Inc . . . 1940 and 41," TLF, 3.

15. Ibid., 4–7, emphasis in original. The taxpayer here is Flotill Products, Inc.

16. Kwolek-Folland, *Incorporating Women*, 150.

17. Ibid., 149–50.

18. Ibid., 141.

19. For World War II as a turning point, see Chafe, *American Woman*. For one example of an interpretation that significantly downplays the impact of World War II, see Goldin, "The Role of WWII."

20. Flotill 1948 stock prospectus, TLF, 18–19.

21. Flotill 1948 stock prospectus, TLF.

22. One study found that executive compensation declined in the 1940s. It is possible that the reduction in Lewis's salary reflected this decline. See Frydman and Molloy, "Pay Cuts for the Boss."

23. Lewis's board of directors was comprised of five of the company's officers, including Lewis and her two nephews as well as her attorney and Carol Byoir, a public relations expert who she would later hire to oversee her marketing and public relations for the launch of Tasti-Diet, per chapter 4. Flotill 1948 stock prospectus, TLF.

24. Lorillard example is from Larcker and Tayan, "A Historical Look at Compensation."

25. Lewellan, "Executive Compensation Patterns." Unfortunately, the chapter does not clarify how "large" and "small" manufacturing firms were determined and categorized.

26. This figure is for 1955 and comes from Institute for Women's Policy Research, "Fact Sheet: The Gender Wage Gap."

27. Flotill 1948 stock prospectus, TLF; U.S. Department of Labor, "CPI Inflation Calculator."

28. Lewellan, "Executive Compensation Patterns," 43.

29. See, for example, May, *Homeward Bound*, for analysis of the dominant national narrative focused on containment and domesticity, as well as Laville, "Gender and Women's Rights in the Cold War." See Meyerowitz, *Not June Cleaver*, for counterexamples to the dominant domestic narrative.

30. Laird, "Making a Hero of Horatio Alger." Laird argues that Alger was recast from his Progressive-era, morality-tale roots by anti–New Deal businessmen and their supporters and came to symbolize a form of individual achievement that contradicted the content of his actual stories, which emphasized the help of kindly, wealthy benefactors as key to the turnaround success of their protagonists.

31. "Who Is Tillie Lewis?" 1976, Folder 8, Box 1, SJCHS. According to Wood, Lewis submitted an application for the Horatio Alger Award. This was likely part of the material prepared for that purpose. Wood, *Tillie Lewis*, 262–63.

32. Uttaro, "Voices of America," 108, 116.

33. "Tillie's Unpunctured Romance," 103–5.

34. Alice Packard, "Women Who Do: The Extraordinary Story of Tillie Lewis," published in unknown source, 116, TLF. This story erroneously reported that she had studied at New York University.

35. Dorothy Walworth, "First Lady of San Joaquin," *Everywoman's Woman*, August 1952, TLF.

36. "Success Story: Tillie and the Pomidori," *Sunday News* (New York), 18 November 1951, 14, gift from Judy Schiffner in possession of author.

37. Transcript of "Tillie Lewis Speech for Pilot Club, New York City," 15 January 1968, TLF. For headline, Dorothy Walworth (adapted from *Everywoman* article), "How a (Female) High School Dropout Built a Business That Does More Than $150 Million a Year," *New Woman*, November/December, 1973, pages unavailable, TLF.

38. Kwolek-Folland, *Incorporating Women*, 194.

39. Transcript of "Tillie Lewis Speech for Pilot Club, New York City," 15 January 1968, TLF. For headline, Walworth, "How a (Female) High School Dropout Built a Business," TLF.

40. Wyndham Robertson, "The Ten Highest-Ranking Women in Big Business," *Fortune*, April 1973, 82, TLF.

41. "Who's News: Commerce and Industry," *Wall Street Journal*, 31 May 1966, and "Ogden Corp. Stockholders Elect a Woman to Board," *New York Times*, 28 May 1966, both clipped and sent to Tillie Lewis from the publicity department at Ogden, TLF.

42. "The Tillie Lewis Story," *Spectrum* (Ogden Foods newsletter), (1967 or 1968), 4, TLF.

43. "1977 Semi-annual Report and Report of Annual Meeting," Ogden Corporation, TLF.

44. White, "Even One Woman."

45. Rayasan, "Do More Women on the Board Mean Better Results?"; Credit Suisse Research Institute, "Gender Diversity and Corporate Performance"; Carter and Wagner, *Bottom Line*.

46. Terry Allen Kramer first became a director of the Ogden Board in 1977. The next female board member, Judith D. Moyers, was appointed one year later in 1978. Information from the SEC archives, http://www.sec.gov/Archives/edgar/containers /fix011/73902/0001047469-98-016492.txt (accessed 21 October 2014).

47. See the image and caption showing Lewis as commissioner, cover of the Stockton Port's newsletter, *Tideways* 19, no. 1 (1970), TLF; "International Food Agricultural Organization Meets in Rome," press release, Ogden Corporation, TLF; information about the FAO and FAO meeting from the Food and Agricultural Organization website, http://www.fao.org/about/en/ (accessed 21 October 2014).

48. Robertson, "Ten Highest-Ranking Women in Business," TLF; Packard, "Women Who Do," TLF.

49. Robertson, "Ten Highest-Ranking Women in Business," 81–83, TLF; Donna Israel Berliner and David C. Berliner, "36 Women with Real Power Who Can Help You," *Cosmopolitan*, April 1975, 191–98, TLF.

50. "Ike Appoints Mrs. Beech One of 12 Named to Advisory Board," newspaper clipping, 4 February 1959, and photo of swearing-in of members of the board by Secretary of State Dulles, stamped on back as Department of State photo, 3 February 1959, Series 2.2, Box 7, Folder 5, WOABC; letter to Olive Ann Beech from Harry A. Bullis, 6 August 1959, Series 2.2, Box 7, Folder 4, WOABC.

51. "Honors: Olive Ann Beech," Box 18, Folder 20, WOABC. The records for neither Tillie Lewis nor Margaret Rudkin contain such a list. They both received awards and honors to be sure, but neither of them seemed to methodically document those awards. In addition, the archival records of P. W. Litchfield, president of Goodyear Tire and Rubber Company, a contemporary of Beech, contain a variety of awards he received but also do not seem to contain a list indicating that he methodically documented his awards and honors. See "Inventory of the Goodyear Tire and Rubber Company, 1899–1993."

52. Elias, "Learning to Lead," 5.

53. Letter to Olive Ann Beech from Mrs. William H. Whipple, 24 February 1980, Box 15, Folder 8, WOABC.

54. Olive Ann Beech, "The Woman Executive," *Michigan Business Review* (May 1961), 20, Box 28, Folder 24, WOABC.

55. Gerard, *Point Blank*. The book and author are referenced in archival material; I purchased a copy from a used bookseller.

56. Advertisement for the *Wall Street Journal* in *U.S. News & World Report*, 16 August 1979, Box 18, Folder 21, WOABC.

57. Soroptomist Club speech, 1–2, Box 6, Folder 3, WOABC.

58. Beech, "Woman Executive," 20, 24, WOABC.

59. "The Gallagher President's Report," supplement to 6 January 1976, Vol. 12, No. 1, Box 19, Folder 31, WOABC.

60. "Win Some, Lose Some: Executives Bare Their Best and Worst Investments," *Wall Street Journal*, 13 November 1987, 20D, Box 24, Folder 9, WOABC.

61. "Remarks for the Dedication of the Olive Ann Beech Gallery," Box 1, Folder 1, WOABC.

62. Beech, "Woman Executive," 20, WOABC.

63. Peter Wyden, "Danger: Boss Lady at Work," *Saturday Evening Post*, 8 August 1959, Box 7, Folder 4, WOABC.

64. See, for example, Deland, *Iron Woman*.

65. Letter to Olive Ann Beech from Lucille (Mrs. Jack) Spines, 2 August 1959; letter to Olive Ann Beech from Warren E. Blazier, 4 August 1959; letter to Olive Ann Beech from Mason Shehan and Your Washington Staff, 5 August 1959; letter to Olive Ann Beech from Louise Thaden, 4 August 1959; letter to Olive Ann Beech from Mary Lynn Beech, 5 August 1959; letter to Olive Ann Beech from June H. Mayer, 5 August 1959; letter to Olive Ann Beech from Yvette Ward, Brown & Bigelow, 6 August 1959; and letter to Olive Ann Beech from Louise Dawson, Refining and Marketing Division of Colorado Oil and Gas Corporation, 7 August 1959, Series 2.2, Box 7, Folder 4, WOABC. There is a whole scrapbook of responses regarding the *Saturday Evening Post* article; these are but a sample.

66. Nocera, "Still Searching for Lee Iacocca."

67. "Aviation: Will Olive Ann Marry?" *Time*, 18 July 1977, 72, Box 18, Folder 21, WOABC.

68. "Marrying Money," *Fortune*, November 1979, Box 15, Folder 7, WOABC; Gerald F. Seib and Kathryn Christensen, "Beech Aircraft Courted Its Buyer," *Patriot Ledger* (Quincy, Mass.), 16 October 1973, reprinted with permission of *Wall Street Journal*, Box 15, Folder 7, WOABC.

69. Lew Townsend and Dan Bearth, "Personalities Played Big Role," *Wichita Eagle-Beacon*, 7 October 1979, 2B, Box 15, Folder 7, WOABC.

70. "Marrying Money," WOABC; Seib and Christensen, "Beech Aircraft Courted Its Buyer," WOABC.

71. Transcript of executive meeting, 27 May 1982, Box 26, Folder 27, WOABC.

72. Merger scrapbook, Box 15, Folder 8, WOABC.

73. Ibid. Scrapbook contains handwritten notecard as well as Raytheon Organization Chart dated 1 September 1979, attendee list and photograph of "Special Beechcraft Luncheon, April 7, 1980, honoring Mr. Thomas L. Phillips, Chairman of the Board, Raytheon Company and Mrs. Phillips, and Mr. D. Brainerd Holmes, President, Raytheon Company and Mrs. Holmes."

74. "A Chronological List of Events at Pepperidge Farm," compiled by H. A. Baldwin, Box 2, Folder 8, ELS.

75. Letter from Margaret Rudkin to Stanleigh Friendman, 27 December 1957, MHRC.

76. Letter to David Ogilvy from Margaret Rudkin, 1 November 1957, Box 58, Folder 1, DOP.

77. David Ogilvy to Reva Korda, internal memo, 19 April 1960, Folder 2, DOP.

78. David Ogilvy to Jim McCaffrey, Reva Korda, internal memo, 6 February 1961, Folder 2, DOP.

79. Letter to Mrs. Henry Rudkin from David Ogilvy, 20 February 1961, Folder 2, DOP.

80. Ogilvy, *Confessions of an Advertising Man*, chap. 3 ("How to Keep Clients"), 16.

81. Note to Mrs. Henry Rudkin Sr. from David Ogilvy, 12 November 1962, Folder 2, DOP.

82. Letter to David Ogilvy from Margaret Rudkin, 1 November 1957; letter to David Ogilvy from Henry A. Rudkin Sr., 23 December 1964, Folder 2, DOP.

83. Ogilvy, *Confessions of an Advertising Man*, 81, 148, 86.

84. David Ogilvy to Bill Blair, internal memo, 27 June 1956, Folder 1, DOP.

85. David Ogilvy to Dave McCall, internal memo, 3 March 1958, Folder 1, DOP.

86. James J. McCaffrey to David Ogilvy, internal memo, 13 March 1962, Folder 2, DOP.

87. John Bainbridge, "Profiles," Striking a Blow for Grandma," *New Yorker*, 22 May 1948, 40, ELS.

88. "Margaret Rudkin: Champion of the Old-Fashioned."

89. Interview, digitized from original vinyl recording, undated but conducted approximately 1958 per content, ELS.

90. Bainbridge, "Profiles," 40.

91. In her speech at the Harvard Business School, she in fact asserted that her initial reaction to the suggestion that she begin baking bread for sale was: "I was much too busy. I had three children, I had to play bridge, I had to do my gardening—I couldn't do any such thing as that." "Address by Mrs. Margaret Rudkin to Harvard Business School," 1960, MHRC.

92. Bainbridge, "Profiles," 40.

93. Schulte, "The Second Shift at 25."

94. Bainbridge, "Profiles," 44.

95. Ibid., 45.

96. See Coca Cola's website for how it presents and protects its "secret formula" (Coca-Cola Company, "Secret Formula"). For coverage of the recent attempt to steal the secret formula from the company, see Day, "3 Accused in Theft of Coke Secret."

97. For a discussion of the difficulties of patenting a recipe, see "Can Recipes Be Patented?"

98. Interview, digitized from original vinyl recording, undated but conducted approximately 1958 per content, ELS.

99. "Harvard Business School's Baker Library."

100. Bainbridge, "Profiles," 42, ELS.

101. "Address by Mrs. Margaret Rudkin to Harvard Business School," 1960, MHRC.

102. "Speech Given by Margaret Rudkin at Drexel Institute of Technology," 17 May 1962, MHRC.

103. Dorothy Roe, "Keep Busy and Look Your Best to Stay Young, 'Grandma' Advises," newspaper clipping from the (likely Norwalk) *Post*, November 1955, PFBC. Thank you to Elizabeth Van Tuyl for providing me with copies of the articles in the file.

104. Bainbridge, "Profiles," 40, ELS.

105. "Address by Mrs. Margaret Rudkin to Harvard Business School," 1960, MHRC.

106. Fox, "Erik Blegvad."

Conclusion

1. Mayo and Nohria, *In Their Time*, xxi, xv.

2. Laird, *Pull*.

3. Ibid.

4. Give Me 5%, http://www.giveme5.com/.

Bibliography

Archival Collections

Bridgeport, Conn.
  Bridgeport History Center, Bridgeport Public Library
    Clippings File, Pepperidge Farm, Bridgeport, Connecticut (PFBC)
College Park, Md.
  National Archives and Records Administration
    Quartermaster General Records (QMG)
    Securities and Exchange Commission: Annual Reports, Prospectuses (SEC)
Fairfield, Conn.
  Fairfield Museum and History Center
    Fairfield Buildings Collection (FBC)
    The Margaret and Henry Rudkin Collection, on loan from Thomas Rudkin
      and his family (MHRC)
    E. Lee Schneider Pepperidge Farm Collection (ELS)
Lodi, Calif.
  San Joaquin County Historical Society
    Tillie Lewis Food Collection (SJCHS)
San Francisco, Calif.
  Labor Archives and Research Center, San Francisco State University
    Cannery Workers Union Collection (CWUC)
Stanford, Calif.
  Special Collections Library, Stanford University
    Mexican Legal Defense and Education Fund Collection: *Alaniz v. Tillie Lewis
      Foods Inc.* (MALDEF).
Stockton, Calif.
  Haggin Museum
    Tillie Lewis Foods/Flotill Cannery Collection (TLF)
Washington, D.C.
  Library of Congress
    The Papers of David Ogilvy (DOP)
  National American History Museum, Smithsonian Archives Center
    National Association of Manufacturers, *Industry on Parade* Film
      Collection (IOP)
  National Archive and Records Administration
    Records of the National Defense Committee, U.S. Senate (NDC)

Wichita, Kans.
  Wichita State University Library, Special Collections
    Walter & Olive Ann Beech Collection (WOABC)

Interviews by Author

Rudkin, Tom (grandson to Margaret Rudkin), August 2013.
Schiffner, Judy (great-niece to Tillie Lewis), April 2014.

Government Documents

Fifteenth Census of the United States, 1930—Population, electronic database,
    Ancestry.com.
Fourteenth Census of the United States, 1920—Population, electronic database,
    Ancestry.com.
New York State Census, 1915, electronic database, Ancestry.com.
New York State Census, 1920, electronic database, Ancestry.com.
New York State Census, 1925, electronic database, Ancestry.com.
New York State Census, 1930, electronic database, Ancestry.com.
Thirteenth Census of the United States, 1910—Population, electronic database,
    Ancestry.com.

Passport Application

"1924 Passport Application for Tillie Weisberg." National Archives and Records
    Administration (NARA), Washington D.C. NARA Series: *Passport Applications,
    January 2, 1906–March 31, 1925*, Roll #: *2513*, *Certificates: 413850-414349, 13
    May 1924-13 May 1924.* Ancestry.com. *U.S. Passport Applications, 1795–1925.*

Ship Passenger Lists

Corte di Savoia (departing Genoa 16 November 1933). Records of U.S. Customs
    Service, Washington, D.C.
Corte Grande (departing Naples 13 June 1928). Records of U.S. Customs Service,
    Washington, D.C.
Duilio (departing Naples 19 June 1926). Records of U.S. Customs Service,
    Washington, D.C.
Passenger Lists of Vessels Arriving at New York, New York, 1897–1957. Digital
    images, National Archives (www.ancestry.com).
Roma (departing Naples 8 July 1932). Records of U.S. Customs Service,
    Washington, D.C.

Directories

(Trow's) *General Directory of New York City*, 1920. (R. L. Polk & Co.) New York Historical Association, New York, N.Y.

(Trow's) *General Directory of New York City*, 1925. (R. L. Polk & Co.) New York Historical Association, New York, N.Y.

(Trow's) *New York Business Directory*, 1912. (R. L. Polk & Co.) New York Historical Association, New York, N.Y.

(Trow's) *New York Business Directory*, 1913. (R. L. Polk & Co.) New York Historical Association, New York, N.Y.

(Trow's) *New York Business Directory*, 1915. (R. L. Polk & Co.) New York Historical Association, New York, N.Y.

(Trow's) *New York Business Directory*, 1916. (R. L. Polk & Co.) New York Historical Association, New York, N.Y.

Stockton City Directory, 1955, electronic database, Ancestry.com.

Wichita City Directory, 1945, electronic database, Ancestry.com.

Wichita City Directory, 1946, electronic database, Ancestry.com.

Wichita City Directory, 1955, electronic database, Ancestry.com.

Published and Unpublished Sources

Abbott Nutrition. "About Us." Accessed 14 July 2014. http://abbottnutrition.com/about-us/about-abbott-nutrition.

"Actor Parker W. Fennelly, 96; 'Titus Moody' of Allen's Alley." *Los Angeles Times*, 24 January 1988. http://articles.latimes.com/1988-01-24/news/mn-38173_1 _titus-moody.

Adapa, Sam, and Kumaresh Chakraborty. "The Supermarket Industry—Private Label Brand Development." In *Case Studies in Food Product Development*, edited by Mary Earle and Richard Earle, 69–74. Cambridge: Woodhead Publishing Limited, 2008. http://plma.com/.

Albala, Kenneth. "The Tomato Queen of San Joaquin." In "Entrepreneurs." *Gastronomica: The Journal of Food and Culture* 10, no. 2 (2010): 55–63.

Amelia Earhart Museum. "Ninety Nines." Accessed 17 September 2014. http://www.ameliaearhartmuseum.org/NinetyNines/NinetyNines.html.

Amoury, Gloria. "New Girl." *Saturday Evening Post*, 8 August 1959, 20, 79–81.

Aron, Marc De Swann. "How Brands Were Born: A Brief History of Modern Marketing." *The Atlantic*, 3 October 2011. http://www.theatlantic.com/business/archive/2011/10/how-brands-were-born-a-brief-history-of-modern-marketing/246012/.

Bailey, Brandon. "Yahoo CEO Marissa Mayer's Ban on Telecommuting Sparks a Firestorm." *San Jose Mercury News*, 25 February 2013. http://www.mercurynews.com/2013/02/25/2013-yahoo-ceo-marissa-mayers-ban-on-telecommuting-sparks-a-firestorm/.

Baldwin, Hanson W. "Our Fighting Men Have Gone Soft." *Saturday Evening Post*, 8 August 1959, 13–15, 82–84.

"Battle of the Bulge." *Time*, 10 August 1953. http://www.time.com/time/magazine /article/0,9171,817679,00.html.

Beck, Koa. "10 Fast Facts about Ginny Rometty, the First Female CEO of IBM." *Daily Worth*, 30 April 2015. https://www.dailyworth.com/posts/3475-10-fast -facts-about-ginni-rometty-the-first-female-ceo-of-ibm.

Berebitsky, Julie. *Sex and the Office: A History of Gender, Power, and Desire.* New Haven, Conn.: Yale University Press, 2012.

Blackford, Mansel. *A History of Small Business in America.* 2nd ed. Chapel Hill: University of North Carolina Press, 2003.

Blair-Loy, Mary. *Competing Devotions: Career and Family among Women Executives.* Cambridge, Mass.: Harvard University Press, 2003.

Blau, Eleanor. "Parker W. Fennelly Dies at 96; Was Actor in Radio, Film and TV." *New York Times*, 23 January 1988. http://www.nytimes.com/1988/01/23 /obituaries/parker-w-fennelly-dies-at-96-was-actor-in-radio-film-and-tv.html.

"Books: Faith for Straphangers." *Time*, 18 March 1946. http://www.time.com/time /magazine/article/0,9171,934510,00.html.

Brown, Carolyn M. "How One Female Business Owner Won Government Contracts." *Black Enterprise*, 8 October 2014. http://www.blackenterprise.com /small-business/how-this-woman-business-owner-won-million-dollar -government-contracts/.

Brown, Martin, and Peter Philips. "The Decline of the Piece-Rate System in California Canning: Technological Innovation, Labor Management, and Union Pressure, 1890–1947." *Business History Review* 60 (Winter 1986): 564–601.

———. "The Evolution of Labor Market Structure: The California Canning Industry." *Industrial and Labor Relations Review* 38, no. 3 (April 1985): 392–407.

Brown, Mary Elizabeth. "Little Italy." In *Encyclopedia of New York*, edited by Kenneth T. Jackson, 758. New Haven, Conn.: Yale University Press, 1995.

Buder, Stanley. *Capitalizing on Change: A Social History of American Business.* Chapel Hill: University of North Carolina Press, 2009.

Bureau of Labor Statistics. "Inflation Calculator." Accessed 12 March 2015. http://www.bls.gov/data/inflation_calculator.htm.

Butkiewcz, James. "Reconstruction Finance Corporation." *EH-Net Economic and Business History Encylcopedia.* Accessed 17 July 2015. https://EH.net /encyclopedia/reconstruction-finance-corporation.

Cain Miller, Claire. "For Incoming I.B.M. Chief, Self-Confidence Is Rewarded." *New York Times*, 27 October 2011. http://www.nytimes.com/2011/10/28 /business/for-incoming-ibm-chief-self-confidence-rewarded.html?_r=0.

Campbell, D'Ann. *Women at War with America: Private Lives in a Patriotic Era.* Cambridge, Mass.: Harvard University Press, 1984.

"Can Recipes Be Patented?" *Inventor's Eye* 4, no. 3 (June 2013). http://www.uspto .gov/custom-page/inventors-eye-advice-1.

Carter, Nancy M., and Harvey M. Wagner. "The Bottom Line: Connecting Corporate Performance and Gender Diversity." Catalyst, 1 March 2011. http://www.catalyst.org/knowledge/bottom-line-corporate-performance-and -womens-representation-boards-20042008.

Cha, Youngjoo. "Reinforcing Separate Spheres: The Effect of Spousal Overwork on Men's and Women's Employment in Dual-Earner Households. *American Sociological Review* 75, no. 2 (April 2010): 303–29.

Chafe, William. *The American Woman: Her Changing Social, Economic, and Political Role, 1920–1970.* New York: Oxford University Press, 1972.

Chizek, C. F. "Review of *Tax Relief under Section 722* by Paul W. Ellis." *Journal of Business of the University of Chicago* 18, no. 4 (1945): 223–24.

Cinotto, Simone. *The Italian American Table: Food, Family, and Community in New York City.* Urbana-Champaign: University of Illinois Press, 2013.

Clark, Patricia. "Government Agencies Fail to Hire Women-Owned Businesses, Again." *Bloomberg's Businessweek*, 4 August 2014. http://www.businessweek .com/articles/2014-08-04/government-contracts-fall-short-on-women-owned -businesses-again.

Cobble, Dorothy Sue. *The Other Women's Movement: Workplace Justice and Social Rights in Modern America.* Princeton, N.J.: Princeton University Press, 2005.

Cobble, Dorothy Sue, Linda Gordon, and Astrid Henry. *Feminism Unfinished: A Short, Surprising History of American Women's Movements.* New York: Norton, 2014.

Coca-Cola Company. "Secret Formula." Accessed 4 April 2015. http://www.coca -colacompany.com/stories/the-secret-is-out-coca-colas-formula-is-at-the-world -of-coca-cola.

Cofield, Natalie Maderia. "Minority Women Entrepreneurs: Go-Getters without Resources." *Forbes*, 28 August 2013. http://www.forbes.com/sites /meghancasserly/2013/08/28/minority-women-entrepreneurs-go-getters -without-resources/#4bd67d894a22.

Cohen, Lizbeth. *A Consumer's Republic: The Politics of Mass Consumption in Postwar America.* New York: Vintage Books, 2003.

Cowley, Stacy. "Government Hits Goal Set in 1994 Women's Business Contracts." *New York Times*, 2 March 2016. http://www.nytimes.com/2016/03/02 /business/government-meets-goal-set-in-1994-for-womens-business-contracts .html?_r=0.

Credit Suisse Research Institute. "Gender Diversity and Corporate Performance." August 2012. http://www.calstrs.com/sites/main/files/file-attachments/csri _gender_diversity_and_corporate_performance.pdf.

Davies, Margery W. *Woman's Place Is at the Typewriter: Office Work and Office Workers, 1870–1930.* Philadelphia: Temple University Press, 1982.

Day, Kathleen. "3 Accused in Theft of Coke Secret." *Washington Post*, 6 July 2006. http://www.washingtonpost.com/wp-dyn/content/article/2006/07/05 /AR2006070501717.html.

Deland, Margaret. *The Iron Woman.* New York: Harper & Bros., 1911.

"Del Monte Foods Company History." Accessed 25 May 2013. http://www
.fundinguniverse.com/company-histories/del-monte-foods-company
-history.

Deutsch, Sarah. *Women and the City: Gender, Space, and Power in Boston, 1870–1940*. New York: Oxford University Press, 2000.

Donaldson, Blake F., and Charles Gordon Heyd. *Strong Medicine*. New York: Doubleday & Company, Inc., 1962.

Earle, Mary, and Richard Earle, eds. *Case Studies in Food Product Development*. Cambridge: Woodhead Publishing Limited, 2008.

Edwards, Jim. "Meet the 10 Most-Liked Ad Agency CEOs." *Business Insider*, 3 April 2013. http://www.businessinsider.com/the-10-most-liked-ad-agency-ceos -2013-4.

Elias, Allison. "Learning to Lead: Women and Success in Corporate America." *Business and Economic History On-Line* 13 (2015): 1–9.

Ellison, Glenn, and Edward L. Glaeser. "Geographic Concentration in U.S. Manufacturing Industries: A Dartboard Approach." *Journal of Political Economy* 105, no. 5 (1997): 889–927.

England, Kim, and Kate Boyer. "Women's Work: The Feminization and Shifting Meanings of Clerical Work." *Journal of Social History* 43, no. 2 (Winter 2009): 307–40.

Farney, Dennis. *The Barnstormer and the Lady: Aviation Legends Walter and Olive Ann Beech*. Kansas City, Mo.: Rockhill Books, 2010.

Fenster, Julie. *In the Words of Great Business Leaders*. New York: John Wiley & Sons, 2000.

Fischler, Marcelle S. "Long Island Journal: At LaSalle, Tears at Reveille's Last Call." *New York Times*, 3 June 2001. http://www.nytimes.com/2001/06/03 /nyregion/long-island-journal-at-la-salle-tears-at-reveille-s-last-call.html.

Fones-Wolf, Elizabeth. Review of *The Business of Benevolence: Industrial Paternalism in Progressive America*, by Andrea Tone. *Journal of Interdisciplinary History* 30, no. 1 (Summer 1999): 150–51.

——. Review of *Creating the Corporate Soul: The Rise of Public Relations and Corporate Imagery in American Big Business, H-Business and EH.net*, by Roland Marchand. EH.net, January 1999, http://eh.net/book_reviews/creating-the -corporate-soul-the-rise-of-public-relations-and-corporate-imagery-in -american-big-business.

——. *Selling Free Enterprise: The Business Assault on Labor and Liberalism, 1945–60*. Urbana: University of Illinois Press, 1994.

——. *Waves of Opposition: Labor and the Struggle for Democratic Radio*. Urbana: University of Illinois Press, 2006.

Fox, Margalit. "Erik Blegvad, Children's Book Artist with a Subversive Wit, Dies at 90." *New York Times*, 10 February 2014. http://www.nytimes.com/2014/02/11 /arts/design/erik-blegvad-childrens-book-artist-dies-at-90.html?_r=0.

Frank, Robert H. *Success and Luck: Good Fortune and the Myth of Meritocracy.* Princeton, N.J.: Princeton University Press, 2016.

Fraterrigo, Elizabeth. *Playboy and the Making of the Good Life in Modern America.* New York: Oxford University Press, 2009.

Frydman, Carola, and Raven Molloy. "Pay Cuts for the Boss: Executive Compensation in the 1940s." *Journal of Economic History* 72, no. 1 (March 2012): 225–51.

Fuss, Diana. *Essentially Speaking: Feminism, Nature and Difference.* London: Routledge, 1989.

Gamber, Wendy. *The Female Economy: The Millinery and Dressmaking Trades, 1860–1930.* Urbana: University of Illinois Press, 1997.

Gartner, William B. "Who Is an Entrepreneur? Is the Wrong Question." *American Journal of Small Business* 12, no. 4 (1988): 11–32. Reprinted as the Best Article of 1988 in *Entrepreneurship Theory and Practice* 13, no. 4 (Summer 1989): 47–67.

"Gemeinschaft and Gesellschaft." *Encyclopedia Britannica Online.* Accessed 12 March 2015. http://www.britannica.com/EBchecked/topic/228066 /Gemeinschaft-and-Gesellschaft.

Gentilcore, David. *Pomodoro! A History of the Tomato in Italy.* New York: Columbia University Press, 2013.

Gerard, E. F. *Point Blank.* New York: Executive Company Publishers, 1964.

Gerber, David. "Cutting Out Shylock: Elite Anti-Semitism and the Quest for Moral Order in the Mid-Nineteenth-Century Marketplace." *Journal of American History* 69 (December 1982): 615–37.

Gilbert, James. *Men in the Middle: Searching for Masculinity in the 1950s.* Chicago: University of Chicago Press, 2005.

Give Me 5%: Education and Access for Women in Federal Contracts. Accessed 19 January 2015. http://www.giveme5.com/.

Goffman, Erving. *The Presentation of Self in Everyday Life.* New York: Anchor Books, 1959.

Goldin, Claudia. "America's Graduation from High School: The Evolution and Spread of Secondary Schooling in the Twentieth Century." *Journal of Economic History* 58, no. 2 (June 1998): 345–74.

———. "The Meaning of College in the Lives of American Women: The Past One-Hundred Years." Working Paper 4099, National Bureau of Economic Research, June 1992. http://www.nber.org/papers/w4099.pdf.

———. "The Role of WWII in the Rise of Women's Employment." *American Economic Review* 81, no. 4 (1991): 741–56.

———. *Understanding the Gender Gap: An Economic History of American Women.* New York: Oxford University Press, 1990.

Goldman, Amy. *The Heirloom Tomato: From Farm to Table.* New York: Bloomsbury Publishing, 2008.

Goldstein, Carolyn M. *Creating Consumers: Home Economists in Twentieth-Century America*. Chapel Hill: University of North Carolina Press, 2012.

Gottfried, Paul. "Harry Jaffa and the American Conservative Movement." *Imaginative Conservative*, 9 February 2015. http://www.theimaginativeconservative.org/2015/02/harry-jaffa-american-conservative-movement.html.

Gray, Christopher. "Inside the Union Club, Jaws Drop." *New York Times*, 11 February 2007. http://www.nytimes.com/2007/02/11/realestate/11scap.html?_r=0.

Grove, Robert D., and Alice M. Hetzel. "Vital Statistics Rates in the United States, 1940–1960." U.S. Department of Health, Education and Welfare, Public Health Service, National Center for Health Statistics. Accessed 2 March 2015. http://www.cdc.gov/nchs/data/vsus/vsrates1940_60.pdf.

Groysberg, Boris, and Robin Abrahams. "Manage Your Work, Manage Your Life." *Harvard Business Review*, March 2014. https://hbr.org/2014/03/manage-your-work-manage-your-life.

Gurock, Jeffrey S., Calvin B. Holder, Durahn A. B. Taylore, and Kenneth T. Jackson. "Harlem." In *Encyclopedia of New York*, edited by Kenneth T. Jackson, 1402–3. New Haven, Conn.: Yale University Press, 1995.

Hacker, Meg. "When Saying 'I Do' Meant Giving Up Your U.S. Citizenship." *Prologue*, Spring 2014, 56–61. National Archive. https://www.archives.gov/files/publications/prologue/2014/spring/citizenship.pdf.

Hamilton, Brady E., Joyce A. Martin, Michelle J. K. Osterman, and Sally C. Curtin. "Births: Preliminary Data for 2013." *National Vital Statistics Reports* 63, no. 2 (29 May 2014). U.S. Department of Health and Human Services. http://www.cdc.gov/nchs/data/nvsr/nvsr63/nvsr63_02.pdf.

Hartigan O'Connor, Ellen. *The Ties That Buy: Women and Commerce in Revolutionary America*. Philadelphia: University of Pennsylvania Press, 2009.

"Harvard Business School's Baker Library Receives Papers of Professor Georges Doriot" (Press Release). Harvard Business School, 23 April 2012. http://www.hbs.edu/news/releases/Pages/georgesdoriotpapers042312.aspx.

Hegewisch, Ariane, and Asha DuMonthier. "The Gender Wage Gap: Annual Earning Differences by Gender, Race and Ethnicity." Institute for Women's Policy Research, September 2016. http://www.iwpr.org/publications/recent-publications.

Hoos, Sidney. "The Determination of Military Subsistence Requirements." *Journal of Farm Economics* 28, no. 4 (November 1946): 973–88.

Hurt, R. Douglas. *The Great Plains during World War II*. Lincoln: University of Nebraska Press, 2008.

"Inventory of the Goodyear Tire and Rubber Company, 1899–1993." Record Group Number 99/106. University of Akron, University Library, Archives. Accessed 11 October 2015. https://www.uakron.edu/libraries/archives/files/DOPs/special/Goodyear_for_Web.pdf. 11.

Jacobs, Meg. "'How about Some Meat?': The Office of Price Administration, Consumption Politics, and State Building from the Bottom Up, 1941–1946." *Journal of American History* 84, no. 2 (December 1997): 910–41.

Jacoby, Sanford M. *Employing Bureaucracy: Managers, Unions, and the Transformation of Work in the 20th Century.* Rev. ed. Mahwah, N.J.: Lawrence Erlbaum Associates Publishers, 2004.

———. *Modern Manors: Welfare Capitalism since the New Deal.* Princeton, N.J.: Princeton University Press, 1997.

Kanter, Rosabeth Moss. *Men and Women of the Corporation.* New York: Basic Books, 1993. Originally published 1977.

Kellems, Vivien. *Toil, Taxes and Trouble: One Woman's Crusade to End the Federal Income Tax.* Yorba Linda, Calif.: Davidson Press, 2001. Originally published 1951.

Kessler-Harris, Alice. *A Woman's Wage: Historical Meanings and Social Consequences.* Lexington: University of Kentucky Press, 1990.

Kruse, Kevin M. *One Nation under God: How Corporate America Invented Christian America.* New York: Basic Books, 2015.

Kwolek-Folland, Angel. *Engendering Business: Men and Women in the Corporate Office, 1870–1930.* Baltimore, Md.: Johns Hopkins University Press, 1994.

———. *Incorporating Women: A History of Women and Business in the United States.* New York: Twayne Publishers, 1998.

Laird, Pamela Walker. *Advertising Progress: American Business and the Rise of Consumer Marketing.* Baltimore, Md.: Johns Hopkins University Press, 1998.

———. "Making a Hero of Horatio Alger: How a Progressive Reformer Came to Symbolize Inequality." Paper presented at Business History Conference, Miami, Fla., June 24–27, 2015.

———. "Parallel Ladders to the Glass Ceiling: Presidential and Corporate Executive Appointments," 1–25. Unpublished essay shared with the author.

———. *Pull: Networking and Success since Benjamin Franklin.* Cambridge, Mass.: Harvard University Press, 2006.

Larcker, David F., and Brian Tayan. "A Historical Look at Compensation and Disclosure: Cool and Refreshing!" *Stanford Closer Look Series: Topics, Issues, and Controversies in Corporate Governance and Leadership.* 15 June 2010, 1–6. https://www.gsb.stanford.edu/faculty-research/publications/historical-look -compensation-disclosure-cool-refreshing.

Laville, Helen. "Gender and Women's Rights in the Cold War." In *The Oxford Handbook of the Cold War,* edited by Richard H. Immerman and Petra Goedde. New York: Oxford University Press, 2013. doi:10.1093/oxfordhb/ 9780199236961.013.0030.

Leff, Mark. "The Politics of Sacrifice on the American Home Front in World War II." *Journal of American History* 77, no. 4 (March 1991): 1296–1318.

Lewellan, Wilbur G. "Executive Compensation Patterns." In *The Ownership Income of Management,* 38–77. New York: National Bureau of Economic Research, 1971. http://www.nber.org/chapters/c6440.

Lewin, Tamar. "Partnership in Firm Awarded to Victim of Sex Bias." *New York Times,* 16 May 1990. http://www.nytimes.com/1990/05/16/us/partnership-in -firm-awarded-to-victim-of-sex-bias.html.

Lewis, Susan Ingalls. *Unexceptional Women: Female Proprietors in Mid-Nineteenth-Century Albany, New York 1830–1885*. Columbus: Ohio State University Press, 2009.

"Lifetime Achievement: Mary Wells." *Adweek*, 20 May 2011. http://www.adweek.com/sa-article/lifetime-achievement-mary-wells-131861.

Longfellow's Wayside Inn. "The Grist Mill (1929) and Pepperidge Farm (1951–1967)." Accessed 13 March 2015. http://www.wayside.org/history/gristmill.

"Lydia Estes Pinkham (1819–1883)." Women Working, 1800–1930. Harvard University Library Open Collections Program. Accessed 15 August 2016. http://ocp.hul.harvard.edu/ww/pinkham.html.

Mandell, Nikki. *The Corporation as Family: The Gendering of Corporate Welfare, 1890–1930*. Chapel Hill: University of North Carolina Press, 2002.

Marchand, Roland. *Creating the Corporate Soul: The Rise of Public Relations and Corporate Imagery in American Big Business*. Berkeley: University of California Press, 1998.

Martin, Philip. *Promise Unfulfilled: Unions, Immigration, and Farm Workers*. Ithaca, N.Y.: Cornell University Press, 2003. Excerpted in *Rural Migration News* 12, no. 2 (April 2006). https://migration.ucdavis.edu/rmn.

"Mary Wells." *Adweek*, 20 May 2011. http://www.adweek.com/sa-article/lifetime-achievement-mary-wells-131861.

"Mary Wells Lawrence." *Encyclopedia Britannica*. Accessed 5 December 2014. https://www.britannica.com/biography/Mary-Wells-Lawrence.

Matzek, Amanda E., Clinton G. Gudmunson, and Sharon M. Danes. "Spousal Capital as a Resource for Couples Starting a Business." *Family Relations: Interdisciplinary Journal of Applied Family Studies* 59 (February 2010): 60–73.

May, Elaine Tyler. *Homeward Bound: American Families in the Cold War Era*. New York: Basic Books, 1988.

Mayo, Anthony J., and Nitin Nohria. *In Their Time: The Greatest Business Leaders of the Twentieth Century*. Cambridge, Mass.: Harvard Business School Press, 2005.

McCart, Neil. *SS Aquitania: Cunard's Atlantic Lady (Famous British Liners)*. Fan Publications, 1994. http://www.liverpoolships.org/aquitania_cunard_line.html.

"Measuring Worth" calculator. EH.net. Accessed 26 October 2010. http://eh.net/hmit/.

Meyerowitz, Joanne, ed. *Not June Cleaver: Women and Gender in Postwar America*. Philadelphia: Temple University Press, 1994.

Moon, Youngme. *Different: Escaping the Competitive Herd*. New York: Crown Business, 2010.

Murphy, Patrick J. "The Golden Age: Service Management on Transatlantic Ocean Liners." *Journal of Management History* 13, no. 2 (2007): 172–91.

Murphy, Patrick J., Jill Kickul, Saulo D. Barbosa, and Lindsay Titus. "Expert Capital and Perceived Legitimacy: Female-Run Entrepreneurial Venture

Signaling and Performance." *International Journal of Entrepreneurship and Innovation* 8, no. 2 (2007): 127–38.

Museum of Flight. "Beech C-45H Expeditor." Accessed 2 March 2015. http://museumofflight.org/aircraft/beech-c-45h-expeditor.

"National Affairs: Barrel No. 2." *Time,* 23 June 1947. http://cotent.time.com/time/magazine/article/0,9171,797962,00.html.

National Association of Women Business Owners. "Federal Procurement." Accessed 13 June 2016. https://www.nawbo.org/advocacy/policies-and-positions/federal-procurement.

National Aviation Hall of Fame. "List of Enshrinees." Accessed 2 March 2015. http://www.nationalaviation.org/enshrinees/.

Nocera, Joseph. "Still Searching for Lee Iacocca." *Fortune,* 8 November 1987. http://archive.fortune.com.

Nohria, Nitin, Boris Groysberg, and Linda-Eling Lee. "Employee Motivation: A Powerful New Model." *Harvard Business Review,* July–August 2008. https://hbr.org/2008/07/employee-motivation-a-powerful-new-model&cm_sp=Article-_-Links-_-Top%20of%20Page%20Recirculation.

Ogilvy, David. *Confessions of an Advertising Man.* London: Southbank Publishing, 1963.

Olegario, Rowena. *A Culture of Credit: Embedding Trust and Transparency in American Business.* Cambridge, Mass.: Harvard University Press, 2007.

Olmsted, Kathryn S. *Right out of California: The 1930s and the Big Business Roots of Modern Conservatism.* New York: Basic Books, 2015.

Olson, James S. *Saving Capitalism: The Reconstruction Finance Corporation and the New Deal, 1933–1940.* Princeton, N.J.: Princeton University Press, 1988.

Ott, Julia. *When Wall Street Met Main Street: The Quest for an Investor's Democracy.* Cambridge, Mass.: Harvard University Press, 2011.

Peiss, Kathy. *Hope in a Jar: The Making of America's Beauty Culture.* New York: Owl Books, 1998.

"Pepperidge Farm." *Advertising Age,* 15 September 2003. http://adage.com/article/adage-encyclopedia/pepperidge-farm/98814/.

Pepperidge Farm. "Margaret Rudkin." Accessed 8 July 2015. http://www.pepperidgefarm.com/MargaretRudkin.aspx.

Peril, Lynn. "Sex and Secretaries: The Rise and Fall of the Office Wife." *Business Insider,* 15 June 2011. http://www.businessinsider.com/secretary-the-rise-and-fall-of-the-office-wife-2011-6. Originally published in Lynn Peril, *Swimming in the Steno Pool: A Retro Guide to Making It in the Office.* New York: Norton, 2011.

Pesce, Nicole Lyn. "Marissa Mayer Bans Telecommuting at Yahoo! and Becomes the Mother of Dissension." *New York Daily News,* 4 March 2013. http://www.nydailynews.com/life-style/n-y-moms-react-yahoo-ban-telecommuting-article-1.1277492.

Place, Irene, and Sylvia Plummer. *Women in Management.* Chicago: National Textbook Company, 1987.

Putnam, Robert. *Bowling Alone: The Collapse and Revival of American Community.* New York: Simon & Schuster, 2000.

Private Label Manufacturers Association. Accessed 14 September 2015. http://plma.com/.

Rayasan, Renuka. "Do More Women on the Board Mean Better Results?" *New Yorker,* 19 November 2013. http://www.newyorker.com/business/currency/do-more-women-on-the-board-mean-better-results.

"Regulation V Loans in the Fifth District." *Monthly Review, Federal Reserve Bank of St. Louis,* May 1947, 3–5. http://fraser.stlouisfed.org/.

Rose, Gerald A. "The March Inland: The Stockton Cannery Strike of 1937," Parts 1 and 2. *Southern California Quarterly* 54, nos. 1 and 2 (Spring and Summer 1972): 67–82, 155–76.

Rudkin, Margaret. *The Margaret Rudkin Pepperidge Farm Cookbook.* New York: Grosset & Dunlap, 1963.

Ruiz, Vicki. *Cannery Women, Cannery Lives: Mexican Women, Unionization, and the California Food Processing Industry, 1930–1950.* Albuquerque: University of New Mexico Press, 1987.

Saker Woeste, Victoria. "Insecure Equality: Louis Marshall, Henry Ford, and the Problem of Defamatory Antisemitism, 1920–1929." *Journal of American History* 91, no. 3 (December 2004): 877–905.

Salcedo, Anastasia Marx de. *Combat-Ready Kitchen: How the U.S. Military Shapes the Way You Eat.* New York: Penguin Random House, 2015.

Sandberg, Sheryl. *Lean In: Women, Work, and the Will to Lead.* New York: Alfred Knopf, 2014.

Scanlon, Jennifer. *Bad Girls Go Everywhere: The Life of Helen Gurley Brown.* New York: Penguin Books, 2009.

———. *Inarticulate Longings: The Ladies' Home Journal, Gender, and the Promises of Consumer Culture.* New York: Routledge, 1995.

Schipani, Cindy A., Terry Morehead Dworkin, Angel Kwolek-Folland, and Virginia Maurer. "Women and the New Corporate Governance: Pathways for Obtaining Positions of Corporate Leadership." *Maryland Law Review* 65, no. 2 (2006): 504–37.

Schleier, Merrill. "Tillie the Toiler or Tillie the Tomato: The Production of Food and the Construction of Gender by Stockton's Tillie Lewis of Flotill Foods." *Far-Westerner,* Spring/Summer 1997, 9–23.

Schulte, Brigid. "The Second Shift at 25: Q&A with Arlie Hochschild." *Washington Post,* 6 August 2014. http://www.washingtonpost.com/blogs/she-the-people/wp/2014/08/06/the-second-shift-at-25-q-a-with-arlie-hochschild/.

Schwartz, Hillel. *Never Satisfied.* New York: Doubleday, 1986.

Sergio, Lisa. "Biographical History." The Dorothy Thompson Papers, Syracuse University Libraries. Accessed 2 October 2014. http://library.syr.edu/digital/guides/t/thompson.

Sewell, Jessica Ellen. *Women and the Everyday City: Public Space in San Francisco, 1890–1915*. Minneapolis: University of Minnesota Press, 2001.

Shapiro, Laura. "'I Guarantee': Betty Crocker and the Woman in the Kitchen." In *From Betty Crocker to Feminist Food Studies*, edited by Arlene Voski Avakian and Barbara Haber, 29–40. Amherst: University of Massachusetts Press, 2005.

Sharpe, Rochelle. "As Leaders, Women Rule: New Studies Find That Female Managers Outshine Their Male Counterparts in Almost Every Measure." *Businessweek*, 19 November 2000. http://www.bloomberg.com/news/articles /2000-11-19/as-leaders-women-rule.

Showalter, Elaine. Review of *Feminism Unfinished*, by Dorothy Sue Cobble, Linda Gordon, and Astrid Henry. *Washington Post*, 29 August 2014. http:// www.washingtonpost.com/opinions/review-feminism-unfinished-by -dorothy-sue-cobble-linda-gordon-and-astrid-henry/2014/08/29/ababf1de -1cdf-11e4-82f9-2cd6fa8da5c4_story.html.

Smith, Gary Scott. *Faith and the Presidency: From George Washington to George W. Bush*. New York: Oxford University Press, 2006.

Sparberg, Andrew. "Hudson Yards." In *Encyclopedia of New York*, edited by Kenneth T. Jackson, 627. New Haven, Conn.: Yale University Press, 1997.

Sparks, Edith. *Capital Intentions: Female Proprietors in San Francisco, 1850–1920*. Chapel Hill: University of North Carolina Press, 2006.

Starr, Kevin. *The Dream Endures: California Enters the 1940s*. New York: Oxford University Press, 1997.

Stengel, Geri. "How Women Can Up Their Chances of Winning Government Contracts." *Forbes*, 6 August 2014. http://www.nytimes.com/2016/03/02/business /government-meets-goal-set-in-1994-for-womens-business-contracts.html?_r=0.

Stewart, James B. "A CEO's Support System, aka Husband." *New York Times*, 4 November 2011. http://www.nytimes.com/2011/11/05/business/a-ceos-support -system-a-k-a-husband.html?_r=0.

Stone, Pamela. *Opting Out? Why Women Really Quit Careers and Head Home*. Berkeley: University of California Press, 2007.

Strom, Sharon. *Beyond the Typewriter: Gender, Class, and the Origins of Modern American Office Work, 1900–1930*. Urbana: University of Illinois Press, 1992.

Surowiecki, James. "Face Time." *New Yorker*, 18 March 2013. http://www .newyorker.com/magazine/2013/03/18/face-time.

Sutton, Denise H. *Globalizing Ideal Beauty: How Female Copywriters of the J. Walter Thompson Advertising Agency Redefined Beauty for the Twentieth Century*. New York: Palgrave Macmillan, 2009.

Taylor, Christiane Diehl. "The Worth of Wives: 1950s Corporate America 'Discovers' Spousal Social Capital." *Essays in Economic & Business History* 26 (2008): 33–46.

Thomas de la Peña, Carolyn. *Empty Pleasures: The Story of Artificial Sweeteners from Saccharin to Splenda*. Chapel Hill: University of North Carolina Press, 2010.

Tone, Andrea. *The Business of Benevolence: Industrial Paternalism in Progressive America*. Ithaca, N.Y.: Cornell University Press, 1998.

Truitt, Richard H. "Byor, Carl." In *Encyclopedia of Public Relations*, edited by Robert L. Heath, 105–8. Thousand Oaks, Calif.: Sage Publications, 2004. http://books.google.com.

Ultan, Lloyd. "Belmont." In *Encyclopedia of New York*, edited by Kenneth T. Jackson, 114. New Haven, Conn.: Yale University Press, 1995.

———. "Williamsbridge." In *Encyclopedia of New York*, edited by Kenneth T. Jackson, 573–75. New Haven, Conn.: Yale University Press, 1995.

U.S. Department of Labor. *Women in Higher-Level Positions*. Bulletin of the Women's Bureau No. 236, 82–83. Washington, D.C.: U.S. Government Printing Office, 1950.

U.S. Department of Labor, Bureau of Labor Statistics. "CPI Inflation Calculator." Accessed 12 March 2015. http://www.bls.gov/data/inflation_calculator.htm.

U.S. Environmental Protection Agency. "Selling Greener Products and Services to the Federal Government." Accessed 19 January 2015. https://www.epa.gov/greenerproducts/selling-greener-products-and-services-federal-government.

U.S. Senate Historical Office. "Harry S. Truman, 34th Vice President (1945)." Accessed 11 March 2015. https://www.senate.gov/artandhistory/history/common/generic/VP_Harry_Truman.htm.

Uttaro, Ralph A. "The Voices of America in International Radio Propaganda." *Law and Contemporary Problems* 45, no. 4 (Winter 1982): 103–22.

Vecchio, Diane C. *Merchants, Midwives, and Laboring Women: Italian Migrants in Urban America*. Urbana: University of Illinois Press, 2006.

Warfel, Susan. Review of *Breaking the Glass Ceiling: Can Women Reach the Top of America's Largest Corporations?*, by Ann M. Morrison, Randall P. White, and Ellen Van Velsor. *Los Angeles Times*, 26 July 1987. http://articles.latimes.com/1987-07-26/books/bk-1589_1_general-management.

Weinstein, Stephen. "Flatlands." In *Encyclopedia of New York*, edited by Kenneth T. Jackson, 459. New Haven, Conn.: Yale University Press, 1995.

Weiss, Jessica. *To Have and to Hold: Marriage, the Baby Boom, and Social Change*. Chicago: University of Chicago Press, 2000.

Wetzel, James R. "American Families: 75 Years of Change," *Monthly Labor Review*, March 1990, for the Bureau of Labor Statistics. http://www.bls.gov/mlr/1990/03/art1full.pdf.

White, Martha C. "Even One Woman on the Board Makes a Difference." *NBC News*. Accessed 21 October 2014. http://www.nbcnews.com/business/business-news/even-one-woman-board-makes-difference-n158846.

"Wichita Tries to Boost Its Aviation Industry with Smaller Planes." *National Public Radio*. Accessed 18 November 2014. http://www.npr.org/2014/11/18/365016009/wichita-tries-to-boost-its-aviation-industry-with-smaller-planes.

Williams, Joan C. *Reshaping the Work–Family Debate: Why Men and Class Matter*. Cambridge, Mass.: Harvard University Press, 2010.

Wilson, Mark. "'Taking a Nickel out of the Cash Register': Statutory Renegotiation of Military Contracts and the Politics of Profit Control in the United States during World War II." *Law and History Review* 28, no. 2 (May 2010): 343–83.

"Women and Minority Small Business Contractors: Divergent Paths to Equal Success." Research summary for the American Express OPEN for Government Contracts: Victory in Procurement (VIP) for Small Business Program, 2011. https://c401345.ssl.cf1.rackcdn.com/pdf/VIP_Survey2_Final.pdf.

"Women in Business." Episode in *Makers: Women Who Make America*. PBS Video, aired 28 October 2014. http://video.pbs.org.

"Women 'Take Care,' Men 'Take Charge': Stereotyping of U.S. Business Leaders Exposed." Catalyst, 2005. http://www.catalyst.org/knowledge/women-take -care-men-take-charge-stereotyping-us-business-leaders-exposed.

Wood, Kyle Elizabeth. *Tillie Lewis: The Tomato Queen*. North Charleston, S.C.: CreateSpace Independent Publishing Platform, 2016.

Zahavi, Gerald. *Workers, Managers, and Welfare Capitalism: The Shoemakers and Tanners of Endicott Johnson, 1890–1950*. Urbana: University of Illinois Press, 1988.

Ziegelman, Jane. *97 Orchard: An Edible History of Five Immigrant Families in One New York Tenement*. New York: Harper, 2011.

Index

Donaldson, Blake F., 37–39, 183, 184, 250n101
Doriot, George, 233
Draper, Andrew J., 66

Earhart, Amelia, 168
Education: in aviation, 174, 271n74; of Beech, 216; of Lewis, 199, 209; for women, 5, 241n8
Edwards, Lucille Winters, 121
Ehrlich, Jacob, 17, 19
Ehrlich, Myrtle. See Lewis, Tillie
Eisenhower, Dwight, 35, 73, 74, 127, 213, 255n76
Elias, Allison, 275n5
Emergency Price Control Act, 79, 84
Employee communication, 128–29
Endicott Johnson shoe company, 96–97, 102, 258n12
Enterprising Women (Bird), 164–65
Entrepreneurial pathways, 11–16, 48–49; of Beech, 25–36; of Lewis, 14, 16–25; of Rudkin, 36–48
Equal Employment Opportunity Commission (EEOC), 114
Evans, Gordon E., 219
Everywoman's Magazine, 99, 101, 154
Excess profits tax (EPT): about, 57; applications for relief from, 58, 59, 252n20; and Beech, 54, 75–76; and Lewis, 54, 55, 57–59, 252n21
Executive wives, 172–73, 199, 224, 236, 237–38
Expert capital, 9, 15, 25, 49

Factory Management and Maintenance, 124
Fairfield County Times Monthly, 181
Farney, Dennis, 249n92
Federal Bureau of Investigation (FBI), 252n29
Federation of Business and Professional Women's Clubs (BPWC), 6

Female entrepreneurs: in beauty industry, 199; competitors of, 6, 65, 156; contemporary advocacy for, 50–51, 239–40; as dangerous "boss ladies," 1, 2, 6, 220, 238; entrepreneurial pathways for, 11–49; gender as brand management strategy for, 50–91, 148–49, 238, 267n5; gender deemphasized by, 27–28, 36, 217–20, 239, 240; and government, 50–91, 238; husbands as pathway for, 5–6, 9, 11–14, 48–49; and labor management, 92–146, 238; literature on, 7–8, 237–38; privilege as pathway for, 15–16, 17–18, 34; resistance to, 29, 30–31, 32, 211; scarcity of in manufacturing, 6–7, 15, 199–200; self-advocacy by, 33, 197–236. See also Beech, Olive Ann; Lewis, Tillie; Rudkin, Margaret
Feminism, 8–9, 94, 205–6, 211, 276n11
Fennelly, Parker, 191–92
Ference family, 133
Fixed price contracts, 115, 119
Fleming, Marjorie, 228
Flotill Products, Inc.: advertising by, 57, 151, 154, 155, 158–60, 164; and Banco di Napoli, 25, 248n64; board of directors of, 276n23; compensation for Lewis from, 202–5, 206; competitors of, 6, 65, 156; and Del Gaizo, 23, 247n54; family metaphors within, 102, 110; fight over excess profits tax by, 54, 55, 57–59, 252n21; founding of, 2; government relationship with, 55–67; labor force at, 98–99, 108–9; loans to, 24–25, 55–56, 59–62, 253n31; marketing efforts by, 57, 151–54, 156–62, 268n28, 269n39; Mexican laborers working for, 106–7; and Meyer Lewis, 103, 105, 106, 113, 153, 269n44; as military contractor, 53,

56–57, 62–63, 66–67, 254n50; national distribution of, 23–24; PR firm for, 153–54, 155, 268n22; as private-label canner, 67, 254n51; production and sales by, 66–67, 155, 254n50, 267n16; production facilities of, 63, 67, 108; quality control by, 63–65; renamed Tillie Lewis Foods, 2, 113–14, 151, 157; seasonal and unskilled workers for, 113–14; strike by workers at, 103, 259n29; and Tasti-Diet, 151, 154–62, 166; unionization of, 103, 111, 112–13; wartime stamp purchase program, 105, 259n38; welfare capitalist policies of, 101–2, 109, 110–11, 146; "Who Is Tillie Lewis?" biography by, 206–8. *See also* Lewis, Tillie

Flushing Bank, 40, 230

Fogarty, Margaret. *See* Rudkin, Margaret

Food, Tobacco, Agricultural, and Allied Workers of America (FTA), 111–12, 260n62

Ford, Henry, 106, 190

Fortune, 9, 221; on Beech, 27, 72, 222; on Lewis, 151, 162, 164, 211–12, 270n46; "The Ten Highest-Ranking Women in Big Business" article in, 14–15, 164, 211–12

Frank, Robert H., 16

Freedom Foundation, 73, 97, 127

Fringe benefits, 117, 141, 143

Garrett Corporation, 141

Gaty, John "Jack," 30–31, 120

Gemeinschaft, 96

Gender roles and stereotypes: and Beech, 166, 168–69, 170–72, 177, 212–13, 220–23, 224–25; and businesswomen's behavior, 197–98, 275n5; as caretakers and nurturers, 37, 48, 92–94, 194–95, 230–32, 280n91; as dangerous "boss ladies,"

1, 2, 6, 220, 238; and female office workers, 1–2, 5–6, 215; and female seasonal unskilled workers, 98–99, 104, 113–14; of "girls," 2; as hostess, 149–50, 166, 168–69, 170–72, 177; and Lewis, 149, 151, 152–53, 157, 158, 160, 161–63, 164–65, 211–12, 258n20; and marketing strategy, 149–51, 150; and Rudkin, 37, 48, 135–36, 149–50, 192, 194–95, 230–32, 280n91; Supreme Court ruling on, 198; of women and detail work, 26–27; of women as bad with numbers, 209. *See also* Brand management

General Mills, 192, 196

General Motors, 127, 130

Gerard, E. F. G., 217

Gift-giving: at Beech Aircraft, 121–22; at Pepperidge Farm, 137, 140–41, 142

Gilbert, James, 241n2

Goldman, Amy, 247n51

Gordon, Richard, 42

Government programs and agencies, 50–55, 91; and Beech, 67–78; investments in business by, 51, 67, 251n6; and Lewis, 55–67; loans from, 53–54, 56, 59–62, 70–72; and military contracts, 52–53, 56–57, 62–63, 66–67, 68–69, 174, 254n50, 271n77; price controls by, 52, 57, 79, 86–88; rationing by, 84–85, 86, 89–90; regulation by, 51–52, 54–55, 56, 78, 79, 84, 88, 90, 91; and Rudkin, 78–90; scholarship on, 51, 60, 251n6

Grant, LaKeisha, 50

Great Depression, 20, 42, 53

Green, William, 105, 111, 259n38

Greener, Violet, 62, 253n31

Gristede Bros., 82–83

Harvard Business Review, 11

Harvard Business School, 233–34

Hedrick, Frank E., 118, 120, 224

Tomatoes, 21–22, 23, 24, 247n56
Top Management: The Officers and Principals, 214–15
Trademarks, 181, 232
Training Within Industry (TWI), 123
Travel Air Co., 26, 27, 28, 33
Truman, Harry S., 118, 256n94
Turner, Pat, 160

Vanderbilt, Amy, 137
Vecchio, Diane, 258n12
Virtual Enterprise Architects (VEA), 50
Voice of America (VOA), 207–8
VT loan program, 70, 71

Wallick, Bob and Joan, 178
Wall Street Journal, 210, 217
Walworth, Dorothy, 99, 101
Weast, Clair and Elsie Orr, 154, 157
Weisberg, Louis, 17–18, 19, 243n17; and Mossalina Products Corporation, 21, 245n38; Tillie marriage to, 17, 19, 20–21, 243n18, 244n27
Weisberg, Tillie. *See* Lewis, Tillie
Weiss, Jessica, 16, 48
Wells, T. A., 32, 33
Western Canner and Packer, 108
White bread, 190, 192, 272n93
"Who Is Tillie Lewis?," 206–8
Whyte, William H., 172–73
Wichita, Kans., 116

Wilson, James R., 184
Wilson, Mark, 51, 54, 58, 59, 252 n21
Women in Management (Place and Plummer), 197
Women's jobs: at banks, 40; at Beech Aircraft, 120–21; as clerical and office workers, 1–2, 5–6, 215; at Flotill, 98–99, 104, 113–14; and prohibition of married women, 4–5, 18, 244n25
Women's pay, 204; as unequal, 97, 113, 205–6
Wood, Kyle, 244n27, 245n38, 258n18; on Del Gaizo, 23, 243n22, 244n24, 245n36, 247n54; on FBI investigation of Lewis, 252n29
World War II, 51, 52; military contracts during, 52–53, 56–57, 62–63, 66–67, 68–69, 254n50; postwar adjustments following, 76; price controls during, 52, 57, 79; rationing during, 84–85, 86, 89–90; soldiers' rations during, 86, 257n98; women's salaries during, 204
Wyden, Peter, 220–22

Yahoo, 92
Yankey, C. G., 33
Young, Charles, 24, 248n64
Young, Claude O., 204

Zerillo, Lorenzo, 22

Manufactured by Amazon.ca
Bolton, ON